Haunting the World

THE SUNY SERIES
HORIZONS OF CINEMA
MURRAY POMERANCE | EDITOR

RECENT TITLES

Gohar Siddiqui, *Déjà-Viewed*

Stanley Cavell, *Cavell on Film*

Saverio Giovacchini, *The Celluloid Atlantic*

John Caps, *Overhearing Film Music*

Hannah Holtzman, *Through a Nuclear Lens*

Benedict Morrison, *Eccentric Laughter*

Matthew Cipa, *Is Harpo Free?*

Daniel Varndell, *Torturous Etiquettes*

Seth Barry Watter, *The Human Figure on Film*

Jonah Corne and Monika Vrečar, *Yiddish Cinema*

Jason Jacobs, *Reluctant Sleuths, True Detectives*

Lucy J. Miller, *Distancing Representations in Transgender Film*

Tomoyuki Sasaki, *Cinema of Discontent*

Mary Ann McDonald Carolan, *Orienting Italy*

Matthew Rukgaber, *Nietzsche in Hollywood*

David Venditto, *Whiteness at the End of the World*

Fareed Ben-Youssef, *No Jurisdiction*

Tony Tracy, *White Cottage, White House*

Tom Conley, *Action, Action, Action*

Lindsay Coleman and Roberto Schaefer, editors, *The Cinematographer's Voice*

A complete listing of books in this series can be found online at www.sunypress.edu.

Haunting the World
Essays on Film after Perkins and Cavell

Dominic Lash

SUNY PRESS

Published by State University of New York Press, Albany

© 2025 State University of New York

All rights reserved

Printed in the United States of America

No part of this book may be used or reproduced in any manner whatsoever without written permission. No part of this book may be stored in a retrieval system or transmitted in any form or by any means including electronic, electrostatic, magnetic tape, mechanical, photocopying, recording, or otherwise without the prior permission in writing of the publisher.

Links to third-party websites are provided as a convenience and for informational purposes only. They do not constitute an endorsement or an approval of any of the products, services, or opinions of the organization, companies, or individuals. SUNY Press bears no responsibility for the accuracy, legality, or content of a URL, the external website, or for that of subsequent websites.

EU GPSR Authorised Representative:
Logos Europe, 9 rue Nicolas Poussin, 17000, La Rochelle, France
contact@logoseurope.eu

For information, contact State University of New York Press, Albany, NY
www.sunypress.edu

Library of Congress Cataloging-in-Publication Data

Name: Lash, Dominic, author.
Title: Haunting the world : essays on film after Perkins and Cavell / Dominic Lash.
Description: Albany : State University of New York Press, [2025]. | Series: SUNY series, horizons of cinema | Includes bibliographical references and index.
Identifiers: LCCN 2024053703 | ISBN 9798855803105 (hardcover : alk. paper) | ISBN 9798855803112 (ebook) | ISBN 9798855803129 (pbk. : alk. paper)
Subjects: LCSH: Film criticism—Philosophy. | Cavell, Stanley, 1926–2018. | Perkins, V. F., 1936–2016
Classification: LCC PN1995 .L336 2025 | DDC 791.4301—dc23/eng/20241126
LC record available at https://lccn.loc.gov/2024053703

for Alex Clayton and Hoi Lun Law,
sine quibus basically none of this

Contents

List of Illustrations   ix

Acknowledgments   xiii

Introduction: Naive Film Criticism   1

Part One. V. F. Perkins

1 *Film as Film* in the Twenty-First Century   19

2 V. F. Perkins and the Redescription of Films   41

Part Two. Stanley Cavell

3 "Not Yet the Last": On a Paragraph by Stanley Cavell   65

4 Cavellian Reflections on Privacy, Consent, and Expression
   in Ildikó Enyedi's *On Body and Soul* (*Teströl és lélekröl*)   89

5 (Re)producing Marriage: Stanley Cavell and
   Paul Thomas Anderson's *Phantom Thread*   107

6 Experience, Skepticism, and Idolatry in Stanley Kubrick,
   Nicholas Lash, and Stanley Cavell   129

Part Three. Figurations

7 The Shape of It All: Priorities and Completeness in Nicole Brenez's Work on Abel Ferrara 151

8 Rupture, Suture, Nietzsche: Impossible Intersubjectivity in Ridley Scott's *Alien* 171

9 Hypnosis-Images: Indiscernibility and Hypnotic Agency in Gilles Deleuze's *Heart of Glass* 195

Part Four. Tarkovsky and Reichardt

10 "You Can't Imagine How Terrible It Is to Make the Wrong Choice": Faith, Agency, and Self-pity in Andrei Tarkovsky's *Stalker* 217

11 Kelly and Andrei in the Zone 241

12 "A Fair Curve from a Noble Plan": Kelly Reichardt's *Certain Women* 249

Notes 275

Works Cited 303

Filmography 317

Index 321

Illustrations

1.1	We are shielded from the conversation.	27
1.2	Martha is blocked from the conversation.	28
2.1	Lisa and the lieutenant.	53
2.2–2.7	A series of smiles.	60
3.1	"Falconetti at the stake looks up . . ."	87
3.2	". . . to see a flight of birds wheel over her with the sun in their wings."	87
4.1	Endre and Mária.	90
4.2	"A pair who recognize themselves as having known one another forever."	91
4.3	Taking an inquisitive pleasure in the other's pleasure.	94
4.4	On body and sole—expressive feet.	105
5.1	Reynolds recognizes Alma.	111
5.2	Substitution.	112
5.3	A staring contest.	122
5.4	Public and private (note the spyhole to the left of the image).	123
5.5	Equilibrium through disequilibrium.	126
6.1	Theatricalization . . .	143

6.2	. . . has already been thematized with abundant clarity.	144
6.3	Addressed in the dark.	146
7.1	"Figurative prolepsis" and "analepsis."	155
7.2	"Passing from the recto to the verso."	158
7.3	"The fifty most terrifying, synthetic seconds in narrative cinema."	165
7.4	Is it "all the nightmare of a young boy"?	165
7.5	An abundance of phallic signifiers.	168
8.1	Physical rupture and cinematic suture.	175
8.2	Physical suture and cinematic rupture.	175
8.3	Our last view of Ash in the chestburster sequence.	187
8.4	Intersubjectivity without subjects.	190
8.5	Impossible suture?	192
9.1	*Heart of Glass*'s opening figure of vision . . .	196
9.2	. . . and its final prophetic vision.	197
9.3	Spreading snow in *Citizen Kane* and spreading fire in *Heart of Glass*.	204
9.4	Hypnotic visions at the beginning of *Heart of Glass*.	206
10.1	Petulance.	223
10.2	Self-pity.	224
10.3	"You awake?"	227
10.4	"This is the Zone."	234
11.1a–11.1d	Creatures of the watery Zone.	242
11.2	*Old Joy*: aftermath.	244
12.1	A momentary expression.	249

12.2	Gina, Ryan, and the sandstone.	253
12.3	"He grinned at her. . . ."	253
12.4	"When do you need it?"	256
12.5	Working "on the margins of American life."	260
12.6	Our last glimpse of Gina.	262
12.7	"It doesn't have to be a tome."	265
12.8	"Boats to build."	270

Acknowledgments

I'm enormously grateful to Murray Pomerance for the alacrity and enthusiasm with which he responded to my proposal of this project. Working with James Peltz on the development and production of this book has been a pleasure.

Most of the book's chapters first appeared elsewhere in versions which have been lightly, or in some cases slightly more heavily, revised for their publication here. I am very grateful to all the editors and journals for publishing this work in the first place, and for permission to reprint material from it here.

The details of the original publications are as follows:

"*Film as Film* in the Twenty-First Century: The Function and Evaluation of Diegesis and Disruption." *Screen* 58, no. 2 (2017): 163–79.
"V. F. Perkins and the Redescription of Film." *New Review of Film and Television Studies* 21, no. 3 (2023): 479–504.
"'Not Yet the Last': Idiom, Privacy, and Mortality in a Paragraph by Stanley Cavell." *Angelaki: Journal of the Theoretical Humanities* 29, no. 5 (2024): 81–96.
"Stanley Cavell on Body and Soul: Privacy, Consent, and Expression in Ildikó Enyedi's *On Body and Soul* (*Testről és lélekről*, 2017)." In *Stanley Cavell and World Cinema: Beyond Hollywood*, edited by Paul Deb. Edinburgh University Press, forthcoming.
"(Re)producing Marriage: Stanley Cavell and *Phantom Thread*." *Film and Philosophy* 25 (2021): 1–21.
"Experience, Scepticism, and Idolatry in Stanley Kubrick, Nicholas Lash, and Stanley Cavell." In *The Oxford Companion to Theology and Film*, edited by Gerard Loughlin. Oxford University Press, forthcoming.

"Fold upon Fold: Figurative Logics and Critical Priorities in Nicole Brenez's Work on Abel Ferarra" *Movie: A Journal of Film Criticism*, no. 8 (2019): 14–22.

"Rupture, Suture, Nietzsche: Impossible Intersubjectivity in *Alien*." *Film-Philosophy* 25, no. 3 (2021): 229–50.

"Hypnosis-Images: Indiscernibility and Hypnotic Agency in Gilles Deleuze's *Heart of Glass*." In *Gilles Deleuze and Film Criticism: Philosophy, Theory, and the Individual Film*, edited by Dominic Lash and Hoi Lun Law, 193–213. Palgrave Macmillan, 2023.

"'You Can't Imagine How Terrible It Is to Make the Wrong Choice': Faith, Agency and Self-pity in Tarkovsky's *Stalker*." *Quarterly Review of Film and Video* 36, no. 4 (2019): 264–85.

"'A Fair Curve from a Noble Plan': *Certain Women*." *Movie: A Journal of Film Criticism*, no. 9 (2020): 11–20.

Introduction

Naive Film Criticism

THE PHILOSOPHER Michael Thompson is fond of defending philosophical positions that he describes as naive; he has referred, for example, both to "naive action theory" (Thompson 2008, 83–146) and to a "naive Aristotelianism" (Thompson 2022, 40). He is not alone in this—Jennifer Hornsby has written a book called *Simple Mindedness* whose subtitle tells us that it defends "naive naturalism in the philosophy of mind" (Hornsby 1997). Given the complexity, rigor, nuance, and sophistication of the arguments of both philosophers, their choice of the word "naive" is surely made with their tongues at least in the vicinity of their cheeks. What the declaration of naivety is intended to accomplish is, in fact, to flag up its absence. These philosophers want to indicate both the plausibility and the richness of certain ways of thinking about the world that philosophers desperately searching for radically new perspectives have tended to dismiss as simple-minded, theoretically inadequate, insufficiently sophisticated—in a word, naive.

In calling the introduction to this book "naive film criticism" I want to make a similar gesture with regard to the philosophically informed criticism of film. This book recommends and tries to exemplify critical engagements with narrative film that do not take it for granted that thinking about, for example, a film's characters as (fictionally) real people (with memories, experiences, expectations, intentions, prejudices), who inhabit (fictionally) real worlds, is necessarily less conducive to critical accuracy, incisiveness, or political acuity than is conducting ones analysis in terms of, say, discursive procedures, functional narrative schemas, cultural stereotypes, ideological residues, or one of any number of other alternatives. Nor does it want to argue that such engagements never display such weaknesses; the point is simply that it depends on the film in question and on the kind of claims that the critic is attempting to sustain. (Although this book *does* argue that naive approaches to film may be able to contribute to the study of a wider range of films than may be immediately apparent; see chapter 1 for more discussion of this.) To put the point another way: nothing contained in this book is intended in itself as a rejection of sophisticated theories, of whatever stripe (although it includes plenty that will be incompatible with one or another specific theory). Its premise, rather, is that we need continually to remind ourselves that any theory will be hamstrung, possibly fatally, should its account of what it is a theory *of* be too sketchily or too hastily drawn. Sophisticated film theory and criticism can only be enhanced by more patient and nuanced naive accounts of movies.[1]

At this point, some readers may wish to skip the rest of this preamble and dive straight into the book proper. I would be delighted for them to do so. Although *Haunting the World* is designed to be a satisfying read from cover to cover, its chapters can also be read in any order. The remainder of this introduction sketches aspects of the book's unity and motivations as I see them, but if readers prefer to begin by gaining a more detailed familiarity with its content, they should feel free to proceed straight to chapter 1, or indeed any other chapter that catches their eye. None of the chapters herein rely so heavily on material in previous chapters as to be unintelligible without prior familiarity with it; the text is also lightly sprinkled with references to other chapters to give some assistance to readers taking their own nonlinear route through the material. For those readers who do decide to come to it later, my hope is that what is presented here as an introduction should serve equally well as an afterword. I should also say that although this book is not intended as an introduction either to Perkins or Cavell, I have tried not to make extensive familiarity with their writings a prerequisite. But it is possibly true that readers who have no acquaintance at all with the work of either man might do best to start with one of the chapters that concentrates on an individual film. The best introduction to the work of either writer is, in my view, to plunge straight in, perhaps with some of their shorter pieces. For what it's worth, my personal recommendations would be Perkins's "Moments of Choice" (2020, 209–19) and Cavell's "Leopards in Connecticut" (1981b, 111–32).

※

There are many inquiries into film—some of them, for example, historical or institutional—in which the ways in which ordinary filmgoers (who-, where-, and whenever they may be) watch and interpret films are, quite appropriately, either treated with a great deal of caution or serve chiefly as data to be analyzed. But careful critical engagements with specific films are not, and logically *cannot*, be examples of such inquiries. There simply is no route towards aesthetic analysis of individual films which does not pass through the critic's own experience of, and response to, the film in question. This does not mean that the result must tell us more about the critic than the film; the film remains the object of study.[2] But any attempt to remove the subjectivity from the critic's observations, and by such deletion to avoid vulnerability to personal idiosyncrasy, cannot achieve "objective" analysis; at best it will simply switch the object of analysis from *the film* to *other people's responses to the film*.[3]

Naive film criticism suggests that we still have much to gain by reading with the grain of a film in a sustained fashion. Compare D. A. Miller's sophisticated claim that "everything we *are* asked to see in Hitchcock feels a bit disappointing," which prompts him to suggest that "Hitchcock would cultivate, alongside his manifest style with its hyper-legible images, a secret style that sows these images with radical duplicity" (Miller 2016, 3–4; emphasis in original), with Robert B. Pippin's naive claim that, in *Vertigo*, "the point of showing us just this narration in just this way . . . has a great deal to do with . . . a general, common struggle for *mutual interpretability*" (Pippin 2017, 10; emphasis in original). This is not for a moment to deny the excitement or the perceptiveness of Miller's critical virtuosity; it is merely to say that to think we have superseded or outgrown the kind of inquiry that Pippin engages in would be to let our sophistication get the better of us.

The dismissal of naive readings of film takes many forms. It may, as Steven Rybin has written in paraphrase of my own work, lead to the creation of "critical hierarchies whereby consideration of figures in the diegeses of the films themselves—including the idea of the diegesis as a representation or narration of reality—is set aside as somehow less sophisticated than the apparently higher-order contemplation of cinematic tropes, such as matters of camera movement, mise en scène, or gesture" (Rybin 2024, 5–6).[4] I would certainly want to resist such hierarchies, and the recurrent tendency within film studies to dismiss some extremely insightful analyses of narrative and character (some of them written by Stanley Cavell) simply because their authors do not explicitly discuss film form at length hamstrings the discipline's ability to profit from such insights. The position this book starts from (which follows on from the chapter on figuration in Lash 2020, 91–104), however, resists Rybin's sharp distinction between the "representation or narration of reality" and "cinematic tropes." On the contrary, it is *by means of* such tropes that films both represent and inflect (we could reasonably say comment on) reality. (Part 3 of this book contains three concrete explorations of this idea.) Thus thinking in terms of character—say—is in no way opposed to thinking in terms of figuration.[5]

Another form of resistance to naive film criticism can be found in many discussions of specific cinematic moments, in which it is common to find the overall narrative of a film represented as unworthy of serious interest. In such analyses, specific moments—often resonating with particular personal experiences of the critic—are isolated from their surroundings. The last chapter of this book attempts to show how the closeness of our engagement with one moment in one film can, on the contrary, be enriched by paying attention to that moment's place in the film as a whole, as well as contributing to our understanding of that whole. This involves thinking both about the progression of the film, moment by moment, and its patterning, as well as about the world which it thereby brings into being for its viewers. As V. F. Perkins once wrote, "[l]ack of attention to the world—what makes it a world rather than what makes it fictional—may be one product of the field's recoil from all that smells of realism" (Perkins 2020, 277). Thus, just as figuration is not opposed to characterization, neither are moments opposed to narratives.

The work of Perkins (1936–2016) and Cavell (1926–2018) is exemplary in demonstrating that naive approaches to film criticism can be anything but.[6] On the contrary, the risk of not thinking about films naively is that we do not, in a sense, think about them at all—not, that is, as the kind of aesthetic creations that they were intended to be.[7] That is why Perkins called his first book *Film as Film*, and why Cavell's first book on film is subtitled "Reflections on the Ontology of Film." Cavell's subtitle is intended on the assumption that one cannot find out anything about what film, as film, *is* (and ontology, after all, is simply the attempt to address the question of what something is) without watching a lot of films and trying to get to grips with them on their own terms. Cavell's subtitle continues to lead to a great deal of confusion and misrepresentation because of the widespread belief that "film ontology" must essentially have to do with the physical and institutional aspects of the medium, and thus be a subject that could potentially be pursued without actually watching any films at all. A naive approach to film criticism fundamentally disputes such a view. (See chapter 6 for more discussion of film ontology, allied to a reconsideration of the notion of film experience.)

The most concrete link between the investigations of film conducted by Perkins and Cavell is their shared passion for Max Ophüls's 1948 film *Letter from an Unknown Woman*, to which Perkins dedicated three full articles and a number of other briefer examinations, and which is the subject of the second chapter of Cavell's *Contesting Tears*. Cavell's discussion of the film is informed both by Perkins's writing on the film and by conversations with him that took place "in the early spring of 1992" (Cavell 1996, xv). Perkins's 1990 article "Film Authorship: The Premature Burial" acknowledges its debt to Cavell, "especially his essay 'A Matter of Meaning It' in his *Must We Mean What We Say?*" (Perkins 2020, 239n7).[8] Another article by Perkins—one of his most important, "Must We Say What They Mean? Film Criticism and Interpretation"—originally published in the same year, 1990, pays direct homage to the title of Cavell's first book. Given what was clearly a serious investigation of Cavell's work on Perkins's part at the end of the 1980s, the ground must have been well-prepared for that meeting in 1992. We are not, however, dealing merely with a case of mutual influence but also of congruent perspectives which were in place long before there was any contact; after all, as William Rothman points out, "Stanley Cavell hadn't read a word of Victor Perkins's writings when he published *The World Viewed*, nor had Perkins read any of Cavell's writings when he published *Film as Film*" (Rothman 2021, 251).

How did those congruent perspectives manifest themselves? Let us begin with Perkins. In the piece just cited, Rothman notes that

"Perkins didn't actually write criticism as if its primary task were *judging* films or directors, in effect weighing how many Michelin stars, if any, to award them" (252; emphasis in original). Certainly, Perkins wasn't in the business of awarding cinematic "Michelin stars," but if this is so, on Rothman's account it is odd that *Film as Film* should be subtitled "Understanding and Judging Movies," let alone that its very first sentence reads: "This book aims to present criteria for our judgment of movies" (Perkins 1972, 7). Was Perkins mistaken about what he was up to in his own book? On the contrary, I want to claim that it is another, more philosophical sense of judgment that is most relevant here, one that marks a fundamental affinity of orientation between Perkins and Cavell. One explanation of the apparent discrepancy noted by Rothman would be that Perkins's position changed over time. Douglas Pye has investigated Perkins's later reconsideration of *Film as Film*, according to which the book's emphasis on criteria is perhaps its chief deficiency. Perkins refers in a footnote to the "Film Authorship" piece to his "unease about the concept of an evaluative 'criterion'" (Perkins 2020, 238n2); it seems evident that had he rewritten *Film as Film* in the 1990s he would not have begun with the sentence quoted above. Pye extrapolates from some later lecture notes of Perkins's that, on the most interesting account of evaluation (which we could also call judgment), "what counts as value is not predetermined but remains to be uncovered"; this is referred to in the lecture notes as evaluation in the sense of "effort to define kinds of value," as opposed to "pass/fail or good/bad"—the latter being precisely the sense of judgment that Rothman distances Perkins from (Pye 2023, 22). This is not to say for a moment that Perkins ever thought that criticism could, or should, be neutral on matters of value; the "Film Authorship" article includes the delicious remark that "[w]anting a value-free auteurism is like wanting one's ice a bit warmer" (Perkins 2020, 230).[9] As I will try to explain below, however, Perkins's own self-understanding of his development risks obscuring important continuities in his critical practice, in the judgments he makes and in what he takes himself to be about in so doing; aspects of Cavell's philosophical work can help to bring this out.

In bringing Perkins and Cavell together my intention is, then, to emphasize philosophical affinities which move between positions that are made explicit and methodological presuppositions which shape and guide the writing from the ground up. I claim that they *did* share an understanding of "judgment" and of "intention" and they *could* have shared an understanding of "criteria."

I have already said something about judgment, and will say a little more below when we come to the question of criteria. But first, some remarks on intention. Cavell writes in "A Matter of Meaning It" (a text to which, as we have seen, Perkins explicitly acknowledged his debt) that "a certain sense of the question 'Why this?' is essential to criticism," as well as that "the correct sense of the question 'Why?' directs you further *into* the work" rather than outside it, towards—say—biography, history, or sociology (Cavell [1969] 2015, 210; emphasis in original). If such a claim seems "false or contentious or paradoxical," Cavell insists, this is not merely the consequence of "a bad picture of intention" but also of "a bad picture of what a poem is. It is the picture of a poem as more or less like a physical object, whereas the first fact of works of art is that they are meant, meant to be understood" (210). To think of films this way is precisely what Perkins means by wanting to consider "film as film." On such an understanding, criticism is an attempt to come to terms with the ways in which works of art are "meant to be understood": "That one is locating intention is what accounts for the fact that a piece of criticism takes the form of an interpretation" (217).

That it can seem counterintuitive, or even straightforwardly false, that we might discover intention *in* a film, rather than having to investigate (say) production documents, diaries, or other material contemporary with its making, is an indication of how firmly entrenched is the view of intention as something internal to the psyche, which—when successful—causes the actions which it prompts. Cavell's view, however, is crucially shaped by G. E. M. (Elizabeth) Anscombe's very different picture of what we are doing when we talk about intention, as found in her extraordinary monograph *Intention*, which Cavell describes as "a work which no one involved in this topic will safely neglect" (Cavell [1969] 2015, 217n).[10] It is quite beyond me to offer a summary of Anscombe's very short, endlessly stimulating, but immensely difficult book (Wiseman 2016 is strongly recommended for readers seeking assistance with it); suffice it to say that it represents a sustained attack on what Anscombe calls "Cartesian psychology," according to which "an intention was an interior act of the mind which could be produced at will" (Anscombe 1981, 59). Instead of thinking—as is, she admits, "quite natural"—that something intentional must possess "an extra property which a philosopher must try to describe" (that is, the property of being intentional), Anscombe's insight is that "the term 'intentional' has reference to a *form* of description of events" (Anscombe [1957] 2000, 84 [§47]; emphasis in original). Thus, as Rachael Wiseman puts it, the "investigation into the concept of intention" that we find in Anscombe's book "reveals a complicated linguistic practice, embedded in a complicated form of life" (Wiseman 2016, 180), one in which "a very large, and the most important, section of those descriptions of things effected by the movements of human beings which go to make up the history of a human being's day or life" are descriptions that are "dependent on the existence of this form [that is, 'the form of description "intentional actions"'] for their own sense" (Anscombe 2000, 85 [§47]). This is of relevance to narrative film because both the production of such films, and much of what takes place within them, would be similarly unintelligible in the absence of such descriptions.

To understand intention in these terms (rather than as a mental state or event that exists internally within a person) is extremely illuminating both, for example, when Cavell asserts his confidence "that when I experience a work of art I feel that I am meant to notice one thing and not another, that the placement of a note or rhyme or line has a *purpose*, and that certain works are perfectly realized, or contrived, or meretricious" (Cavell [1969] 2015, 168–69; emphasis in original) and when Perkins declares that "[i]n order to recognise particular sets of choices, one has to have some sense of available choices," which will involve "systems of rhetoric and viewpoint, concepts of plot construction, and, particularly, of continuity" and, "in the ideological area . . . what can function as a focus of dramatic interest, and under what conditions" (Perkins et al. 1975, 13–12). Remarks such as these are sometimes dismissed or ridiculed on the basis that we cannot have the kind of access to a filmmaker's interior life that would enable us to check whether they "meant" what is claimed, or that they thought in terms of these particular "available choices." Anscombe's account of intention allows us to see both Cavell and Perkins as interested not in fleeting moments of psychological experience but in forms of description of films that interrogate their intelligibility and their meaningfulness in the context of shared human lives.[11]

So much for intention. What about criteria? Perkins was quite right to want to move away from criteria in the sense in which they frequently appear in *Film as Film*, but Cavell suggests he may have gone too far in wanting to ditch evaluative criteria entirely. Something akin to Cavell's alternative account of criteria, outlined below, is not in fact entirely absent from *Film as Film*. See, for example, the remark that, in the most positive sense, criteria "relate to claims which the critic can sustain rather than to demands which he must make" (Perkins 1972, 59). In context, this remark is meant to indicate critical humility ("we can evolve useful criteria only for specific types of film, not for the cinema" [59]) and also to criticize more all-encompassing manners of theorizing. (Chapter 1 has some criticisms to make of the first of these aims.) We might see *Film as Film*'s weaknesses regarding criteria as related not so much to the theoretical deficiencies of the idea of evaluative criteria as to those moments when Perkins slips into *making demands* rather than keeping the focus on *sustaining claims*. (Again, chapter 1 has more to say about this.) But Perkins's later repudiation of criteria neglects a different set of implications that might be drawn from his own remark. As Pye puts it, what Perkins was really concerned with were "[c]laims that can only be defined and sustained by detailed critical engagement with the film," which means that they "can only emerge from—are formulated in—that engagement" (Pye 2023, 24). The phrasing "formulated in" is very well-chosen, and of the greatest importance. It is *in* "detailed critical engagement" that critical claims *and* the criteria which they require for their coherence and comprehensibility are *both* "defined and sustained." The criteria are not formulated in a separate theory and then brought to bear, but this does not imply that criteria are irrelevant.

Even though they don't focus on aesthetic criticism, the early parts of Cavell's *The Claim of Reason*—whose very first chapter is called "Criteria and Judgment"—rebut the claim that criticism doesn't, and shouldn't, "proceed through the use of anything that can reasonably be described as criteria" (Pye 2023, 22) by presenting an account of what criteria might be that, I claim, Perkins *would* have been willing to accept. (Or perhaps it would be more correct to say *should*. I do not know what Perkins himself would have made of *The Claim of Reason*, but my claim is that the philosophy it makes explicit is, in this regard, in accord with what is implicit in the best of Perkins.) Cavell's account is presented as an interpretation of the later Wittgenstein's "recurrent idea of a criterion" (Cavell 1979b, 6). He makes a distinction between criteria and standards: "Both criteria and standards are means by which or terms in which a given group judges or selects or assesses value or membership in some special status; but criteria, we might say, determine whether an object is (generally) of the right kind, whether it is a relevant candidate at all, whereas standards discriminate the degree to which a candidate satisfies those criteria" (11). The judge in, say, "Kennel Club or Horse Shows, or diving competitions" turns out to have "a more or less clear area of discretion in the application of standards, but none whatever over the set of criteria he is obliged to apply" (12). This is the kind of judging that Rothman is quite right to say that Perkins has no interest in. However, in Wittgenstein's idiosyncratic use of the notion of criteria there is never "a separate stage at which one might, explicitly or implicitly, appeal to the application of standards" (13). The first example Cavell offers of such a case is, suggestively, an aesthetic question: "Is Schoenberg's *Book of the Hanging Garden* a tonal work?" (13). A useful answer to such a question will have much more to do with "claims which the critic can sustain" than with "demands which he must make" (Perkins 1972, 59). We might say that the weakness of Perkins's early work was not that it involved criteria but that it confused them with standards—"We have a duty to ourselves to ensure that our standards are as clear and consistent, as perceptively implied, as we can make them" (Perkins 1972, 190)—whereas the kind of criteria that are involved in Perkins's (and in Cavell's) best criticism are much more like those at play in the following: "In judging (saying something true or false) you have to be able or willing to judge a contraction of the face as a wince, to recognize a smile as forced, to find a slap on the forehead to express the overcoming of stupidity by insight, a fist to the heart to express the overcoming of stiff-neckedness by contrition, a tone of voice to be that of assertion" (Cavell 1979b, 35). I hope I have said enough by now for it to be apparent how relevant this is to film criticism in its naive form. (If not, chapters 4 and 5 have more to say about these matters.) Non-naive criticism is naive in thinking that this dimension of our understanding of films is unproblematic, that it can be skipped or presumed.

The passage from Cavell just quoted will strike a familiar note to those acquainted with Wittgenstein's discussion of seeing aspects in part 2 of the *Philosophical Investigations*. This kind of seeing is intimately connected to acting; there would be little point in judging "a contraction of the face as a wince" were it not to have consequences for one's dealings with the person judged to have winced. Also worth noting in this regard, therefore, are Anscombe's remarks about interpretational motives and their complexity. She points out that "if we wanted to explain e.g., revenge, we should say it was harming someone because he had done one some harm; we should not need to add to this a description of the feelings prompting the action or of the thought that had gone into it. Whereas saying that someone does something out of, say, friendship cannot be explained in any such way" (Anscombe 2000, 20 [§13]). I take from this that something as apparently straightforward as friendship cannot be factored into its internal and external dimensions.[12] There is no account of an act of friendship that does not take heed of "feelings" or "thought," but that does not make the action we are concerned with into mere *evidence* of friendship. An act can be, precisely, an act *of* friendship; one might see such a thing in a film. Anscombe goes on to remark that "[t]he motives admiration, curiosity, spite, friendship, fear, love of truth, despair and a host of others" are for these reasons very often "extremely complicated" (21 [§13]); as a result, she is "very glad not to be writing either ethics or literary criticism" (19 [§12])—or, presumably, film criticism! This all suggests an important way in which the interpretation of narrative (whether in film or elsewhere) holds out the promise of genuine philosophical insight and thereby suggests another line one might take in defending naive approaches to film.[13]

I cannot here work out these claims about criteria, nor about intention, in the detail they deserve, but they underpin much of this book.[14] The work collected here did not, in the main, set out from an explicit recognition of these links between Perkins and Cavell; what I have been saying in these few paragraphs represents a sketchy attempt to bring out something of the basis of the important affinities I have consistently, if often inchoately, perceived between these two bodies of work. Which is to say that the book spends very little time arguing that it is illuminating to bring Cavell's work on film together with Perkins's; the test of that particular pudding must be in the eating.

In bringing this introduction to a close, an account of the structure of the book will be useful. The two chapters that comprise its first section engage directly with Perkins, setting out some issues that are central to the continuing value of naive film criticism. "*Film as Film* in the Twenty-First Century" disagrees with Perkins on some points of detail in order to subscribe all the more strongly to what I take to be the fundamentals of his approach. The second chapter, "V. F. Perkins and the Redescription of Films" attempts to do for the notion of description something similar to what Alex Clayton has done with "aesthetic suspense" (see Clayton 2016), drawing out some insights and implications that Perkins left largely implicit in order to extract critical resources from his writing without hardening it into a rigid methodology.

The book's attention then moves to the work of Stanley Cavell. Chapter 3, "'Not Yet the Last': On a Paragraph by Stanley Cavell" is a very close reading of the final paragraph of the original version of Cavell's first book on film, *The World Viewed*, the paragraph in which, as Cavell put it much later, his "preoccupation with ghosts and the spectral began to take on explicitness" (Cavell 2005c, 108). The chapter aims to bring out both the fact and the way—neither, I think, sufficiently appreciated—that this paragraph brings together many of the book's themes (which are also themes of wider importance in Cavell's philosophy). Chief among them is the importance to Cavell of mortality. The chapter also endeavors to counter the unfortunately persistent tendency to distort the interpretation of Cavell by treating the form of his writing as too easily and too neatly separable from what it attempts to convey and to accomplish; the position that this book takes on cinematic figuration (which is articulated in more detail in later chapters) is thus shown to have relevance also to criticism itself.

With the fourth chapter, the book moves into the mode in which it will remain for the majority of what follows: namely, extended readings of individual films. The films discussed range fairly broadly historically (the films discussed in the greatest detail were released in 1948, 1963, 1976, 1979, 2006, 2016, and 2017) and rather less broadly geographically (the majority of them originate in the United States), but there is no particular significance to the specific grouping of films covered. They are simply all films worthy of sustained attention. Although these chapters (I hope) bear out what is said in the earlier ones, they should not be thought of as applying a theory of philosophical criticism which is set forth at the beginning of the book. *Haunting the World*, throughout, is more concerned with proposing and exemplifying methods and attitudes than it is with constructing theories, although many of the book's claims certainly have theoretical implications, and these are by no means confined to the first three chapters. Indeed, aside from Cavell—who was professionally a philosopher—and Perkins (whose work is philosophically very astute), various other philosophers make an appearance, including Nietzsche, Wittgenstein, and Hegel, as well as the aforementioned G. E. M. Anscombe, whose work on agency and intention particularly informs chapters 6 and 9. Rather than setting out a theory per se, then, the first three chapters are intended to set the scene, after which issues of theoretical and philosophical importance are allowed to emerge via close engagement with individual films. That such engagements can all-too-easily be distorted by getting our theoretical priorities wrong is a thought that lies just beneath the surface of the entire book.

The engagements with Cavell to be found in part 2 concentrate much less than does most Cavellian work in film studies on Cavell's most influential contributions to thinking about film, his proposal of the genres of remarriage comedy (in Cavell 1981b) and the melodrama of the unknown woman (in Cavell 1996)—although both chapters 4 and 5 do engage with the comedy of remarriage. In both cases, however, my claim that the films discussed are related to remarriage comedy has more to do with setting the stage for an engagement with other Cavellian themes than it does any attempt to engage directly with Cavell's thinking on genre. Cavell's thought has much more to offer the study of film beyond these two categories (intriguing and productive though they certainly are); these chapters are attempts to indicate what some of these offerings might be. In chapter 4, Cavellian (and Wittgensteinian) themes of privacy, consent, and—most centrally—expression are discovered within Ildikó Enyedi's *On Body and Soul* (*Testről és lélekről*, 2017). Chapter 5 addresses Cavell's reading of Wittgenstein's thinking about criteria and their relationship to crisis as this informs Paul Thomas Anderson's *Phantom Thread* (2017) and the kind of remarriage comedy I believe it to be, after which chapter 6 addresses themes in Cavell's work that are of theological relevance, exploring their application to the films of Stanley Kubrick. (There is a little more theological material in chapter 10.) Chapter 6 also speaks to questions of experience and ontology in film as well as picking up the theme of Cavell's interest in human finitude which was central to chapter 3.

Haunting the World's third part addresses the work of some very different thinkers on film—all of them, as it happens, French—whose work is much more connected to non-naive domains of film theory: Nicole Brenez, Jean-Pierre Oudart, and Gilles Deleuze. But although it contains criticisms of this work, the function of this section is by no means to set up Perkinsian or Cavellian criticism as superior to or incompatible with this kind of work. Instead, it collects investigations into the films of Abel Ferrara, Ridley Scott, and Werner Herzog, all of which develop threads that began earlier in the book concerning questions of critical priority, agency, and intersubjectivity. These three chapters are united by a concern for figuration taken in the sense I have already touched on sketchily earlier in this introduction—in which figuration involves attention to the film's shape and its processes of shaping, rather than being a way of signifying that operates separately from, or even in opposition to, narrative and characterization—a sense which is indebted to the work of Brenez and which the first chapter in this section articulates in more detail. This is developed in chapter 8, which approaches Scott's *Alien* (1979) by means of a fresh approach to the once much-championed, and equally much-maligned, notion of cinematic suture. Chapter 9 reconsiders Deleuze's famous distinction between the movement-image and the time-image, and in particular its implications for our understanding of agency, in the light of his remarks about Werner Herzog's *Heart of Glass* (1976). Perkins and Cavell are not always prominent in this section, but the insights gleaned from their work that are set forth in parts 1 and 2 ground all the thinking here. For example, the conclusion of chapter 9 implies that the accounts of cinematic agency that we find in Perkins and Cavell are to be preferred over that which we find in Deleuze.

The fourth and the final part of the book concentrates on questions of agency and psychology in the work of two filmmakers: Andrei Tarkovsky and Kelly Reichardt. Chapters 10 and 12 are concerted attempts to demonstrate in concrete detail some of what a naive approach to film criticism has to offer. (Between them there is a short chapter connecting some of the themes that chapter 10 identifies in Tarkovsky's *Stalker* with aspects of Reichardt's work.) Recalling issues that I touched on at the beginning of this introduction, the first of these chapters attempts to demonstrate that detailed psychology and irony are not irrelevant to Tarkovsky's cinema, and the second argues against the view that an interest in individual moments of a film must tend to direct us away from a concern with wider patterns of narrative and action.

A concluding word on the book's title is in order. Lola Seaton notes that the poet Louise Glück once answered a demand for a definition of poetry with the claim that it "is that which haunts." Seaton goes on to remark: "That which is memorable—one is tempted to say, 'merely' memorable—stays with you; that which haunts won't leave you alone. That which haunts affects, consumes, disquiets, returns unbidden, perhaps unwelcome. . . . [I]n fact, we may be haunted by what we would prefer to forget, or are in danger of forgetting (or fear we are: Hamlet's father's ghost commands him to 'Remember me')" (Seaton 2023). The films discussed in this book, in their various ways, wouldn't leave me alone; in this may lie something of their poetry. The specific phrase "haunting the world" was a favorite of Cavell's, for whom it refers chiefly to the isolation and disconnection, the "sense of human strangeness to itself" (Cavell 2005c, 44) that can be the result—or the manifestation—of skepticism, a theme which runs through *Haunting the World*. (Particularly detailed accounts of what this can look like are to be found in chapter 10, which shows how the Stalker's self-pity becomes his way of haunting the world, and chapter 12, which presents Reichardt's *Certain Women* as a detailed study of some of the ways in which the plans via which we navigate our lives—carefully considered, hastily improvised, or somewhere in between—can isolate us from one another as easily as bring us together, or even achieve both at once.) But Cavell's use of the phrase also relates to his sense of what films are, that they offer each of us "[a] world complete without me which is present to me" (Cavell 1979a, 160). This haunting is multidirectional: in watching films we haunt other worlds, but every lover of film knows how readily the worlds that we have thereby haunted can come to haunt our own, in terms similar to those that Seaton outlines. As Cavell puts it: "The impact of movies is too massive, too out of proportion with the individual worth of individual movies, to speak politely of involvement. We involve the movies in us." (154). One of the morals that Cavell draws from all of this is that film, and our experience of film, has a profound and serious connection to the ways in which we so easily come—problematically, sometimes tragically—to haunt our own world, and that film can therefore not merely illustrate but also illuminate this phenomenon. Haunting the world is, of course, not merely a state we can find ourselves in, but something we *do*; it is in order to explore this idea further that the later chapters of *Haunting the World* become more and more explicitly concerned with questions of agency. To say this is to offer a hint as to why I believe that it would be a mistake to characterize what I have been calling a naive approach to film criticism as, in and of itself, an attempt to evade the political.

Part One

V. F. Perkins

1

Film as Film in the Twenty-First Century

The English critic V. F. Perkins was never a prolific writer, although his passion for teaching—he taught at the University of Warwick for almost forty years—has produced more than one generation of film scholars shaped by his patience of mind and acuity of vision.[1] His work first came to attention via his contributions to *Movie*, a journal he cofounded in 1962 with Ian Cameron, Mark Shivas, and Paul Mayersberg (and soon to be joined by Robin Wood), in which much of his work appeared.[2] Yet it was only with his first and only full-length book, *Film as Film* (originally published in 1972) that Perkins fully set out his philosophy and methodology of criticism. (Since his death, Douglas Pye has done the world an immense service by collecting Perkins's shorter criticism into a single volume; see Perkins 2020.) Although he reviewed and refined some of the positions taken in that book over the years that followed—some important revisions are contained in his 2005 piece "Where Is the World?"—he never deviated from its central vision. That vision involved a commitment, both patient and passionate, to a method of interpretation which combined vivid imagining of the fictional world with close attention to artistic techniques of signification. A single sentence from an article originally published in *Movie* in 1963 will perhaps serve to demonstrate this vision in microcosm: "Much of the meaning of [Nicholas Ray's] *King of Kings* is contained in its intricate pattern of looking, glancing and staring" (Perkins 2020, 163–64). We cannot, according to Perkins, fully appreciate the meaning (either as noun, in the sense of that which a film conveys, or as participle, as in how a film goes about being meaningful) of a fictional film without both imaginatively inhabiting its fictional world *and* paying the closest possible attention to its formal patterning.

A dedication to clarity was also an abiding feature of Perkins's work. He spoke in a 2011 interview of his interest in "a clarity that can articulate subtlety," but also of his sensitivity to the fact that "it's easy to achieve clarity if you crudify" (Zehle 2011). Perkins was determined to involve himself in what a very different type of critic, whose work is discussed later in this book—namely, Nicole Brenez—has referred to as "tak[ing] the risk of the work itself" (Brenez 2011). He remained adamant that oversimplification was not a price worth paying for clarity; hence his resistance to David Bordwell's formalism, about which he observed in 1990 that, "[a]s in many other efforts to put work in the humanities on a Sensible Footing, the task is assumed to involve drawing criticism closer to the natural sciences but according to an all-clocks-and-no-clouds model that scientists themselves reject" (Perkins 2020, 254). The arguments put forward in *Film as Film*, then, still have much to offer the thoughtful film student. Revisiting them now is perhaps particularly timely, when it is in some quarters apparently regarded as the case that "it can surely be said that we are some decades past the time when judgement and taste constituted crucial parts of art criticism and theory" (Chakravorty 2017, 153). Assertions of taste dressed up as arguments are indeed to be deplored; but so is the notion that "judgement and taste" can, let alone should, be simply and neatly excised from criticism and theory. Perkins's body of work stands as a peerless example of the role judgment and taste can play in reasoned argument.

In what follows, however, rather than simply enumerating the strengths of *Film as Film*, I want to suggest some of its limitations, or rather some ways in which it might be seen not fully to follow its own proposals. I will defend two related propositions: firstly, that some of the readings the book proposes could be otherwise framed, given an adjusted set of assumptions (chiefly regarding the nature of diegesis and artifice), without thereby departing from the book's general tenor; and, secondly, that the book's fundamental methodological recommendations are more widely applicable than the author himself allows.

Film as Film begins by sketching the early histories of film and of thinking about film, and in doing so makes some sound observations concerning the ontology of cinema. Perkins's contest with "established theory" may perhaps seem a little brittle to today's reader, when the theoretical landscape looks so very different, but criticisms such as the following (of Rudolph Arnheim) remain valuable: "The manner of recording, here and throughout established theory, is given a quite artificial precedence over what is recorded. It is as if a theory of poetry were to acknowledge that words refer to things but insist that the critical reader should be concerned with their sounds alone" (Perkins 1993, 17). This should be remembered in the context of current debates about "medium specificity" (see, for example, Turvey 2022). To say so is not to deny the importance of the medium, simply to argue that its relevance and significance are always relative to the particular questions being asked. The central purpose of *Film as Film* is to argue for a methodology in which it is incumbent on the critic to frame their judgments—which is to say any and every evaluation of the relevance and significance of an element of a film—within the context of the questions that are at issue. But if we are not to give automatic precedence to the cinematic apparatus, how should we consider the ontology of film? We should, suggests Perkins, recognize and celebrate its hybridity: "The movie incorporates the real object or fictional event into the medium itself" (Perkins 1993, 24), and hence that which is "presented becomes a part of the manner of presentation" (25). Respecting the nature of film is an admirable intention for a critic (hence the book's title), but this respect can easily go astray; the critic should remember that to "search for grace through purity contradicts the cinema's hybrid character" (58). If there is to be a striving for grace, it needs to happen otherwise than through purity.

Perkins's reminders about the history of film are helpful in this context because of the need always to be sensitive to the complexity of the relationship between what is called illusion and what is called reality when dealing with film: "In its conception and at its birth, the motion picture was a curious hybrid: the magic lantern was crossed with the optical toy, and the offspring of this liaison was mated with the camera. The cinema bears to this day (and for the foreseeable future) every mark of its mixed parentage. The relationship between illusion and reality is usually ambiguous and often chaotically muddled" (42). This is well put, but I have reservations about Perkins's subsequent argument. He writes that "[t]he attempt to show 'how the very properties that make photography and film fall short of perfect reproduction can act as the necessary moulds of an artistic medium' [Arnheim] puts the emphasis in the wrong place, by making temporary limitations of the cinema's mechanism stand in for a coherent view of its *artistic* disciplines" (57; emphasis in original). Granted, the disjunction between "perfect reproduction" and artistic reproduction is unhelpful, and Arnheim himself hypostatizes a particular state of cinematic imperfection. But in countering him Perkins, it seems to me, risks implying that the history of cinema's technical devices is one of simple addition—everything as before, plus new possibilities: "Devices which are necessitated by one set of mechanical limitations become optional, but not unusable, when those limitations are removed" (56). But the significance of shooting a film on black-and-white celluloid today—when to do so is a choice not to use cheaper and more flexible digital means—is not the same as it was when that was the only option available. *Film as Film* recognizes this, but still sees only gain: "Only with colour as an available resource can we regard the use of black-and-white photography as the result of an artistic decision" (54). Options, however, have been not only gained but lost. Those specific uses of black and white that take their meaning from the presumption that all other films are also black and white are no longer possible: try making a black-and-white film today and not signifying "art film," at least to some extent.[3] To oppose Arnheim's claim that the situation was previously more limited, and therefore better, with the view that the situation is less limited now, and therefore an improvement, is undialectical and unsatisfactory. Possibilities change their meaning when limitations change, and vice versa.

But let us move to Perkins's proposals regarding the nature of criticism. He suggests the following: "To regard criticism positively, as a search for the most satisfactory definitions of function and value, allows an escape from academic systems of rules and requirements. Criteria then relate to claims which the critic can sustain rather than to demands which he must make. . . . Anything possible is also permissible, but we still have to establish its value. We cannot assess worth without indicating function" (59). This proposition gets to the heart of *Film as Film*'s continuing usefulness. The last sentence, in particular, of the above passage crystallizes the book's fundamental insight, one that is a powerfully productive guideline for critical writing of any kind. Value is relative but not untethered: we must indicate function, after which it may become possible to assess worth. But, of course—and this will be central to my argument—any indication of function stands just as open to challenge as any assessment of worth. The critic would do well to bear in mind Nietzsche's insistence that valuing is always valuing-over. Thus positive criticism cannot escape a simultaneous devaluation, because the very selection of criteria devalues those criteria not selected. Sensible as Perkins's suggestion to regard criticism "positively, as a search for the most satisfactory definitions of function and value," is, such an approach risks a vulnerability to the charge of turning its own presuppositions into prescriptions if some account is not taken of whatever it is that the act of valuing something positively has thereby *de*valued.

Perkins argues that it follows from his position that "the critic cannot require a movie to fit his definitions; it's his task to find the description which best fits the movie. The most he can 'demand' from a film is coherence: a structure which points consistently towards the performance of comprehensible functions. Without that, judgement becomes impossible" (62). This is also a very reasonable assessment of the critic's situation, but the introduction of notions such as "coherence," "consistency," and "comprehensibility" makes the situation very tricky if we are to avoid inadvertently imposing a particular view of what such things might be. (It is worth noting that Perkins himself came to have reservations about this aspect of *Film as Film*; he said to John Gibbs in 1997 that "I think that *Film as Film* slightly overdoes coherence really" [Gibbs 2019, 48]. A project complementary to the one undertaken in this chapter would be to articulate Perkins's career—and particularly his tendency to keep returning to certain films over and over—as a continual struggle against critical prescriptiveness, an attempt to take as seriously as possible what is involved in taking a film on its own terms; the following chapter has more to say on this issue.) The argument against imposing definitions onto a film also applies to metacritical statements such as this, and we need to be just as careful about the definitions of the terms by which we regulate our criticism as we are about those we use to conduct it. The relationship between coherence and consistency, in terms of how we judge divergence of tone, diegetic mode, and so forth, is particularly delicate. Perkins's associate at *Movie*, Robin Wood, once declared—and I think the Perkins of *Film as Film* would have entirely agreed—that he does not "see how incoherence can possibly ever be regarded as an asset" (Wood 1976, 19).[4] Wood's examples of instances where incoherence mars but does not ruin great works (D. H. Lawrence's *The Rainbow* and F. W. Murnau's *Sunrise*) might, however, be better described as instances of inconsistency. If coherence can only be predicated of a whole (can anything be *partly* incoherent?), then nothing prevents coherence being developed precisely via inconsistency (which certainly *can* be local—or might even necessarily be so).[5] *Pierrot le fou* (Jean-Luc Godard, 1965), which Wood declares to be "a film that teeters on the brink of chaos, its compositional principles being barely adequate in strength or definition to hold together the complex impulses at work," might be an example of this: from "barely adequate" it surely follows that the film's "compositional principles" *are* adequately cohesive (20).[6] If, then, a successful film is *necessarily* (in some sense) coherent, coherence (or its absence) becomes something that can be declared—albeit perhaps provisionally—at the conclusion of a critical investigation (or demonstrated during the account of one) rather than a critical criterion in itself with any obvious local application.[7] At any rate, if our definitions of coherence and comprehensibility are themselves too rigid, we will end up, in spite of everything, requiring films to fit our definitions. This would be precisely what Perkins strives to avoid in *Film as Film*, which he claimed "is, as far as I know, the first attempt at an aesthetic and evaluative theory of film which is not prescriptive," in contrast to some of his earlier, "dogmatically prescriptive" writing in *Movie* (Perkins 1972, 147).[8]

That prescriptiveness is a genuine risk is illustrated by Perkins's treatment of *Play* (Dusan Vukotic, 1962), a short film in which the drawings made by two young children come to life and interact with one another. Perkins states of the film that the "only rational explanation for its events is that the battle takes place in the children's minds," which is apparently contradicted by the fact that it nevertheless "puts the real boy and girl on exactly the same level as the animated drawings" (Perkins 1993, 63). Aside from the fact that there is not really anything stopping us using the first explanation if we wish (we would just have to see the film as a composite representation of two minds: "My car runs over your flower!" "Well then I'm slashing your car's tires!"), Perkins here appears to confuse a certain mode of diegesis with rationality itself. That which is shown might well be *impossible* in "real life," but there is nothing *irrational* about a representation which begins in a realistic mode and then moves into the realm of fantasy or imagination ("What if our drawings could come to life?"). To equate diegetic consistency with rationality risks confusing the notion, or the illusion, that a consistent and coherent diegesis directly presents a consistent and coherent world with the notion of reality itself. Perkins could be seen to imply that cinematic enunciation is only rational when it pretends not to be enunciation at all. However, the effectiveness of the surprise elicited by the transition between diegetic modes that happens in *Play* is predicated precisely on the *reasonableness*, not exactly the *rationality*, of the expectation that a narrative mode, once introduced, will be maintained, as well as, crucially, the subsequent recognition that another (equally comprehensible and thus equally rational, though clearly not realistic) mode has been entered.[9] That we are both surprised by *and understanding of* such a transition indicates its rationality. Perkins claims that *Play* "might be expected to irritate its audience by requiring simultaneous belief in actions which exist on two different levels of credibility," though he does not criticize it for this (his criticisms lie elsewhere, in the fact that, for him, it eventually "declines into a pretentious cold-war allegory"):[10] "In fact the cinema's magic is powerful enough to overcome purely rational objections of this sort" (63). Imagine, however, that the narrative was presented as a short story. Would we be likely to raise such "rational objections"? Would we not simply say that the narrative procedure chosen by the author began in a realistic manner and moved subsequently into what we could perhaps call magic realism? Perkins's presuppositions about the nature of diegetic coherence are indicated by his distinction between rationality and magic, which muddles the distinction between the rational and the irrational, in terms of the way we comprehend narrative, with that between realistic and fantastic (or magical) modes of diegesis. (The novelist John Barth has written that he finds "the fantastic device of Hamlet's father's ghost a good deal more believable than the realistic device of the accidental exchange of poisoned swords in the midst of Hamlet's duel with Laertes in Act V" [Barth 1984, 223].) In this context, the rational and the magical are two sides of two quite different distinctions, but Perkins treats them as two sides of a single distinction. It seems to be this confusion that leads him to attribute irrationality, quite inappropriately, to *Play*.

This might seem to be a minor quibble about a particular understanding of the word "rational," but I think it has reverberations elsewhere in the view of diegesis that permeates *Film as Film*. Let us look at Perkins's treatment of *The Children's Hour* (William Wyler, 1961), which he refers to by its British title, *The Loudest Whisper*. This is the story of the destructive effects that a rumor of homosexuality spread by a young girl has on the lives of two schoolmistresses, Martha (Shirley MacLaine) and Karen (Audrey Hepburn). Perkins objects to the way in which, when Mary (Karen Balkin) whispers the fateful gossip to her grandmother Amelia (Fay Bainter), we cut from the back of the car in which they are traveling to the front with the driver, shielded from the crucial conversation by a pane of glass (fig. 1.1). Perkins objects that this is an unmotivated transition that exists simply to prevent the audience hearing what the granddaughter says: "There is, literally, no excuse for the device: we are deprived of what we want to hear and offered no compensatory distraction" (Perkins 1993, 125). This is not quite correct: Mary begins to whisper *before* the cut; her mouth, shielded by her hand, is pressed right up to her grandmother's ear, so that we cannot hear what she says in any case. Well, Perkins might say, that only makes the device both arbitrary *and* superfluous; and as he rightly notes, we do not need to hear the words "since we are well enough aware that the accusation is of homosexuality" (125). But what *is* the effect of our being placed next to the chauffeur? I suggest that it evokes something of the nature of gossip. We are aware that a secret (an exciting, shocking secret) is being exchanged, but simultaneously made conscious of our exclusion from that exchange, as well as of the frustration and the desire to be *in*cluded that such an exclusion provokes. The front of the car feels airless in its isolation from the communication occurring in the back, making us desperate for the oxygen of inclusion: when the grandmother slides back the glass panel, after the secret has been transmitted, the acoustic changes and we are able to hear more ambient sound. We have been let in to the space of transmission, but all too late. Since the actual nature of the secret is clearly predictable, far from being a ham-fisted method of controlling audience knowledge, the device is in fact an effective way of generating a particular set of sensations and significations.

Nor is this an isolated incident; a very similar device is used later. All the girls are being pulled out of the school by their parents

Figure 1.1a and 1.1b. We are shielded from the conversation. *Source: The Children's Hour* (1961).

in response to Amelia's spreading of the rumor. Martha and Karen are beside themselves with anguish and confusion, having no idea what could be behind it all. They implore the parents to let them know why they are removing their daughters, but nobody will tell them. Finally, Karen manages to persuade one father, who tells her the reason on the path outside the front door of the school. The camera, however, remains behind with Martha, standing just inside the building behind the closed screen door (fig. 1.2). Once again the device evokes the feeling of exclusion and the desire to know, but our position as spectators is shifted. In the earlier scene we were placed with the driver, a member of the little society in question (the society

Figure 1.2a and 1.2b. Martha is blocked from the conversation. *Source: The Children's Hour* (1961).

that will be titillated and supposedly threatened by the rumor) but one who is, at this point, excluded from the gossip. The way it provoked our desire to be included illustrates something about the impulse which causes gossip to spread. But now the desire to know belongs to one of the offending parties, who are in fact the wounded parties, and the exclusion is even more damaging: denying the accused any knowledge of the charges against them means that the gossip is able to spread unchecked. The fact that a very similar narrative device is used in both instances underlines the formal parallels between these two situations while also emphasizing their emotional and ethical disparity—precisely the kind of meaningful and economical patterning that Perkins praises so highly in other films.[11]

It is somewhat curious that Perkins's criticism of Wyler's device is contrasted with Alfred Hitchcock's practice in *Rope* (1948). In that film there is a sequence in which the housekeeper comes close to opening the chest in which the victim's body lies. The camera angle prevents us from seeing what the two protagonists (and murderers) are doing: "The suspense of the scene depends on our being made to wait for the moment when the housekeeper opens the chest. It is heightened by the frustration of our desire to know whether either of the heroes is in a position to observe what is happening and so intervene to prevent catastrophe" (125). This really is a case of withheld information, unlike the example from Wyler, in which we are so readily able to infer the content of the whisper. Perkins admires the pervasiveness of Hitchcock's control: "He has placed his actors in such a way that within this setting there is no angle from which the camera could embrace both the corner where the heroes are standing and the housekeeper's passage from sitting-room to dining-room" (126). This has been well established long before the sequence in question. Hence, for Perkins, the artifice is not as intrusive as it is in Wyler. But one could easily counter that *Rope* is, on the contrary, *saturated* with artifice. The fact that Hitchcock goes to such lengths to engineer the visual restriction in question is only one example among many. The virtuosity is extraordinary, but whether it is felt to result in an engrossing economy of means, a distractingly hypercontrolled atmosphere, or some other possibility is an open critical question.[12]

We might compare Perkins's comments on *The Children's Hour* with those on the ending of *La notte* (Michelangelo Antonioni, 1961), which he also sees as an instance of arbitrary exclusion. For him, the film ends "when it has served the director's purpose but before it has satisfied the spectator's requirements" (149). "In *La Notte* the 'real ending' is knowable but has been withheld. The picture would need to cover at most another two or three hours in its protagonists' lives in order to resolve the ambiguities of its last sequence" (149). Thus different viewers have different feelings about "what 'actually' happens after the end of the picture, and, as a result, whether the conclusion is optimistic or otherwise" (148). Could not the stimulation of such a situation have been one of the director's intentions, rather than it being the case that Antonioni's interest was only "in the crisis itself . . . not in how it can be resolved" (147)? Of course, Perkins is comparing *La notte* with the exemplary integration of narration, diegesis, and theme he discovers in *Anatomy of a Murder* (Otto Preminger, 1959). But no film is fully narratively closed, and the amount of diegetic time necessary for a fuller resolution is irrelevant because diegetic time is only ever a construction. A similar argument could be made about the ending of, say, *My Darling Clementine* (John Ford, 1946). Will Wyatt Earp ever return to Clementine? A simple cut to a scene two or three years later could equally well have resolved the ambiguities of that film's final sequence.[13]

Perkins is also critical of a lighting change and closeup in *The Criminal* (Joseph Losey, 1960): "Since the effectiveness of the film depends on our being literal-minded in our response to the image there is nothing to be gained by the deliberate creation of discrepancies" (83). It is not quite clear to me whether Perkins means that the effectiveness of Losey's film in particular relies on a certain literal-mindedness in the audience (in which case he does not argue why this should be the case), or that the effectiveness of all films relies on this (in the sentence before the one quoted he refers to "the director" and "the film" in what are clearly general terms), in which case I think he is simply wrong. Consider another case of dramatic and unmotivated lighting change in a different film from the same year: *Sergeant Rutledge* (John Ford, 1960). In this courtroom drama, transitions from scenes set in the courtroom to scenes that directly represent the events being described by the witnesses are preceded by the witness being isolated in a pool of bright light, surrounded by darkness. There is clearly no diegetic motivation for this device. It draws attention to the artifice of the film at the expense of the diegesis. But, equally clearly, it was never intended to represent a diegetic change in lighting, nor was it intended to disrupt the diegesis in such a way that we might begin to doubt its coherence or reliability. It represents, instead, the intensity of each witness's attempt to focus on their memories and the way that their present surroundings fade from their consciousness as they do so. It also, through its repetition, creates a formal device that marks off the two different timescales of the film, that of the continuing trial and that of the events which led to the trial in the first place. Clearly there can be critical debate on the effectiveness of such a device, about whether its positive qualities do or do not outweigh the disruption of diegesis that it involves, but I do not see how we are justified in making blanket statements such as that the "effort of adjusting to an incredible lighting scheme is not conducive to concentration" (83). Surely the question here has to be "concentration on what?" Incidentally, shortly after his criticism of *The Criminal*, Perkins disparages the use of color effects in *Red Desert* (1964) in a similar fashion: "We are so busy *noticing* that we respond rather to our awareness of the device than to the state of mind it sets out to evoke" (85; emphasis in original). Given *Film as Film*'s frequent praise for Hitchcock's *Marnie* (1964), from the same year, it is odd that nowhere is there any mention of its similarly dramatic color effects, which are also motivated by character psychology (Marnie's phobia of the color red).[14]

All narrative is artifice, and Perkins argues for a certain kind of artifice, since there cannot be none at all. But an alternative artifice could also have been effective, and justifiable. The critic cannot merely state that a device is intrusive, but must evaluate how intrusive it is, and to what purpose. Perkins applauds instances where a desired narrative effect, or effect of mise-en-scène, is achieved in a diegetically justifiable manner, such as when the lighting of the chicken-run sequence in *Rebel without a Cause* (Nicholas Ray, 1956) "is traced to a quite credible source: the headlamps of the cars which other gang members, spectators, have drawn up along the sides of the course" (84). Such devices, used well, are indeed excellent instances of creative and diegetic economy. But it is equally conceivable that a contrived diegetic excuse for some narrative effect would draw more attention to itself (distractingly and unhelpfully) than a device without any strictly diegetic motivation. Imagine that in the Wyler film we had been prevented from hearing the girl's whisper because another car passed by on the other side of the road, the noise of its engine drowning out the conversation. In such an instance it is at least possible that the introduction of a diegetic event *purely* for a specific narratological purpose would, though entirely "plausible," be far more artificial than the use of a device without diegetic motivation. Perkins in fact insists on a related point: "The fictional world is not some inert matter to be galvanized into significance by the rhetorical manipulation of the movie's language" (130). Certainly the resistances of diegesis to manipulation are very interesting, and this is because the fictional world only exists through the collaboration of the viewer's imagination (and imagination has its limits—not in the sense of external boundaries but in the sense that we cannot *simply* imagine anything we wish in connection with anything else; the imagination is not a free-for-all). But the film's rhetoric also helps *produce* the world: we cannot entirely separate world and rhetoric because the nature of the world can only be inferred from what the film shows us.[15] This is not to say we cannot feel rhetoric and world to have an unhappy relationship, but rather that if we wish to claim this about a film, we need to recognize that this unhappy relationship itself comes about through the film's rhetoric.

This fact could, I feel, have been given greater emphasis in an interesting alternative account of the question of films and worlds: Daniel Yacavone's 2015 book *Film Worlds*. Yacavone's distinction between the "world-of" and the "world-in," between "films as artistic worlds distinct from fictional story-worlds," sidesteps exactly the questions of diegesis and credibility with which I am concerned here, and in fact often displays a surprisingly untroubled view of the ontological stability of the fictional world (Yacavone 2015, xxi). He writes, for example, that "[c]inematography, camera placement and movement, editing, staging, design, music, and lighting may all be seen to take up what amounts to a particular *perspective upon* the represented *world-in* of some films" (124; emphases in original). But these elements are also the only means by which we have access to the world-in at all! Yacavone is talking here about devices that draw attention to themselves, but this relies on a background of standard narrative strategies, which must themselves give a particular "perspective upon" the world-in. Hence the world-of is logically (at least with regard to reception) prior to the world-in: we postulate the world-in as a consequence of the world-of, rather than seeing the world-in and then examining what sort of perspective on it we are afforded by the world-of.[16] Hence the critic cannot merely identify diegetic motivation or the lack thereof when judging such instances of tension between diegetic credibility and evident artifice. Indeed, in his later work Perkins recognized this and articulated the situation thus: "Because the world is created in our imaginations it need not suffer damage from any foregrounding of the devices that assist its creation. We can, if we will, glide over inconsistencies and absorb ruptures, or delight in them. It is not difficult to see the image on the screen simultaneously as a world and as a performance. We do it all the time" (Perkins 2020, 296). Shortly afterwards, Perkins declares in conclusion that "understanding the events of a movie as taking place in a world is a prerequisite of the intelligibility not only of plot but also of tone, viewpoint, rhetoric, style and meaning" (297). I would only amplify or qualify this (I am not quite sure which of these Perkins would deem the following claim to be doing) by saying that the possibility of making inferences based on our world that are appropriate to a given fiction is not predicated on the completeness, coherence, or consistency of the fictional world, nor is it undermined if the relationship of that world to our own is symbolic or allegorical. Consider, for example, the emotional intelligibility of Beckett's *Waiting for Godot*, or of *Holy Motors* (Leos Carax, 2012).

Both in *Film as Film* and in his later writing on film worlds, Perkins omits any serious consideration of the extent to which what he proposes applies to less naturalistic or more fantastic cinema. He does consider *The Wizard of Oz* (Victor Fleming, 1939): "The physiologies of a man of tin and a man of straw—together with the threats from rust, fire or loss of stuffing—are easy to comprehend; and in Oz, as in Kansas or Coventry, the same things count as evidence of nerve, brain or heart" (Perkins 1993, 284). This is quite right, but the danger of extrapolating such a position is that it could easily slide into an excessive literal-mindedness that would, for example, fundamentally misconstrue allegorical worlds. In *Film as Film* Perkins strays near this territory with his criticism of the stone lions in *Battleship Potemkin* (Sergei Eisenstein, 1925): "If we interpret the image in context, the lion has dozed contentedly throughout the massacre" (104). This is obviously a deliberately lumpen objection, intended to highlight the artificiality of the effect. But it is a very curious objection to make to a film whose every shot, as Sam Rohdie puts it, is "at once within the diegetic boundaries of the film and going beyond it" (Rohdie 2006, 34). Hence Perkins's objection that "[u]nattached stone lions had no place in a film which undertook to convey ideas and experiences through the presentation of experiences believably undergone by a group of rebel sailors" (Perkins 1993, 189) is bizarre, because the film clearly does *not* attempt exclusively so to do. Eisenstein's focus on the shock of confrontation, on the creation of new effects and the generation of response in the viewer precludes any such overriding commitment to the "believable"; he wrote in 1926 of the way that "individual elements of affect" do not, in *Potemkin*, appear "within the story (in the generally accepted sense of the term)" but are, rather, "strung along the 'story carcass'" (Eisenstein 1968, 14). In this context we should also note that we cannot a priori even assume that the people who appear in a film are meant to be characters as we ordinarily understand that word, and thus to possess, fictionally, a world. Not all theaters work that way—certainly not Noh theater, or indeed the Proletkult theater in which Eisenstein worked before moving into cinema. Nor did he forget all that he learned there: "The characters in *Strike* are not characters in the usual way. Essentially they are exaggerations, caricatures and in that sense rather than the actors seeking to realistically play a part, create a 'person,' they act to distort, to make emphatic (over-acting), grotesque and comic (in the sense of clowning about)" (Rohdie 2006, 39).

Given his preference for synthesis, Perkins is approving of instances where the narration reinforces what other elements of the film are telling us about a character or situation. He writes of another sequence in *Rope* that "the flashy precision of the camera effect informs our view of Brandon; the split-second control of the image becomes a projection of Brandon's evil assurance and calculation" (Perkins 1993, 88–89). It seems, then, that stylistic excess is acceptable if motivated diegetically (like those car headlamps in *Rebel Without a Cause*), or by character, whether metaphorically (Emma losing her hat in *Johnny Guitar* [Nicholas Ray, 1954]; see 78) or mimetically, as in *Rope*. But what of irony or other narrative "comment"? Perkins does claim that his view can incorporate irony, speaking for example about an ironic effect of editing in *Marnie* (100). But does not irony often rely on just the kind of separation between diegesis and narration that Perkins so often criticizes? Nobody would expect a narrator in a novel to eschew explicit or implicit comment on the action or characters, whether or not the narrator is an identified diegetic character. What prevents something analogous from happening in film?[17] Perkins asserts that synthesis, "where there is no distinction between how and what, content and form, is what interests us if we are interested in film as film" (133). Such a situation is predicated on "our common experience of the world" (187). But what are we to do if a director is interested in that in our experience of the world which is *not* held in common? Or if, as Rohdie argued in his review of *Film as Film*, a director (such as, he suggests, "Eisenstein, Vertov, Makavejev, Straub, Marker, Rocha") attempts not to collapse content and form, not to synthesize, but instead to work directly with the earlier stages of the dialectic, to "present a conflict in the film text, or, more precisely, locate contradictions between, in *Movie* terms 'device' and 'content'" (Rohdie 1972, 139)?

Film as Film occasionally strays too close for comfort towards the profoundly ideological position of arguing for the possibility of a nonideological standpoint: "It is a man's own, and legitimate, decision whether to concern himself with any medium for its own sake.... He may have no use for the cinema except as moral propaganda, or as an elaborate light show" (Perkins 1993, 187). Must we dismiss such films from consideration as films? On the contrary, given that the "weakness of much criticism is its insistence on imposing conventions which a movie is clearly not using and criteria which are not applicable to its form" (188), the task is to search for appropriate and applicable criteria. Such a search need not lead us merely to exchange Perkins's interest in synthesis for an approach which, as Rohdie characterizes modernism, treats "the art object as the prime material reality" and therefore concentrates "on the 'text' as a construct of signs and as the locus of any problem about art and aesthetics" (Rohdie 1972, 135). Terry Eagleton argued many years ago that the very concept of the aesthetic (which any interpretation and evaluation of cinema can never wholly escape, should it even try) "offers a generous utopian image of reconciliation between men and women at present divided from one another" at the same time as it "blocks and mystifies the real political movement towards such historical community" (Eagleton 1990, 9). We might find this too schematic, but Eagleton draws the correct moral, namely, that "[a]ny account of this amphibious concept which either uncritically celebrates or unequivocally denounces it is thus likely to overlook its real historical complexity" (9). Tracing the way that particular films take particular positions or use particular strategies with respect to this dichotomy is surely preferable to focusing either on film as world or film as text to the exclusion of the other position.

The strongest criticism of disruptive effects in *Film as Film* might be the following: "As an illusion-spinning medium, film is not bound by the familiar, or the probable, but only by the conceivable. All that matters is to preserve the illusion. . . . [T]he created world must obey its own logic. There is no pretext, whether it be Significance, Effect or the Happy Ending, sufficient to justify a betrayal of the given order. In a fictional world where anything at all can happen, nothing can mean or matter" (Perkins 1993, 121).[18] The penultimate sentence here is predicated on the final sentence: the reason why the "given order" can never justifiably be betrayed is because if it is, then all criteria for significance become empty. But at what point can one say that the "order" has been "given"? Would it be possible to provide examples of meaningless films where anything can happen?[19] They cannot exist because films are not infinitely long! Rewatching can always reveal new logics. We might still feel a film was excessively indulgent or insufficiently integrated—perhaps calamitously so—but to say so would be a judgment relative to function (as Perkins insists all judgments must be) and to the balance between various tensions in the film. Indeed, tension and release is (as Perkins would, I am sure, wholeheartedly agree) crucial both to the construction and the effect of any successful film. Why should a variation in degrees of credibility not itself be a source of drama? (The chapter on *Holy Motors* in Lash 2020 represents an investigation into something like this.)[20] This is, once again, a question of film worlds. In some stories, asking for certain consistencies to apply to the world is not simply unnecessary but inappropriate. This can be demonstrated negatively by the fact that a narrative can surprise us or make a joke by answering questions about its world which we had, quite reasonably, been happy to leave unasked: much of Terry Pratchett's career was based on doing just that ("A Thaum is the basic unit of magical strength. It has been universally established as the amount of magic needed to create one small white pigeon or three normal-sized billiard balls" [Pratchett (1986) 2012, 47].) Does a film's reliance on our knowledge of our world mean that it *has* to postulate a gap-free world of its own? To say that Godot exists somewhere in the play's world, and that reasons for his nonappearance must also exist, would be to misunderstand the play entirely—but this does not mean that we therefore see Vladimir and Estragon as merely allegorical or absurdist ciphers that do not inhabit a world.

In "Where Is the World?" Perkins suggests that imagination might cut through this kind of difficulty:

> If we insist too much on reason here we shall divorce criticism from experience. It is normal for a movie to stress and sustain the separation between the fictional world and the world of the viewer. Imagination allows the movie to work within that register. But imagination makes other registers available as well. In one such, a world may be suggested whose beings can respond to our watching. In another, the film may have its actors step aside from their character roles and move apart from the fictional world so as to appear or confront us in their own right. (Perkins 2020, 293)

But this rests on a distinction between reason and imagination as unhelpful as that we saw earlier between reason and magic. To imagine is not to cease to use one's reason; indeed much—one might even say all—rational activity is impossible without the use of the imagination. Perkins might reply that in *Film as Film* he clearly states that he is not providing standards of judgment for any and every film: "The values I have claimed for *Rope*, say, or for *Johnny Guitar*, cannot be claimed, in the terms of this study, for a picture like Godard's *Les Carabiniers*, where the fictional action attempts neither credibility nor the absorption of personal meaning into a dynamic pattern of action. The degree to which *Les Carabiniers* is to be valued will have to be argued in terms other than those proposed here" (Perkins 1993, 190). This passage indicates Perkins's sensitivity to an issue I earlier suggested that he is at times in danger of occluding, namely, that without a recognition of the critic's own hierarchy of value, the (inevitable) presence of presuppositions are liable to decay into (unwarranted) critical prescriptions. In claiming that his critical values (those of "credibility" and "the absorption of personal meaning into a dynamic pattern of action") are utterly irrelevant to Godard's film, however, Perkins's medicine is too drastic. An admirable attempt at methodological humility ends up exaggerating the differences between Godard's work and that of the filmmakers for whose work Perkins's methods are most evidently suited. *Les carabiniers* (Jean-Luc Godard, 1963) has a great deal to do with credibility, even if it is in the way it becomes strained, stretched, or even destroyed; and the film is certainly concerned with relationships of meaning arranged in dynamic patterns. Susan Sontag interprets the return of Michel-Ange and Ulysse from their travels with nothing but a collection of postcards as a "gag" which "vividly parodies the equivocal magic of the photographic image" (Sontag 1977, 2). But the gag would have no meaning if it did not discover something absurd in how they (and we, with our own holiday snaps) treat images of valuable things as themselves valuable. The length of the scene and the level of delight the postcards generate are obviously incredible. This means that credibility is not irrelevant to the fictional action, something it does not even barely touch upon; rather, the fictional action's purpose and effect are inexplicable without addressing the question of credibility.

There is, then, no reason why the method of *Film as Film*, broadly conceived, could not be brought to bear on, for example, what Perkins himself beautifully describes as "the shattered continuities of Alain Resnais's *Last Year in Marienbad*" (Perkins 1993, 56). Perkins's belief "that a longing for an all-embracing aesthetic of *the cinema* is the worst part of our inheritance from the major theorists, and a symptom of the immaturity of the discipline of film criticism" (Perkins 1972, 149; emphasis in original) does not preclude a wider applicability for his methods of articulating and evaluating the aesthetics of certain films than he himself seemed prepared to grant, certainly at the relatively early stage in his career that *Film as Film* represents. The fundamental motivation for these criticisms of Perkins's book, then, is not because its project is misguided, but precisely because it is so well-founded. To insist that it is not possible to "assess worth without indicating function" (Perkins 1993, 59) means that if we seem to encounter something that impedes a particular function, it is incumbent upon the critic to search for alternative motivating functions. These functions might be found to relate to any aspect of our world and any way of existing in or interpreting it. Close reading and detailed investigation of function, pattern, and effect in any film need in no way predispose one, *pace* the Rohdie of 1972, "to ignore modern theory and to reject most of the past" (Rohdie 1972, 143).

There is a famous story about Theodor W. Adorno at the 1951 Darmstadt summer school for new music. Adorno strongly criticized a piano sonata by Karel Goeyvaerts for its lack of motivic development. It fell to a young Karlheinz Stockhausen to defend the work, pointing out that Adorno was criticizing the work for not being something it was not attempting to be: "Professor, you are looking for a chicken in an abstract painting" (Stockhausen 1989, 36). Perkins might be seen as recommending us to do our utmost to avoid such wild poultry chases, which is certainly good advice. But following this advice does not mean that if we cannot see a chicken at first glance, we must assume all our accumulated avian knowledge to have become instantly irrelevant. On the contrary, we may simply have to think a bit harder about the ways we can put it to good use. I hope to have begun to demonstrate that Perkins's method is *not* inextricably tied to the notion that "we can value most the moments when narrative, concept and emotion are most completely fused . . . where there is no distinction between how and what, content and form" (Perkins 1993, 133). Or, to put it another way, that we can consider such statements as hyperbole, reading "no distinction" as "little distinction" or, better, as "no straightforward distinction." This kind of remark might then be seen less as indicating that Perkins's approach is only applicable to films whose attitude mirrored that exhibited by his writing (films whose efforts are aimed, as Perkins said his were, at "mak[ing] the labor disappear" [Zehle 2011]) than as demonstrating the importance of developing and deepening our sense of the complexity of such distinctions. My purpose in showing that some of the things criticized by Perkins can be defended without departing from his fundamental methodology has been to demonstrate that the limitations of some of the critical judgments in *Film as Film*, if considered rightly, serve only to highlight the book's undiminished vitality.

2

V. F. Perkins and the Redescription of Films

VICTOR PERKINS'S WORK always stood, and continues to stand, at (at least) one remove from the mainstream of film studies. His interest in paying the closest possible attention to the life of the fictional worlds depicted in films and his aversion to the construction of elaborate theoretical edifices put as much distance between him and so-called *Screen* theory (the 1970s amalgam of semiotics, Althusserian Marxism, and Lacanian psychoanalytic theory named after the journal once much associated with this kind of theorizing) as it did between him and the cognitivist theories initiated in the later 1970s and the 1980s by scholars such as David Bordwell and Noël Carroll, with their interest in the way films exploit—and hence give us insights into—the normal workings of the human perceptual, cognitive, and emotional apparatus. Perkins's consistent lack of interest in theory (qua theory) has contributed to a caricature that paints him as an old-fashioned moralizing formalist, interested primarily in aesthetic synthesis and suspicious of the irresponsibility of modernist dissonance and fragmentation. I hope the preceding chapter has helped to demonstrate that—although, as with all caricatures, this one is not based on *sheer* fabrication—it is a misleading and unhelpful distortion of Perkins's work, and one which risks obscuring the valuable contributions his thought, and work inspired by his thought, have to make to film studies today.

Indeed, there is a growing body of work aimed both at correcting this view and at demonstrating the wider contemporary relevance of

Perkins' work.[1] This chapter is intended to contribute to this development by concentrating on the perhaps innocuous-sounding subject of description; it will use Perkins's work to assist in constructing some proposals about the function and value of description in film criticism. I will argue that it is possible to use Perkins's practice as a model in which film-critical description serves as a fulcrum between some quite different, but nonetheless intimately connected, senses of description. Perkins shows that description in film criticism can illuminate both (1) what we might refer to as the descriptions traced *by films themselves* (I will clarify this slightly obscure phrase in what follows) and (2) the moral agency and psychology of the characters in films, the understanding of which is very largely a function of appropriate *act descriptions*.

This chapter aims, then, to bring out coherences in V. F. Perkins's writings on film that he did not himself thematize or bring to the foreground, coherences that are grounded in connections between the role that description plays in Perkins's writing and that writing's ethical concerns. These connections can be clarified by exploring the intersection between a range of senses of the word "description," and particularly its close relation, "redescription"; or so I will argue. If it is fruitful—as, following Raymond Williams, I believe it is—to think of redescription as a fundamental practical ethical operation, then Perkins's work demonstrates that narrative films can be remarkably rich sites for the exploration of this operation. Specifically, I will argue that Perkins's criticism suggests the existence of a very interesting subclass of such explorations that I will refer to as "failures of redescription."[2]

The structure of the chapter is as follows: after briefly introducing the topics of description and redescription in Perkins's writing, the next two sections survey pertinent accounts of description in film criticism and theory and in moral philosophy. The chapter then arrives at its central topics—failures of redescription and Perkins's interest in them—which are explored chiefly through his writings on two films: *Letter from an Unknown Woman* (Max Ophüls, 1948) and *America, America* (Elia Kazan, 1963).

Perkins and Redescription: Introduction

Perkins was clear from early on in his career that value-free description is impossible. He declares in *Film as Film* that the temptation is to deny the validity of judgement altogether and to confine criticism to a descriptive role with no claim to be able to evaluate. But this position turns out to be a sham. Even description depends upon forms of evaluation which are no less "subjective" than judgement. A descriptive analysis will need at the least to make claims about the distribution of the film's emphasis; and emphasis is as subjectively perceived, relies as much on a personal response, as judgement. (Perkins 1993, 191)[3]

Description is therefore not, for Perkins, something preliminary to be got out of the way as quickly as possible so that we can move on to the serious business of analysis. Nor need it diminish the particularity of its object. Whereas the narrator of Olga Tokarczuk's novel *Flights* claims that "[d]escribing something is like using it—it destroys; the colours wear off, the corners lose their definition, and in the end what's been described begins to fade, to disappear," Perkins feels something like the opposite to be the case (Tokarczuk 2017, 75). Description is a crucial pivot between the aesthetic demands the critic feels that the film places on them (the need to do justice to the film) and the question of *what it is* that is placing these demands. Without accurate description—without persuasive "claims about the distribution of the film's emphasis"—we have little chance of achieving an accurate sense of what, exactly, is placing the aesthetic demand to which the critic was responding in the first place. Both these questions, as Robbie Kubala has argued, involve practical reasoning. (So, for example, those questions of emphasis which a description brings out relate to what we have to *do* to watch a film with understanding.) On Kubala's account of aesthetic obligation, "the considerations that have the decisive force of obligations—the *focus* of aesthetic obligations"—are not "features of aesthetic objects by themselves, or features of persons as such, but the connections that features of aesthetic objects bear to the practical identities of persons" (Kubala 2018, 279; emphasis in original). Kubala gives an example of the narrator's response to having to leave his beloved hawthorns, early in Proust's *À la recherche du temps perdu*, arguing that he "may not yet know precisely which features of the hawthorns give them their importance for him, but in finding out he will discover more about what he is responding to" (279).

It is the practical side of this process of "finding out" that I propose to refer to as *redescription*. Perkins's former student Andrew Klevan writes, apropos of a description by Perkins of a scene from Orson Welles's *The Magnificent Ambersons* (1942), that "[d]escription is not simply a matter of telling us accurately or evocatively what we can see, but what we may come to see" (Klevan 2011, 83). Description is important largely because of the constant possibility of *re*description—if we "come to see" things differently we have redescribed them—and the shifts in perspective and insight that redescription can facilitate. I say "constant possibility" because, as J. L. Austin puts it, "no situation . . . is ever 'completely' described" (Austin 1970, 184). Supplementing a previous description is itself a form of redescription. The medium of film is profoundly well-suited to the exploration of description and redescription through its combination of visual motifs with a host of other forms of patterning, something Nicole Brenez refers to as "constructing a film through the form of a passage between altered images" (Brenez 2007, 21), and that Perkins emphasizes when he states that "[b]asic to the synthetic approach to movies which I believe most productive is the claim that significance, emotional or intellectual, arises rather from the creation of significant *relationships* than from the presentation of things significant in themselves" (Perkins 1993, 106–7; my emphasis). Critical description is not, therefore, merely a tool for reminding the reader of details of the film under discussion; descriptive writing about film can help elucidate the senses in which films themselves can plausibly be said to "redescribe" characters, situations, and events. In what follows, I will suggest that Perkins's descriptive practices in his critical writings represent a site in which different senses of description powerfully intersect, thereby serving to express continuities between the activities of film, viewer, and critic.[4]

Description in (Film) Theory and Practice

In this section I want to examine some ways in which aesthetic theory has claimed that description is not only something that one can do to artworks, in writing, but also something that artworks can do themselves. There has recently been a resurgence of critical interest in description, responding to a perceived upswing in the prominence of descriptive practice. Stephen Benson summarizes this history efficiently:

"The notion of a so-called 'descriptive turn,' first proposed in the 1990s, originated in the social sciences and has spread thence across the disciplines and their objects, including most recently to literary criticism and literary history; has spread, that is, both to the descriptive practice of a discipline and to the objects of that discipline understood as being themselves descriptive" (Benson 2018, 46).[5] This particular trend has not, thus far, had much impact on film studies.[6] However, as I have already indicated, Perkins's work serves to demonstrate both the potential virtues of "the descriptive practice" of the film-critical discipline, and some ways in which its objects—that is, films—can be "understood as being themselves descriptive." Benson suggests that a distinctively descriptive mode can be found in the work of such disparate contemporary writers as T. J. Clark, Wayne Koestenbaum, Lisa Robertson, Kathleen Stewart, Timothy Morton, Timothy Bewes, and David James. While I would not claim that every aspect of the descriptive mode that Benson proposes applies to Perkins's work, the overlap is sufficient for us to see him as operating within the orbit that Benson describes. It is, I think, plausible to see Perkins's work as "suggestive of an experiencing and writing first person . . . [as] tending to avow and affirm rather than . . . critique; and, regarding classification as creative or critical, decidedly open" (44).[7] I find all three of Benson's tendencies borne out in a passage such as this, from Perkins's short book on *The Magnificent Ambersons*:

> The film's game with time has become boisterous and unpredictable. We are invited to share in pleasure at the plasticity of the image and sound, their openness to interruption, displacement and manipulation. . . . There is continuity in the world represented but not in the means or the density of representation. Some episodes are fully realised although uprooted, their characters active in identifiable social settings—the barber's, the dressmaker's. At other points the speakers are speakers only, isolated from their own lives and contexts against blank backgrounds of empty sky to deliver their views of Amberson actions and prospects. (Perkins 1999, 38)

The first person is clearly present, albeit in plural form, suggesting, it seems to me, an invitation to test the description against one's own experience rather than a prescriptive assertion. The passage also, via descriptive nouns and adjectives ("boisterous"; "unpredictable"; "plasticity"; "interruption, displacement and manipulation"; "blank"; etc.), "affirms" rather than "critiques" the film's "game with time." This description aims at critical accuracy and yet it is also a passage of creative prose; in this regard it is, as Benson put it, "decidedly open." Perkins's description aims both to specify ("Some episodes . . . At other points . . .") and to evoke ("uprooted"; "blank backgrounds of empty sky") the exhilarating collision between the "continuity" of the world depicted in Welles's film and the discontinuity of that very depiction. The passage does not want us to return to the film unchanged; it seeks to render more exact our sense of the film's address to its viewers. The description attempts neither to replace the film with language, somehow to "translate" it into description without remainder; nor does it want merely to append the author's subjective impressions to our memories of *The Magnificent Ambersons*. Instead, it proposes new ways of seeing the film. If its proposals succeed, it is indeed Welles's film that we will see anew (herein lies the criticism), but it is Perkins's description that will have helped us so to see it (herein lies the creativity).[8]

A different sense of the role of description in film and film theory was proposed by Raymond Durgnat in 1982. Durgnat objects to Christian Metz's comparison of shots in films to sentences in language: "Had he said 'the shot is a description' it would have been easy to see that narratives are made up of descriptions, and that a narrative is simply the description of a series of events (which are usually implied to constitute one entity of some sort). But whether we stress that entity or those events, narrative is simply a subtype of description" (Durgnat 1982, 109–10).[9] It is not at all clear that narrative is helpfully understood as a subtype of description,[10] but Durgnat's comments are nonetheless very valuable in suggesting that films *themselves* might be understood to constitute, or perhaps to be constituted by, acts of description. In this they seem richer in potential consequence than Frank P. Tomasulo's discussion of narration and description in a sequence from Welles's *Citizen Kane* (1941). Tomasulo concludes that we are dealing with "an authorial agency that alternately, and sometimes simultaneously, narrates from the points of view of the participating characters and describes from the viewpoint of a more impersonal author" (Tomasulo 1996, 516).

By associating narration with diegetic characters and description with the film's "author," this formulation does not appear to allow for the possibility that characters might describe (isn't Thatcher describing Kane when he tells him that he's "one of the largest stockholders in the Public Transit Company"?) and authors narrate. (Tomasulo's title refers, of course, to the classic statement of opposition between narration and description, one that comes down firmly on the side of narration, namely, the 1936 essay "Narrate or Describe" by Georg Lukács [Lukács 1970].)

It is true that narration and description are often held to be in some kind of opposition, because narration implies propulsive action of some kind, which needs to be paused in order for description to take place. As the art historian Svetlana Alpers puts it, "[t]here seems to be an inverse proportion between attentive description and action: attention to the surface of the world described is achieved at the expense of the representation of narrative action" (Alpers 1983, xxi). Durgnat appears to subscribe to a similar view when he claims that "Rossellini . . . rather flattened 'classical' emphases under a kind of description, in contrast to Hollywood, which accelerated and simplified description for the sake of fast-moving stories" (Durgnat 1982, 118), as does Seymour Chatman when he argues that "what happens in description is that the time line of the story is interrupted and frozen" (Chatman 1980, 123). Both these facets of description—its narratological and dramatic dimensions—are rich and interesting but, although they have been central to what study there has been of the descriptive activity of films themselves, neither is my primary focus here.[11]

It might be useful at this point to recall that to describe can mean to mark out or draw, as in the geometrical sense of the word. As a narrative film progresses it describes—in the sense of outlining and filling in—a whole range of persons, events, attitudes, and so on. To return to the distinction between showing and describing: we can be shown something without having specific features pointed out, but a description must of necessity select and emphasize some such features, even if this emphasis happens only by means of selection; recall Perkins's claim that "descriptive analysis will need at the least to make claims about the distribution of the film's emphasis" (Perkins 1993, 191). Of course, films *do* show, but they *also* describe. And they do so, I want to argue, by means of what we have already seen Brenez refer to as "a passage between altered images" (Brenez 2007, 21); it is in the process of this passage that they perform the acts of selection and emphasis necessary for description to take place. (Another way of articulating the relationship between showing and describing might be to say that the sense in which films describe is closer to the way an argument can show something to be the case, or even, perhaps, the way a hotel employee might show you to your room, than to the way we might show a friend our new car. But films are obviously excellent at this last kind of showing as well.)

D. P. Fowler has compared verbal description with what goes on in photography: "The same photograph can be read as a sign of triumph or an indictment of crime, but verbal description has to take a stand, however 'objective' it attempts to be. Again, there is an obvious sense in which description in language inscribes a point of view more forcefully and more unambiguously than plastic art" (Fowler 1991, 29). Because they take place in time in a way that photographs do not, even though our contemplation of them must necessarily do so, films have to "take a stand" in a manner analogous to Fowler's account of verbal description, and thus can meaningfully be said to engage in acts of description. Later I shall give some examples of how they do so, by means of the descriptive criticism of V. F. Perkins, but first I need to set out the second of the two senses of description which his critical descriptions of films intersect with, namely, description as an aspect of moral philosophy.

Description and Moral Philosophy

A tradition within moral philosophy that draws on the likes of Hegel, Nietzsche, and Wittgenstein, and includes figures such as Elizabeth Anscombe, Iris Murdoch, Bernard Williams, Cora Diamond, and Robert Pippin, among many others, has emphasized the centrality of appropriate act description to our understanding of intention and agency.[12] One of the fundamental insights of Anscombe's work on intention—which if not, in and of itself, an example of moral philosophy, was centrally concerned with demonstrating, as Rachael Wiseman puts it, that "discharging the . . . tasks of conceptual clarification required for moral philosophy to be possible and describing the unity of the concept of intention are the very same project" (Wiseman 2016, 65)—is that actions can be intentional under one description but not under another.[13] I might be intentionally keying a car, but not intentionally keying *your* car, if I do not know that the car which I am keying is yours.

In a chapter on the relationship between literature and moral philosophy whose insights are just as pertinent with respect to film, Diamond (whose work in this area is deeply influenced by Anscombe) defends "a particular view of moral philosophy, of how far it is concerned with a world whose deepest difficulties include difficulties of description" (Diamond 1991, 378). Such a view is offered in opposition to one that sees moral philosophy as concerned with matters of choice, narrowly construed. Instead, argues Diamond, moral philosophy must concern itself with ways of seeing the world. Following Murdoch, she objects that "[i]f we treat action as the central notion in defining the sphere of morality, this may . . . have as one of its sources a view of the world as in a fundamental sense comprehensible, and of the facts constituting the situations in which we act as straightforwardly describable" (377).[14] In many a concrete situation, whether fictional or real, it will be very difficult to determine quite how to describe what is going on; doing so is both ultimately unavoidable and of fundamental ethical significance.

Looking at things this way, argues Diamond, suggests a particular sense of "the moral interest of literature," one that involves the recognition of "gestures, manners, habits, turns of speech, turns of thought, styles of face as morally expressive"; she concludes that "[t]he intelligent description of such things is part of the intelligent, the sharp-eyed, description of life, of what matters, makes differences, in human lives" (375). Recognizing "gestures," "turns of speech," and "styles of face"—not to mention "manners," "habits," and "turns of thought"—are, of course, what we spend much (perhaps even most) of our time doing when watching narrative films.[15] Pippin has argued that films are excellent sites for the dramatization and exploration of the—often profound—difficulties that arise when finding appropriate act descriptions ceases to be straightforward. He claims, for example, that "film noirs' narrative structure continually raises questions about the identifiability of reliable act descriptions . . . in a way that challenges widely held, conventional views about the nature of action and agency" (Pippin 2012, 114n11).

Murdoch expresses a consequence of the type of position outlined in the previous three paragraphs as follows:

> In short, if moral concepts are regarded as deep moral configurations of the world, rather than as lines drawn round separable factual areas, there will be no facts "behind them" for them to be erroneously defined in terms of. There is nothing sinister about this view; freedom here will consist, not in being able to lift the concept off the otherwise unaltered facts and lay it down elsewhere, but in being able to "deepen" or "reorganize" the concept or change it for another one. On such a view, it may be noted, moral freedom looks more like a mode of reflection which we may have to achieve, and less like a capacity to vary our choices which we have by definition. I hardly think this a disadvantage. (Hepburn and Murdoch 1956, 54–55)

Before finally getting round to looking at Perkins's work in some detail, I want to bring in a name from a slightly different tradition: Raymond Williams, who proposes a sense of description which is, I think, quite helpful in bridging the gap between the ways that films "describe" and the ethical aspects of finding appropriate act descriptions.[16] In the first chapter of *The Long Revolution*, entitled "The Creative Mind," Williams argues that "each one of us *has to learn to see*. The growth of every human being is a slow process of learning . . . 'the rules of seeing,' without which we could not in any ordinary sense see the world around us" (Williams 1961, 33; emphasis in original). He goes on: "We learn to see a thing by learning to describe it; this is the normal process of perception, which can only be seen as complete when we have interpreted the incoming sensory information. . . . The process of interpretation is neither arbitrary nor abstract; it is a central and necessary vital function, by which we seek so to understand our environment that we can live more successfully in it" (39).[17] This kind of description is, for Williams, something epistemological and adaptive; if we want to adapt to something new, we will have to engage in acts of redescription. Elsewhere, in the context of a discussion of Ingmar Bergman's *Wild Strawberries* (1957), Williams argues that

that film is a distinctive and powerful form because the competent film viewer "has learned the conventions of this highly mobile and flexible form, and sees *with* it, in a radical way" (Williams 1968, 163; emphasis in original).[18] Thus, in my terms, the viewer is guided to see *by* the descriptions that make up the film, the way its "highly mobile and flexible form" traces similarities and differences in meaningfully productive ways—and a good critic's descriptions will help clarify the ways that this happens.

Critically evaluating aesthetic function involves, then, assessing these acts of description and their consequences; as Perkins once remarked during a roundtable discussion, "in attempting to produce some kind of evidence to criticism, one is taking positions about ways of recognising" (Perkins et al. 1975, 13). This sense of recognition seems to me very close to what Williams calls description. Accurate recognition relies, for Perkins, on a continual awareness of the possibility of alternative descriptions, or redescriptions. A film could be said to describe things in a certain way or ways, and the film viewer has an awareness both of the way the film does this and of the other ways it might have been done. For example, Alex Clayton has elucidated Perkins's notion of "aesthetic suspense," responding to a passage that describes the music in Nicholas Ray's *Johnny Guitar* (1954): "The hyperbolic quality of Young's score is appreciated even as it contributes to the urgency of conflict and the vividness of emotional depiction. Intensification is calculated to arrive at, but not to pass, the edge of absurdity. The daring in this process constructs an aesthetic suspense that defines the film's special thrill" (Perkins 2020, 360).[19] Clayton makes it clear that this aesthetic suspense operates precisely because of our awareness of the possibility of alternative descriptions; as he puts it, in the sequence in Nicholas Ray's *Johnny Guitar* when Emma and her mob confront Vienna, "[a]esthetic suspense results from the perception that we are only a whisker away from risibility" (Clayton 2016, 212). That is to say, the suspense results from our sense that there is a myriad of different ways the scene could have been portrayed, many of them differing only minutely from one another; we get a sense of the particularity of the scene partly by means of our awareness of the paths not taken that hover somewhere in our awareness. The sense the critic has in writing about a film that it resists paraphrase need not generate the sense that the film could have taken no other form than the one it does. On the contrary, our sense of the possibilities not actualized, the roads not taken, the descriptions not selected, very frequently *sharpens* our sense of a film's achievement (or, just as likely, its failure to achieve something).

But it is not only a question of the most successful films describing "accurately," as it were. We must also come to terms with the fact that, for Williams, we *can't not* describe, if we want to see anything at all: "We learn to see a thing by learning to describe it" (Williams 1961, 39). So this is another reason why it is reasonable to speak about films as descriptive: because they so often adopt the stance of a describer, whether that position is occupied at a given time by a particular character, a narrator or "monstrator," or—most broadly—"the film itself."[20] Fowler points out that "description is rarely 'pure,' because the way that narrative impurity is introduced is often through the figure of an observer" (Fowler 1991, 27), an observation that resonates with Perkins's sense of one of the distinctive aspects of film: "The movie can explore the opportunities of unembodied viewpoint but it can never escape the necessity of viewpoint itself. So one of the arts of the movie is to turn this condition to advantage" (Perkins 2020, 275).[21]

Failures of Redescription

How, according to Perkins, do films "turn this condition to advantage," and to what extent is this a matter of description? Andrew Klevan argues that "Perkins demonstrates that good description . . . puts the matter of what is present at stake" (Klevan 2011, 83). In what remains of this chapter I want to suggest that Perkins had a particular interest in films that dramatize what I will call *failures of redescription*, precisely because such films provide rich opportunities for the critic to explore what, precisely, is at stake. In narrative films we encounter another layer of description to those already mentioned because characters within the film are constantly engaged in acts of description, redescription, or misdescription, either explicitly or in something like Williams's sense. When dealing with failures of redescription, criticism is concerned with describing the way that a particular film's aesthetic function involves dramatizing instances of moral failure, by which I do not mean simple lapses of behavior on the part of particular characters, but a much more multifaceted phenomenon that intertwines the social and systemic with the personal and involves the intersection of multiple forms of value and valuing. Two instances of an attention to failures of redescription are, I think, Perkins's essays on Max Ophüls's *Letter from an Unknown Woman* (1948) and on Elia Kazan's *America, America* (1963). I will begin with the earlier film, looking in detail at Perkins's writing, before a discussion of *America, America* that takes his essay a little more as a starting point for a further investigation of the issues raised.

Letter from an Unknown Woman

Ophüls's film, based on a novella by Stefan Zweig, tells the story of Lisa (Joan Fontaine) and her long-unrequited love for Stefan Brand (Louis Jordan), which begins when she is very young. They do eventually spend one night together, after which Stefan leaves and Lisa gives birth to a son. Years later they meet again, but Stefan does not recognize her, after which Lisa writes him a letter explaining everything, which is sent to him after her death; it is this letter which narrates and structures the whole film. An article by Perkins, originally published in 1982, focusses on a sequence set in Linz that occurs a third of the way through the film (see fig. 2.1 and Perkins 2020, 311–33),

Figure 2.1. Lisa and the lieutenant. *Source: Letter from an Unknown Woman* (1948).

during which Lisa refuses a proposal from a young lieutenant called Leopold (John Good) because of her love for Stefan (even though Stefan has, at this point, barely any idea of her existence).

Perkins is sensitive both to what he calls the "motif of non-recognition" running through the film (314)—which is in my terms already a failure of redescription—and to the way the film articulates the *construction* of supposedly instinctive responses, the way we more or less deliberately adopt the viewpoints that lead us "unavoidably" to see things, to describe things, in a certain way. He refers, for example, to what the film shows us of "what Leopold will become once the authority of his sex and rank has been so internalised as to emerge as 'innate' confidence and steely poise" (325). In a different way, Lisa thinks she is overpowered and overcome but in fact has strict criteria for the description of the relationship she so passionately envisages: "Lisa believes in the recklessness of her passion. She believes that she must have Stefan come what may. But she does not, in fact, want him on any terms. She wants him on very strict terms indeed" (328). Perkins goes on to say that "[i]t is equally part of [Lisa's] charm and a source of her deadliness that she is so locked into her role as to preclude her achieving the perspective on her predicament that the film gives us" (332)—she fails to achieve the necessary redescription of her changing predicament.

The film is so structured as to describe a process of transition between crucial moments of recognition and misrecognition; hence its deployment of repeated situations and images. Famous among the latter is the repetition of what Perkins describes in a later article as "the matched camera movements over the staircase as first the adolescent Lisa watches Stefan's return from a night on the town in the company of a giggling mistress and then, years later, as he is seen to lead Lisa herself up the same stairs" (419). Perkins's description of these paired shots is too rich for me to go into detail about here, but I want to highlight the way that the detail of his description facilitates the subtlety of his interpretation. Equipped merely with the description quoted above, we might think it obvious that the second scene deploys repetition with a difference in order to comment ironically on the former: Lisa has become just another lover, but cannot recognize this fact. This is not untrue, but Perkins makes clear that to stop there would be grossly reductive:

It [the repeated shot] comes as the culmination not of Lisa's watching and waiting but of her, shall we say, courtship of Stefan. All that was sordid has become sacramental. There is no rush. The movements have a solemn, considerate grace. Lisa's hesitation at the top of the stairs is grave rather than coy, a moment of commitment with no demand to be coaxed. Her dress and hat are in undecorated black with a chaste simplicity of line. Stefan's clothing too has been softened and simplified so that clumsy urgency may be the more visibly replaced by attentiveness. . . . So the assertion of similarity is put in tension with the sense of transformation. (422)

This last sentence once again highlights Perkins's sensitivity to the constant pressure exerted by the possibility of redescription. The film forces us to see that to understand the latter scene we cannot merely describe it, but we have to recognize that such a description must be a redescription of the first staircase scene. Perkins's own descriptive practice then demonstrates for us the necessity of an attentive patience in so doing. If we simply assume we know instantly how the two scenes relate we risk misrepresenting them; we will find ourselves describing the film we *think* we are watching rather than the film we are actually watching.

But it is not the case that once we have achieved a certain kind of description, our task is complete. Perkins returned to *Letter from an Unknown Woman* again and again in his teaching and writing because he found more to be described, and redescribed, in it. A crucial aspect of the subtlety of both Ophüls's film that Perkins's analysis perceives clearly is that, while a central aspect of *Letter from an Unknown Woman* is the exploration of Lisa's failure to gain the perspective that we, the viewers, enjoy, the film does not hold out this possibility as the solution to all her problems, could she only have achieved it. Redescription (or the failure to achieve it) is fundamental to the experience of being human—an experience that Perkins thinks it is the function of films to explore—but the avoidance, or the remedy, of misdescription is not necessarily efficacious, in and of itself. And thus both viewer and critic would be well-advised to avoid smugness about the accuracy of their own descriptions. It would grossly underestimate the film's complexity to see it simply as a tragedy of misrecognition, or of misdescription. Or, to be more precise, if the film is a tragedy, it is not *simply* because a redescription fails to be achieved but because the film indicates the limits of what redescription *can* achieve, in and of itself. Immediately after claiming, in the earlier of the two articles we have looked at, that Lisa "is so locked into her role as to preclude her achieving the perspective on her predicament that the film gives us" Perkins goes on to remark dryly that "[w]e should not pretend that the achievement would necessarily have done her much good" (332). Perkins focuses on the way the film's structure and patterning describe and clarify the descriptive behavior of its protagonists, the complicated patterns of recognition and misrecognition that characterize not only the lives of Lisa and Stefan but also *Letter from an Unknown Woman* itself. A focus on redescription does not provide Perkins with an opportunity of indulging a facile existentialism, but rather of exploring the reciprocal—mutually shaping—impacts of people and environments, selves and systems, personal stories and sweeping histories.

America, America

Elia Kazan's *America, America* is explicitly concerned with the relationship between personal stories and sweeping histories. Set at the very end of the nineteenth century, it tells the story—inspired by the life of Kazan's own uncle—of its young protagonist Stavros's (Stathis Giallelis) progress from rural Turkey, to Constantinople, and—eventually—to New York City. In his essay on the film, originally published in the Winter 1971–72 issue of *Movie*, Perkins observes that "[w]hat Stavros would most like is to 'start this journey over,' to make a fresh start on the quest for a fresh start" (Perkins 2020, 199). This is of course impossible—one must always start from here, wherever "here" might be, as in the old joke wherein somebody asking for directions is told "I wouldn't start from here if I were you." Stavros has a fantasy of beginning from a clean sheet, wiping away all previous descriptions and starting afresh, but the film is clear that any supposedly fresh start would simply be another redescription. As we shall see, Kazan's film is, for Perkins, centrally concerned with the clashes between mutually incompatible descriptions.

Sylvie Rollet describes the opening images of the film as follows: "It is via a series of static, distance shots, diving alternately in and out, that we are shown the image of the uninhabited mountains. At no point can we identify the adopted viewpoint as relevant to an individual or even a group of people. We cannot even find continuity between the shots that would enable us to piece together a landscape" (Rollet 2007, 170). The film moves from this mode, which seems to strive to show without the need for an agent doing the showing, into a more documentary mode (as Kazan's voiceover narration sets up the historical and geographical situation), before finally introducing us to our protagonist and entering into his narrative. When we first see Stavros, however, it is in the distance; we have no way of knowing that he will be the protagonist and could not describe him if asked. Rollet claims that the film is positioned between two fantasies: Kazan's "lost, forgotten, Anatolia," and the America that Stavros is so desperate to reach, which "is the basis for the contradictory demands of fiction and documentary to which the direction of the film must comply" (168). The arc that the film describes—from rural Anatolia to, eventually, the heart of New York City—intertwines Stavros's movement from one descriptive fantasy to another with the historical facts that his story also represents. At the risk of seeming to play with words, I think we could fairly say that there is in the film a dialectic between what the poet R. F. Langley has called, in relation to Caravaggio, "a consistently recorded world" and the almost-anagrammatic idea of a consistently *reordered* world (Langley 2006, 55). This is reflected in the lapse of Stavros's father Isaac (Harry Davis) almost into incoherence as he tells his son to take the family's valuables with him to Constantinople in order to contribute to his uncle's carpet business; his second sentence chaotically jumbles up his first: "You will take with you everything this family has of worth. You will . . . I set everything up . . . of worth . . . this family has."

The central instance of what, as mentioned earlier, Nicole Brenez calls "a passage between altered images" in *America, America* is Stavros's smile (the film was called *The Anatolian Smile* when it was released in Britain); the film is almost a compendium of different smiles, chiefly—but not exclusively—belonging to its protagonist. Smiles—like all other facial expressions, of course—can be either expressive or performative, or indeed both at once. A smile can express genuine feeling, but it can also attempt to influence others (by expressing agreement, sarcasm, submission, fear, or any number of other states, not to mention all the complex combinations or in-between positions that are possible). This is one reason why smiles can be so hard to describe in words. They may also be hard to fully comprehend, even for the smiler; they may express the difficulty of responding to the fact that, as Perkins puts it, "'[e]xplain yourself' is an imperative but also an impossibility since 'you have to be a person like I am to understand'" (Perkins 2020, 199). We strive to make our descriptions compatible with one another, but we must deal with the fact that, as Williams insists upon, we can't *not* describe; we are always in the midst of a description and there is no such thing as a fresh start. Thus, what might seem to be the rather on-the-nose material in *America, America* about Stavros's desire to be "washed clean" and start again, or the explicit reference of the officer on Ellis Island to baptism, could be seen ironically to underline the impossibility of such a fresh start, rather than indicating the film's capitulation to this myth.

Perkins writes that "[t]he tip-gatherer's smile of Stavros the Yank offers a new, aggressive, and mercenary gloss on the smile of the Anatolian Stavros with its suggestion of anxious complicity in his own exploitation, of proclaimed gratitude and inner revulsion" (198). A gloss is, of course, a kind of redescription.[22] But it is not simply a case of an early smile and a late smile; the film proceeds by a whole series of smiles, each glossing or redescribing its predecessors. The smiles also, Perkins recognizes, take their place as part of an ethical thread running through the film concerning the many attempts "by one character to absorb another into his scheme of life without disruption, by assigning an identity which fits the other comfortably into his own plan" (202)—which is to say, by attempting to force a description onto another, who may or may not resist.

Rather than pursuing this aspect more widely, however, I want to conclude by attending closely to a few of the film's important smiles, in the hope of both giving something of the flavor of the way the film describes its progress between them and showing what we might conclude from this. (The still images don't, unfortunately, capture much of them since it is how they come into being and cease to be that really distinguishes them and makes them meaningful.) Stavros's first smile is a fake one, when the ice he and his Armenian friend Vartan (Frank Wolff) are transporting is inspected. We know it is fake because his face falls flat immediately afterwards when the officer isn't looking (fig. 2.2). This smile is followed soon afterwards by a more ambiguous one in response to the officer's question as to whether he had anything to do with an arson attack on a bank in Constantinople, two weeks' journey away (fig. 2.3). The first smile literally puts on the right kind of face for authority, while the second is a more complex way of negotiating threat. It is at this point that the officer asks, "Why do you smile?"—which of course is the question that runs through the whole film. To describe these initial smiles in exhaustive detail would be a complex operation, but they are relatively easy to understand: they are under Stavros's control, deployed deliberately to negotiate his relationship to antagonistic forms of authority. The same is true of the bitter half-smile he puts on after the Turkish authorities have massacred groups of Armenian Christians, telling his father, "they're saving the Greeks for the next holiday" (fig. 2.4).

But we also need to compare Stavros's smile with that of his father. His grandmother (Estelle Hemsley) tells him that he has his father's smile. This smile is, as we shall see, a capitulatory smile. So another important question becomes whether or not the film describes the transformation of this smile into another kind of smile. Two clear instances of his father's smiles that occur in close succession are seen when Isaac is forced to smile by the Turkish governor when he has managed to get Stavros released after he has been arrested for associating with Vartan and the Armenians ("Smile? Smile?")—a smile which Stavros himself witnesses (fig. 2.5)—and then his rather different smile immediately afterwards when he drinks with the Turkish authorities (fig. 2.6). The second is the subtler; it is the more hesitant but also the more craven because it seems to express the belief—or at least the desire to believe—that at some level what is going on is sincere. (Later the father tells his son, excruciatingly, "But Stavros, I've always kept my honor safe inside me.")

As we have seen, very early in the film we are prompted to consider Stavros's motivation for smiling. In the middle of the film, his future father-in-law tells him that he never smiles. Then the film concludes with a final, "American" smile (fig. 2.7), the smile that Perkins thinks "offers a new, aggressive and mercenary gloss on the smile of the Anatolian Stavros with its suggestion of anxious complicity in his own exploitation, of proclaimed gratitude and inner revulsion" (198). This is a persuasive reading and yet I am not sure that it is the only one possible. I find myself wanting to redescribe Perkins's description, to suggest that the film's ending is all the more unsettling because

Figures 2.2 to 2.7. A series of smiles. *Source: America, America* (1963).

it is not clear whether or not Stavros's final smile *does* express "inner revulsion" beneath its "proclaimed gratitude." If it does, Stavros has ended up reinhabiting a form of his father's painfully craven smile; yet it is also possible that Stavros has managed to *avoid* revulsion. This might seem to be an achievement, and yet—given the realities of his still-exploited situation—it is hard to see this transformation as wholly to the good. His father's hypocrisy and Stavros's lack of it might simply represent two different forms of capitulation.

Stavros's smile does not, then, simply reappear by the time he gets to America, nor has a genuine smile simply been replaced by a compromised smile; we have seen both that his first smile in the film is fake, and that it is not clear exactly how and to what extent his final smile is compromised. But, certainly, each smile in the film, and particularly the final smile, prompts us to reconsider and redescribe his earlier smiles. It is, then, appropriate that the name of the supposed promised land is repeated in the title—that the film is not *America*, or even *Anatolia, America* but *America, America*—because this leaves ambiguous whether or not the two repetitions of the word are synonymous. Has Stavros redescribed his America by the end of the film? Perhaps, rather than the scales falling from his eyes when confronted with the unreality of his fantasies about the possibility of an American fresh start, Stavros manages to redescribe his exploited situation as one that somehow *conforms* to his initial fantasies. If so, the whole film describes a colossal failure of redescription, not in the sense that he fails to achieve a redescription, but rather in that the redescription he does successfully manage *itself* represents a kind of failure, an abandonment of an ideal by means of the pretense that it has been achieved.[23]

To conclude very briefly. The genitive in this chapter's title is, obviously, intentionally ambiguous. Films, I have been arguing, are not only *objects* of description and redescription, but can also meaningfully be thought of as themselves the *agents* of acts of description and redescription, as well as excellent sites for the dramatization of ethical activity in terms of (successful and unsuccessful attempts at) act description.[24] Perkins's writings demonstrate that successful attempts to describe the descriptions and redescriptions that films both undertake and dramatize are one of the means by which criticism can best come to terms with and evaluate the relationship in narrative film between aesthetic and ethical redescription. This also, finally, suggests another perspective on Perkins's tendency continually to return to the same films over the course of his career: each return took the form of a new description that was necessarily a redescription, making criticism itself exemplary of a sustained ethical procedure wherein attempting to get things as precisely *right* as one possibly can is in no way synonymous with aiming to solve a problem once and for all. Lee Wallace says something similar when she observes, in a Cavellian mode, that "[p]rose imperfectly captures the register of film but . . . the pursuit of perfection relies on getting things wrong as a way towards getting them right" (Wallace 2020, xii). Continual redescription, in film criticism as in life, offers a way of submitting neither to relativism nor positivism, and V. F. Perkins's lifelong practice of film criticism is evidence that such an achievement is possible.

Part Two

Stanley Cavell

3

"Not Yet the Last"

On a Paragraph by Stanley Cavell

THE FINAL PARAGRAPH OF the original 1971 edition of Stanley Cavell's influential and controversial book *The World Viewed: Reflections on the Ontology of Film* reads as follows:

> A world complete without me which is present to me is the world of my immortality. This is an importance of film—and a danger. It takes my life as my haunting of the world, either because I left it unloved (the Flying Dutchman) or because I left unfinished business (Hamlet). So there is reason for me to want the camera to deny the coherence of the world, its coherence as past: to deny that the world is complete without me. But there is equal reason to want it affirmed that the world is coherent without me. That is essential to what I want of immortality: nature's survival of me. It will mean that the present judgment upon me is not yet the last. (Cavell 1979a, 160)[1]

Even by Cavell's standards, this passage exhibits both an elegance of phrase and a sinuousness of structure that it would be an understatement to describe as complicated. As well as the difficulties of the paragraph's argument, there is a further challenge in accurately grasping its tone and register. Its final words seem to strike a note of hope ("the present judgment upon me is not the last"), but it also talks about "my haunting of the world," and about "danger." The idea that "the world is coherent without me" can hardly be described as straightforwardly reassuring, and Mark Greif has even referred to "the still somewhat terrifying and unexpected last words of Cavell's book" (Greif 2020, 89). In an aphorism written around the same time as *The World Viewed*, Cavell proclaimed: "I myself am better at beginnings than endings. I mean in my life with others. In writing I am better at endings" (Cavell 2010, 484). Emboldened by a well-known piece by Stephen Mulhall that discusses the first five paragraphs of Cavell's *The Claim of Reason* (Mulhall 2005) but responding to a sense that beginnings in Cavell have tended to garner more attention than endings, I want here to attempt to unpack some of the complexity and richness to be found in these one hundred and twenty-four words.[2]

I should probably declare at the outset that I have no general answer to give to the question of why Cavell writes as he does. His own response to the charge of obscurity in *The World Viewed* can be found at the beginning of "More of *The World Viewed*" (Cavell 1979a, 162–63). Nobody (not even Cavell himself) would dispute that he can be difficult to understand, and even if my own experience is that George M. Wilson overstates matters when he wonders whether "the author gave a single thought to that part of his audience who, struck by the interest of his work, desire to understand it better," one can sympathize with the sentiment (Wilson 1974, 244). Contra a view that is widespread in certain academic quarters, paraphrase is always at least *possible*—if never perfect—so it is not that Cavell could not have said what he wanted to say in different words. But it is my view that, in the main, his style represents an attempt to wrestle seriously with his subject, to pay its difficulties the respect they deserve, rather than an instance of obfuscation for the glory of it (or for the cover that obscurity can provide).[3] If read patiently, Cavell can be seen to pay more attention to, and to attempt to offer more assistance with, the reader's difficulties than many philosophers of equal, or greater, reputation; Wittgenstein, for one. (It is also true that Cavell's body of work is not stylistically monolithic; despite—or possibly because of—its brevity, I find *The World Viewed* to be a more regularly elusive text than the much longer *The Claim of Reason*.) But, as I say, I do not attempt a general defense here. If my arguments in this chapter are convincing, they will demonstrate something of how, in one important instance, Cavell's style goes about its business and counts its costs. This may at least encourage the unpersuaded to attempt a renewed reading of other passages that have also tended to elude them. If it does not, nothing more general that I could say would be any more effective.

⁂

My thesis is that the paragraph with which we are concerned unites a number of the central concerns of Cavell's thought (the ontology of film; the nonproposal of philosophical theories; questions of finitude and mortality) in a fashion that is remarkable considering its brevity. Also, although I am sensitive to the danger of adding to the body of work on Cavell that originates in the belief that his philosophy "is insufficiently read, either too narrowly or too hastily, and that if it were explained just a little more clearly, its readership would suddenly become fruitful and multiply" (Cavell 2010, 514), it is nevertheless the case that this paragraph has been egregiously misunderstood. I do not claim here that just a little more clarity will instantly open up new vistas of understanding, but I do claim that the juxtapositions in this paragraph express persistent themes in Cavell's work in ways worthy of our close attention.

Robert Pippin has recently summarized Cavell's account of skepticism in the cinema, providing, in the process, a useful précis of the paragraph that is our concern here: "That the world or a 'projected world' can be present to us without our being present to it can on the one hand intensify a feeling of privacy and anonymity, and on the other undermine our sceptical assumption about the unavailability of the world itself, its availability only as inflected by our viewing it, and so our inability to know the world of others" (Pippin 2021, 141). Pippin captures the ambivalence and flavor of paradox in Cavell's arguments about skepticism and cinema in *The World Viewed*, and in this paragraph in particular, with its "on the one hand . . . on the other" structure; "there is reason," apparently, for me to want one thing as well as "equal reason to want" something incompatible.[4] Our encounters with film can make us feel all the more private and anonymous, excluded from the world we can see and hear onscreen, but they can also "undermine" our resignation to the fact that the only world we can ever know is the world as we receive it, our sense that, as Kant puts it, "our representation of things as they are given to us does not conform to these things as they are in themselves but rather that these objects as appearances conform to our way of representing" (Kant 1998, 112 [Bxx]). For Pippin, it seems, Cavell combines these two experiences; the price of undermining our sense of our own "inability to know the world of others" may be to "intensify a feeling of privacy and anonymity," but this might be a price worth paying, particularly if we need only pay it in full while sat in the movie theater.[5]

As will become clear, I have some reservations about this sketch, but it is certainly preferable to glosses such as the following, recently offered by Noël Carroll:

> In contrast to solipsism, where nothing would survive me, film symbolizes the possibility that I can at least live on in memory, a promise of immortality, quite different from the one Bazin identified, but which offers, nevertheless, consolation. That is, in viewing a world past from which I am absent my desire that there be a world apart in which I am remembered symbolizes a way in which the human desire for immortality might be satisfied. Film as such does not prove this. Rather, it is a powerful—and for that reason—welcome symbol of it. (Carroll 2020, 54–55)

Carroll conveys the gist of the passage as, I suspect, many readers understand it, and not unhelpfully so, but the purpose of reading Cavell's own prose with something akin to the attention he gives to the writings of others is to demonstrate that the nub of the matter often lies, precisely, in the difference between the gist and what the passage's words in fact say. Something Rachael Wiseman has written about Anscombe's *Intention* is pertinent here: "The difficult thing . . . is not the arguments or the concepts, but the difficulty of paying close and unwavering attention to what Anscombe *actually says* rather than what one *suspects she must mean*" (Wiseman 2016, 5; emphases in original). To point out two things that Carroll says that Cavell does not say, and one thing that goes in the other direction: Carroll refers to a contrast with solipsism, while Cavell does not; Carroll mentions the idea of symbols, or symbolization, three times, Cavell not at all; and finally, and most significantly, while Cavell insists that there is "equal" reason for me to want it *denied*, rather than affirmed, "that the world is complete without me," there is no mention of this in Carroll's discussion. These paragraphs by Pippin and Carroll will be very useful as specimens of how Cavell's paragraph can be read, but clearly there is much more to be said.[6]

In what follows, I will discuss Cavell's paragraph under five headings, each taking their cue from some of the most striking features of its language. The first of these is what we might call the passage's deceptively idiomatic quality, the way it sits just next to what we expect it to say; this will lead to some thoughts about Cavell's understanding of privacy and fantasy. Secondly, the way the paragraph plays with pairings and oppositions which can seem clear enough at first blush, but which shift around elusively when subjected to pressure, will help clarify one of the most characteristic gestures made by Cavell's writing and thinking. The third section connects ideas of haunting and betrayal, while the fourth points out and explores connections between this paragraph and what Cavell says earlier in *The World Viewed* about abstract painting. The final section discusses the paragraph's concern with last things, which will help clarify Cavell's perspectives on ontology and temporality. It brings together the paragraph's concerns with privacy, difficulty of comprehension, haunting, and abstraction in the claim that the way Cavell ends his first book on film—far from demonstrating his belief that film provides what Carroll calls a "welcome symbol" of "the human desire for immortality" (Carroll 2020, 55)—serves on the contrary to indicate the centrality to his thinking (about film, certainly, but by no means only this) of finitude and mortality.

Deceptively Idiomatic: Privacy and Fantasy

To get us started, let us note some of the paragraph's ambiguities and some of the things it comes close to saying but in fact carefully does *not* say. The "world of my immortality" with which the first sentence ends cannot simply be assumed to refer to a world in which I am immortal. For one thing, given that such a world is defined as "a world complete without me," the idea appears incoherent. How on earth could the world of "my immortality" be a world "without me"? How we answer this question is crucial to how we understand not only this paragraph but also *The World Viewed* as a whole. We are not yet, however, in a position to do so. At the other end of the paragraph, despite Carroll's reference to "the human desire for immortality" (Carroll 2020, 55), Cavell does *not* write, say, "why I want to be immortal" but "what I want of immortality." It almost sounds as if immortality is on the cards, like it or not, but that I may or may not get what I want from the condition. Alternatively, even though the paragraph begins very clearly with "my immortality," things seem to have shifted by the time we reach the end. If what immortality offers is "nature's survival of me," this might suggest that the immortality at issue is *nature's* immortality; I am mortal—something will outlive me—and that thing is nature. Furthermore, "essential to what I want" is very easy to read as a reference to the essence of what I want, or as a way of stating what it is that I want. Whereas Cavell's actual words seem closer to (though they do not, of course, say) "essential *for* what I want"; that what I want (which is what?) would not be possible without "nature's survival of me." But it is still ambiguous, under this interpretation, whether or not the idea that "the present judgment upon me" is "not yet the last" is itself a statement of "what I want of immortality" or merely its corollary.

It has only taken me a paragraph (albeit one almost three times as long as Cavell's) to plunge us into confusion. Even innocuous-looking articles are treacherous here: in the very first sentence there is a shift from "a world" to "the world." Is there only one "world of my immortality," but many worlds "complete without me which [are] present to me"? (One for each film, perhaps?) In "More of *The World Viewed*," Cavell indicates how crucial the distinction between definite and indefinite articles can be for him: "I speak of 'a world past,' and the idea of pastness threads through my books, as does the idea of presentness and of futurity. But I do not say that this is *the* past, that it is history" (Cavell 1979a, 210; emphasis in original). But there seems to be a slippage within the paragraph; how do we move from "*a* world complete without me" to the thought "that *the* world is complete without me" in its fourth sentence? Another shift is from completeness to coherence and back again; we move from "complete without me" to "coherence of the world," then to "coherence as past," "complete without me," and finally "coherent without me." The paragraph implicitly raises, but does not answer, the question of the relationship between completeness and coherence; must that which is complete necessarily be coherent, and vice versa?[7]

Just two more observations before we start to leave (I do not, as Cavell might put it, say solve) this quagmire of interpretational instability. At various points familiar or idiomatic phrases are almost, but not quite, stated. "It takes my life," for example, alludes to death (to take someone's life is, usually, to kill them) without directly referring to it; what immediately follows the phrase is the notion of "haunting," again both an allusion to, and a kind of denial of, death. And in the final sentence, the "yet" at the end both defers and insists on the eschatological notion of a last judgment. Compare: "It would mean that the present judgment upon me is not the last." This would leave whether or not there will be a last judgment undecided, whereas Cavell's formulation implies (does it not?) that there certainly will be, but that it has not "yet" arrived.

I have drawn out all these knotty instabilities of meaning and instances of the "fracturing of idiom" (Cavell 1981a, 16) because I want to claim that there is a relationship between the deceptively idiomatic (or deceptively *un*idiomatic) features of our paragraph and Cavell's ideas about privacy, a topic that was important to him throughout his philosophical career. (This is how I read his claim in "More of *The World Viewed*" that "in writing about film I felt called upon to voice my responses with their privacy . . . on their face" [Cavell 1979a, 163].) Trying to understand Cavell by "close and unwavering attention to what [he] *actually says*," as Wiseman puts it, we are forced to question whether we can share what he says, not only in terms of whether or not we agree with it, but of whether we share his language sufficiently as to grasp what it is he "*actually says*" (Wiseman 2016, 5). Privacy is explicitly important, even central, in Cavell's work on the interpretation of Wittgenstein's *Philosophical Investigations*, in relation to which Cavell's account of Wittgenstein's (it is now customary to say so-called) private language argument relates privacy directly to fantasy:

> One fantasy [of a private language, that "of inexpressiveness"—the other private language fantasy is "one in which what I express is beyond my control"] may appear as a fear of having nothing whatever to say—or worse, as an

> anxiety over there being nothing whatever to say. . . . A fantasy of necessary inexpressiveness would solve a simultaneous set of metaphysical problems: it would relieve me of the responsibility for making myself known to others—as though if I were expressive that would mean continuously betraying my experiences, incessantly giving myself away; it would suggest that my responsibility for self-knowledge takes care of itself—as though the fact that others cannot know my (inner) life means that I cannot fail to. (Cavell 1979b, 351)

I will return to the question of betrayal. But we can, I think, already see that these fantasies are related to—I do not say map directly onto—the two wishes described in our paragraph, either for "the camera to deny the coherence of the world," or for it to be "affirmed that the world is coherent without me." If the world is "complete without me" then surely there can be no question of my having "the responsibility for making myself known to others"; experiencing a sense that "the present judgment upon me is not yet the last" might well suggest that "my responsibility for self-knowledge takes care of itself," although perhaps not because "I cannot fail to know" my "(inner) life" but rather because it is up to "nature," which has survived me, to judge me. Alternatively, if my life is "my haunting of the world" (either like the Flying Dutchman or like Hamlet's father), perhaps this is because "what I express is beyond my control"; ghosts do not, I think, usually get to choose who or why they haunt. So, although the remarks about film predate the remarks about the private language fantasy, what they collectively suggest is that the experience of film addresses the same anxieties as does indulging in fantasies of private language. If we have been guided either by Pippin's or by Carroll's summaries of what Cavell is saying here (according to which the projected world either helps "undermine our sceptical assumption about the unavailability of the world itself" or, "in contrast to solipsism," offers "consolation") we ought to find this surprising. But must we then conclude that the two things—watching films or fantasizing about private languages—represent comparably misguided indulgences? Is film perhaps a better—a more, we might even say, *sustainable*—way of responding to these anxieties than are fantasies of private language? Or perhaps the "danger" Cavell refers to in this paragraph marks the fact that we are, in the cinema, continually on the edge of slipping into fantasy. As he writes in "More of *The World Viewed*," when watching films "our normal senses are satisfied of reality while reality does not exist—even, alarmingly, *because* it does not exist" (Cavell 1979a, 188–89; emphasis in original). But, of course, what is a danger of film is also "an importance."[8]

There are, then, complex connections between the fantasy of a private language (my own language, unshared and unshareable) and that of "a world complete without me which is present to me." Rather than pursuing the relevance to Cavell's work on film of the details of his reading of Wittgenstein, however, I want instead to emphasize the centrality to his thought of fantasy and desire. What has come to be known as psychoanalytic film theory operates at such a distance from Cavell's work that to describe him as a psychoanalytic film theorist almost sounds like a joke. This is despite the fact that he hardly makes a secret of it; the chapter of *Contesting Tears* on Max Ophüls's *Letter from an Unknown Woman* (1948) is called "Psychoanalysis and Cinema," and—even though, as Catherine Wheatley points out, it is with *Contesting Tears* that "psychoanalysis becomes more central to Cavell's work" (Wheatley 2019, 148)—there are only three times as many references in *The World Viewed* to Bazin (who everybody mentions in relation to Cavell's theories of film) as there are to Freud, who almost nobody mentions.[9] We should not, therefore, neglect the emphasis in our paragraph on "what I want"; this is not a mere turn of phrase but is central to what it is that Cavell is trying to say.

Self-stultifying Pairings?

That Cavell's paragraph sets up some kind of binary opposition is clear enough; we have seen how it is structured around two things that "I" have "equal reason to want." It also evokes similar relationships in its very vocabulary. This becomes apparent if we arrange the paragraph's pairings into two columns. The italicized items in square brackets are terms that do not appear in the paragraph, but which are suggested by the presence of their corresponding term. Most of these pairs (with the important exceptions of "importance" and "danger" and—just possibly—"past" and "present") strike one as mutually incompatible; surely nothing can be both "complete" and "incomplete" or "coherent" and "incoherent"?

Table 3.1. Pairs (explicit and implied) in the final paragraph of *The World*

Complete	[*Incomplete*]
Without	[*With*]
Immortality	[*Mortality*]
Importance	Danger
Haunting	[*Dwelling(?)*]
Unloved	[*Loved*]
Unfinished	[*Finished*]
Want	[*Do not want*]
Affirmed	Deny
Coherence	[*Incoherence*]
Past	Present

Note: I suggest "dwelling" as a contrasting pairing for "haunting" because of the reference to Heidegger in the penultimate paragraph of *The World Viewed*.

To this list we might also add a different kind of pair, namely, ambiguous words with (at least) two distinct meanings. Think, for example, of the ambiguities of "left" ("I left it unloved"/"I left unfinished business") or of the (surely very deliberate) fact that "present" is used in a different sense in the first sentence of the paragraph to that with which it is used in the last. In the first sentence it seems both spatial and temporal ("present to me"), while in the last it is primarily temporal ("the present judgment"). Almost everything in the paragraph can either be taken in (at least) two different ways, or conjures up an obvious complement of potentially equal weight.

What I want to emphasize is the reliance of this paragraph—both at the microlevel and at the level of its overall structure—on opposed pairs that threaten to cancel one another out, or to become, as Cavell's great influence J. L. Austin puts it, "self-stultifying" (Austin 1975, 51). What are we to make of the fact that there is "equal reason" for me to want two incompatible things (either, that is, that there is or is not a world "complete without me")? As we have seen in the summaries quoted earlier, Carroll simply ignores one side of the equation, whereas Pippin (usually an excellent reader of Cavell) risks implying that the two can be added together relatively straightforwardly. I want both to suggest that we should pay more attention to the difficulty of knowing how to handle these oppositions, and to point out quite how pervasive such structures are in Cavell's work. Here are a few examples not quite at random. Early in *The Senses of Walden* we read that we can find in *Walden*, *Leaves of Grass*, and *Moby Dick* a "mood at once of absolute hope and yet of absolute defeat" (Cavell 1981a, 9). In "The Thought of Movies" we are told about a kind of knowledge of the ordinary that film "at once blesses and curses us with" (Cavell 2005a, 96). Obviously resonating with our paragraph, "What Becomes of Things on Film" claims that films by Hitchcock and Capra "make nakedly clear the power of film to materialize and to satisfy (hence to dematerialize and to thwart) human wishes that escape the satisfaction of the world as it stands" (2005a, 6). Finally, to return to *The World Viewed*, we find that not only do "movies have an inherent tendency toward the democratic," they also have "opposite tendencies toward the fascistic or populistic" (Cavell 1979a, 35).

A skeptic might wonder if this recurrent tendency is not, at best, a Cavellian tic to be ignored or, at worst, a strategy for avoiding committing to really saying anything at all. We may, for example, want to know whether film is a democratic or a fascistic medium. How does it help us to be told that it has "inherent ... tendencies" in both directions? Doesn't that just get us back to where we started? Cavell will, of course, want to say no, for reasons that resonate with some of the central insights of psychoanalysis and are also very important for properly grasping what he means by referring to the "ontology" of something—such as, in the subtitle of *The World Viewed*, "the ontology of film." I will address the latter issue in the final section of this chapter, but regarding the first: the contradictoriness of what it is to be a human being, to be a subject, is central to psychoanalysis.[10] After Freud it no longer sounds peculiar to claim that, for example, the reason we fantasize about something—say, a private language—might be precisely because we fear it, nor that this fear itself could be complicatedly contradictory: "So the fantasy of a private language ... turns out, so far, to be *a fantasy, or a fear*, either of inexpressiveness ... or one in which what I express is beyond my control" (Cavell 1979b, 351; my emphasis). That we are contradictory hardly cancels each of us out; contradictory is exactly what it is to be each of us.

A similar structure is at the heart of what Cavell has to say about skepticism: "If one has felt both of these ways about skepticism [that is, has felt both that it has 'power and subtlety' and that it instances 'intellectual frivolity'], then one may come to sense that this very conflict itself may be displaying, or concealing, some critical fact about the mind, and one which neither side has been able, or willing, to contemplate" (Cavell 1979b, 159). Would it be reasonable to extrapolate this observation and say that if one has "felt both . . . ways" about wanting film to show a world that is and is not "complete without me," that this "conflict itself" might also indicate "some critical fact"?[11] What fact would that be? I suggest that a fruitful answer is to be found in Cavell's reading of Kant's transcendentalism, in whose "systematization" he finds "[t]he intuitive idea . . . of the human creature as essentially *restless*" (Cavell 2004, 128; emphasis in original). What Cavell calls Kant's "motto" of this idea is to be found at the beginning of the first edition of the *Critique of Pure Reason*: "Human reason has the peculiar fate in one species of its cognitions that it is burdened by questions which it cannot dismiss, since they are given to it as problems by the nature of reason itself, but which it also cannot answer, since they transcend every capacity of human reason" (Kant 1998, 99 [Avii]). Cavell further observes that "[w]hat I am calling human restlessness is for me a fundamental, motivating idea of Wittgenstein's *Philosophical Investigations*, a perpetual seeking, perpetually undermined, for what Wittgenstein calls rest, or peace" (Cavell 1979b, 128). This restlessness might also be connected with a "restiveness" that Cavell discusses in his memoir, in which he refers to the importance of a "dialectical impasse" according to which dissatisfaction with philosophy comes to seem itself philosophical: "From the first essay of mine that I still use, "Must We Mean What We Say?" the writing expresses restiveness with philosophical professionalism. Of course I felt I was managing to express this very restiveness philosophically—importantly by not denying that the philosophical was precisely what was in question" (Cavell 2010, 182). I am tempted to describe these oppositional structures (which I am claiming to be both rhetorical and philosophical, as well as at least potentially psychoanalytical) as instances of a distinctive—though I certainly do not say unique—Cavellian dialectic, one that is intimately related to his Wittgensteinian sense that philosophy is not in the business of proposing theories, which he himself describes as resulting in his attempt "to write without contention, neither denying nor affirming" (515).

At least two things, then, are useful to me here in these passages. First, that the rhetoric of Kant's sentence recalls the rhetoric of many of Cavell's sentences, and perhaps also indicates further ways in which this kind of rhetoric doesn't *simply* cancel itself out, because it is expressive of the way we pursue our lives, buffeted by incompatible desires and contradictory phenomena. And yet, the charge of self-cancelling is not wholly inappropriate, because Cavell, like Wittgenstein, sees his philosophical goal as therapeutic rather than theoretical; as a matter of divining the source of persistent problems rather than of deciding which side of a perennial debate is in the right. And second, that they suggest it may be helpful to regard the final paragraph of *The World Viewed* as expressive of "a perpetual seeking, perpetually undermined." Given that ghosts are often "restless," is the restlessness that Cavell finds so well expressed by Kant connected to the idea that we might "haunt our existence"?

Ghost Stories: Haunting and Betrayal

We have seen that our paragraph is structured according to various oppositions, most significantly between something that I have "equal reason" to want affirmed and to want denied. This something is, of course, that "[a] world complete without me which is present to me is the world of my immortality." Surprisingly, however, this immortality does not seem to signify either an endless life (an existence without death), nor an afterlife in something like the traditional Christian sense.[12] Instead we learn that "it"—that is, the opening sentence of the paragraph, just quoted—"takes my life as my haunting of the world." We have already seen various ways in which this paragraph resonates with Cavell's central interest in skepticism. There is one place I have found in Cavell's work in which haunting and skepticism are explicitly brought together: "Emerson [in 'Self-Reliance'] goes the whole way with Descartes's insight—that I exist only if I think—but he thereupon denies that I (mostly) do think, that the 'I' mostly gets into my thinking, as it were. From this it follows that the skeptical possibility is realized—that I do not exist, that I as it were haunt the world, a realization perhaps expressed by saying that the life I live is the life of skepticism" (Cavell 1988, 108). A life without thought is a life in which I merely haunt the world; applied to film this might sound like a condemnation of film's inherent mindlessness, which cannot be right, because such a view is precisely what *The World Viewed* sets out to demolish. But, just as in my first section I discovered connections between our paragraph and what Cavell says elsewhere about skeptical fantasies of private language, bringing this passage from *In Quest of the Ordinary* together with *The World Viewed* (as Cavell's decision to echo his phrasing from almost two decades previously surely invites) does seem to suggest that if film is "a moving image of skepticism," it is so in the sense that it brings it about "that I as it were haunt the world." This, in turn, suggests that it is film's image of *skepticism* (rather than of skepticism's defeat) according to which "the present judgment upon me is not yet the last."[13] All of which ought once again, I think, to surprise us much more than it seems to have done.

Later in *In Quest of the Ordinary*, discussing romanticism, Cavell notes that his "favorite romantics are the ones (I think the bravest ones) who do not attempt to escape these conditions by taking revenge on existence. But this means willing to continue to be born, to be natal, hence mortal" (1988, 143). We will come back to the question of mortality in the final part of this chapter. First, however, we need briefly to discuss betrayal. Betrayal is a central feature of the penultimate paragraph of *The World Viewed* (which of course directly precedes our paragraph), in which Cavell discusses Alain Resnais's *Hiroshima Mon Amour* (1959) in Heideggerian terms. This suggests that the notion of betrayal may be helpful in understanding the book's final paragraph. The penultimate paragraph begins as follows:

> To satisfy the wish for the world's exhibition we must be willing to let the world as such appear. According to Heidegger this means that we must be willing for anxiety, to which alone the world as world, into which we are thrown, can manifest itself; and it is through that willingness that the possibility of one's own existence begins or ends. . . . The wish for total intelligibility is a terrible one. It means that we are willing to reveal ourselves through the self's betrayal of itself. (Cavell 1979a, 159)

This passage resonates with the passage about fantasies of private language in *The Claim of Reason* that was cited in the first section of this chapter.[14] But what is the connection between betrayal and the haunting that we have been discussing in this section? It seems to be that, unless we are "willing to let the world as such appear," which means being "willing for anxiety"—a willingness through which "the possibility of one's own existence begins or ends"—we will end up haunting the world. But "total intelligibility" does not offer any safeguards against this haunting. Cavell's exploration of betrayal makes use of the kind of double meaning discussed earlier, in that betrayal as giving oneself away is connected to betrayal as unfaithfulness: "'I betrayed you tonight,' she [the woman in *Hiroshima*] says in a monologue to her dead lover, looking at herself in the mirror" (159). The "you" here is ambiguous between the lover and herself; she has betrayed—or is betraying—them both, in more than one sense. But the fact that "[t]he wish for total intelligibility is a terrible one" does not mean that Cavell thinks we can avoid betrayal by refusing such a wish. (That we cannot might be another way of saying that we are mortal.) He draws a perfectionist moral, long before he described his philosophy as a perfectionism: "The knowledge of the self as it is always takes place in the betrayal of the self as it was" (160).

Is "the betrayal of the self as it was" what "nature's survival of me" would allow me to avoid, and is this why film "takes my life as my haunting of the world" (160)? But if this is so, does not what Carroll calls a "consolation" start to sound more like a delusion—or like an image, once again, of skepticism, rather than skepticism's defeat—or even like a way of "taking revenge on existence"? And is this not a disappointing—not to say distressing—conclusion to a book about film?

Painting

It may seem peculiar that the final paragraph of a book on film contains direct references to an opera by Wagner (*The Flying Dutchman*) and a play by Shakespeare (*Hamlet*) but mentions no films whatsoever. But it also seems—or should seem—odd that a book about film, particularly one that has not infrequently been understood to argue for a realist classicism in cinema contains an entire chapter entitled "Excursus: Some Modernist Painting" (108–18). In a recent article, however, Daniel Morgan carefully and convincingly demonstrates that questions of modernism are central to *The World Viewed*, because in it "Cavell is using the terms of modernist aesthetics, centrally the view that the terms of past art can no longer be assumed, as a way to reframe central questions posed by film (and by films)" (Morgan 2020, 211).[15] Seen in this light, it is less surprising that Cavell should turn to one of the paramount examples of twentieth-century modernism, namely, abstract expressionist painting, in order to explore what it means to say "that the terms of past art can no longer be assumed."

There are two verbatim anticipations of the final paragraph of *The World Viewed* in its chapter on painting, namely, the phrases "complete without me" and "nature's survival of me." Discussing "the post-Pollock paintings I have responded to—especially those of Morris Louis, Kenneth Noland, Jules Olitski, Frank Stella," Cavell declares that these paintings achieve a "quality" that "might be expressed as openness achieved through instantaneousness—which is a way of characterizing the *candid*. The candid has a reverse feature as well: that it must occur independently of me or any audience, that it must be complete without me, in that sense *closed* to me" (Cavell 1979a, 111; emphases in original). Shortly afterwards he claims, apropos of modernist paintings such as those by Louis, that their "declaration of my absence and of nature's survival of me puts me in mind of origins, and shows me that I am astray. It faces me, draws my limits, and discovers my scale; it fronts me, with whatever wall at my back, and gives me horizon and gravity" (114).

What are we to make of these repetitions, or rather these preparations (seedings, one might almost call them) of crucial phrases from the book's final paragraph five chapters earlier (that is, some fifty pages—almost a third of the book)? The remarks that include these phrases emphasize specificity and finitude. The return not "*to* nature but . . . *of* it" (113; emphases in original) that Cavell finds in the experience of these paintings emphasizes both his location and his limitations; it "draws my limits . . . discovers my scale . . . gives me horizon and gravity" (114). In contrast to minimal art such as, presumably, the work of Carl Andre or Donald Judd, "in response to [which] I am deployed, dematerialized, unidentifiable," modernist painting, Cavell claims, renders him "concretized, finitized, incarnate" (117). What the echoes of his remarks about modernist painting that Cavell incorporates into his book's final paragraph should therefore do, I suggest, is qualify or inflect the remarks about immortality that it contains by reminding us of his earlier emphasis on *mortality* ("finitized") instead. This makes it all the more unclear that our paragraph offers consolation, as Carroll suggests, or at the very least renders any apparent consolation it contains extremely questionable. At the end of the chapter on painting, Cavell asks with impassioned rhetoric: "Is there no way to declare again the content of nature, not merely its conditions; to speak again from one's plight into the heart of a known community of which one is a known member, not merely speak of the terms on which any human existence is given?" (118). The obvious answer one would expect in a book on film is surely: "Yes, there is, and its name is cinema!" But Cavell pointedly does not answer these questions directly, deliberately leaving open the question of whether or not cinema is able to do such things. And if one were to look to the book's conclusion for hints as to an answer, the idea of "a world complete without me which is present to me" seems an extremely unlikely candidate for a means whereby one might "speak again from one's plight into the heart of a known community of which one is a known member." Even if "the present judgment upon me is not the last," is this sufficient compensation for an expulsion from any "known community" so extreme that "the world is coherent without me"? The force of this question is one of the reasons for the mutually exclusive rhetoric of *The World Viewed*'s final paragraph ("there is reason . . . there is equal reason").

Last Judgments

In "More of *The World Viewed*," Cavell declares that "a certain obscurity of prompting is not external to what I wished most fervently to say about film (and hence cannot have been cleared up before I commenced writing, nor at any time before I called the writing over)" (162). Does the original book's final paragraph clear anything up? What I have been saying thus far in this chapter has aimed at demonstrating that it clears up much less than readers seem often to have assumed. I want to conclude by looking at the role of finality in the paragraph. Its final word is, of course, "last" but—entirely characteristically—this emphatic termination is qualified by the fact that what is being declared is "that the present judgment upon me is not yet the last." This, of course, is the source of the reassuring tone that some have discovered in the paragraph. Yet again, however, turning for interpretational cues to other writing by Cavell complicates such a discovery.

In many places throughout his oeuvre, Cavell refers to his discomfort with notions—such as he finds in Derrida—of endlessly deferred judgment. He refers in his memoir, for example, to his "suspicion of certain current ideas of meaning as always deferred. Perpetual deferral suggests that the meaning of what we say and do is perpetually open to the future. This is crucial, but it slights the equally obvious fact that meaning is at the same time perpetually encircled by the present" (Cavell 2010, 110). Or, to give just one more example, the postscript to Cavell's essay on "Hamlet's Burden of Proof" ends by declaring that he takes "Shakespeare's practice (interpreting, interpreted by, Freud's), call it the practice of comedy and of tragedy, to show that, even if you say that some meaning is always deferred, all meaning is not always deferred forever" (Cavell 2003, 191). Despite the truth that there certainly is in the claim that "some meaning is always deferred," a misplaced emphasis on such notions risks becoming an evasion of mortality, which is the very thing that Cavell's interest in the acknowledgment of finitude seeks to avoid. He finds a more valuable model for thinking about the interminability of interpretation in the writing of Wittgenstein, whose philosophy

> lies in the practice, the commitment to go on in a certain way, call this discontinuously, which is to say, not in an endless deferring of claim that might well be a gesture toward infinity, say transcendence; it lies rather in a particular refusal of endlessness, in an unguardedness, an openness. . . . It is not that philosophy ought to be brought to an end, but that in each case of its being called for, it brings itself to an end. (Cavell 1989, 73–74)[16]

With this in mind, we should be cautious of concluding that *The World Viewed* "brings itself to an end" by affirming the endless possibility of reassessment. (Recall my remarks in the first section about the way that "not yet the last" both declares that there are judgments to come, and that there *will*, eventually, be a last.) This is relevant to the ontology of film, about which we are surely entitled to expect the final paragraph of a book subtitled "Reflections on the Ontology of Film" to have something to say. To show this, I want to disagree with something Morgan says in his article about the book's modernism. He claims that "perhaps the strongest transhistorical claim in the book [is] that cinema's ontological foundation is the presentation of a world" and, further, that this world "is one that is screened from us and thereby—necessarily—of the past" (Morgan 2020, 229). When, therefore, Cavell goes on to say that color films create "a world of the immediate future" (Cavell 1979a, 82), Morgan finds this deeply perplexing: "It seemed that the world of cinema being a world of the past was a necessary feature of the medium; now that has changed" (Morgan 2020, 230). Aside from the pedantic point that the remarks early in *The World Viewed* to the effect that "a world I know, and see, but to which I am nevertheless not present . . . is a world past" (Cavell 1979a, 23) are about photography, not cinema, there is a more substantive remark to be made here about ontology. Morgan goes on to argue that when we notice this odd shift taking place within the book, "we can no longer treat the fact that we take the world of the cinema, in classical Hollywood film, to be a world past—one that is sealed off from me—as a given feature of the medium. It is, rather, something like a deep convention" (Morgan 2020, 232). Morgan is at pains to point out that "everything Cavell says seems to suggest that this argument [about cinema's world being a world past] has an ontological foundation, that it is what it is for something to be cinema—and, in a sense, the answer to the subtitle of *The World Viewed* itself" (229–30), and that the later parts of the book therefore undermine this claim.

However, this distinction between a "given feature of the medium"— what Morgan earlier refers to as "cinema's ontological foundation"—and a "deep convention" is, it seems to me, profoundly un-Cavellian.[17] Morgan implies that ontology must be without time, which is precisely what Cavell is denying; we could put the point very simply by saying that cinema can change. Indeed, the history of the cinema shows quite clearly that it *has* changed; note Cavell's remark that "the movies have been what they have been" (Cavell 1979a, 232n8). Early in the book, Cavell declares that "[t]he first successful movies . . . were not applications of a medium that was defined by given possibilities, but the *creation of a medium* by their giving significance to specific possibilities" (32; emphasis in original). It is helpful here to take Cavell literally—there *was no medium* until "specific possibilities" were given "significance." Later, Cavell reiterates this point in a way that I read as directly rejecting the sharp distinction that Morgan makes between a "given feature" and a "deep convention": "nothing is a 'possibility of the medium' unless its use gives it significance" (133).

To use the example of a game, beloved of course of Wittgenstein, one could say that what Morgan says here implies that he would understand the ontology of a game in terms of its rules as they stand at a given time, which is to say the conditions for something to count—at that time—as an instance of such a game. For Cavell, however, understanding a game's ontology would, at least potentially, involve every instance of its being played, rather than merely the contents of its rulebook. What a game is can change over time—its rules can be revised without it ceasing to be the same game—and this is also true of cinema (the nature of such change is clearly a pressing concern in today's unstable so-called "media landscape"). This underlines, I think, how central to Cavell's thought is *what happens*, other words for which might be finitude or mortality.[18] If film's ontology were timeless, then the medium of film could never suffer damage or degradation; nothing that happens to "actually existing cinema" could affect the medium itself. But Cavell does not believe this, neither about film nor about the "medium" (if we can call it that) of humanity. As he puts it in his memoir: "Have I become the one who has done all and only what I have done, accepted that what I have done is no better and no worse than it is?" (Cavell 2010, 517). For Cavell, the ontology of film cannot be conceived purely as a matter of the apparatus, because what film is cannot be something separate from what films are, when watched ("viewed"). Such a view is entirely compatible with Cavell's interest in psychoanalysis; what people are makes no sense other than in terms of what happens to them, what they do, as well as what they *think* they do and have had happen to them, or think they think (and so forth). This may be frightening, precisely because it is not at all the same as saying that things could not have been otherwise. Cavell remarks in "More of *The World Viewed*" that "[i]n the closing pages of my book I note a certain anxiety in the participation and perception of the audience of a film and I characterize that as an experience of my contingency" (Cavell 1979a, 212). And yet what generates anxiety can also have different effects. Towards the end of his chapter on modernist painting, Cavell goes as far as to associate the perpetual deferral of judgement with a kind of childishness: "The idea of infinite possibility is the pain, and the balm, of adolescence. The only return on becoming adult, the only justice in forgoing that world of possibility, is the reception of actuality—the pain and balm in the truth of the only world: that it exists, and I in it" (117).[19]

Films both are and are not endlessly repeatable. Hence their "importance" and their "danger," their special value in coming to terms with what, in a discussion of Freud, Cavell once referred to as "a quest for one's own death, one that, as it were, would make sense of the singularity of life" (Cavell 2022, 285). If comprehension involves bringing particulars under generalities, how are we to make sense of the utter singularity of our existence, given that—as the cliché goes, and as Fritz Lang once titled a movie—"you only live once"? Does film provide a means for subverting this singularity and its contingency, or merely the illusion of such a possibility? Cavell, of course, wants to avoid taking this as a simple choice between mutually exclusive options; hence the complexity of our paragraph. In this short phrase we see many of the themes I have been emphasizing in the paragraph which concludes *The World Viewed*, including privacy (is "one's own death" a private matter or not?); difficulty of comprehension (the wish to "make sense"); and perhaps even haunting (is that what "a quest for one's own death" is, or risks becoming?).

To describe the end of a book as similar to a death might seem either banal or overblown (or indeed both). And yet, Cavell was prepared to write about the *Philosophical Investigations* that its 693 sections demonstrated Wittgenstein's "willingness to come to an end 693 times," which—as a result of his understanding "the current over-insistence (so I judge it) on the idea of meaning as the deferral of significance, to be an expression of the fear of death"—Cavell interpreted as "a memorable realization of Montaigne's assignment of philosophy as learning how to die" (Cavell 2022, 67). I suggest that the end of *The World Viewed* is another such "memorable realization." The book's penultimate page refers twice to "absolute isolation." Isn't *that* what the experience of being "present" to "a world complete without me" would most likely resemble? Cavell declares that "[f]ilm's promise of the world's exhibition is the background against which it registers absolute isolation: its rooms and cells and pinions hold out the world itself" (Cavell 1979a, 159). Here is yet another binary ambiguity—does film "hold out the world" in the sense of offering it to us, or of keeping it back from us? Cavell immediately goes on to claim that "[t]he fullest image of absolute isolation" in cinema is to be found at the end of Carl Theodor Dreyer's *Joan of Arc* (1928) in the image of "Falconetti at the stake look[ing] up to see a flight of birds wheel over her with the sun in their wings"; I suggest that we might read this description as a figure for the viewer, who, like Joan, knows that such "free" creatures could only "accompany" them if their body had been "gone through utterly" (159). Whether or not we share Joan's faith—and although this might not appear to get us much closer to an answer as to how "the world of my immortality" can be "a world without me" (which is to say that film remains mysterious)—this might at least help us recognize that the reason that Cavell closes his first book on film with a discussion of immortality is because his real interest is in mortality.

In his very first book, Cavell declared that the "punchline" of Samuel Beckett's *Endgame* "is that there is no other but this to come, that the life of waiting for life to come is all the life ever to come" (Cavell [1969] 2015, 112). That this is so easy to overlook, to misunderstand, or to resist is both dangerous and important. The very difficulty we have distinguishing revelation and fantasy in our experience of films is central to their value. I suggested earlier that Cavell's work shows how the experience of film addresses the same anxieties as does indulging in fantasies of private language; the seriousness of these anxieties means that no mere refusal of fantasy can be sufficient to clear up the problems to which they are a response (an indication, once again, of Freud's importance to Cavell). We gravely mistake Cavell's meaning if we read him here as interested in fantasies of eternal life, rather than as meditating on what it means for meaning to be "perpetually encircled by the present" (Cavell 2010, 110) and how it is that we can so easily find ourselves, in response, haunting the world. Cavell finds in Dreyer's film, and the other films he values so highly, serious explorations of the fact that—like it or not—the world of my mortality (which is the only world we are given to know) is a world *with* me.

Figure 3.1. "Falconetti at the stake looks up . . ." *Source: The Passion of Joan of Arc* (1928).

Figure 3.2. ". . . to see a flight of birds wheel over her with the sun in their wings." *Source: The Passion of Joan of Arc* (1928).

4

Cavellian Reflections on Privacy, Consent, and Expression in Ildikó Enyedi's *On Body and Soul (Teströl és lélekröl)*

THE FIRST CONVERSATION between Endre (Géza Morcsányi) and Mária (Alexandra Borbély), the protagonists of Ildikó Enyedi's 2017 film *On Body and Soul (Teströl és lélekröl)*, is an elegant study of the role in human conversation of the implicit and the explicit; the true and the false; the aggressive and the phatic.[1] Endre is the chief financial officer at a Hungarian abattoir; Mária is its temporary meat quality inspector, filling in for another woman who is on maternity leave. The conversation is constructed around simple shot/reverse-shot exchanges, presented in shallow focus with plausible but elegant side lighting which models the characters' faces clearly; the cinematography and mise-en-scène gently but firmly distinguish between Endre, Mária, and their environment. It's lunchtime, and Endre sits down opposite Mária in the cafeteria without being invited, his "bon appetit" denying her the opportunity of saying she would rather be left alone. Rather embarrassingly for him, she proceeds to stand up, formally introduce herself, and shake his hand. Endre is in his fifties, or even sixties, but displays a calm energy that belies his age. Mária appears to be in her early thirties, at most. Her straight blonde hair, simple grey T-shirt, floral skirt, and facial expression that initially appears somewhere between blank and uncertain also make her appear younger than she is, even a little childlike. (Later in the film we discover that she is still seeing the same psychiatrist she has been consulting since childhood.) Endre asks her why she thinks he chooses the lunch he does, and without hesitation she replies: "Perhaps because your arm is crippled. It's easier to eat mash with one hand." Mária says this without meeting Endre's gaze. Taken aback, his eyes flicker from her face to the table as he responds to what he perceives as her gratuitous insult by calling her Marika, a diminutive he has already been told that she dislikes. (It may well be a childish name, or at least one that she associates with childhood; later in the film, her psychiatrist calls her by the same name.) It is Mária's turn to be taken aback; she looks directly at him and responds that he has surely been told that she doesn't like the name. Endre denies this, and with a surprising lack of suspicion she immediately apologizes: "Then I was wrong. Pardon me. I find it unpleasant."

Figure 4.1a and 4.1b. Endre and Mária. *Source: On Body and Soul* (2017).

This is an undemonstrative exchange in which, nevertheless, each contribution by one party startles and wrongfoots the other; there is an understated but pervasive comedy of misunderstanding. Both these people are seen by others (and, indeed, initially by each other) as somehow "defective," Mária because of what we come to recognize as her autism spectrum disorder (hence her bluntness about Endre's arm and her readiness to believe his denial about her name) and Endre thanks to his paralyzed left arm. As Saige Walton puts it, referring to some remarks by the film's director, the two of them "are not just introverts. They are wounded. They 'react to an environment . . . which is not cut for them [*sic*]—or anybody'" (Walton 2020, 351).² The woundedness that Enyedi refers to is clearly, I think, to do with the characters' histories and their implications for the way they relate to other people, which is to say that his arm and her autism are not, in themselves, their wounds. And yet the film has to strike a difficult and delicate balance, because these attributes do clearly condition the characters' being-in-the-world as well as, to some extent, figuring their woundedness. During the film, Mária and Endre discover that they have been sharing the same dream, which leads to a hesitantly blossoming romance, only for the relationship to break down. (The breakdown is precipitated by precisely the same kind of misfiring connection between statement and implication that their first conversation sets up as a theme of the film: Mária tells Endre that she doesn't have a phone and he takes this claim not so much as a lie but as a rejection.) A tragic conclusion appears inevitable, only for a happy ending unexpectedly to ensue.

Figure 4.2. "A pair who recognize themselves as having known one another forever." *Source: On Body and Soul* (2017).

On Body and Soul partakes of both of Stanley Cavell's famous genres of film, the comedy of remarriage and the melodrama of the unknown woman. Not only is the latter part of the film the story of the two protagonists getting *back* together, but the dream that they literally share (in which they are a male and female deer in a snowy forest, and which is the first thing we see in the film) seems to indicate that they have some kind of primal connection, that they have somehow known each other forever, without knowing it. (The film gives little indication of when they first began having these dreams.) This echoes the first part, at least, of the "myth" that Cavell proposes as "the common inheritance of the members" of the remarriage genre: "A running quarrel is forcing apart a pair who recognize themselves as having known one another forever, that is from the beginning, not just in the past, but before there was a past, before history" (Cavell 1981b, 31). Mária is also, clearly, taken by almost everybody she encounters in the film to be some kind of "unknown woman." Fascinatingly with regard to the interpretation of the shared dream, Cavell "associate[s] melodrama with the contest of interpretations and with marriage as made of, and unmade by, mind reading" (Cavell 1996, 27).[3] Endre and Mária's first conversation clearly sets up the film's interest in "the contest of interpretations," and its latter sequences, in particular, evoke melodramatic conventions (although the happy ending then challenges them).

The specifics of *On Body and Soul*'s relation to Cavell's genres are not, however, my main interest here; rather, I am concerned with how they open up onto broader themes found within Cavell's work, and not only in the writing that explicitly focusses on cinema. These themes are *privacy*, *consent*, and *expression*, all of which we see in operation in Endre and Mária's first conversation. Cavell's thinking on all these topics—as well as on the ways in which they relate to one another—is profoundly indebted to the work of Ludwig Wittgenstein. Privacy is a Wittgensteinian preoccupation familiar from what has become known, not altogether happily, as the *Philosophical Investigations*'s private language argument. Although he acknowledges that Wittgenstein "rather cultivates the impression . . . that he denies language is private," in Cavell's reading Wittgenstein's "teaching is that the assertion or the denial either of the publicness or the privateness of my language is empty" (Cavell 2003, 228). There is not a *fact* to be determined philosophically as to whether language is private or whether it is public; it is instead a question of what we want to say to each other when, and why.

It is this question which motivates Cavell's discussions of the relationship between marriage and mind reading. He discovers the idea in *Macbeth*; in that play, Macbeth and Lady Macbeth consistently say "what the pair already knows or has already said; or [do] not say something the other does not say, either assuming the other knows, or keeping a pledge of silence," meaning that we are presented with an idea of "reading the text of another as being read by another" (Cavell 2003, 238). Endre and Mária's relationship is marked as much by its difference from as by its similarity to this situation. As we have seen, initially their reading of each other provokes consistent misreading; hence the distance they have to cover when they come to discuss their shared dream and discover that, with regard to the dream, they do indeed know something that each of them "already knows." It is this discovery that prompts them to make the effort to begin to read one another correctly, but despite the magical realist conceit of the shared dream, the film does not at all indulge in the sentimental idea of a connection beyond—or more direct and more profound than—that which can be established through language. The couple need to talk to each other about their dreams, underscoring Cavell's claim "that there is no human desire without the capacity to make oneself intelligible," which "amounts to saying that there is no human desire without the imagination of one to whom one may be intelligible" (Cavell 1996, 37). This same idea underpins Cavell's idea of the soul: "If the body individuates flesh and spirit, singles me out, what does the soul do? It binds me to others" (Cavell 1979b, 411).[4] The film expresses the nonmetaphysical (which is to say relative, or nonabsolute) privacy of their shared dream when, halfway through the film, Endre writes down what he dreamed the night before and invites Mária to write down what she dreamed before reading his account. They read each other's descriptions and smile at the way they accord with each other ("see you tonight then," says Endre), but the film maintains their privacy by not showing us what they have written. And yet it also insists that what they have written is not something utterly private, incommunicable to anyone but each other, by showing us, in image and sound, exactly what they do dream.[5]

As the film proceeds from this point it increasingly plays variations—in ways that may be uncomfortable, to say the least, for some viewers—on a key aspect of Cavell's comedy of remarriage, namely, "the education of the woman, where her education turns out to mean her acknowledgement of her desire," which "in turn will be conceived of as her creation, her emergence, at any rate, as an autonomous human being" (Cavell 1981b, 84). Just as in Cavell's remarriage comedies, this education is not exactly carried out *by* the male partner; hence, for example, the presence in *It Happened One Night* (Frank Capra, 1934) both of lessons that Peter (Clark Gable) needs to teach Ellie (Claudette Colbert)—such as how to dunk doughnuts—and of those in which his lecturing leads to his humiliation, such as when he tries to demonstrate how to hitchhike. The male lecturing that is so prominent in Cavell's comedies is absent from the central relationship in *On Body and Soul*, but Mária's self-education is very prominent. Her autism expresses itself partly as a profound discomfort with physical contact, but she is clear that a relationship with Endre must involve sex. She initially attempts to educate herself by watching pornography, until her psychiatrist tells her that he doesn't recommend it. She has more success with plunging her hand into a plate of mashed potato (which might seem to be a solely physical therapy until we remember Endre's fondness for mash, as expressed in their first conversation), and later delights in her surprise at being caught unawares by a sprinkler while lying in a park.[6] She also, to her other colleagues' intense amusement, experiments with running her hands over one of the cows in the abattoir. When, after their final reconciliation, the couple do finally sleep together, Mária's face shows fleeting indications of her own physical pleasure, but her thoughtful curiosity about, and enjoyment of, Endre's pleasure is much more prominent.

Figure 4.3. Taking an inquisitive pleasure in the other's pleasure. *Source: On Body and Soul* (2017).

The reason that all this may be difficult for some viewers is, of course, that Mária's education in the physical aspects of a loving relationship seems to be entirely a matter of conforming to Endre's terms. Not that he explicitly demands this; rather, she makes no attempt to express a different vision of what their relationship might entail. She knows she is in love with him, and therefore goes through what she needs to go through in order to be able to love him on terms that he can understand, without ever questioning whether or not these are the only terms possible. Does all this amount to a very dark reading of the film's sexual politics, in which the woman is so sure that the relationship's very possibility rests on her consenting to the man's terms that the idea of these terms including room for negotiation never occurs to her?[7] I will have more to say about this later, but part of our answer must involve an account of what we imagine her alternative terms—those which her willing acceptance of his terms is presumably precluding—might, or could, have been. Such an account is not at all easy to produce. Before considering this, however, I want to step back from the film for a while and say more about the third Cavellian theme I mentioned above (after privacy and consent), namely, expression. How is it, for example, that we understand Mária's expression while she has sex with Endre, and how does it relate to whatever it is that the film is expressing in that moment?

In a chapter on expression in the work of Wittgenstein and Maurice Merleau-Ponty, Kathleen Lennon writes that the two philosophers' shared position is that "[e]xperiences, sensations, emotions are visible on the body for us all to see" (Lennon 2017, 32). We do not, for example, see purely physical movements of the face, from which we *infer* that somebody must be experiencing a particular emotional state. As Wittgenstein puts it in his *Remarks on the Philosophy of Perception*, "We see emotion. . . . [W]e do not see facial contortions and make inferences from them . . . to joy, grief, boredom." Or as Merleau-Ponty says in the *Phenomenology of Perception*, "I do not see anger or a threatening attitude as a psychic fact hidden behind the gesture, I read anger in it." (Both passages cited in Lennon 2017, 32.) Wittgenstein believes, as Marie McGinn puts it, that "[o]ur sense that we do not really *see* the friendliness in a face, or that 'He gave a friendly smile' is not really a perceptual report, is seen to lie in nothing more than a mistaken idea of how the concept of visual experience functions" (McGinn 1997, 204; emphasis in original). (This insight has profound implications for our understanding of what we perceive in the cinema which have not, I believe, been sufficiently appreciated. I will have a little more to say about this shortly.) Despite denying that understanding a facial expression or a gesture is a matter of inference, however, neither Wittgenstein nor Merleau-Ponty wish in any way to sidestep or to downplay the fact that it involves interpretation, nor that we have to learn how to understand such things. As Lennon puts it, "[b]odily expressions are . . . public and observable, not hidden, though . . . there are circumstances in which we might find them difficult to read, or we might be mistaken about them" (Lennon 2017, 33). When this proves to be the case, "inference to something supposedly lying behind the expressions will not help. What is necessary is to be able to *see* the gestures in a certain way" (37; emphasis in original).[8] And in order to do so, "to grasp expressive content as expressive, we must be engaged" (36). The connection between an expressive gesture and our response is a matter of "a normative, rather than a causal relation" (36), which means that we can talk about—for example—appropriate and inappropriate responses.[9]

The question of the difference between the appropriate response to an expression of pain by somebody in the room next to you and the appropriate response to an expression of pain on a cinema screen is once again beyond the scope of what I can say here. I want, instead, to emphasize the similarities between understanding an expression or a gesture in "real life" and understanding them in film, in terms of the role of interpretation. Note, for example, the resonance between Lennon's paraphrase of the view, shared by Wittgenstein and Merleau-Ponty, that "[e]xperiences, sensations, emotions are visible on the body for us all to see" (32) and Perkins's well-known remark—made in response to David Bordwell as part of an article (already cited in chapter 1) that pays very close attention to gesture—that the meanings he articulates in his discussion of Max Ophüls's *Caught* (1949) "are not hidden in or behind the movie, and that [his] interpretation is not an attempt to clarify what the picture has obscured" (Perkins 2020, 248). As Alex Clayton puts it, Perkins "was the first to really demonstrate the significance of the fact that films do not merely give views of things but also embody the viewpoints from which those things are seen" (Clayton 2022a, 216). I want to suggest that, although while watching films we often need to make inferences (about character motivation, for example), we primarily understand the viewpoints that films "embody"—when we do understand them—not by, as Lennon puts it, "inference to something supposedly lying behind" the film, but rather by coming to see a film, or a sequence within a film, *as* expressing a certain viewpoint, by (to use Lennon's words again) "grasp[ing] expressive content as expressive."

Although filling out such an account would take us too far away from *On Body and Soul*, my proposal (explicitly here, and implicitly throughout this book), is that filmic expression, understood in quite a general sense, has more in common with facial expression, so understood, than has often been recognized. In contrast to Kyle Stevens's view that "[w]e do not *see* the film cutting or the camera panning. We see one shot after another and objects drifting out of frame in just that way" (Stevens 2022, 4; emphasis in original), by analogy with Wittgenstein's account of expression I want to say that there is a sense in which "the film cutting or the camera panning" are precisely what we *do* see. We understand films as expressions of intention (however thorny it can be to pin down precisely what is entailed by this), and hence see them *as* expressive, not merely as facilitating inferences as to their expressivity. (As James Conant writes, "[t]he real underlying confusion" at issue here, such as I find in Stevens's claim, "is not one about art, but one about intention" [Conant 2018, 309n77].) I find a similar line of thought expressed in Cavell's discussion of the relationship between body and soul in part 4 of *The Claim of Reason*, in which he argues that to think about the mind and the body in terms of "closeness" is not the issue. He illustrates this with examples taken both from aesthetic expression and facial expression: "I expect that the relation between the stone and the statue is pervasive, but they are not close to one another, they do not touch at every place, or at any place. The smile is not close to the face" (Cavell 1979b, 398).[10]

But *On Body and Soul* not only bears out such an approach to cinematic expression; it also reminds us that this account is in need of a very considerable caveat. We need to ask how neurodiversity complicates both how we understand the interpretation of human expression and my extension of a particular way of thinking of this to cinematic expression. Autistic people do sometimes need to infer emotions from facial expressions; Mária says to her psychiatrist at one point, "No, I made eye contact, I remember. His pupils dilated."[11] Is this (uncomfortable as it might be to say) where the Cavellian "education" comes into *On Body and Soul*? Does Mária eventually learn to see expression in a manner that is closer to the way a nonautistic person sees it, and if so—combined with the questions of sexual consent and desire we explored above—should we agree with Lilla Tőke's claim that the film's "celebration of the complex relationship between body and soul, between dreams and reality, and most importantly perhaps, between the tenuous work that goes into the making of human relationships, happens in a framework that is as gendered as it is ableist" (Tőke 2024, 47)?

I have no simple answers to these difficult questions. Certainly, what seem to be jokes at the expense of masculinity can look a little different at second glance. Endre's colleague Jenö (Zoltán Schneider) has his sexist boasting undercut by his meek acquiescence to his wife's request that he pick up their children so she can go out with her girlfriends; but is the film puncturing his posturing or inviting us to laugh at him for being henpecked? The investigation into the theft of some mating powder which provides the plot mechanic for Endre and Mária to discover their shared dreams (a psychologist is brought in to examine all the employees, whose questioning involves asking what they dreamed the night before) ends up identifying Jenö as the culprit, and not Sanyi (Ervin Nagy), the arrogant young man that Endre had suspected. The film thus implies that Endre's wearily superior reaction to Sanyi's alpha-male performances have prejudiced him against the younger man. Even the well-constructed scene of sexual embarrassment during Endre's interview with the psychologist Klára (Réka Tenki), in which she catches him staring at her breasts ("Well, are they satisfactory?"), could plausibly be understood as coming closer to taking his side (in finding her reaction unreasonable) than hers. (Her pleasure in his discomfort is evident in the glint in her eye and the wry hint of a smile in the corner of her mouth.)

An important shortcoming in Tőke's account, however, is its neglect of what Robert Pippin would call the film's "reflective form," which is to say that Tőke pays insufficient attention to the ways in which the film "embodies a formal unity, a self-understanding that it is always working to realize," a unity which "requires investigative works . . . covering as many details as possible" if we are to appreciate the ways in which the film "*is the movie it is* only by means of this emerging, internal self-conception" (Pippin 2020, 8; emphasis in original). This is to say that Tőke is rather indifferent to the ways in which *On Body and Soul* addresses its audience and to the sense that the audience derives from this of the film's attitude towards itself. Tőke writes, for example, about how, during the unsuccessful date that leads him to break off his relationship with Mária, Endre acts in "typical sexist fashion . . . blam[ing] Mária for stirring up his appetite for romance," but offers no discussion of the way the film presents this behavior, or of the attitude it adopts concerning it (Tőke 2024, 47). This is clearly because Tőke's position is that the film ultimately endorses "his unwillingness to learn Mária's needs or to break away from normative romantic love" (47), but I think it is worth proceeding a little more slowly. It is surely important that the film makes a point of highlighting Mária's powers of judgment. Her colleagues complain because she marks some carcasses as Grade B despite their fat content only exceeding regulations by two to three millimeters. She classifies strictly according to a rule, allowing herself no interpretative flexibility. (See the introduction for more discussion of the relationship between criteria and standards.) And yet, as far as we can see, she judges the fat content by eye, rather than with a ruler or a similar device; we see her look closely at one of the carcasses before printing out the label indicating its quality rating. She appears, then, to judge intuitively, not by inference. I am reminded of the carpenter Olivier (Olivier Gourmet) in the Dardenne brothers' film *The Son* (2002), who—as Pippin puts it—"has a remarkable ability to estimate distances intuitively," something which Pippin understands as "a reference to a kind of intuitive, nondiscursive knowledge" (Pippin 2020, 250n39). Her inflexibility on the quality grading of course also indicates her autistic discomfort with ambiguity, but I take the point of her intuitive calculation of the fat content to be that Mária is not devoid of noninferential knowledge. When Endre challenges her about her grading with a pretense of being impressed by the precision of her vision she responds, "Yes, I have good eyes. I know."

The question of Mária's instinct relates, of course, to the way that the film often figures her as animallike; specifically, as like a deer. As Walton observes, when Endre first approaches her in the cafeteria, as she "reaches for a glass in the cafeteria, her hand visibly halts in midair, preternaturally aware of the fall of Endre's footsteps behind her" (Walton 2020, 353). This might seem only to compound the film's problems; not only does Mária attempt to make her desires conform to Endre's, but she is apparently figured here as a helpless doe, a creature of instinct.[12] And yet I do not find Tőke's description of the scene in which she attempts suicide to be convincing: "Like the animal trapped in the back of the truck, Mária is awaiting her cruel death. Her eyes, just like the animal's in the film, are enormous and they stare unabashedly at the camera; however, in the bathtub, the eyes display a sense of panic and pain" (Tőke 2024, 48). I certainly think it is right that we are invited to compare the expression in her eyes with those we have seen earlier in the eyes of cows awaiting slaughter, and it is quite right to say that "[t]he sharp contrast between the white bathroom and her deep red blood reminds viewers of the contrast between the sterile, white wall tiles and the cows' rich red blood that covered the ground of the slaughterhouse" (48) but Tőke once again seems to me to underestimate the richness of the film's reflective form, simply assuming that the point of the comparison is to assert a direct equation between cow and woman.[13] But the complexity of the range of emotions that we see successively in Mária's eyes as she sits in the bath with the blood gushing from her slashed wrist—calm deliberation; pain; sorrow; regret; fear; curiosity; surprise; resignation—is in sharp contrast with what we can see in the eyes of the cows we have seen earlier.[14]

It seems to have been less frequently noted that the film also figures Endre's connection to the stag; in the sex scene mentioned previously (which follows Endre's unexpected phone call to Mária, which gets her out of the bath and off to A&E) his breathing is clearly reminiscent of the stag in the shared dreams—so much so that we might wonder whether this is one of the things that Mária is thinking about as she looks up at him with curiosity.[15] We should also think about the way that the film presents the stag and the doe in the dream scenes. The way these scenes are constructed, particularly their use of the animals' gazes and their proximity, very clearly indicates their awareness of each other, even their awareness of each other as a couple. It is possible that a viewer might take this, during the film's opening scene, as verging on the anthropomorphic; and yet, as we come to realize, we are not looking at wild animals (even if wild animals were filmed to produce these scenes). We are, instead, looking at two people who are dreaming that they are deer. To adapt a remark of Cavell's about a frog who had been turned into a prince, I feel inclined to say of the figures in the dreams that they have the consciousness of deer, though they have the self-consciousness of human beings; the film's use of shot/reverse-shot editing patterns structured around eyeline matches expresses this (see Cavell 1979b, 396).

Where are these dreams happening? We might want to say that they are happening somehow in Mária and Endre's heads, but to say so would be to open up difficult questions of so-called "other minds skepticism" which Cavell spent a great deal of time thinking about. *On Body and Soul* was filmed in a real abattoir and includes graphic footage of cattle being slaughtered, decapitated, and otherwise dismembered. Given the film's title, these scenes surely invite us to think about what it is we might expect to learn by seeing the inside of an animal.[16] If the soul is something internal, will cutting the body open show it to us? I see this footage as resonating with the sequence in *The Claim of Reason* in which Cavell engages in an elaborate parable exploring the possibility that a human being could be counterfeit. He both recognizes and satirizes our instinct that we would want to settle the question by looking inside, giving us a version of the story in which the craftsman "rips open the friend's shirt to reveal a chest of hammered brass which, prompted by the craftsman's prying knife inserted into an all but invisible seam running straight down from the pit of the arm, snaps off to reveal something like clockwork," then asks what difference it would make if the craftsman developed his skill further so that when "[t]he brass chest snaps off . . . to my horror, I see no clockwork, but for all the world, the insides of a human being" (Cavell 1979b, 404).[17] For Cavell, "[t]he myth of the body as a veil expresses our sense that there is something we cannot see, not merely something we cannot know. It also expresses our confusion about this: Is what we cannot see hidden *by* the body or hidden *within* it?" (368; emphases in original).

This section of *The Claim of Reason* explores the question of whether it is correct to say that understanding another to be a human being is a matter of knowledge by means of a whole series of potentially humanlike figures: from frog princes we move to statues and finally to automata, but not without a fascinating discursion on dolls. Cavell points out that, for someone—clearly figured as an adult—relating to a doll that is not their own (it belongs to a child), there is no question of simply stipulating things to be true about the doll: "If I say 'See. Now she's comfortable,' something must have changed, or I must have done something, put a pillow under her head, or rearranged her so that she is no longer sitting on her foot. . . . At some point my say comes to an end. I defer to the one whose doll it is" (402). We have already noted Mária's childlike qualities. They are developed further in that she still plays with dolls, or specifically with Playmobil figures. She does so not with others, however, but in order privately to rehearse encounters that have happened and to practice for those that might ensue. Actually, she initially uses salt and pepper shakers to replay her first conversation with Endre (about which, as with everything else, she has perfect recall; the film makes no attempt to avoid the trope of the autistic savant). When she does so she adds her interpretation of the unspoken thoughts of her two "protagonists." ("Endre" says, for example, "She seems to be lonely . . . that's why I came over here," while "Mária" declares, "I'm a bit scared. I don't know what he wants.") The scene indicates that her grasp of the unspoken implications of interpersonal interaction are more sophisticated than we may have initially given her credit for. She is perfectly capable of understanding such things, it can just take her a little longer to think them through, and she benefits from making her understanding of them explicit to herself. It is the speed of response required ("I should answer something now . . . and then we'd be conversing already") that led to the remark about Endre's arm that he took as hurtful.

Later, Mária rehearses a conversation she has not yet had with Endre, using Playmobil figures. She has to get them from a box in her garage, so this is clearly not something she is in the habit of doing regularly. Something more anthropomorphic is required for this important bit of preparation. Endre is represented by a one-armed knight; this choice strikes me more as a knowing allusion to fairy tales on Mária's part rather than an indication that she lives in a fairy tale. She represents herself beginning to tell him three signs that reveal whether somebody is lying, the first of which is that the pupils dilate, but the playacted conversation is derailed (or, rather, it gets on track) by making explicit Endre's jealousy of the younger Sanyi, who he assumes that Mária finds more attractive than him; on being assured that he does not—which requires more than a simple denial, but also the explanation that she is afraid of him—the relationship is, within the playacted scenario, repaired. In her tableaux, "Endre" gets up when "Mária" tells him she is afraid of Sanyi, whereas in their actual conversations Mária tended to get up to express formality.

When she attempts to play out the conversation in reality, however, Endre doesn't respond in the way she had prepared for and remains seated. Her attempt to force the matter by declaring "I think you are beautiful" predictably misfires. The conversation that Mária acts out is an attempt at wish fulfilment, certainly, but it is also perfectly plausible. It is not *sheer* wish fulfilment but a kind of rehearsal for engagement with the world; we understand that although she has a kind authority over the Playmobil that another person could not have (they would have to "defer" to her, as Cavell puts it), her authority over the plastic figures is not absolute. They do not represent the creation of a world subject purely to her whim, but a means of some preparatory engagement with the world we all have in common. She might, perhaps, have learned more by playing with her Playmobil with somebody else; but could she have done that she would have had no need for it.[18]

I have been attempting to demonstrate the complexity of the film's representation of Mária, that although she exhibits features familiar from other cinematic representations of autism, the film neither patronizes nor underestimates her. I realize, though, that none of this may seem to touch the fundamental charge that the film endorses her submission to the conditions of a nonautistic, and male-dominated, world. In fact, I think that the charge is probably justified. But, although the film may not expose Endre's lack of self-critique in the way we might wish, neither does it hide it, or explain it away. The alternative to Mária submitting to Endre's terms can't be simply to insist on her own; then there would be no relationship. But neither can there be bland compromise, because that would be something contractual, rather than a mutual discovery. (Cavell makes the important point that "our consent or agreement in words cannot be contractual" [Cavell 1990, 64]; hence, we cannot enter into a contract to call—say—"love" that which we do call love, but must instead find ourselves in agreement about the matter; or not.) The ending of the film indicates that something of the mutuality that drew Endre and Mária together has been lost: they can't remember what they dreamed the night before, and the film ends with an empty image of the snowy forest, the deer nowhere to be seen, before fading to a blinding white. Is this a version of what Cavell calls the tendency of some remarriage comedies to end either "by declaring us to be witnessing a film" or "by telling us otherwise to mind our own business" (Cavell 1990, 125–126)? Perhaps it suggests that their relationship will now be something ordinary, which does not mean that it will not be special, but does mean that it will have no guarantees, not being underpinned by a magical connection. And so Endre will surely have to come to adjust to Mária, as well as the other way round, or it will not be able to continue.

I will end with two tiny moments of cinematic expressiveness in *On Body and Soul* which seem to me to be notable achievements. After Endre and Mária first learn that they are sharing a dream (irritating the psychologist who assumes, quite reasonably, that this is a private joke between them), they both prepare for bed. Endre's anticipation is indicated, quite conventionally, by a shot of him sitting on his bed looking thoughtfully out of the window. Mária's excitement, however, is shown delightfully obliquely, slightly comically, and yet with perfect clarity, in a shot from under her bed of her taking off her sandals. She slips each foot out, then rests them both on top of the shoes, before pulling them suddenly up into bed. She is careful and methodical, and yet her excitement is apparent in the speed with which her feet disappear. She turns the light off, and in the next shot we are in the snowy forest, the doe looking up suddenly to catch sight of the stag already looking at her. When, therefore, much later in the film we get a similar shot of Mária stepping out of her sandals, this time as she gets into the bath to kill herself, the film efficiently evokes the whole history of their relationship and the very different sense of anticipation she now feels. Feet, in a film, can be as expressive—if very differently so—as a face.

We might, or might not, have to make a specific inference in order to appreciate this connection and what it expresses; or we might miss it entirely. But even if we are such as to need to make inferences in order to understand the emotion expressed in a face or in a gesture, certain things—such as the humanity of another—cannot be a matter of inference. Beyond, that is, the question of the relationship between expression, inference, and seeing-as, which attention to autistic experience very importantly complicates, there will always remain issues of what Cavell calls acknowledgment, which are not questions of knowledge, and which no inference could settle; "[c]riteria come to an end" (Cavell 1979b, 412).[19] As uncomfortable as the apparent asymmetry of adjustment on the part of its two protagonists may make us, I take the disappearance of the deer at the conclusion of *On Body and Soul* to indicate a recognition of this.

Figure 4.4a and 4.4b. On body and sole—expressive feet. *Source: On Body and Soul* (2017).

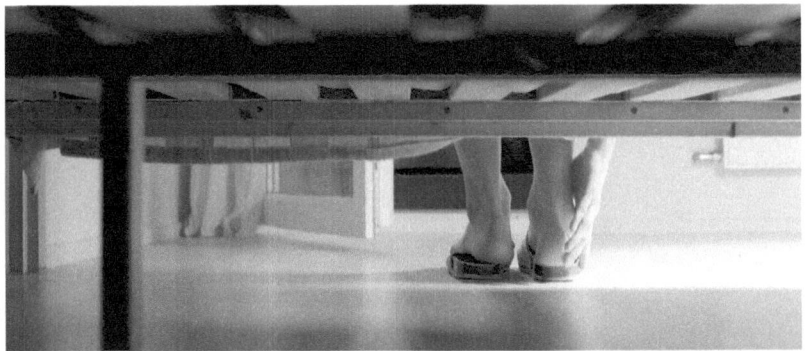

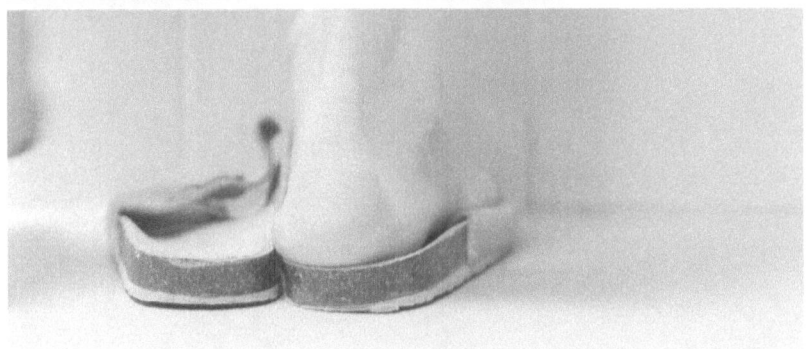

That is to say that the film makes clear that our acknowledgment of one another must take place in and through our shared language (which does not of course mean that it is nothing but language), as well as that it relies on the risky matter of shared understanding, not being based on any kind of magical guarantee. If we are lucky, our words and gestures will come to express to one another our mutual consent to share our privacy. Cavell responds to a famous remark of Wittgenstein's as follows: "It may seem that you could believe that the human body is the best picture of the human soul and yet deny that anything corresponds to the picture. My intuition is that this is false, that not to believe there is such a thing as the human soul is not to know what the human body is, what it is of, heir to" (400). *On Body and Soul*, despite everything about it that might give us pause, offers a picture of that intuition.

5

(Re)producing Marriage

Stanley Cavell and Paul Thomas Anderson's *Phantom Thread*

DANIEL SHAW HAS ARGUED that, for Cavell, films "inspire us to see our lives as worth living . . . by restoring our faith in the wellsprings of human value: romantic love, individual autonomy, nonconformity, and the search for self-improvement" (Shaw 2017, 116). This chapter proposes that although movies certainly *may* achieve this, Shaw's formulation risks giving the impression that films serve mainly to generate a kind of therapeutic—and perhaps rather bland—optimism. I want, instead, to emphasize the importance, in Cavell's work, of doubt, difficulty, and provisionality.[1] Cavell once remarked that he "might describe his philosophical task as one of outlining the necessity, and the lack of necessity, in the sense of the human as inherently strange, say unstable, its quotidian as forever fantastic" (Cavell 1986, 85). Given this, do we know—and if so, *how* do we know—what "romantic love, individual autonomy, non-conformity, and . . . self-improvement" would look like, were we to encounter them? I draw inspiration from Steven G. Affeldt's account of Cavell's investigation of what Wittgenstein called criteria, according to which "the search for criteria . . . occurs in response to a crisis"

(Affeldt 1998, 12). I will pursue this idea via a close reading of aspects of Paul Thomas Anderson's film *Phantom Thread* (2017), in which a celebrated dressmaker and his wife eventually achieve a strange and delicate equilibrium in their relationship via periodic food poisoning.

I will first demonstrate the relevance of *Phantom Thread* to some of Cavell's central interests in film by exploring the ways it could be said to belong to, or at least exist in the orbit of, his crucial genre of remarriage comedy. After this, I will explore the relevance to film philosophy of some aspects of *The Claim of Reason*, a book that a number of commentators (see, for example, Rudrum 2013, 11) have called Cavell's masterpiece, but which has to date not made much of an impression on Cavellian work in film. (Though for some exceptions, see Shuster 2015; Moran 2017, 88–100; Russell 2018; and Macarthur 2016, which I discuss in some detail below.) I will pursue some of the implications of what I claim is the delicate pun that Cavell makes by referring to the "production" of criteria (see, for example, Cavell 1979b, 22).[2] Do we *discover* or *construct* criteria—or is this a false distinction? I propose that we might read *Phantom Thread* as the story of the production of criteria in response to a situation of interpersonal confusion and disorientation, criteria according to which a remarriage—it seems—takes place. To see the film as obviously working in terms of a perversion or subversion of "romantic love, individual autonomy, [and] nonconformity" would be to assume that criteria already exist that are being subverted or perverted. This chapter will, instead, argue that investigating the ways in which criteria are (or fail to be) produced and shared is something explored by films themselves as well as a task to which a criticism informed by humanism still has a great deal to contribute.

Poisonous Remarriage

Phantom Thread is set in England in the 1950s, and centers on three protagonists: Reynolds Woodcock (Daniel Day-Lewis), dressmaker to the great and the good; his sister and business partner Cyril (Leslie Manville); and his lover, model, muse, and eventual wife, Alma (Vicky Krieps). Woodcock is demanding, fussy, and inflexible; at the heart of the narrative are Alma's attempts to fashion a relationship between them that is mutually tolerable. Noticing how much more "tender" he becomes when ill, Alma responds to the disastrous failure of her attempt to surprise Reynolds with dinner for two by poisoning him with mushrooms. This has the desired effect and leads, upon his recovery, to a proposal of marriage, in order "to break a curse." (Notably, Alma responds with to this with her own proposal: "Yes. Will you marry *me*?") But their relationship subsequently deteriorates once more, and Alma poisons Reynolds again. This time, however, she lets him know that this is what she is doing. We are led to believe that a cycle has been established; whenever Reynolds becomes too unbearable, Alma will make him ill so that he will "settle down a little."

The film is thus clearly a story of "remarriage," of the reestablishment of a relationship; in a sense even the actual marriage is a remarriage, a refounding of the relationship that is somehow in place even when Reynolds and Alma first meet. It is also a comedy, not just because it is funny, but because, I will argue, it proposes an essentially comic vision—it has, to put it more than crudely, a "happy ending," albeit a complicated one. (Michael J. Meyer has argued that remarriage comedies participate in "an important and yet underappreciated aesthetic category" that he dubs "anxious happy endings" [Meyer 2008, 77].) But it certainly is extremely, if dryly, funny. (A favorite line: as Alma removes some tea that Reynolds didn't ask for, he tells her that although "the tea is going out, the interruption is staying right here with me.") Richard Porton describes the film as a "frequently laugh-out-loud sendup of a ludicrously fastidious British couturier's more than slightly sadomasochistic relationship with his reluctant muse," which seems to me about three-quarters right (Porton 2018, 49). Reynolds is certainly "ludicrously fastidious" and sent up by the film, but it is less clear in what sense his *relationship* is sent up; and Alma is far from "reluctant," as we shall see. Sheila O'Malley has rightly observed that "[t]here are vestiges of the classic screwball formula in *Phantom Thread*, where a workaholic nerd (like Cary Grant in *Bringing Up Baby*) is overrun by a free-spirited dame who will not take no for an answer" (O'Malley 2018, 28).

Bringing Up Baby (Howard Hawks, 1938) is one of a group of seven films made between 1934 and 1941 that Cavell refers to as the genre of remarriage comedy. Of all Cavell's work on film, his invention (or discovery) of this genre has garnered the most attention. Why are marriage—and remarriage—so important to Cavell? Catherine Wheatley explains that it has to do with the central Cavellian concept of acknowledgment, of what it is truly to live *with* other people. In contrast to Shakespearean tragedy, which is "the result of a failure of acknowledgement," the comedies of remarriage instead present us with "models of acknowledgement" (Wheatley 2019, 103–104). I cannot, however, show that *Phantom Thread* is a remarriage comedy simply by listing its features, because, as Cavell argues, there is "nothing one is tempted to call *the* features of a genre which all its members have in common" (Cavell 1981b, 28; emphasis in original). He suggests instead that each new addition to the genre somehow reworks it, until "the state of saturation, completeness of expression, has been reached" (30). There is no way to know for sure that this "saturation" has taken place; it would merely take the production of a new member of the genre to show that it has not. The fact that *Phantom Thread* was made so much later than the films Cavell discusses is, therefore, no barrier to its membership of the genre: "[I]t is not clear that the genre has yielded itself up completely" (26).

Cavell suggests that we "think of the common inheritance of the members of a genre as a story, call it a myth" (31). Let us look at some of the elements involved in Cavell's setting-up of this myth:

> A running quarrel is forcing apart a pair who recognize themselves as having known one another forever, that is from the beginning, not just in the past but in a period before there was a past, before history. This naturally presents itself as their having shared childhood together, suggesting that they are brother and sister. . . . Something evidently internal to the task of marriage causes trouble in paradise—as if marriage, which was to be a ratification, is itself in need of ratification. So marriage has its disappointment—call this its impotence to domesticate sexuality without discouraging it, or its stupidity in the face of the riddle of intimacy, which repels where it attracts, or in the face of the puzzle of ecstasy, which is violent where it is tender, as if the leopard should lie down with the lamb. . . . Upon separation the woman tries a regressive tack, usually that of accepting as a husband a simpler, or mere, father-substitute, even one who brings along his own mother. (31–32)[3]

Figure 5.1. Reynolds recognizes Alma. *Source: Phantom Thread* (2017).

One can certainly make the case that Reynolds and Alma "recognize themselves as having known one another forever." Their first meeting takes place at breakfast in a hotel, after Reynolds has followed Cyril's advice to refresh himself with a visit to his country house. Alma, a waitress in the hotel restaurant, comes in rather noisily, glances at Reynolds and immediately—and embarrassingly—trips up. She looks at him, looks down, laughs at herself. He looks at her and smiles while also looking down. One could call it love at first sight, but they do not gaze, stupefied, into each other's eyes; there is a definite sense of *recognition* in these glances. Reynolds smiles wryly, as if to say, partly to himself and partly to her, "she's always doing this kind of thing."

But *Phantom Thread* also registers important differences from Cavell's myth. It displaces the combination of lovers and siblings by including a real sister (who Reynolds repeatedly refers to as "my old so-and-so").[4] When Reynolds first takes Alma back to his country house he tells her about the many superstitions associated with making wedding dresses; it is hinted that Cyril may have been cursed never to marry by helping the young Reynolds make the dress for their mother's second wedding. When Alma first poisons Reynolds, the film cuts directly from her discovery and removal of a label reading "never cursed" to Reynolds, in bed, having a vision of his dead mother; the

Figure 5.2. Substitution. *Source: Phantom Thread* (2017).

editing suggests that Alma's action may have prompted this vision. When Alma subsequently enters the room, we initially see both her and the vision of the mother in her wedding dress, only for the mother to disappear. Rather than temporarily accepting a "father-substitute," Alma makes herself into both a mother-substitute and a sister-substitute, one able to overcome the taboo on incest, thereby ambiguously either removing the curse (exorcising the mother's ghost) or perhaps merely replacing it with another (bringing him under her spell; there is clearly something of the witch and her potions in Alma's play with mushrooms and teapots).

Whereas Cavell sees his other major film genre, the melodrama of the unknown woman, as the "negation" of the remarriage comedy—by means of "the negation of marriage itself"—*Phantom Thread* performs these reworkings of the remarriage myth so as to reflect critically upon the genre (Cavell 1996, 6).[5] One common criticism of Cavell's readings concerns his insistence that it is always the female who is educated by the male; that structure is here emphatically reversed (see Wheatley 2019, 126–32, for a lucid discussion of gender in the remarriage comedies). Cavell also makes another observation that is turned upon its head in *Phantom Thread*: "This male of remarriage comedy . . . is shown to be nurturant, either literally cooking for the woman, or cooking with her, never cooked for, somehow assured of sustenance" (Cavell 1996, 173), something that is most forcefully underlined by Katharine Hepburn's spectacular "incompetence" in cooking breakfast for Spencer Tracy in what Cavell calls "a relatively minor member" of the remarriage genre, *Woman of the Year* (George Stevens, 1942) (Cavell 1986, 116). And yet this element of the myth is not straightforwardly reversed, because Alma's cooking is, in the literal sense at least, decidedly *not* "nurturant." Most cases of food poisoning are indeed brought about by either inattention or "incompetence," so Alma's skill and deliberation here constitute a crucial aspect of the variation the film plays on this theme.

Food is quite explicitly linked in the film both to sexual appetites and to creativity: the note that Alma leaves Reynolds at the end of their first meeting, telling him her name, is addressed "to the hungry boy"; he tells her, before they sleep together for the first time, "you look beautiful. . . . You're making me extremely hungry"; Cyril tells Alma that Reynolds "likes a little belly," which associates his desire for Alma with both food and pregnancy; there is an ill-tempered conversation about "taste" early on when Alma says she doesn't like the fabric of one of the dresses; and, of course, the argument over the disastrous surprise dinner she cooks him is over *his* taste, namely, his dislike for butter with asparagus.[6]

This obviousness is, it seems to me, something that the film manipulates quite consciously, asking the audience how sure they are that they recognize what is going on. The whole film plays on the cliché that "the way to a man's heart is through his stomach," and the way that the rather pathetic side of Reynolds lurking behind the stormy-tempered genius is revealed evokes the notion that "his bark is worse than his bite." (Reynolds even says to Dr. Hardy [Brian Gleeson], "I seem to remember barking at you.") Words are literalized so as to turn them inside out: Alma literally poisons Reynolds but, if we believe that this film is a comedy, this is because she *doesn't* poison their relationship. Instead she succeeds, at least temporarily, at making him "tender" (something we often want to achieve with our food; certainly our meat, implying a predatory side to Alma's character). Recall Cavell's remark about "the riddle of intimacy . . . in the face of the puzzle of ecstasy, which is violent where it is tender"; Alma is, instead, tender where she is violent (Cavell 1981b, 31). To be tender is to be soft and pliant; the opposite is to be rigid and inflexible. Reynolds's surname, Woodcock, suggests inflexibility (as well as evoking a—rather juvenile—image of male sexual potency). This rigidity is the threat that the couple must learn to keep at bay. As Louise Dumas aptly puts it, "the couple enter a spiral between life and death, domination and submission, creation and petrification" (Dumas 2018, 8; my translation).

Skepticism

Cavell connects rigidity and petrification directly with his central theme of skepticism when he remarks of *The Winter's Tale* that it illustrates "the imagination of the body's fate under skepticism," a fate that is remedied by the undoing of petrification, as Hermione is turned back from a statue into a woman of flesh and blood (Cavell 1979b, 481). Skepticism in philosophy usually takes one of two forms: skepticism about the existence of the external world and skepticism about the existence of other people, or, as it is usually put, other minds. Cavell had a perennial fascination with both issues as well as equally perennial senses that much of this philosophy was profoundly misguided, that Wittgenstein spoke a great deal of sense on the subject, and that he was frequently misread and misunderstood. All these subjects are central to Cavell's 1979 book *The Claim of Reason: Wittgenstein, Skepticism, Morality, and Tragedy*. Wheatley writes that Cavell sees the remarriage comedy as representing successful instances of couples acknowledging one another, and thus avoiding skepticism: "In order to avoid the tragedy of skepticism, Cavell thus concludes, we must be willing to let go of our desperate desire for knowledge" (Wheatley 2019, 104). This is entirely accurate but could be misleading. "The tragedy of skepticism" is not simply a synonym for skepticism; what we try to avoid is *succumbing* to skepticism, being defeated by it. (It is relevant to *Phantom Thread*, I think, that Cavell refers to a "*recovery* from skepticism" [Cavell 1988, 26; my emphasis].) These matters are closely related to another ambiguous genitive that Cavell deploys frequently, "the truth of skepticism." Too many commentators have carelessly misread this as the claim that skepticism is true. But Cavell nowhere proposes that we should "let go of . . . knowledge" either because there is no such thing to be gained, or in the sense of just putting our heads in the sand (refusing to find out when we perfectly well could, if we wanted to), but rather that we need to recognize those situations in which thinking in terms of knowledge is simply not appropriate. As he puts it, "the truth of skepticism [is], namely, that the human creature's basis in the world as a whole, its relation to the world as such, is not that of knowing, anyway not what we think of as knowing"; this—contrary to much philosophical discussion of the topic—means that skepticism "cannot be combatted through simple 'refutations'" (Cavell 1979b, 241, 109).[7]

An interesting discussion of these issues is provided by an article that seems to me illuminating and misleading in roughly equal measure. David Macarthur has argued for the relevance of *The Claim of Reason* to Cavellian reflections on film, insisting that "[t]o see Cavell as aiming to overcome skepticism is to miss one of his deepest impulses. The glory of Cavell's writing is how assiduously it works to keep philosophy *open* to skepticism" (Macarthur 2016, 134n18; emphasis in original). On Macarthur's reading, Cavell's first book on film, *The World Viewed*, argues that the situation of the film viewer enforces a kind of temporary skepticism about the external world, one about which no discussion is required: "Cavell concludes that the cinematic respite from the ordinary ethical precondition of society—according to which 'something [is] owed another simply as a human being, the failure of which reveals the failure of one's own humanity' (*Claim* 434)—does not need accounting for" (121). Macarthur thinks that this is mistaken, arguing that Cavell's work on skepticism in works such as *The Claim of Reason* is of profound relevance to film, but that to say so is to disagree with Cavell.

It is true that Cavell says things like this: "The fact that I am invisible and inaudible to the actors, and fixed in position, no longer needs accounting for; it is not part of a convention I have to comply with. . . . In viewing a movie my helplessness is mechanically assured: I am present not at something happening, which I must confirm, but at something that has happened, which I absorb (like a memory)" (Cavell 1979a, 25–26). But Macarthur misinterprets the sense in which, for Cavell, this "does not need accounting for"; by saying this Cavell does not mean that there is nothing to say about it. It is the viewer's invisibility to, or absence from, the actors that does not need accounting for, and by no means "the cinematic respite from the ordinary ethical precondition of society," which seems to me a profoundly un-Cavellian idea. There is no reason to think that Cavell would disagree with Macarthur's proposal that in watching films "the issue of acknowledgement is, as in the case of theater, not canceled but transmuted into a form of self-revelation" (Macarthur 2016, 124).[8] The language Macarthur uses to describe the relationship of the viewer to the human activity we watch on the film screen ("null and void"; "no question of acknowledgement"; "without . . . even attempting to"; "no need to account for" [128, 122, 126, 127]) seems to me very hard to square with the paragraph to which chapter 3 was devoted:

> A world complete without me which is present to me is the world of my immortality. This is an importance of film—and a danger. It takes my life as my haunting of the world, either because I left it unloved (the Flying Dutchman) or because I left unfinished business (Hamlet). So there is reason for me to want the camera to deny the coherence of the world, its coherence as past: to deny that the world is complete without me. But there is equal reason to want it affirmed that the world is coherent without me. That is essential to what I want of immortality: nature's survival of me. It will mean that the present judgment upon me is not yet the last. (Cavell 1979a, 160)

My absence from the world of the film I am watching is anything but "null and void" as a topic for reflection; instead it generates a complicated and contradictory set of desires. Macarthur offers, supposedly in opposition to Cavell's views, what seems to me a pretty good paraphrase of this very passage:

> Indeed, the powerful allure of film can be explained precisely by our desire to view others whilst at the same time escaping the ordinary burden of viewing (i.e., viewing *seen*), being relieved of our endless responsibility to acknowledge others whom we confront in daily life. In providing a way of viewing others that is, at the same time, a refuge from the acknowledgement that ordinary everyday viewing of others demands (i.e., viewing *unseen*), film invites an exploration of the very conditions of acknowledgement themselves. (Macarthur 2016, 130; emphases in original)

Cavell does not emphasize relief and refuge in quite the way Macarthur does; instead he indicates that they are both "an importance . . . and a danger." But Macarthur is sensitive to important parallel dangers in our relations with others: "Our knowledge of others, if we want to call it that, is not assured, not guaranteed, not authoritative, is endlessly open to question, courts disharmony and discord, is reflectively opaque, and without clear limits. Our skepticism of others is more a matter of disappointment than doubt. Moreover, we do not have generally applicable standards for what would count as establishing genuine or better acknowledgment of another" (131). It is precisely this situation that, I am claiming, *Phantom Thread*—in keeping with the other remarriage comedies, but in darkly distinctive ways—is concerned to explore.[9]

Disorientation and the Production of Criteria

As Cavell and Macarthur both emphasize, the renewability of skepticism means that the emergence of disappointment and disorientation is a standing possibility. As Affeldt puts it, "the search for criteria . . . occurs in response to a crisis—either confusion in the face of some empirical phenomenon or philosophical disorientation" (Affeldt 1998, 12). The word "criteria" is something of a Wittgensteinian term of art that can be a little confusing. (I discuss it further in the introduction.) Criteria, in Cavell's reading, relate to the means by which we assure ourselves of, for example, the existence of the external world, the personhood of other people, or of "the difference between the waking world and the world of dreams, or between natural things and mechanical things, or between the masculine and the feminine, or between the past and the present" (Cavell 1986, 101), not to mention many apparently more mundane phenomena. As we have seen Macarthur point out, Cavell's point is precisely that these criteria are not "generally applicable" but always specific and in need of being found anew in each situation (Macarthur 2016, 131); in some cases they may never be found.[10] Nor are they simply lists of features that can be ticked off: "Perhaps the most direct evidence that, for Cavell, Wittgensteinian criteria are not marks or features is simply his claim that 'of course feelings are included among the criteria for applying a concept' (*CR* p. 48)" (Affeldt 1998, 9).[11] They are closely bound up with questions of language, of description, and for making ourselves accountable to one another: "In calling *that* a wince, a flirtatious overture, an appropriate gift, an unresolved conclusion, a table, enough fish for two, I reveal, or begin to reveal, what counts for me in what ways, and I open myself to questions and to requests for elaboration in response to which I will, if I can, say more about how and why I am counting something as I am" (22; emphasis in original).[12] It is, I hope, clear why this is a matter both for people, in their relations with one another (is what Reynolds and Alma have a marriage?) and for film critics (is what Reynolds and Alma have a marriage?), and why a loss of confidence in this kind of mutually intelligible description can be profoundly disorientating. "What is this?" Reynolds asks multiple times at the surprise dinner, and the viewer cannot help but ask a similar question. What is going on, and how can we tell?

Cavell remarks that "in using official criteria we *start out* with a known kind of object whereas in using Wittgensteinian criteria we *end up* knowing a kind of object" (Cavell 1979b, 16; emphases in original). In this context, I think his delicate ambiguity in speaking of *producing* criteria is very helpful: "[T]he best proof that there are such things as Wittgenstein calls criteria is to produce some" (28). When we successfully do so, have we produced them in the sense that we might produce an aspirin from our bag if somebody has a headache, or in the sense that a factory produces a car? We do not have to decide between these two senses, but the ambiguity serves to remind us not to think too simplistically in terms of one or the other. Just as Cavell's language of "recalling criteria" should, says Affeldt, not be thought of as "a matter of recalling a given order of criteria which is separable from and which under-girds" (Affeldt 1998, 12) our forms of life, when we "produce criteria" we both discover them (come upon them; they preexist us and our situation) and create them (bring them into being; their applicability to precisely *this* situation does not preexist). We could make a similar point by speaking of criteria as "found"—found like a coin down the back of the sofa, or founded like a nation or an institution?

But why would we want to produce such criteria in the first place, rather than just attempting to suppress, ignore, or dismiss skeptical questions when they arise? The answer, of course, is that "the philosophical search for our criteria is a search for community" (Cavell 1979b, 22). What kind of community do Reynolds and Alma manage to find (or to found) in *Phantom Thread*? Is it a genuine community? Alma certainly thinks that the earlier, intolerable state of their relationship is not, that it is perverse and artificial. During the disastrous surprise dinner, she tells Reynolds that "nothing is normal or natural; everything is a game." It is at least a relatively open question whether she responds to the situation by finding a way for them to know one another that *is* normal and natural, that is not a game, or whether she merely replaces one unnatural game with another.

Another way of phrasing this question would be to ask what kind of community they are looking for. Cavell notes both that, in remarriage comedy, "the happiness of marriage is dissociated from any *a priori* concept of what constitutes domesticity" and yet that "our grammar"—understanding that word in an expanded, Wittgensteinian sense—"is in some sense to be understood as *a priori*," namely, "the sense in which human beings are 'in agreement' in their judgments" (Cavell 1986, 117, 106). Human beings are *both* somehow "in agreement" *a priori* (Cavell is here referring to the famous §242 in the *Philosophical Investigations*; see Wittgenstein 2009, 94) and can have no a priori concept of what it is truly to agree with one another. It does not seem helpful to think of relationships as necessarily based *either* on the satisfaction of definite plans *or* on the emergence of situations that could not have been predicted in advance, each option excluding the other. *Phantom Thread* further complicates our understanding of this by means of ambiguity about Alma's desires and plans. When exactly she formulates the plan to poison Reynolds is, for example, left ambiguous. After the failure of the surprise dinner for two, we see Alma in the kitchen of the country house preparing poisonous mushrooms. But she gives him the tea containing it back in the London townhouse. The scene of preparation might, or might not, represent a flashback. If we decide that it does, Alma will appear much more deliberately calculating than if it does not.[13] Also, the issue of Alma's professional ambitions is very understated but definitely present. She wears a dress of her own design at the surprise dinner, which is what first brings Reynolds out of his angry bewilderment. ("Hmm. It's rather interesting. Very good work.") Does she perhaps recognize Reynolds Woodcock, the dressmaker, on their first meeting, as do the two young women in the restaurant? In which case, does her final vision in which she "take[s] care of [his] dresses" represent a surrender of her ambition to his, or a fulfilment of it?

And what of Alma's insistence that she knows what Reynolds wants? She tells Cyril that "I have to know him in my own way." What does this mean? Compare it to, for example, "I have to *get to know* him in my own way," which would be subtly different and not as open to our hearing in it the undertone that knowing somebody one's own way might be not really a form of knowing at all. *Phantom Thread* explores something Robert Pippin finds in Henry James, namely, "the thin line . . . between interpreting and understanding, on the one hand, and manufacturing and imposing, on the other" (Pippin 2000, 63). We might also ask whether imposing oneself on another is or is not, if not a way of coming to know, at least a way of coming to *be known*. The sadomasochistic aspects of the relationship are not merely an inversion of ordinary power relations but constitute an exploration of the relationship between what Cavell calls the active and passive forms of skepticism. As Richard Moran explains, these are "roughly, the form where the question for me is whether I can gain access to or conviction in the mind of another, and the form where the question for me is whether *anything* I do or manifest could possibly make my *own* mind known to another" (Moran 2017, 100; emphases in original). Does Reynolds come to know Alma's mind, or does she simply orchestrate a situation in which they can both entertain the fantasy that he does?[14] In pursuing these questions *Phantom Thread* also bears out Cavell's observation that "it is an essential feature of the genre [of remarriage comedy] . . . to leave ambiguous the question of whether the man or the woman is the active or the passive partner, whether indeed active and passive are apt characterizations of the difference between male and female" (Cavell 1981b, 82).[15]

As with the relationship between Reynolds and Alma, so with the viewer's relationship to the film. It can be difficult to work out what kind of film we are watching, quite how "normal" or "abnormal" it is. Some viewers have taken it for a stodgy costume drama, others for a deeply disturbing sadomasochist fantasy, or even an apologia for toxic masculinity (more on this in a moment).[16] The film's fluidity of structure is relevant here. It is hard to predict what will happen next, and yet when it does happen it can seem like simply repetition—why two poisonings, for example?[17] In this apparent amorphousness and play with abnormality *Phantom Thread* has affinities with Cavell's suggestion that

> it is the task of the modernist artist to show that we do not know a priori what will count for us as an instance

of his art.... And only someone outside this enterprise could think of establishing new conventions as a matter of exercising personal decision or taste. One might rather think of it as the exploration or education or enjoyment or chastisement of taste and of decision and of intuition, an exploration of the kind of creature in whom such capacities are exercised. (Cavell 1979b, 123)

This is not to take a position on whether or not *Phantom Thread* is accurately described as a "modernist" art work, but to say that Reynolds and Alma collectively occupy a position analogous to that of the artist Cavell describes here, engaged in "the exploration or education or enjoyment or chastisement of taste," and so that the challenge for the film viewer is to some extent whether or not we can see things from inside their "enterprise." These issues help indicate why it is so important that what goes on in *Phantom Thread* at least *risks* looking unnatural or abnormal: because otherwise the most important questions would have been decided in advance. (Perhaps the film also indicates that the *ordinary*—another of Cavell's most recurrent themes—is not an antonym for the *abnormal*; Cavell's Tanner Lectures were entitled "The Uncanniness of the Ordinary" [see Cavell 1986].)

Some responses to the film have, as I said above, seen it as an apologia for toxic masculinity (see Hemon 2018 in particular). While good work has been done countering this kind of view (see Siemienowicz 2018), it certainly could be argued that Alma helps to perpetuate Reynolds's toxic masculinity. See, for example, the painful scene in which she removes a Woodcock dress from a drunken American heiress, a procedure that has aphrodisiac properties, as the couple's subsequent kiss—and Alma's rather strangulated proclamation "I love you"—demonstrate. There are also, though, definite senses in which Alma *defeats* Reynolds. On that first date, she tells him that he would lose a staring contest with her. Later, after they have been married but with their relationship again on the rocks, she goes out dancing alone on New Year's Eve, because he will not accompany her. When he tracks her down they have what is clearly a staring contest (see fig. 5.3). It is only at the very end of the film—after the second poisoning—that we are shown that he did dance with her, and that he must therefore have lost the staring contest.

Figure 5.3. A staring contest. *Source: Phantom Thread* (2017).

If Alma helps Reynolds to continue as he is, it is only by introducing a novel distinction between public and private. There is no indication that Reynolds will behave differently in public in the future—whether towards her or towards anybody else—only that he will periodically need to be brought down to earth by Alma. Having said this, the public world in the film is an odd one. Porton notes the film's disconnection from the world at large; though set in 1955, "[t]here isn't a peep about Prime Minister Anthony Eden, who took over from Churchill in 1955. Even Queen Elizabeth II, who was crowned two years earlier, goes unmentioned" (Porton 2018, 49). Before Alma comes into his life there is not really, for Reynolds, any distinction between public and private; or, rather, he simply avoids the public unless it is entirely on his own terms. His townhouse is his home, his workplace, and his exhibition space. The townhouse and the country house sometimes feel like the only two real *places* in the film. They are almost the only locations we see both from the inside and the outside; other locations—a registry office; Devonshire Hall; somebody else's country house; the Swiss Alps—are given no establishing shots.[18] These spaces do not, therefore, feel entirely real, solidly connected to the rest of the world, but are more like transitory environments that exist only briefly in the interim before Reynolds can get back to the safety and solidity of his usual surroundings.

Figure 5.4. Public and private (note the spyhole to the left of the image). *Source: Phantom Thread* (2017).

The emerging distinction between public and private is indicated during the scene of the fashion show in the townhouse. A public (or semipublic—certainly everybody present has been invited) event is taking place in a private house. Reynolds looks at Alma through a peephole; he is looking privately at somebody that the others present are looking at publicly, making his looking somehow perverse, even though what he is looking at—Alma—is available to general view. Of course, he looks at all the models that way, but the scene hints that he does so in a distinct way with Alma, and that she is aware of this. But for their relationship to be able to continue, for "remarriage" to take place, a more fundamental division than this will have to take place, one in which Reynolds will have to surrender some control of his privacy, a surrender which constitutes an at least partial recognition of the fact that his independence was always artificial, a construction—something Cyril is well aware of. But whereas Cyril prefers to carry on as they always have and avoid conversation (she tells him that hearing his complaints "hurts my ears"), in making her poisoning explicit Alma finds a way for conversation to take place.

I have been arguing that the remarriage narrative is that of the coming-to-be-shared of Reynolds's and Alma's criteria. At the time of the first poisoning, they are not shared. Rather than a communal practice, Reynolds thinks he has simply made a discovery—about his relationship with Alma, certainly, but chiefly about himself and his own projects: "I have things I want to do. . . . The mistakes I've made and made again, they can no longer be ignored. There are things nagging at me. Things that now must be done. Things I simply cannot do without you." But he comes to see the wedding as just one more mistake, as he confesses to Cyril: "I've made a terrible mistake in my life. . . . I can't work. I can't concentrate, I have no confidence." He is too cowardly to tell this to Alma directly, but she overhears him; his inadvertent making-explicit must be countered by her deliberate act in revealing the poisoning, which is of course not only a revelation about what she is about to do, but about what she has already done. Their marriage—or we might call it their first remarriage—did not come about as a result of his insight following a chance occurrence but was engineered by Alma.

The political implications of this process of sharing, and thereby of division (into public and private) might well seem troubling, and not merely because Reynolds surrenders in private without having to surrender in public. Cavell has been criticized by Joshua Foa Dienstag for his belief that films, including the remarriage comedies, offer the viewers "a lesson that will reconcile us to our democracy" (Dienstag 2016, 10). Cavell himself, however, offers a very different view in "More of *The World Viewed*":

> For movies are inherently anarchic. Their unappeasable appetite for stories of love is for stories in which love, to be found, must find its own community, apart from, but with luck still within, society at large; an enclave within it; stories in which society as a whole, and its laws, can no longer provide or deny love. . . . The myth of movies replaces the myth according to which obedience to the law, being obedience to laws I have consented to and thus established, its obedience to the best of myself, hence constitutes my freedom—the myth of democracy. In replacing this myth, it suggests that democracy itself, the sacred image of secular politics, is unlivable. (Cavell 1979a, 214)

It certainly seems to me plausible that *Phantom Thread* makes such a suggestion. How we react to this suggestion may depend on how much we feel the film to, as Porton puts it, "send up" the relationship between Reynolds and Alma—which, if it does so, may therefore also be a sending-up of this attempt to replace "the myth of democracy"—as opposed to merely sending up Reynolds, in which case the film might come closer to endorsing the attempted replacement, as long as the former masters—the white male geniuses—are suitably chastised and mortified.

Eternal Return

I want to conclude by making very brief reference to another philosopher of great importance to Cavell, but one less discussed—either by Cavell or his commentators—than Wittgenstein, namely, Nietzsche, and specifically his idea of the eternal return, the notion that "[t]his life as you now live it and have lived it you will have to live once again and innumerable times again" (Nietzsche [1887] 2001, 194). Cavell writes that "the willing acceptance of repetition, or rather eternal recurrence, is the recipe Nietzsche discovered as the antidote for our otherwise fated future of nihilism, the thing Nietzsche calls 'the revenge against time and its "It was"'—a revenge itself constituting a last effort not to die of nostalgia" (Cavell 1996, 82–83). At the end of *Phantom Thread* we are in a situation of eternal return: it is clear enough that poisonings (or their equivalent) will have to recur periodically in order to achieve equilibrium through repeated disequilibrium, a structure that is represented visually by the way Alma's hand disturbs the lampshade when pouring water after serving Reynolds his second helping of poison.[19] The film seems to dispute Tracy's remark to Hepburn in *Woman of the Year* that if patching things up were to "become a habit, then we'd wind up with a patchwork quilt instead of a marriage."

The sense of eternal return is further underlined, in case we missed it, by Alma's remark to the doctor that Reynolds will be "waiting" for her "in this life, and the next, and the next one after." (She has transformed the situation from one in which she is waiting to one in which it is he who waits; see note 15.) But it is important to register that the vision of their life together in the future that she goes on to describe to Reynolds is just that, a *vision*; it may not come to pass. As in Nietzsche, the eternal return is a metaphor for a kind of test, an image of ethical and psychological commitment in which "all our lovers and children and friends come back and are welcome," rather than any kind of ontological or mythological fact (see Pippin 2010, 69–70). Alma's devotion to "the nuptial ring of rings: the ring of recurrence" (Nietzsche 2006, 184–87; see also Cavell 1986, 114–15), her use of poison as an "antidote for . . . nihilism," is an attempt to create a collective "immortality" for her and Reynolds (unlike the intimations of solitary immortality that Cavell sees in the viewer's relation to film), one that can only exist by being continually affirmed and reaffirmed.

Marriage, like skepticism, is constantly renewable (as well as in need of constant renewal), and *Phantom Thread* connects the unavoidable threat of the renewal of skeptical disorientation to the continual renewal that constitutes a successful marriage, something for which—to keep with the culinary metaphors—there is no recipe. The fact that the film ends "happily" does not mean that disorientation is banished; indeed, this very happiness, given how it is constituted, is likely to provoke a lingering aftertaste of disorientation in the viewer.[20] It is certainly true that the poisoning exploits Reynolds's egotism. Rather than removing that egotism, as many viewers might have wished, the poisoning turns from an egotism built on a fantasy of self-sufficiency into a willingly dependent egotism, a

Figure 5.5. Equilibrium through disequilibrium. *Source: Phantom Thread* (2017).

surrender to Alma's ministrations. Nicholas Spice has observed that "[t]o be a patient is to be a solipsist: for a while, the world revolves around you. This is why being ill as a child was so special—I had my mother to myself" (Spice 2020, 37). Though exactly which is never confirmed, we can be confident that Alma ends up either replacing the role Reynolds's mother took whenever he was a sickly child or compensating for the fact that she refused to do so. Poison creates an enforced need for nurture, and therefore if Reynolds is a "solipsist" it is only in a qualified sense; he can focus on himself only because of another, and he becomes completely aware of this with Alma in a way he never could with Cyril.[21]

Between the two poisonings, when their relationship is at a low ebb, Reynolds and Alma play backgammon. She remarks that it is a "stupid game," to which he replies, "If you were victorious and confident you'd see it in a different light." Her ultimate achievement, the one that leads to their "remarriage," is to educate him that the opposite is also true. When trying to get out of his marriage he tells Cyril that it is unsustainable because Alma causes him to have "no confidence." But in his discovery of how things look when he is defeated and vulnerable, rather than "victorious and confident," and in his recognition that this is a lesson she has taught him—that in bringing this about she is giving him something he needs—we see Alma and Reynolds managing to produce the criteria according to which their marriage can continually renew itself. Much of *Phantom Thread*'s humor lies in the way it straightfacedly presents this peculiar situation as an image of "romantic love, individual autonomy, nonconformity, and . . . self-improvement" (Shaw 2017, 116).[22] In showing us that we cannot "start out" by knowing what these things are, the question *Phantom Thread* ultimately poses its audience is whether or not we can "end up" recognizing them in it (Cavell 1979b, 16).

6

Experience, Skepticism, and Idolatry in Stanley Kubrick, Nicholas Lash, and Stanley Cavell

THE FILMS OF STANLEY KUBRICK are readily understood as explorations of human knowledge and its limits, whether these limits are conceived of as cosmological, historical, metaphysical (*2001: A Space Odyssey*; *The Shining*); rational, social, ethical (*Dr. Strangelove*; *A Clockwork Orange*); or emotional, economic, and interpersonal (*Barry Lyndon*; *Eyes Wide Shut*).[1] These explorations have been interpreted both as deeply religious and as profoundly atheistic. We need not, however, read *2001* as primarily an investigation of human transcendence (as Suparno Banerjee does, claiming that it presents human evolution as "a mysterious process overseen by some higher existence, with obvious religious undertones" [Banerjee 2018, 44]), nor (as if in some kind of nihilistic recompense) need we see *A Clockwork Orange* as chiefly an expression of humanity's inherent barbarism. This is in no way to deny that there is much to reflect on in these films concerning the ontologies both of film and of religious, or irreligious, experience, as well as about their relationships to the shapes of human knowing and desiring. In making this claim, however, I am drawing on ways of construing what we might mean in speaking about "religious experience" and "the ontology of film" that are at odds with how these notions are most frequently understood. For example, "religious experience," as the term is widely used, can be seen—contrary to the intentions of those who so use it—to describe a form of what Stanley Cavell often calls haunting the world. This chapter will explore some of the implications that these alternative accounts of experience might have concerning how we should regard Kubrick's cinema. It concentrates on *2001* and *A Clockwork Orange* because of the starkness with which these two films, adjacent in Kubrick's career, seem to exemplify the religious and the anti-religious aspects of his oeuvre. First, however, with the help of the work of Cavell and of the theologian Nicholas Lash, I need to outline the understandings of religious experience and film ontology which I want to put in play.[2]

One further preliminary note even before these preliminaries, however. Kubrick has ardent admirers as well as detractors (or skeptics) of varying degrees of fervor. The skeptics tend to find the films limited by their supposed coldness, while the most devoted partisans find in Kubrick's legendary obsessive control the marks not only of filmmaking genius but of genuine profundity. It is therefore quite startling, after spending time reading the literature on Kubrick in academic film studies, to encounter the three densely fascinating pages Cavell devotes to *Dr. Strangelove* during an early essay on Samuel Beckett's *Endgame*. Cavell begins by declaring that the "clearest fact about the film is its brilliance" (so far, so familiar), before going on to clarify the nature of this "brilliance": "It is not, for example, the result of brilliant moviemaking, at which it is quite routine; nor the result of brilliant ideas, for it has no ideas (which is perhaps sufficient reason not to defend it, as has been tried, as satire). Its brilliance is that of farce, with its stringent rhythm of entrances and concealments; and of silent comedy, with its sight gags. Only it is abstract" (Cavell [1969] 2015, 124). I quote this passage (to which I will return later) not to be provocative, but simply in order to remark that Cavell's description of *Dr. Strangelove* might suggest fresh critical avenues by which to approach Kubrick's work. We do not have to commit ourselves one way or another on the brilliance of his "moviemaking" (by which I assume that Cavell principally means to refer to such things as cinematography, editing, and mise-en-scène), nor even of his "ideas"; there may be other virtues, other brilliances, at work and in play within Kubrick's films that merit our attention. But to see this, we need first to turn to the promised preliminaries.

Nicholas Lash on Religious Experience

In his 1988 book *Easter in Ordinary*, Lash observes that "[a]lmost all modern discussion of religious experience" makes two assumptions: first, that "the notion refers to some particular kind or category of 'experience' or psychological state which may be phenomenologically distinguished from *other* kinds of conscious experience" and, second, that the word God "is the name of a particular object or thing which we encounter or come across in enjoying the kind of experience which is called 'religious'" (N. Lash 1988, 128–29; emphasis in original). Lash rejects both assumptions, which leads him to make some apparently paradoxical claims. He argues, for example, that "it is not the case that all experience of God is necessarily religious in form or content" (7). We might have assumed that "experience of God" and "religious experience" are synonyms. If, however, we cannot even coherently distinguish (phenomenologically speaking) a particular type, or set, of subjective, "internal" sensations and experiences—such as, for example, "the feeling of absolute dependence" (128)—which we might label "religious," then it follows that whatever may justly be named experience of God (if there is any such experience) might not fall within the bounds of what we have previously understood "religious experience" to consist of. Given his diagnosis of this confusion, it is unsurprising that Lash's recommendation is that we attempt "simply to dispense altogether with the notion of 'religious experience,'" although he grants that this will prove difficult if not impossible (129).

This, which we might call the negative pole of Lash's account of religious experience, is only fully comprehensible if we consider the positive pole, which concerns the attempt, in our actions and in our words, to avoid idolatry. The work of William James exemplifies the modern accounts of religious experience that Lash deplores. In what he admits is perhaps a caricature, but not thereby a "misrepresentation" (given that "the purpose of a caricature is to highlight the salient features of an object" [80]), Lash responds to the claims we find in James such as that "there *are* religious experiences of a specific nature" from whose evidence we can surmise the existence "of a superior co-conscious being" (79, citing James's *A Pluralistic Universe*; emphasis in original) by concluding that "[t]he God of William James turns out . . . to have been not only a creature, but a thing: a large, powerful, fundamentally friendly material object of which our more elevated elements form part" (80). Given, however, that "the distinction between the world and God is not itself a fact about the world" (something that Lash takes to be an orthodox claim, and one to which all the great religious traditions of the world have consistently subscribed), any such being as that which James describes could not possibly be God (N. Lash 1996, 65).

We will return to Lash's account of the role of idolatry in our lives. (As will, I hope, become clear, I read idolatry as Lash understands it as a form of what Cavell calls haunting the world.) For the present, it remains to make one further point about Lash's account of (what we might now refer to as) so-called religious experience, which is that its attack is crucially directed against contemporary assumptions about the essential *privacy* of experience. Only I, so the thinking goes, can know if I am having a religious experience. James was of this opinion. Lash's view, however, influenced by Wittgenstein, has more in common with that of Wittgenstein's great disciple (and Lash's fellow Catholic) Elizabeth Anscombe. Both believe that our assumptions about religious experience are often misguided a fortiori because some of our basic assumptions about experience are also mistaken. In her book on intention, that supposedly most inner and private phenomenon, Anscombe writes that, although certain features of intention suggest that "if we want to know a man's intentions it is into the contents of his mind, and only into these, that we must enquire," which might appear to entail that "what physically takes place, i.e., what a man actually does, is the very last thing we need consider," her view is that it should rather be "the first" (Anscombe [1957] 2000, 9 [§4]). Lash, similarly, insists that "[f]or *human beings*, experience, at least in the vast majority of its forms, includes a great deal more than mental goings-on" (N. Lash 1988, 92; emphasis in original).[3] It would, for example, be very peculiar to describe "the experience of personal betrayal" solely in terms of "something which went on in our minds"; it surely also includes "all manner of physical features, such as opening letters, finding the door closed in our face or—if the Judas was a business partner—a significant diminution in our bank balance" (92).⁴ (Even though the stunt by which Barry Lyndon [Ryan O'Neal] is brought to think that he has killed Captain Quin [Leonard Rossiter] in a duel hinges on what Barry believes, the deception is a public collective action that does not simply take place in his mind.) At his most polemical, Lash even denies "that there is any such thing as experience," if by this we mean something that can coherently be separated from human goings-on in the world in all their material and social detail: "[T]here is no such thing as pure or raw experience, any more than there is any such thing as pure or raw size or quantity or color" (12).⁵ To assume that there is, says Lash in a very Wittgensteinian idiom, is to be "bewitched by the form of our language" (12).⁶ Neither God nor experience, then, are *things*; but to claim this is not to deny their reality.

Cinematic Ontology and the Experience of Film

I take Cavell's declaration that he could "claim no familiarity with extreme religious states" to indicate a skepticism as to whether they constitute the heart of the matter that resonates with Lash's view (Cavell 2011, 518). For now, I want to step back from explicitly theological concerns and sketch some ways in which the form of Cavell's account of the ontology of film resonates with the shape of Lash's account of religious experience. After this, we will be in a position to turn to Kubrick's cinema and see what kind of theological value it might have in the light of the writings of Lash and of Cavell.

In his book *Film/Cinema/Movie*, subtitled *A Theory of Experience*, Gerald Mast addresses the subtitle of Cavell's first book on film. Mast declares that Cavell "subtitles his study, *The World Viewed*, 'Reflections on the Ontology of Film,' but he actually reflects on the ontology of movies" (Mast [1977] 1983, 14). There is certainly something in this charge; Cavell explicitly denies that what he has to say about film applies to animation (see his response to the charge that this undermines his arguments in Cavell 1979a, 167–74). But the claim as to whether this omission undermines Cavell's arguments hinges on what we understand by ontology. Cavell's account is far too focused on his own experience of films to be an ontology, so one possible objection goes. However, when it comes to film, ontology has fundamentally to do with experience. Cavell counters the assumption, which has affinities with the accounts of religious experience that Lash challenges, that the proper object of the study of the experience of film must, somehow, be the experience of the viewer, per se. Robert Pippin is describing such a position when he notes: "It has become especially popular recently, across a wide range of different theories—affect theory, cognitive science approaches, neuro-aesthetics, feminist criticism, psychoanalytic approaches, postmodernist art, post-Danto philosophical aesthetics—to consider the art work, film in this case, as in the first instance an occasion for an experience, suggesting that our attention should be devoted to understanding that experience" (Pippin 2019, 540). If "the ontology of film" is a fancy way of referring to whatever it is we want to offer in response to the question "What is film?" it cannot merely be a matter of, for example, the physical substrate of the recorded material or the mechanics of its projection. Since films are made to be experienced, an account of the ontology of film—of what films are—must also be an account of the experience of film. On the kind of assumption Pippin describes, there is something that I, and only I, experience when watching a film, which is distinct from the film which the film prompts (or perhaps causes) me to have; this private experience we can call "the experience of film." Cavell, however, insists that what we experience while watching a film *is the film we are watching*.[7]

Cavell's use of the term "ontology" often skews the way that his interpreters, even those sympathetic to his work, understand the references he makes to the material aspects of the filmic apparatus. Cavell's ontology of film is therefore frequently grouped with—or even elided with—other "realist" ontologies such as those of André Bazin and Siegfried Kracauer. Robert Sinnerbrink writes that, for Cavell, "the 'automatism' of the moving image—its mechanical basis as a 'manufactured' artifact, dependent on the relationship between an object, light, and the camera—is a defining element of its ontology and of the medium's ambiguous claims to realism" (Sinnerbrink 2020, 131). Such claims, while not wrong, can easily mislead. They neglect the fact that what Cavell calls automatisms are just as likely—in fact more likely—to be things like genres rather than aspects of the mechanical production and reproduction of films. Cavell's claim is that "[w]hat gives significance to features of this physical basis are artistic discoveries of form and genre and type and technique, which I have begun calling automatisms" (Cavell 1979a, 105).[8]

In her book *Cinema and Experience*, Miriam Bratu Hansen argues that Kracauer's *Theory of Film* is best thought of as offering "not a theory of cinematic realism, but a theory of film experience and, more generally, of cinema as a sensory-perceptual matrix of experience—a project that links Kracauer . . . with Robert Warshow and Stanley Cavell" (Hansen 2012, 255). In her defense of Kracauer's project, Hansen grants the validity of the charge of "a potential methodological circularity—assumptions about the ontological qualities of the medium derived from viewing particular films become the basis for aesthetic norms and critical judgments" (350).[9] Hansen claims that Kracauer "cautions against" this very fallacy (350) when he declares: "The properties of a medium elude concise definition. It is therefore inadmissible to postulate such properties and use them as a starting-point for aesthetic analysis. What is adequate to a medium cannot be determined dogmatically in advance" (Kracauer 1960, 12). Kracauer's formulation of the problem is not, however, quite synonymous with Hansen's. Once again, the precise import of "ontology"—or what Kracauer calls the "properties of a medium"—is crucial. In Hansen's presentation, it seems as if "viewing particular films" must of necessity be a suspect method for making discoveries "about the ontological qualities of the medium." In denying, however, that it is admissible to determine "[w]hat is adequate to a medium . . . dogmatically in advance," we see Kracauer at his most Cavellian.[10] The point here is that watching films in order to learn about the medium is precisely what one *should* do. (In a late piece, Cavell distinguishes his writing on film from that of a writer closely associated with Kracauer, namely, Walter Benjamin, by noting that Benjamin "develops his speculations concerning . . . the technological medium of film without consulting a film's idea of itself, or undertaking to suppose that one or another may have such a thing" [Cavell 2005c, 87].)[11] If we remove the pejorative word "assumptions" from Hansen's formulation, then attempting to discover "the ontological qualities of the medium" by means of "viewing particular films," reflecting on the experience, and then going on to propose "aesthetic norms and critical judgments," is on such an account precisely the *right* way to go about things, and not in any destructive sense circular.[12] Hansen's claim that the heart of Kracauer's theory of film is "a matter of stylistic practice rather than a matter of medium ontology" insists on a distinction between what film (the medium) *is* and what films (as instances of work in that medium) *are* that neither Kracauer nor Cavell would accept (Hansen 2012, 279). Paying attention to the details of individual films is, for Cavell just as it was for Kracauer, not just good scholarly practice; without it any claims about "the experience of cinema" risk emptiness with regard to any of the stakes (philosophical, phenomenological, historical, or ethical) that most matter to him. To paraphrase Anscombe on intention, while on some accounts of the ontology of film our experience of the concrete details of actually existing films are the very last thing we need consider, Cavell suggests that they are the first.

The Experience of Stanley Kubrick

Let us sum up where we have got to. Lash disputes that there is such a thing as religious experience, in part because he claims that experience is not best understood as something private and isolable, while Cavell's work suggests that to understand the ontology of film as something separable from an account of the experience of film is to rely on a similar, and similarly unsustainable, notion of experience. If we grant these two positions, what might we discover about theology, film, and their relationship from the experience of Kubrick's cinema? Most immediately obvious are some negative conclusions. We will not, for example, find in *2001* any *theological* insight into the methodologies of the creator of the world, such as the suggestion that we modify the idea that "the universe has been designed from the beginning by an intelligent being to bring about humans," concluding instead that "the designer's purpose wasn't producing humans in particular, but rather producing intelligent, morally and spiritually accomplished beings whether human or non-human" (Shatz 2021, 257). Such a designer would obviously be, like William James's God, a "powerful . . . material object"—although *2001* is deliberately ambiguous as to whether or not its designer is "fundamentally friendly" (N. Lash 1988, 80; see my Lash 2021a for discussion of this and related ambiguities in Kubrick's work).[13] To see the theological dimensions of this film as located here would be to subscribe to the "current English usage" according to which, as Lash acidly puts it, "the concept of the supernatural, which once referred to that which, by God's redeeming grace, his sinful creatures were enabled to do—namely, to realize their humanity in truthfulness and love—now refers to entities from outer space" (N. Lash 1988, 102).

It may well be that Kubrick did think along these lines. He speculated to *Playboy* that opposition to *2001* on the part of certain critics may have come about because "there is a certain element of the lumpen literati that is so dogmatically atheist and materialist and earth-bound that it finds the grandeur of space and the myriad mysteries of cosmic intelligence anathema" (Kubrick 1968, 94). I am not interested here in the pronouncements of Stanley Kubrick the man, however, but in what we find in his films, and it is far from obvious that a reading of *2001* as first and foremost an investigation into the possibility of such a designer is critically sustainable. Another way of putting the same point would be that it is not a foregone conclusion that the film's value stands and falls on how interesting one finds its treatment of this issue.

It has become a critical commonplace to observe how readily Kubrick's films give rise to diametrically opposed interpretations. It will be clear from the preceding that I do not believe that a privatized account of experience (such as is at least a risk of spectator-centered accounts of film viewing) offers a viable route out of such interpretational conundrums. But I am certainly not suggesting that we ought to discuss films *rather than* our experience of them. Rather, the lesson I draw from Lash and Cavell is that to interpret a film *is* to talk about our experience of it. This in no way entails that we shouldn't focus on "our own experience," as long as we realize that doing so involves an engagement with the kind of textual details that interpretations focus on, rather than comprising a wholly separate and alternative object (there is not the film there and my experience here; my experience is *of* the film).

How, then, might such a stance encourage us to respond to the critical stalemates that Kubrick's work frequently generates? For every claim that we find in his work the traces of "a director who invokes an experience of the numinous and the predestined . . . a mystical experience, an ecstasy at the end of things, that continually threatens to consume or immerse the subjects of his films and ultimately draws us as viewers into this experience of the holy as well" (Keuss 2005, 83) we can find one closer to the view that "Kubrick's adoption of skeptical tropes conjoins the absurdity of human existence to the brutish nastiness of human nature" (Murray and Schuler 2007, 135), in such a way that his work merely recycles a farrago of shallowly pessimistic clichés such as "our proximity to a state of nature, the corruptness of authority and human institutions, disillusionment with ideals such as progress, the banality of the good, the pull of immediate pleasures, the divergence of appearances from reality, the seepage of the nightmare world into daily existence, and the grasping for salvation from beyond the human condition through technology or alien life" (136). The accounts of experience offered by Lash and Cavell that I have outlined above provide an alternative to both these positions. Jeffrey F. Keuss appears to equate "mystical experience," "experience of the holy," and "experience of the numinous and predestined," indicating clearly that he assumes that religious experience takes exactly the forms that Lash wishes to dismantle. *2001* may indeed evoke, or mimic, such experiences but—if Lash is right—this tells us nothing about the film's theological interest. For their part, Murray and Schuler charge Kubrick with an emptily repetitive skepticism but do not even mention Cavell's extremely rich alternative account of the central role that skepticism often plays in our lives, of which more in a moment.

The presence of such divergent accounts of Kubrick's authorship is, however, not best understood simply as a reflection of the perspective of each individual viewer, as it would be according to a privatized account of experience. Nor is to reject these two caricatures to dispute that each of them puts their finger on an important aspect of his oeuvre; as we have seen Lash argue, "the purpose of a caricature is to highlight the salient features of an object" (N. Lash 1988, 80). Indeed, while they might seem to be diametrically opposed—Kubrick either directs us towards the "mystical" or he emphasizes "brutish nastiness"—in a more fundamental sense the two accounts are in agreement. Keuss's admiring discovery of "a profound discontent with the state of modern humanity akin to the fervour of an evangelist calling for an encounter with something more, something larger, and ultimately something transcendent" (Keuss 2005, 83) is a positive evaluation of "the grasping for salvation from beyond the human condition through technology or alien life" which Murray and Schuler also discover in *2001*, but whose shallowness and predictability they attack.

If, then, Keuss, Murray, and Schuler agree in finding in Kubrick's work a dissatisfaction with humanity, then rather than asking which of them evaluates it correctly we could instead explore what role it plays in his films. There are myriad ways in which we can "find something in" a film; are both these accounts correct in seeing the films as *endorsing* such a dissatisfaction? I concluded an earlier study of optimism and pessimism in Kubrick—issues which are fundamentally a matter of the films' vision of humanity—as follows: "Something of the distinctiveness of Kubrick's filmmaking lies in the ways that his films continue to insist upon questions about optimism and pessimism while simultaneously demonstrating their inadequacies. In fully engaging with this body of work, we will not find such questions entirely satisfactory, but we will also find it impossible simply to abandon them" (Lash 2021a, 237). In this I was deliberately (and rather obviously) echoing the famous opening to the preface of the first edition of Kant's *Critique of Pure Reason*: "Human reason has the peculiar fate in one species of its cognitions that it is burdened with questions which it cannot dismiss, since they are given to it as problems by the nature of reason itself, but which it also cannot answer, since they transcend every capacity of human reason" (Kant 1998, 99). This same passage (in a slightly different translation) is one of the two epigraphs to the second part of Cavell's 1979 magnum opus *The Claim of Reason*, which is entitled "Skepticism and the Existence of the World" (Cavell 1979b, 127). Cavell later declared that "philosophy left to itself has been unable to determine whether skepticism is refutable (Descartes, Kant, Moore) or irrefutable (Hume, Wittgenstein) or unworthy of refutation (Husserl, Heidegger, Quine) or self-refuting (Austin, Strawson, Dewey)" (Cavell 2003, xv). Although he takes something from all these philosophers—chiefly Kant, Wittgenstein, Heidegger, and Austin—Cavell does not think it necessary simply to choose between these options. Instead, he finds skepticism to be illuminated by the very range of philosophical responses it has provoked (and continues to provoke).

Rather than seeing skepticism as something either false or to which our human finitude condemns us, Cavell sees in our tendency to succumb to skeptical doubts about the existence of the world and of other people an expression of our finitude. He remarks that "[b]oth Wittgenstein and Heidegger continue, by reinterpreting, Kant's insight that the limitations of knowledge are not failures of it" (Cavell 1979b, 241). Although it is often overlooked, Cavell also sees in this the relevance of religious or theological thought to his central philosophical concerns. As Hent de Vries puts it:

> Not the least innovative aspect of Cavell's thinking is that it takes "religion" . . . not so much as reflecting a tendency towards *otherworldliness*, to *the other than human* or *the beyond of this life, after life*, as it were, but, on the contrary, as hinging on the most intimate and expansive, silent and expressive, aspirations and intimations (call them the *hopes*, sometimes *fears*, rarely *trembling*) inhabiting and surrounding the nonepistemic and fundamentally non-criteriological awareness of our very own finite natures. (de Vries 2011, 465; emphases in original)

In this, Cavell's position is very close indeed to Lash's (which might suggest that Cavell is not quite as "innovative" as de Vries believes). We saw earlier Lash's emphasis on the supernatural as a matter not of extraterrestrials but of how it is that "sinful creatures" might "realize their humanity in truthfulness and love" (N. Lash 1988, 102). *Easter in Ordinary* concludes with a turn to poetry, namely, to a sonnet by George Herbert and to Gerard Manley Hopkins's "The Wreck of the Deutschland," about which Lash emphasizes "the conjunction of Herbert's 'heaven in ordinarie' and Hopkins's use of 'easter' as a verb": "Living in relation, in the way that we do, to the unknown God, we do not possess, nor do we need to know, more of the form which the fullness of his eastering in all our ordinariness may take" (296).[14] Lash's turn to poetry here also resonates with Cavell. The claim is not that what we need is any kind of "flight into feeling," but rather that "at least the metaphorical density of the poetic is some safeguard against the flight into thought" (293). Thinking and feeling can both be used to help us evade the matter at hand. This, in part, is why not *only* philosophy, or theology, will suffice. The same attitude lies behind Cavell's description, quoted above, of what philosophy "left to itself" has made of skepticism, with the implication being that it is best not always to leave philosophy to itself (Cavell 2003, xv). This remark is made in the introduction to a book on Shakespeare; Cavell finds literature, very broadly conceived, as a crucial partner to philosophy in these matters. Of course, this conception is broad enough to include film.

My suggestion at this point, then, is twofold. First, I am proposing that the critical oscillation that we frequently encounter with regard to Kubrick's work (which I have illustrated with chapters by Keuss and by Murray and Schuler) can usefully be seen as having its source in the same aspects of human experience as give rise to the philosophical oscillation diagnosed by Cavell concerning the appropriate response to skepticism. It is because our relationship to skepticism is so conflicted that the ambiguities with which Kubrick's films present their characters can send us scrambling in different directions in order to gain some kind of mastery of our experience of them. (Aaron Taylor reads "the ambiguity of performance" in Kubrick as evidence of his "skeptical classicism," which is "a deliberate affront to the presumptuousness of narration's testimonial function" [Taylor 2016, 24].)[15] Secondly, given that both Lash and Cavell suggest that theology is best seen, ultimately, as a way of exploring and fulfilling (rather than denying or escaping) our humanity—or, to use the familiar Cavellian phase, as an exploration of how best to avoid our haunting the world—this might suggest a way of considering as theological the concern of Kubrick's cinema with humanity and human experience. The problem is one of discovering how we may best acknowledge—live out—our finitude. These two ideas converge in the question of how Kubrick's cinema addresses us, because it is only by developing some kind of account of its rhetoric that we can start to determine whether its display of skepticism merely expresses the films' defeat by it, or whether there is something else going on. At this point I think a distinction that Cavell draws (in the course of a debate with Saul Kripke on the interpretation of a remark of Wittgenstein's whose details need not concern us here) may be helpful:

> Kripke's version of the scene of instruction—concluding "Then I am licensed to say, 'This is what I am inclined to do'"—is, I think importantly, a rendering counter to Wittgenstein's formulation, implying something like, "Do it my way or suffer the consequences." I do not deny the possibility. But I find it at least as plausible to take what Wittgenstein actually writes, namely "Then I am inclined [not: licensed] to say: 'This is simply what I [not: am inclined to] do'" (in which perhaps nothing is imagined to be said) to be a *weak* gesture, even passive, implying something like, "I cannot see here where or how to make myself plainer, but here I am, doing what I do, whenever you find you are interested again." (Cavell 2006, 20; emphasis in original)

I want to ask whether it might be possible to recast the question of Kubrick's supposed coldness in terms of weak or strong gestures. Perhaps, that is, both Kubrick's supporters and detractors have considered his work as in the business of making strong gestures, of making assertions (take it this way or suffer the consequences). But how far would it take us—absurd as the claim might initially seem—were we to think of them as weak, as making gestures closer to the one Cavell ventriloquizes as saying something like: "Here I am, doing what I do."[16] Kubrick's mature cinema takes the risk of not interpreting itself. The ambiguity of these films—of which the clash of responses is evidence—might, I am suggesting, be more a matter of openness to judgment than the assertion of profundity. (In saying this I do not equate ambiguity simply with the possibility of multiple interpretations; rather, I agree with Hoi Lun Law that a "satisfying account" of any given ambiguity "requires us to acknowledge the reason for the doubt and to reason with it" [Law 2021, 177].) This issue, by the way, is a matter of the ontology of film, in the sense defended earlier.

How might such a claim be made more concrete? A good starting point will be to return to Cavell's remarks about *Dr. Strangelove* and his suggestion (which will surely appear heretical to Kubrick afficionados) that the film "has no ideas (which is perhaps sufficient reason not to defend it, as has been tried, as satire)" (Cavell [1969] 2015, 124). That mutually assured nuclear destruction is absurd and farcical can hardly be declared an extraordinary piece of insight on the part either of Kubrick (the man) or of his film. But it is only according to a view of the film's rhetoric as "strong" that it might seem intended to be taken as making any kind of claim to the contrary. This is not to excuse anything that might be found to be clichéd in the film; rather it is to encourage us not to see its value as standing or falling on its conceptual originality.

Let us look at a comparable example from *A Clockwork Orange*. James Naremore characterizes the initial responses to the film in terms of the now-familiar oscillation between alternatives: "Was it an important satire or an immoral, misogynistic and misanthropic fraud?" (Naremore 2007, 154–55). It is obvious that the film explores the theatricalization of violence. This is made clear in the sequence a little over halfway through the film in which Alex (Malcolm McDowell) is paraded on a stage in order to demonstrate the success of the Ludovico treatment, the crudely Pavlovian process he has undergone in order

Experience, Skepticism, and Idolatry 143

to curb his propensities towards sex and violence. If the idea is that the state hypocritically theatricalizes violence, then we might agree with Cavell's hyperbole that the film "has no ideas." But what are we to make of the fact that, long before Alex's cure is theatricalized, the scene in which Alex and his "droogs" come upon a rival gang engaged in attempting to rape a young woman takes place in a theater, staged according to a stock notion (for 1971) of student agitprop?

If we wish to be even moderately charitable, interpretatively speaking, we should not be satisfied with the idea that the latter scene serves merely to make a point that the earlier scene has already made perfectly adequately, not to say crudely. It clearly cannot be designed to point out something hidden, or less than obvious. Certainly, we could say that the later scene shows that the state participates in the same theatricalization as do the young hoodlums, but if that is to be our conclusion it would be hard to deny that it makes the film callow in its nihilism. What, however, if the theatrical settings are not a strong assertion but rather a "weak" gesture? Then the theatricalization would not be an insight but an acknowledgement, not a demand that we *ought* to see things this way, but rather an admission that we *do* see things this way. The film shows us what it looks like so to view things. The repetitiveness lies not so much in Kubrick's treatment as

Figure 6.1. Theatricalization . . . Source: *A Clockwork Orange* (1971).

Figure 6.2. . . . has already been thematized with abundant clarity. *Source: A Clockwork Orange* (1971).

in the outlook itself; it is what the worship of violence looks like. The worship of violence is a form of ideology. So we might also say, as I now want to suggest, that it is not so much that such scenes function as a commentary upon idolatry, but rather that watching them gives us an experience of idolatry.

An Anthropology of Ideology

There is something anthropological about Kubrick's cinema. The fact that it does not present us with intimate accounts of what de Vries calls our "intimate and expansive, silent and expressive, aspirations and intimations" does not mean that it has nothing to do with them (de Vries 2011, 465). Instead, it presents a picture of their causes and consequences. Cavell observes that we are prone to think of society either as a "prison" or as a "school room," but that we should beware of "push[ing] too hard to fix the power between generations . . . since society has also been thought, more or less convincingly, to resemble a hospital, a madhouse, a circus, a herd, a hell, a kaleidoscope, a chorus, a mob, a body, an arcade"; we should note that, between them,

2001 and *A Clockwork Orange* provide instances of almost every one of these possibilities, save perhaps the circus; the Stargate sequence at the end of *2001* is certainly kaleidoscopic (Cavell 2006, 22). There is one anthropological fact about human beings that Lash insists upon: "Whatever names we give to things, we worship things (especially ourselves) as naturally and as spontaneously as we breathe and speak. We have no option but to have our hearts set somewhere, to hold something sacred. . . . We are spontaneously idolatrous" (N. Lash 1996, 49–50). Paul D. Murray wryly refers to this aspect of Lash's thought as the view that "theology is best understood as the critical theory of faith" (Murray 2007, 4). For Lash, the atheist's fundamental mistake is not believing that God does not exist; it is, rather, to think that not worshipping *anything*—let alone a God that may or may not exist—is easy. Lash wants to say that it is so difficult as to be (at least close to) impossible. Finding out what it is appropriate to worship is continuous with the attempt to find out what, and how, it is appropriate to praise. Never to praise anything would be as difficult as never to worship anything, but finding both the right form and object for our praise is a source of great human difficulty. Cavell thus expresses his own version of Lash's claim when he writes, in deliberate echo of a famous remark of Nietzsche's, that "humankind would rather praise the void than be void of praise," and that "the traditional concept for this false praise is idolatry, freeing allegiance into superstition" (Cavell 2005c, 65–66).[17]

The suggestion I ultimately want to make in this chapter, then, is to propose that Kubrick's cinema is open to fruitful theological investigation insofar as it seriously dramatizes that which we are prone to worship, whether (to refer only to *2001* and *A Clockwork Orange*) it is our own technological prowess; an idea of a super-powered being; sex; violence; or power. Thus, when Kubrick declared that *2001* is not concerned with "any traditional, anthropomorphic image of God" (Kubrick 1968, 64), he himself underestimated the difficulty of avoiding idolatry. Even HAL is pertinent here, as the computer comes to worship its own cognitive perfection, with disastrous consequences. One clue as to how we might pursue further the relevance of questions of idolatry to Kubrick's cinema is provided by Lash's account of two different modes in which idolatry may find expression: either "in many forms of worship of the void, of Gnosticism, nihilism and despair" or "in all kinds of fundamentalism, traditionalism and nostalgia" (N. Lash 1996, 63). Would it be reasonable to say that, despite their divergences, critics tend to agree that Kubrick's films *oppose* the second mode of idolatry ("fundamentalism, traditionalism and nostalgia") while remaining divided as to whether his cinema merely *represents* (in the sense of dramatizing) the first mode, or whether it also *expresses* it (in the sense of subscribing to it, rendering the films themselves Gnostic, nihilist, or despairing)? If so, perhaps this reflects the fact that the first mode tended, in the period during which Kubrick was making films—between World War II and 9/11—to seem more alive as a serious possibility than the second. And if *that* is so, more recent history might prompt a reconsideration.

Figure 6.3a and 6.3b. Addressed in the dark. *Source:* For 6.3a, *2001* (1968); for 6.3b, *A Clockwork Orange* (1971).

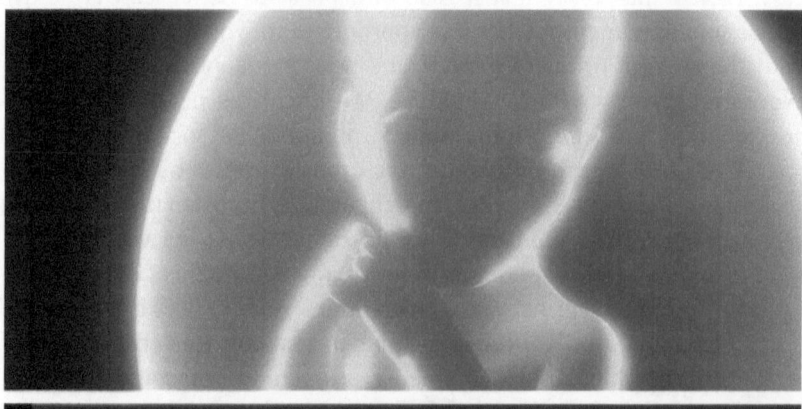

In lieu of a more definite conclusion, let me note a divergence between Lash and Cavell. Lash declares that "[p]hilosophical discourse is soliloquy; in philosophical reflection, the only voice heard is that of the philosopher," whereas theology "is trying to say something sensible in the presence of God. . . . It is, says Anselm, not 'soliloquy' but 'allocution'" (N. Lash 1996, 5–6). Cavell, however, held firm throughout his career to "the idea of philosophy's task as responsiveness" (Cavell 2006, 25). We have noted that much of the difficulty of Kubrick's work lies in our uncertainty about its mode of address to the viewer. *2001* ends with the Star Child staring towards the viewer, dovetailing with Kubrick's next film, which opens with Alex's "unblinkingly ominous impudence" (Taylor 2016, 23); the *fact* of the films' address is clear, but this renders it no easier to parse or to accommodate. At one point, Kubrick presents us with a figure of a cinema turned inside out; as Gerard Loughlin puts it, at the end of *2001* "it is as if Bowman were in an inverted cinema, where the house lights are up, intensely bright, and only the screen is dark" (Loughlin 2004, 72). The camera then enters that screen, plunging into the darkness. Lash declares that in "Christian religious and theological discourse . . . [w]e *address* the dark, respond in wonder to the silence which surrounds us as the voice of God" (N. Lash 1996, 59; emphasis in original). Kubrick's cinema should not reduce us merely to "silence" in response to the "wonder" that it can certainly provoke. It allows us, instead, to ask about how we find ourselves *addressed* in the dark, what it is that we find calling most strongly to us or that we—as Lash puts it—discover ourselves to have our hearts set on. The very fact that his cinema "has no ideas" (Cavell [1969] 2015, 124) but instead puts starkly on display so many of the "frozen positions" (Cavell 2022, 184) out of which we operate means that the weak gestures of Kubrick's films, in themselves, can neither reassure nor lecture us. But therein lie both their anthropological and their theological resourcefulness, the possibility that our experience of these films does not substitute for, but contributes to, our experience of one another and of the world (in) which we worship.

Part Three

Figurations

7

The Shape of It All

Priorities and Completeness in Nicole Brenez's Work on Abel Ferrara

NICOLE BRENEZ IS A VERY different type of critic from either Perkins or Cavell.[1] Her taste in film is declaredly broader, for one thing; it ranges from the action cinema of John Woo to the experiments of Paul Sharits. Indeed, she often delights in bringing together apparently disparate work—a chapter dedicated to "Observations on John Woo," for example, touches along the way on John Cassavetes, Jean-Luc Godard, Pier Paolo Pasolini, Alfred Hitchcock, Howard Hawks, and Roberto Rossellini, not to mention Erich Auerbach and G. W. F. Hegel (Brenez 2023, 3–20). Given this, it is probably unsurprising that she also writes a very different kind of prose; it would be impossible to mistake the work of a writer given to claims such as that John Woo's "masterpieces elaborate an anthropological poetics of funerary rituals" (18) for that of either Perkins or Cavell. (Although the passage just quoted is admittedly a little closer to the kind of thing that Cavell occasionally goes in for; Perkins absolutely eschews this kind of register.) But Perkins and Cavell would heartily agree with the claim that when considering film-critical methodology, "[t]he attention given to the films is what matters most" (ix).

This chapter—which is a study of aspects of the criticism, and critical methodology, of Nicole Brenez, taking her 2007 book *Abel Ferrara* as its primary text—aims to demonstrate that if we look past our initial impression of incompatibility, it can be shown that Brenez's work has important contributions to make to the kind of approach to film that is defended and exemplified elsewhere in this book. Adrian Martin, who translated her book on Ferrara into English, has written that Brenez practices "a mode of film criticism that calls itself *figural analysis*" (Martin 2015; emphasis in original). In what follows I shall argue that, rather than representing a wholly distinct "mode of film criticism," Brenez's work has at least some affinities with, for example, that of critics in the tradition associated with *Movie*. But, although both Brenez and Perkins give, for example, a central role to notions of synthesis, their critical priorities are somewhat different. I shall also, therefore, indicate some important areas of divergence, which could be said to hinge around ideas of credibility and the importance of the viewer's uninterrupted immersion in the fictional world. (See chapter 1 for more on these topics.)

Brenez has published extensively, but her most significant collection remains *De la figure en général et du corps en particulier* (*On the Figure in General and the Body in Particular*) from 1998, a partial translation of which, by Ted Fendt, finally appeared in English in 2023. As the title indicates, the notions of figures and figuration are central to her approach; she frequently makes reference to things like "figurative invention" and "figural logic." Martin remarks that "quite deliberately it seems to me, Brenez never defines the concept of figure in any direct, simple, clear way" (Martin 2012, 7). Others have felt something similar, and Brenez seems to have felt the force of the observation, choosing to begin *On the Figure in General* with a letter to the John Ford expert Tag Gallagher that responds to what she affectionately calls his "threatening" remark that if she can't "define [figurative analysis] briefly in two or three words . . . you'd be better off considering another approach" (Brenez 2023, ix). Martin is quite correct that there is, in Brenez, a deliberate decision not to offer a single, easily digestible definition of figuration (the definition offered by Brenez and Luc Vancheri that is cited in Martin 2012 is anything but simple and digestible), but Martin also reproduces an email he received from Brenez in which she insists that she's "trying to be very clear: the analysis is about the process elaborated by the film to construct its own type of 'figure'" (Martin 2012, 31).[2]

Although it would not, I think, be entirely unfair to see a fondness for theoretical complexity for its own sake in Brenez's resistance to potted definitions of her methodology—"I do not see why an analytic desire should be summed up in a formula (partly watering it down)" (Brenez 2023, ix)—a more charitable interpretation would locate the sources of this reluctance in the fact that figuration is, for Brenez, an absolutely fundamental concept. In illustrating how this is the case I would like to draw attention to the intersection of two familiar senses of the figurative in her work, an intersection that has interesting and important relevance to film criticism considered much more broadly.

In studies of rhetoric or literature, the figurative exists in opposition to the literal: figurative language is language that is *not literal* (or at least not merely, or not entirely literal). In visual art, however, the notion of the figurative exists in opposition not to the literal but to the *abstract*. Figurative art represents people, animals, plants, and objects, whereas abstract art—which does not—is referred to as "nonfigurative." These two senses could be seen as pulling in opposite directions. In visual art figuration moves *towards* some kind of "replication" of the world we know, while in literature it pulls *away* from it; away, that is, from direct, literal, factual statements about the world. These remarks need to be qualified somewhat to emphasize that I am referring to *tendencies*, not mutually exclusive properties. Not all linguistic figures are nonliteral, hence my qualification "not merely, or not entirely"; they are all, nevertheless, distinguished from an idea of plain, "nonfigured" language (even if such a thing could never actually exist in practice). Film is interestingly placed because of the way it makes use of phenomena that can be described using either sense of figuration. It is not unique in this; when illustrated, novels also negotiate the distinction of the figurative from both the "literal" and the "abstract" (think of Lewis Carroll and John Tenniel, for example), and certain genres of painting employ something akin to literary figuration in their use of imagery (Dutch *vanitas* still lives, for example). Nevertheless, although it is only infrequently remarked upon, the fact that fully accounting for many filmic sequences, images, or motifs requires that we attend to both senses of the word is very striking. Brenez's work, I want to argue, suggests that it might be illuminating to think of the role played by what we shall see her refer to as the "plastic" (visual) and "rhetorical" operations in a film as aspects of one broader process, that of figuration.³

Brenez compares Ferrara's *The Blackout* (1997) with George Cukor's *A Star Is Born* (1954) which, she claims, "serves essentially as a 'rough draft' for *The Blackout* to the extent that the common motif of disappearance determines an exigency of figurative invention" (Brenez 2007, 106). In *A Star Is Born*, Judy Garland plays a singer named Esther Blodgett who the alcoholic film-star-on-the-decline Norman Maine (James Mason) discovers, makes a star (after she has been renamed Vicki Lester by the studio), and marries, before his drinking causes her to plan to end her career in order to care for him. Maine overhears this intention on her part, which prompts him to commit suicide in an attempt to liberate her. Towards the end of the film, Maine drowns himself, an event indicated by a shot of Maine walking off into the sea followed by the sight of his dressing gown drifting helplessly among the rocks in the shallows. The film ends with Esther announcing on stage that "This is Mrs. Norman Maine." Brenez writes:

> *A Star Is Born* metaphorizes disappearance before and after the elided suicide. Before, by the transformation of Norman into a reflection: we see him already dissolved in the oceanic image, glazed in the glass window. It is thus an anticipation, a *figurative prolepsis*. After, we witness the return of the deceased on a new stage, that of the music hall where Vicki, before an immense blue background that transposes the Pacific Ocean into an almost fluorescent monochrome, begins her number with the famous words, "This is Mrs. Norman Maine," thus immortalizing Norman in the form of his alter ego. This time it is a case of *figurative analepsis*. (107; my emphasis)

What Brenez intends by the phrase "metaphorizes disappearance" is not entirely clear; it relates to her claim that both *The Blackout* and *A Star Is Born* explore heterosexual couples that somehow fuse—"This is Mrs. Norman Maine"—and that this fusion is achieved first by "each partner playing the other's image" and subsequently "because the event of suicide engenders the visual principle of figurative propagation"

Figure 7.1a and 7.1b. "Figurative prolepsis" and "analepsis." *Source: A Star Is Born* (1954).

(107). This claim is not, however, necessary for the point I wish to demonstrate, which is rather more simple, but also much more general in its application. Norman's suicide is "elided" because it is narratively crucial but only indirectly represented. The scene of the death itself, as I have mentioned, indicates the event by showing only its preparation—Maine walking into the sea—and its aftermath, in which the sodden dressing gown also serves as a metonym for Maine's drowned body. But, Brenez shows, the death is *also* indirectly represented both before and after its occurrence; it is foreshadowed in a "figurative prolepsis" and recalled in a "figurative analepsis." The images mentioned by Brenez are connected figuratively in two ways. First, they predict or recall particular representational images: the actual images resemble each other, which is to say that their figuration—in the sense familiar from visual art—has something in common. Both images represent the sea by featuring a wide expanse of blue, emphasized by the breadth of the CinemaScope image. But the images are also connected figuratively in a second way, by means of their symbolism. A "literal" reflection of the ocean in a window becomes a metaphor for the way Norman will soon meet his death, while the blue of Vicki's stage backdrop is a metonym for the ocean, and hence for that same event (now in the past). This, I think, is partly what Brenez means when she writes that "it is necessary to consider figurative logic not only as the treatment of a motif, theme or singular form, but also in terms of grouping figures in a plastic sense . . . and in a rhetorical sense" (Brenez 2023, xvi–xvii). It is, therefore, entirely appropriate that she uses rhetorical language to make her point—"prolepsis" and "analepsis" are names of rhetorical figures. Given that anticipation and recall of narrative events are part of a film's narration, Cukor's film offers an instance in which such narrational devices require that we attend to figures both in the sense of visual representation (which Brenez refers to as a "plastic" sense) and in terms of pattern and symbol, in a "rhetorical" sense (cognate with the linguistic meaning of "figurative"; attentive to aspects of signification such as metaphor and metonymy). It is not merely that Norman's death by drowning is prettily and poetically evoked by certain figurative (metaphoric or metonymic) procedures, but that *narrative* functions of foreshadowing and recalling his death are achieved by the use of representational images (figuration in one sense) that signify in the way that they do by means of metaphor or metonymy (figuration in the other sense).

For Brenez, then, a film's metaphoric connotations (say) may be crucial to its narrative strategies: "This is not merely a matter of rhymes aiming to establish a thematic coherence but of constructing a film through the form of a passage between altered images" (Brenez 2007, 21). (In the terms of chapter 2, this "passage" is something we could say that the film describes.) We should not, she argues, approach visual or rhetorical echoes or rhymes merely as devices that help generate a supplementary layer of, say, symbolic patterning, but examine the ways in which, as we progress through a film, we encounter images that resemble one another but are "altered" in significant ways. Metaphorical or metonymic meanings, or many other kinds of implicit meaning, can be central to the narrative of a film, and we often understand them by means of the film's "passage between altered images." Brenez's use of the term "figurative" to cover the intersection of the visual and the rhetorical is reminiscent of Perkins's use of the word "image" in the following: "A fur coat provides Max Ophüls with an image for the rewards and limitations of the role of bourgeois housewife in *The Reckless Moment*" (Perkins 2020, 211). The coat is, simultaneously, a *visual* image and a *metonymic* image; Perkins underlines this by choosing not to put all the weight on the rhetorical connotation by saying, for example, that the coat is a "symbol" or an "emblem." Not only this, but Perkins also shows a profound sensitivity to the "passage between altered images," if we take "image" in a broad enough sense. He observes about Ophüls's *Caught* (1949) that the director "uses three different coats to depict the options open to his indecisive heroine. . . . The use of dress here goes beyond working as a simple but effective visual presentation of changing circumstances. It helps also to define an attitude to those changes" (211–12). The passage from one coat to another is central to our understanding of the film on a number of interpretive levels. Another example, from the same article, is Perkins's treatment of three shoulder-clasping gestures at the beginning of Nicholas Ray's *In a Lonely Place* (1950), which help to "establish that neither hero nor heroine is sure whether the man's embrace is protective and loving or threatening, murderous" (215). This is achieved by means of three gestures performed by three different characters, each gesture being "significant in [its] own right" in delineating the boundaries of the film's Hollywood setting, but also—by means of the "passage between" them, Brenez would say—serving "to dramatize the ambiguity of gesture itself" (215).[4]

To repeat: Brenez recommends that we should see our understanding of films—of both their narrative and metaphorical aspects—as coming about by means of our response to the relationships between images which change. Tracing the differences between these images is crucial, and is an operation which she thinks of as elucidating a dynamic process of transformation rather than explaining an abstract scheme of patterning. Articulating the way that this happens is central to her critical project; her references to "figurative logic" very often apply, in a broadly Deleuzian way, to the "logic" of a particular film or group of films. (There is more on Deleuze's treatment of these issues to come in two chapters' time.) The goal is to indicate the distinctive ways that figures (in all senses) transform in the film(s) in question (this is what we saw her refer to above as "the process elaborated by the film to construct its own type of 'figure' "). Having seen how Brenez's understanding of figuration leads her to share key assumptions with Perkins, I shall now offer an example of the kind of figurative logics that particularly interest Brenez, and which often lead her in directions that Perkins might not have found so amenable.

Brenez devotes a number of pages in *Abel Ferrara* to the notion of "figurative anamorphosis": "Ferrara's films are structured like passages through the looking-glass; it is a matter of passing from the recto to the verso of a given situation or image" (Brenez 2007, 15). A clear example of what this means can be found in Ferrara's *Body Snatchers*, Ferrara's version of which owes at least as much to Philip Kaufman's 1978 *Invasion of the Body Snatchers* (in particular its famous pointing and screaming pod people) as it does to Don Siegel's 1956 film. Ferrara's *Body Snatchers* is a film that, for Brenez, "plainly obeys the anamorphic logic of Ferrara's work. At the start, in an eminently familiar domestic

Figure 7.2a and 7.2b. "Passing from the recto to the verso." *Source: Body Snatchers* (1993).

gesture, Marti [Gabrielle Anwar], riding in the back of the family car, pushes away her stepbrother, Andy [Reilly Murphy]; at the end, she hurls him from a helicopter down into a world consumed by blood and fire. The fold is perfect" (20). A simple act of sibling impatience is transformed at the end of the film into something far darker; Andy has to be destroyed because he is no longer Andy, having been replaced by the body snatchers. The image of Marti innocently pushing away her brother has been "anamorphically" transformed into an image of his (replacement's) destruction, in a process that illuminates both images. By referring to this as an instance of "figurative anamorphosis," Brenez, it seems to me, intends the same blend of rhetorical and plastic meanings that we encountered earlier: this kind of pattern is figuratively (metaphorically) anamorphic—the rhetorical sense of figurative—but also operates by means of visual images—the plastic sense. This kind of procedure (of "figurative logic," to use Brenez's own language) she claims to be characteristic of Ferrara's cinema; his "[f]ilms are organized upon a single major fold, where the beginning finally meets or "touches" the ending to offer a striking comparison, or a more gradual pleat, where the major fold is progressively translated throughout in a series of small folds (akin to a pleated skirt) over the entire structure of a film" (15). Such procedures are, of course, not unique to Ferrara: we might see *A Star Is Born* as another example of such a procedure, in which the disappearance and death of James Mason is the central "fold," around which the proleptic and analeptic images mentioned above are organized.

Brenez is also interested in how preexisting figures, such as archetypes, are deployed and transformed within a particular film; she writes that *Body Snatchers* "progresses by superimpositions and slippages from one maternal archetype to another" (84). A distinctive feature of the film, for Brenez, is the dizzying *range* of archetypes it puts into play, connecting one with another and thereby complicating and destabilizing the possibility of using any of them to generate a rigid interpretation of the film—one that, for example, attempted to "decode" the film according to a static set of oppositions. *Body Snatchers* involves, in the first place, "not the double status of mother/ stepmother but that of mother/wife" (84); it is not only a question of the legitimacy of the substitute mother but also the relationship between the female, and her body, as nurturer of children and as erotic being. The false, body snatched version of a woman who was already a replacement, a stepmother—Carol (Meg Tilly)—appears "in the marital bedroom as a nude body, a body posed as improper, suspect, displaced, and menacing," in part because the "erotic vision is attributed to the scared little boy" (84). Andy sees the body of his real stepmother, lying on her bed, crumble into dust, after which her replacement steps out of a closet. We see a naked female body framed from the neck down, emerging from blurred darkness into warmly lit clarity, emphasizing it as an erotic vision. We then cut to the face of a retreating Andy, terrified and disgusted, before cutting back to a close-up of the false Carol's face, indicating the separation between the familiar mother (terrifying *because* she is so familiar to the boy, and yet he knows she cannot be his mother, not even his stepmother) and the eroticized female body. The editing emphasizes both the separation between the two archetypes (the mother and the sexual object) and their connection, because we know they are aspects of a single body. The replacement of the real stepmother is represented in a way which both singles out these two archetypes and rearticulates them in an uncanny, disturbing way. Andy rushes downstairs to his father, screaming that "Mommy's dead," only for the false Carol to descend the stairs in a white dressing gown, now reintegrated into a form that Andy can see is a terrifying substitute, and that his father, Steve (Terry Kinney) can only see as his completely nonthreatening wife, in her familiar role as weary mother.

Brenez also analyses Ferrara's use of "myth, anchoring the film within popular iconography: Carol is Wicked Stepmother, witch, ghost (in her white nightgown, haunting the house with her oppressive presence), ghoul (vampires), succubus (demoness who comes in the night to be united with a man whom she will then eat), Medusa, enigma (her smile, whose trace appears in the final shot of *New Rose Hotel*), and, last but not least, she incarnates death" (84). Rather than simply listing any association that occurs to her, Brenez is attempting here to indicate the richness of the various tropes of illegitimate substitution that the film alludes to. (The list is anchored with concrete details: the white nightgown, the nocturnal setting, the smile.) Furthermore, she does not restrict her interpretation to a simple translation of the narrative into a psychoanalytical, metaphorical or mythic register; it is not merely a question of "timeless" archetypes, but of establishing relationships between them, or transforming one into another. Each viewer is likely to register different associations somewhat differently, at different points of the film, but nevertheless Brenez indicates that the way relationships form between such associations is something that necessarily takes place *in time*, as we watch the film—not only when we contemplate it afterwards—resulting in "a film not of disquieting strangeness but its opposite, abominable familiarity" (85).

For Brenez tracing such procedures can take precedence over the maintenance of the world of the film; this is where the difference with Perkins, who writes in *Film as Film* that "[a]ll that matters is to preserve the illusion," begins to emerge clearly (Perkins 1993, 121).[5] Brenez writes approvingly that "Ferrara's scenes are less plot events than visual echoes. Their logic is not especially Aristotelian, for they are not determined by linkages of cause and effect or before and after. They belong to a psychic process: the *reproduction of a trauma in multiple aftershocks*" (Brenez 2007, 17; emphasis in original). She remarks that we are led, in a number of Ferrara's films, "to the limits of understanding" (129). For Brenez, these films do not merely depict the pathological, but are themselves organized pathologically: "[I]t is no longer the protagonist who becomes delirious but the film itself. Trauma no longer functions merely as a narrative cause or motor; it becomes a structuring principle" (128). She gives an example of this from *The Driller Killer* (1979), in which a painter named Reno (played by Ferrara himself) becomes a serial killer. The film "offers, in visual terms, the passage from local to total delirium": at one point "the link between creative torment (painting a canvas) and murder (drilling a tramp's body) undergoes a lengthy visual elaboration. The rest of the film is devoted to economizing these transitions, directly joining creative act and criminal gesture, neither of which is connoted as more realist than the other. This leads to the formal fusion of both dimensions of experience in the final red monochrome" (129).[6] We are often unable to distinguish between hallucination and reality in Ferrara's films, which can put their narrative coherence at risk. One of the most dramatic instances of this is the conclusion of *New Rose Hotel*, about which Brad Stevens—in a book Brenez describes as "magisterial" (5)—refers to as an instance of "the destruction of narrative: in *New Rose Hotel*'s final section we are presented not with a resolution of the story . . . but rather with a state of total collapse in which the protagonist . . . is simply abandoned at a moment of crisis" (Stevens 2004, 274). But for Stevens, as for Brenez, such procedures do not make the films themselves incoherent—do not turn them into hallucinations—but are tools for a coherent investigation into hallucination itself. For Brenez, what looks at first glance like formal disarray need not be evidence of incoherent unintelligibility but can help us gain an understanding of disorder, particularly ethical and political disorder.

Perkins, on the other hand—as we saw in chapter 1—is of the view that neither effective narration nor effective symbolism are likely to result if the film becomes incoherent or undermines its credibility. A well-known passage in *Film as Film* finds a lighting effect in Losey's *The Criminal* (1960), via which a convict's "face is seen isolated against a black background," to be destructive of "the framework of maintained belief," because although the device is intended, Perkins assumes, "[a]s a means to eliminate distraction," it in fact "merely substitutes one distraction for another" (Perkins 1993, 83). Aaron Smuts, in a critical but sympathetic assessment of Perkins's views on credibility, argues that Perkins uses the word "in at least three different senses and . . . never makes it clear how they all fit together" (Smuts 2006, 86). After exploring credibility in *Film as Film* in the sense of, first, correspondence to reality; second, as a function of internal consistency ("something like playing by the rules of the game"); and, finally, as convention, Smuts argues persuasively that belief is, for Perkins, the goal of credibility, and thus that "[w]hat Perkins' concept of credibility amounts to is a rough composite between internal consistency and correspondence with reality in the form of convention. Perkins is insistent that the filmmaker must remain out of mind" (88, 90).[7] Achieving credibility, for Perkins, is one of the ways films also achieve coherence, and "[c]oherence is the prerequisite of meaning" and "the means by which the film-maker creates significance" (Perkins 1993, 116). Katerina Virvidaki has, however, argued that "if we dissociate a basic aspect of Perkins' understanding of film coherence—namely, a film's 'synthetic' understanding—from a particularly tight form of 'synthesis,' valued by Perkins," it then becomes "possible to argue for a *pliant* and *variegated* understanding of the workings of" coherence and incoherence (Virvidaki 2017, 4, 3; emphases in original). Perkins is willing to grant that incoherence can be significant, but sees it as likely to lead only to profligately unconstrained interpretation: "Meaning may exist without internal relationship; but coherence is the prerequisite of contained significance" (Perkins 1993, 117). One reaction to this claim, pertinent to many of Ferrara's films, might be to wonder whether a film could, somehow, contain—which is to say motivate, make intelligible use of—its *incoherence* or, in Brenez's terms, its *disorder*. Brenez's treatment of credibility, coherence, and synthesis might suggest ways of reconsidering, or resituating, some of Perkins's fundamental claims akin to those I propose in chapter 1. This might, for example, be one way of reading her statement that Ferrara's "work introduces disorder into a cynical world; misunderstandings begin here, since some critics attribute this disorder to the films themselves" (Brenez 2007, 3). She implies that the films' disorder can be seen as *motivated incoherence* that is intelligible in relation to the disorder of the world at large, and would agree with Brad Stevens's claim that "Ferrara imbricates our responses to imagery with our responses to external reality" (Stevens 2004, 272).

Like Perkins, Brenez is concerned with synthesis; one of the great strengths of Ferrara's cinema, for her, is the way it "manifest[s] Ferrara's genius for figurative synthesis" (Brenez 2007, 6). But although Brenez shares some fundamental assumptions with Perkins, she has, as we have seen, a very different attitude with regard to the role played by credibility and the ways in which a truly successful narrative film must efficiently integrate all its elements. What precisely she intends by "figurative synthesis" is not made entirely explicit, but there are clues. She admires *Body Snatchers*, for example, because of the way it maximizes possible interpretive avenues. Is it, diegetically, a fantasy, a "dream of a teenaged girl . . . a lethal fable invented so that she can do away with her brother, mother, and father" (7); is it a science fiction, "a futuristic essay on industrial pollution and global militarization" (6); or is it, perhaps, "a retrospective meditation on 'Hiroshima man'" (6)? Brenez does not ask, like Perkins, for synthesis to be achieved by means of a balance predicated on maintaining the illusion of the fiction but, rather, for a synthesis that comes about via the forging of links between narrative, metaphorical, and visual procedures—even if this process disrupts our involvement with the narrative world; the emphasis is always on movement and transformation, on what we have seen her refer to as "a passage between altered images" (21). This passage may reorientate hierarchies at any moment; even Ferrara's use of allegory she admires because it "is especially kinetic: his characters allegorize not fixed notions but questions or problems" (13). A maximally "figuratively synthetic" film seems, for Brenez, to be one that activates, moves among, and forges connections between, *as many* different narrative, thematic, and visual phenomena as possible—whereas for Perkins, a maximally synthetic film is one whose synthesis is itself maximally *efficient*, as smooth and integrated as possible; for him a synthetic theory is "a theory of balance, coherence and complexity" (Perkins 1993, 189).

This difference in critical priorities can also, I think, be seen in the way Brenez manipulates interpretational priority. Demonstrating the credibility of her critical claims is not always her first priority; there is, in her work, a role for what may initially appear to be rather implausible claims, in the way that they encourage the reader to reconsider their sense of a film's organization or significance. An instance of this can be found in her discussion of a short sequence from *Body Snatchers* that Brenez refers to as "the fifty most terrifying, synthetic seconds in narrative cinema" (Brenez 2007, 10). The young boy Andy lies listening with worry to an argument between his father and sister. There is a dissolve to what Brenez calls the "dark, speckled brilliance" (10) of an asphalted road. The camera moves right to bring Carol, Andy's stepmother—or rather her false, alien replacement—into view, dressed in dark clothes, her dark hair moving slightly in a gentle breeze. She is seen from above, at such an angle that her face is visible but its expression foreshortened and unreadable. The camera lowers itself, getting closer and closer but maintaining the same angle on her face before eventually rotating slowly so that she is presented at eye level in close-up, to the right of the screen. Conventional framing is only achieved at the very end of the camera movement. A military truck can be seen facing us, out of focus and slowly approaching. "Carol" is looking off to screen left; now she turns her face slightly to the right (further towards screen left) and another truck enters the frame from the left. The truck passes her and she hands a soldier at the back of the truck a black plastic bag which contains, we know, the remains of the real Carol.

The way the crane shot transfers our point of view from above the earth—only gradually bringing us into alignment with the false mother's own level—mimics the extraterrestrial arrival of the body snatchers and their adoption of human scale. Mimicry is an entirely appropriate strategy (figurative strategy, Brenez would say) for a film largely concerned with that very process. Brenez emphasizes both the sequence's symbolic dimension and the way it is connected to the preceding sequence:

Figure 7.3. "The fifty most terrifying, synthetic seconds in narrative cinema." *Source: Body Snatchers* (1993).

In a slow-motion sequence-shot, the false, snatched mother, Carol (Meg Tilly), moves toward a truck, carrying a garbage bag that contains the remains of the real mother. Much is fused in this image of man-as-ashes: the Nazi ovens, the obliteration of bodies in Hiroshima, and the contemporary transformation of genetic patrimony into industrial property. . . . But the lap-dissolve that begins the sequence-shot, superimposing the disturbed face of Andy upon the cosmic asphalt, suggests that it is all the nightmare of a young boy. (10)

Figure 7.4. Is it "all the nightmare of a young boy"? *Source: Body Snatchers* (1993).

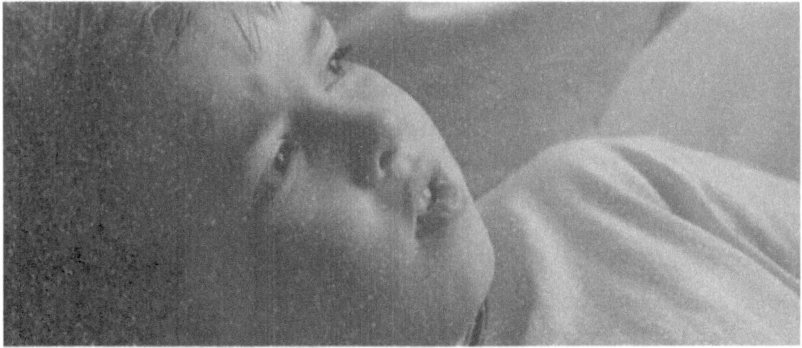

The first part of this passage permits a perfectly conventional division between narrative content and its symbolic resonances which may, out of context, appear a little far-fetched but which Brenez integrates into her wider reading of the film's "figurative synthesis," arguing, for example, that in it "[t]he capitalist system is figured as a toxic military base" (10) and linking an image of the shadows cast by a group of soldiers to "the outlines of bodies imprinted onto Hiroshima's walls" (7). But the point about the nightmare of the young son instead takes its starting point from a purely visual feature of the film: the dissolve superimposes the asphalt on the face of the boy. Brenez is not arguing that, diegetically, what is going on *is* merely a nightmare—"It was all a dream!"—but rather that what she would call the film's figurative invention raises this possibility, or connotes such an idea. It does so because it is a merely one instance of a pattern that Brenez finds in a great many of Ferrara's films. *The Funeral* (1996) ends with the coffin lid being lowered above Johnny's (Vincent Gallo) dead body, leading Brenez to suggest that "the final image suggests that the entire film might have been the dream of a corpse" (77). She also argues that the way that a scene in *Dangerous Game* (1993) in which Harvey Keitel confesses his infidelities to his wife after having just learned from her of her father's death is sandwiched between two shots of air stewardesses offering him a drink gives rise to the idea that he was "dreaming the intervening scene" (97). Brenez's claim is that it is part of Ferrara's style, of his films' figurative logic, to employ certain images in such a way as to evoke a sense of dream or fantasy without going so far as actually to generate a fantastic diegesis. But because films that *do* wish to indicate a diegetic dream or fantasy often use the exact same devices, the result is a curious and distinctive effect that hovers between possibilities, with both the prosaic diegesis and the sensation of a dream active simultaneously; such effects are common even in those of Ferrara's films not primarily concerned with hallucination.

Brenez's mode of writing is, then, related to her critical priorities if we understand that term with reference to the way she structures her arguments. It is true that she doesn't, as a rule, give much attention to detailed description, but her work has other strengths and pleasures. She does at times employ a somewhat apodictic tone, which can result in what might appear to be grandly sweeping claims. Take, for example, her discussion of the scene in the restaurant after crime kingpin Frank White (Christopher Walken) is released from prison in *King of New York* (1990), and the modes of complicity with his criminality that it displays: "There are five orders of complicity: subordination, connivance, collusion, attraction, and embrace" (65). Although, in context, it is relatively clear that the claim about "five orders of complicity" is specific to the restaurant scene, its placement soon after the opening of the section, which refers to Hobbes's view of human nature and its "three principal 'causes of quarrel'" leading to "three modes of behavior involving the use of violence" (64) means that the possibility of reading the claim about complicity as a general one is, one might say, connoted.[8] But it would be a mistake to read the way she structures her arguments as evidence that her criticism begins with the abstract and simply imposes extraneous ideas on the films she discusses. On the contrary, returning to the films after reading her criticism shows how closely attentive she is. Nevertheless, perhaps because she wants to distance herself from an empiricism that might consider itself to be neutral and purely objective, or to dissuade us from thinking that philosophy needs to be "applied" to films—rather than that films can be examined with an eye to determining the philosophical work that they themselves are doing—she tends to introduce specific details as *evidence* for more general claims, rather than as *material* on which to build those claims. This strategy might well make us miss the vivid description of films to be found in other critics, but there is surely no reason to wish for a single model of textually attentive criticism. Brenez, I would argue, draws out lines of thought which one can follow upon returning to the films in question, rather than merely extracting themes or pursuing loose associations. John Gibbs and Douglas Pye correctly observe that "[i]nterpretation has to be rooted in the concrete details of the text (its style) because it is only through these that we gain access to the film's subjects," but there are different ways such a "rooting" might exhibit itself in written critical texts (Gibbs and Pye 2005, 10). Brenez's style is not wholly devoted to demonstration through close reading—though it does do this—but it is nevertheless *based*, throughout, on close reading.

    I want, finally, to ask whether Brenez always fulfils her commitment to fluidity and transformation by examining a single tiny example, which is again an instance of "the movement of one thing towards its other," from *Ms. 45* (1981). This film tells the story of how suffering two rapes on a single day transforms a mute seamstress named Thana

(Zoë Tamerlis) into a vengeful killer, who eventually wants to destroy all men simply for being men. The film's culminating massacre takes place at a Halloween party, at which Thana—who takes on the trappings both of "virgin" and "whore" by dressing as a heavily made-up nun (combining the insignia of the only sexual roles traditionally allowed women by men in order to enact her task of obliterating all men)—is eventually stabbed to death by her friend Laurie (Darlene Stuto). Brenez writes: "By erasing Thana, Laurie bears witness to the gesture—at once castrating (she wields an enormous knife) and protective (without this gesture, society is no longer even possible; it would be the reign of pure violence, Thana's reign)—through which the human creature participates in his or her own enslavement" (Brenez 2007, 90). The gesture is presumably castrating because it puts an end to Thana's use of her (phallic) gun. But what are we to make of the fact, unmentioned by Brenez, that the *knife* is also clearly shown as *Laurie's* symbolic phallus, thereby emphasizing, as Alexandra Heller-Nicholas puts it, "the blurriness of gender that had dominated Thana's killing spree" (Heller-Nicholas 2017, 4)?

Before she stabs Thana, Laurie holds the knife erect at her crotch, accentuated by her black skirt which is open at the front, revealing her legs and underwear. The gesture is not exactly emphasized but the slow motion of the sequence gives us plenty of time to notice it.

Figure 7.5. An abundance of phallic signifiers. *Source: Ms .45* (1981).

Despite the tiresomely familiar misogyny which is on plentiful display elsewhere in the party (two men discuss buying virgins, while another man denies his partner the option not to be a mother by refusing to have a vasectomy despite earlier having promised to), at the moment of her death Thana is positioned between two instances of *subversion* of gender, combinations of supposedly contradictory gender codes in single individuals. Her final victim is a man dressed as a bride in white, who stands in front of her; behind her is Laurie, wielding her knife as surrogate penis. Even given the fact that, as Brenez argues, there is a sense in which Thana "incarnates the logical, politically radical response to an intolerable situation" (Brenez 2007, 89), the consequence of fully enacting this response would, as Brenez says, be the obliteration of all society. Brenez notes that "Thana drifts towards a collective massacre—erasing all masculine bodies suspected of sexual aggression, then any man whatsoever, and finally . . . every kind of body, whether male, female, or transsexual" (42), but she neglects the application of imagery that transgresses gender boundaries to Laurie, the agent of Thana's destruction. Heller-Nicholas puts it well when she refers to Thana's "blind spot to intersectionality leading ultimately to her death" (Heller-Nicholas 2017, 39). Perhaps we could read the gender slippage in this final composition as a whole as giving the lie to Thana's misandry, which dominates her violence. Even if it is initially directed against one man, and eventually becomes indiscriminate, the majority of the film's narrative outlines the way the object of Thana's hatred expands from men who approach her sexually to *all men*, in general. According to this misandry, men are utterly other than women, and therefore utterly unworthy of existence. In fact men and women are *not* wholly other to one another, but this Thana will never understand; hence the complete incomprehension with which, as she dies, she says to Laurie the only word she speaks in the entire film: "sister."

Why, then, does Brenez not mention Laurie's phallic knife? Perkins wrote in his final published piece that "[w]hen some salient detail escapes comment, the omission may as soon result from a writer's decision and priorities as from a failure of observation," but that it is also "[i]nevitably" the case that "we do fall victim to failures of observation" (Perkins 2020, 482). Even if Brenez's omission is the result of an oversight (unlikely as this seems), perhaps she was prompted not to notice it—if one can say such a thing—because of her interpretation of Laurie as an agent of accommodation with regressive norms. In Brenez's reading, Laurie's "irritation and rage in the face of harassment . . . nonetheless expresses itself in a socially admissible way" which serves ultimately to "render the situation tolerable" (Brenez 2007, 89). Thana is, as we have seen, the radical alternative to such behavior, who must ultimately be destroyed, and destroyed by Laurie, the socially acceptable face of protest: "Laurie kills the adolescence that is represented throughout the film by Thana's bodily mutation. This is an adolescence entirely aligned with rebellion. . . . Once dead, Thana can become an adult, that is, servile" (90). It would not have been easy for Brenez's argument to explore the consequences of any transgressive sexuality associated with Laurie while retaining such a firm opposition between two forms of protest as embodied in the two characters.[9] This small example can serve as a reminder of how vigilant the critic concerned with figurative transformation needs to be, because of how seductive static oppositions can be even to those explicitly dedicated to avoiding them.

There does not, then, seem to me to be such a thing as "figural criticism," if it is considered to be an alternative to other, supposedly more traditional, methods. Brenez's approach offers an example of alternative emphasis rather than a wholly distinct approach to criticism. This is not, of course, a weakness because it increases the ways in which Brenez's practice could usefully inform other styles of criticism; to take on board its example does not require that one subscribe fully to her method in all its aspects. Brenez may sometimes invert critical priorities, but she does not do so merely to be different. Her thinking is systematic (in that it makes structurally interconnected theoretical propositions and articulates a strong sense of films as interrelated wholes, as well as parts of an oeuvre that itself forms an interrelated whole) but not in such a way that any omission discovered risks its collapse. There is no essential incompatibility between the nuanced descriptions and sensitivity to pattern and motivation we find in critics such as Perkins, on the one hand, and the explicit theoretical constructions and interest in forms of excess and disorder that motivate Brenez on the other—as long, that is, as our priorities are in order. It is "[t]he attention given to the films" that "matters most" (Brenez 2023, ix).

8

Rupture, Suture, Nietzsche

Impossible Intersubjectivity in Ridley Scott's *Alien*

IN FILM STUDIES, THE CONCEPT of suture has long occupied a prominent position whenever questions about the relationships between narrative comprehension, the construction of diegetic worlds, and the spectator's experience are at issue.[1] It has served, for some theorists, as a fundamental part of their theoretical framework, while for others it represents a prime target for attack. The dominant understanding of suture—among both its proponents and detractors—has, however, paid much more attention to the account given by Daniel Dayan in 1974 than it has to the details of the version of suture initially proposed by Jean-Pierre Oudart in 1969 in a two-part article for *Cahiers du cinéma*, which subsequently appeared in an English translation in *Screen* in 1977. This chapter aims, in a small way, to redress the balance. I hope to demonstrate that making use of Oudart's account does not require one to take a position on psychoanalytic theory, whether Lacanian or any other variety. Certainly, the origin of many of Oudart's ideas can be traced to Jacques-Alain Miller's Lacanian article "Suture (Elements of the Logic of the Signifier)," but Oudart's reworking of these ideas does not stand or fall on our acceptance of any wider psychoanalytic framework (see Miller (1966) 1977). Suture can be seen as one of the most important figurative procedures (according to the sense of figuration developed in the previous chapter) to be found in narrative film, and is therefore independently valuable as a concept for the study of the complex forms of intersubjectivity that narrative cinema so readily and so richly dramatizes. This chapter attempts to demonstrate this by reconsidering the concept of suture as it applies to film via a close reading of some aspects of Ridley Scott's *Alien* (1979) and the ways that their formal operations of suture (and its corollary, rupture) relate to the diegetic procedures of rupture (and suture) that they (re)present.

Suture, Once Again

Suture was one of the most popular, as well as one of the most controversial, concepts to enter film studies in the 1970s. It is often taken to refer to the way that classical continuity techniques, chiefly of editing, create for the film viewer a sense that they are watching a world that is coherent in space and time, while simultaneously concealing and disavowing the artifice by which this very sense of wholeness and coherence is generated. Thinking about suture in this way is closely tied up with the ideas of theorists whose standing in film studies is now rather in dispute: Jacques Lacan and Louis Althusser. Although Markus Kügle has rightly argued that, in comparison to Oudart's presentation, Daniel Dayan "heavily simplified the concept [of suture] in addition to adding the dimension of ideology critique" (Kügle 2020, 215; my translation), some remarks by Dayan on shot/reverse shot editing (from his 1974 article "The Tutor-Code of Classical Cinema") will serve as a helpful example of what has become the "standard line" on cinematic suture (for its defenders and opponents both): "When shot two replaces shot one, the absent-one is transferred from the level of enunciation to the level of fiction. As a result of this, the code effectively disappears and the ideological effect of the film is thereby secured. The code, which *produces* an imaginary, ideological effect, is hidden by the message. Unable to see the workings of the code, the spectator is at its mercy" (Dayan [1974] 1976, 448–49; emphasis in original). The reference to the "absent-one" is a way of speaking about who- or whatever is seeing what the film shows. One answer to the question of the identity of this figure could, of course, be the film viewer, but the film viewer is not part of the film's world. While watching a film, it is always possible to raise the question of who, within the diegesis, is seeing what the viewer is shown. If the answer to this question were to be "no one," the further possibility arises that the viewer's attention would be thereby led towards the nature of the film as a construction, as something fictional and artificial—precisely to the gap between the world within which they are watching the film, and the world that they see *in* the film that they are watching. The second shot in a shot/reverse shot structure ascribes the role of the "absent-one" to a diegetic character in the film, and thus "the absent-one is transferred from the level of enunciation to the level of fiction," meaning that they are "absent" no longer. (Recall Cavell's remarks about a "world complete without me which is present to me" [Cavell 1979a, 160]; see chapter 3.) This process makes it seem as if the question of "Who sees?" is answerable without reference to ticklish questions concerning the viewer's relationship to what they are seeing. In Dayan's version of suture, then, by means of a rhetorical device the film conceals the fact that it is put together rhetorically, that it is *addressed* to the viewer at all. But while shot/reverse shot is an exemplary site for this kind of effect, suture is not just another name for shot/reverse shot editing; it refers instead to a much broader phenomenon to do with the way spectators interact with, and are affected by, narrative cinema.

Before turning to the details of Oudart's account of suture, I want to get some concrete examples on the table by turning to two scenes from *Alien* in which operations of rupturing and suturing are featured diegetically, as well as being at play in the film's form. This will not, I hope to show, be simply a question of punning or playing with words. Scenes that dramatize suture (or rupture) can very usefully serve to highlight what is most interesting about suture as an aspect of the form and rhetoric of narrative cinema; as the narratologist George Butte, to whom I will return, puts it, "suture as form enunciates especially well suture as theme" (Butte 2017, 8). (Oudart himself notes that what he calls suture in cinema is "primarily" a "representation," and that the "play of the cinematic signifier" is "truly scenic" [Oudart 1977, 38, 40].)

The most famous scene in the film, the scene within which Roger Luckhurst claims that "*Alien*'s occupation of our cultural imagination is located" (Luckhurst 2014, 40), is of course that in which the xenomorph bursts out of Kane's (John Hurt) chest—a scene, it might seem obvious, of rupture rather than suture. In a later scene, the android Ash's (Ian Holm) head—having previously been violently removed after he turns against the remaining crew—is reattached (if not to his body, then at least to his power supply) so that he can speak. This second scene, then, is one of suture rather than rupture, of reattachment subsequent to dismemberment. But how are form and theme related in these two scenes? As a first approximation—employing, for the moment, something like Dayan's understanding of suture—we might say that suture as theme serves negatively to highlight suture as form, or that theme and form have an opposite relation. By this I mean that when the xenomorph bursts from Kane's chest, although the character's body is fatally ruptured the film's "body" is sutured. Convincing acting, a mobile camera that puts the viewer in the midst of things, and a rapid and complex pattern of editing based on a range of shot/reverse shot logics all contribute to diminishing the audience's sense of distance, to putting us at the "mercy" of the film, as Dayan puts it (Dayan [1974] 1976, 448–49). (Recall those stories of early audiences throwing up in response to this scene; this might well seem like a particularly merciless deployment of cinematic power.) As mentioned above, the power of this moment comes from what is shown, not how the spectacle has been created: the audience is sutured into the shocking spectacle of the character's rupturing body. In the second scene, however, although what it presents is, diegetically, a kind of suture, this time the filmic body ruptures; the direct cut from a model head to the actor's head is unconcealed, emphasizing its construction and artifice, and serving—just a little—to lessen viewer involvement in the narrative, to render the audience's suturing within it problematic or less effective. I should note at this point that I am fond of both these moments, despite (or perhaps because of) the fact that the first is widely considered a high-water mark in cinema, while the second seems, at best, a forgivable—if a little perplexing—error or lapse of judgment. I do not wish to argue that the second moment must have been artistically intended, but we can certainly see how easily it could have been avoided, as is achieved in a similar scene involving the android Bishop (Lance Henriksen) in *Alien*[3] simply by means of cutting away at the crucial moment. Whatever the reasons behind the decision not to disguise the transition from model to actor, then, we are left at this point in the film with a rupturing transition that need not have been there.

Figure 8.1. Physical rupture and cinematic suture. *Source: Alien* (1979).

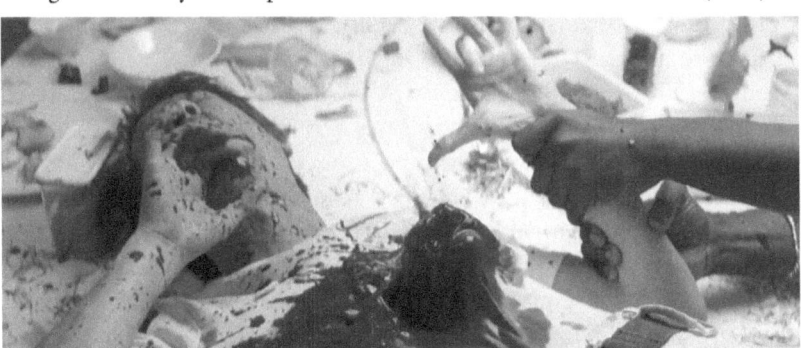

We might, then, want to claim that the first scene represents rupture but sutures us into the narrative, whereas the second represents suture but ruptures our involvement, even if only a little. I think there is something to be said for such a view, although it is rather too neat and schematic. There are other things we might say about the two scenes: the alien that runs away from Kane's corpse is far from convincing, while the white fluid that emerges from Ash's mouth is very convincing, indeed disgustingly so (even though in fact it was only milk). But it is only according to an understanding of suture akin to Dayan's that we are forced to think of suture as successful or unsuccessful in quite these terms, as something that fails as soon as we notice its operation. When, in a later piece, Oudart

Figure 8.2. Physical suture and cinematic rupture. *Source: Alien* (1979).

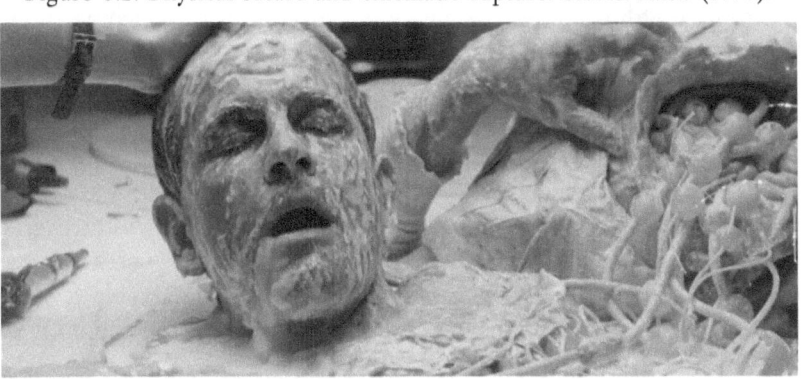

complains about a tendency for critics to overvalue "the iconoclastic vertigo of the deconstruction of reality," this could only come as a surprise to anyone who equates Oudart's view of suture with Dayan's (Oudart 1978, 58; my translation). When discussing Buster Keaton's *The General* (1926) in his original article on suture, Oudart refers to the film's "protagonists who are no longer present, who no longer have the innocent 'being-there-ness' of a moment ago, but instead have a 'being-there-for-ness'" (Oudart 1977, 41). It is precisely this movement between a pure "being-there-ness" (a sheer perception of presence) and a "being-there-for-ness" (a perception that is aware of itself, one which notices that things are there *for* a subject of some kind) which Oudart finds most interesting about what he calls suture.

Oudart introduces suture by means of a discussion of the work of Robert Bresson, claiming that his "fundamental discovery, foreshadowed in *Pickpocket* and asserted in *The Trial of Joan of Arc*, was of a cinematic articulation irreducible to any other, which we shall call suture" (Oudart 1977, 35). If suture, for Oudart, is the "discovery" by a modernist like Bresson of "a cinematic articulation irreducible to any other" it doesn't sound like it has much in common with Dayan's notion of something by means of which "the code effectively disappears and the ideological effect of the film is thereby secured." For Oudart, on the contrary, by means of suture Bresson "puts the filmed subject within a structure and in a symbolic place which are those of cinema per se, no longer as a fictive subject located in an illusory existential relationship with its surroundings, but as the actor in a representation whose symbolic dimension is revealed in the process of reading and viewing" (39). This, rather astonishingly, is not very far from being the opposite of what suture has come most usually to mean in film studies. Kügle notes that "suture, which is often understood in shorthand as a seamless sewing-up of filmic images was, strangely enough, not conceived of [by Oudart] as a seamless sewing-up" (Kügle 2020, 206; my translation). Dayan claims that the formal operations of mainstream classical cinema have the ideological effect of concealing their true function, while Oudart introduces suture as something remarkable and unusual in Bresson which both reveals and exploits (in a nonpejorative sense) the symbolic, figurative operations of cinema. (Oudart does not even find this remarkable feature in all Bresson's mature films; he remarks that the director, regrettably, "neglects" suture in *Au hasard, Balthazar* [Oudart 1977, 39].) Rather than subsuming suture to a form of the Althusserian notion of interpellation, as Dayan does—according to which the subject is ultimately an illusion created by the very discourses by means of which it seems to exist—Oudart is careful to emphasize both the construction of a fictional space and the viewer's recognition that this is, precisely, a construction: there *is* suture, we might say, but it leaves a perceptible scar, and both suturing and scarring are equally important.

Suture and Intersubjectivity

A number of scholars have, of course, noticed how different Oudart's account is from what has become the standard version of cinematic suture, much maligned by scholars including David Bordwell, Noël Carroll, William Rothman, and George M. Wilson (see, for example, Bordwell 1985; Carroll 1996; Rothman 1976; Wilson 1986, 216n2). Richard Allen, for example, observes: "The assumption that the spectator is so readily made aware that her field of vision is the field of the Absent One seems contrary to the assumption that underpins the claim of apparatus theory and Dayan's account; namely, that the spectator in the cinema is not medium aware until her attention is drawn to the image as an image" (Allen 1995, 36). Instead, we can be aware of film as a medium at the same time as we are engaged with it as narrative. (This aspect of Oudart's theories resonates with Robert Pippin's ideas about cinema's "reflective form," which we have already encountered in chapter 4; see Pippin 2020.) Thus, Oudart's account "suggests that even in classical Hollywood cinema there is a latent awareness of the suturing operation" and thus "the value of Oudart's theory (as opposed to Dayan's) lies in its suggestion that a movement in and out of medium awareness is possible in all cinema" (Allen 1995, 36, 38). For Oudart, successful suture represents a delicate balance between two pitfalls to which narrative films are constantly vulnerable: either, on the one hand, falling into a pure illusionism or, on the other, generating an entirely artificial textuality that surrenders all the advantages of narrative absorption. Oudart finds the latter in the work of some modern filmmakers who, he says, "have put cinematic language under exemplary pressure, but at the risk of leading it to the threshold of reification" (Oudart 1977, 44).

With regard to horror cinema, this way of thinking about suture might help us explore the balance between wanting to know how things are done, how effects are achieved, and *not* wanting to know (because this would diminish our suture to the narrative world). This balance might involve a kind of dialectic; if things are too lifelike, too hard to figure out, this can in some cases be more distracting than cases in which we can easily see how it was done, but for various reasons don't care. (If this were not the case then it might be hard to see why older horror films, much of whose artifice is easily apparent to our more knowing eyes, can retain their ability to terrify.) I want, however, to concentrate here on something a little different, which is, as I have said, on the relation of suture to intersubjectivity, and specifically the relationship between represented intersubjectivity and the intersubjectivity (or at least quasi-intersubjectivity) that is in operation in the viewer's relationship to a film. Thinking along these lines, we cannot simply think in terms of a film's ideological, suturing operations being either masked (by the film) or unmasked (by the critic or scholar), because we need to take represented intersubjectivity seriously *as intersubjectivity* (which means being "naive" in the sense explored in the introduction) in order to ask how it relates to the ways in which the viewer and the film confront one another as (quasi-)subjects.

George Butte's work is very helpful in pursuing these questions. If comparing Dayan to Oudart indicates that suture can be a helpful concept if one is not an Althusserian, Butte's work further demonstrates that Oudart's ideas are helpful even if we neglect his Lacanian framework. (Butte himself, with his phenomenological focus, finds Maurice Merleau-Ponty much more helpful.) I should make it clear once again that this chapter takes an agnostic position on the relevance and helpfulness of Lacan and Althusser for film studies; what I want to demonstrate is simply that suture can still be a helpful concept either way, and that—contrary to what is often assumed—work on cinematic suture need not involve extended explication of Lacanian or Althusserian concepts. Butte argues that Oudart's project is "not about space and protocols for making sense of it by viewers; it is about layers of experience. . . . Bordwell, Carroll, and Barry Salt sought outcomes from Oudart's account of experience in and of film that it was never designed to provide. Dayan and [Kaja] Silverman and other Althusserian students of film as ideology have also misread, or underread Oudart, seizing on the Lacanian threads in his essays at the expense of their phenomenological richness" (Butte 2017, 29).[2] For Butte, what is crucial about suture is that it involves the film viewer in a process of looking that involves other subjects—the characters in a film—who are *also* looking, and aware that they are looking, as well as that they are being looked at. The process easily becomes very complex, so complex that even a relatively straightforward example becomes awkward to convey in prose; the notion of suture helps us discuss the fact that one of the most remarkable resources of the language of film is how elegantly and powerfully it can convey these processes. Using an passage from Jane Austen's *Pride and Prejudice* in which "Elizabeth believes she sees that Colonel Fitzwilliam perceives how she thinks he feels about her and has seen (she blushes to think) that she sees he sees," Butte argues that "narrating these phenomenological complexities works best with the strategies of suture: indirection, looking at looking over the shoulder of the observer, and linking bodies and minds imperfectly and sometimes dangerously to other bodies and minds that read and misread" (7). The question of misreading is very important; the process of relating to other people involves constant acts of interpretation and reinterpretation, and these acts always involve risk. Compare Oudart's remark that "[s]uture is best understood through a consideration of what is at stake in the process of 'reading' film" (Oudart 1977, 35).

Central to the process of continual interpretation and reinterpretation that takes place as we watch a film is the question of obliqueness, the gap between what we *want* to see (such as, in the simplest case, what a character is looking at) and what we *do* see, which Butte links to what, as we have just seen, he calls "indirection." The issue of obliqueness initially makes an appearance in Oudart's account in a quite literal sense, in terms of the angle between the gaze of the camera and the gaze of the character.[3] Oudart remarks that there are hardly any shot/reverse shot structures in the strictest sense in cinema because what we see is almost never literally what a particular character would see (Oudart 1977, 37). What happens in shot/reverse shot when it is used interestingly, for Oudart, is that the spectator is "doubly decentred." In the first instance, the viewer "comes to posit the signifying object as the signifier of the absence

of anyone" (38). I take this to mean that in the first shot of a shot/
reverse shot figure we are perfectly happy to read the first image as
showing us what is going on from a kind of "absent" position. We
don't think that anybody is there in the film's world, seeing what we
are seeing; we know that there is no camera in the film's world. But
what happens subsequently, as the shot/reverse shot figure proceeds,
is that "the unreal space of the enunciation leads to the necessary
quasi-disappearance of the subject as it enters its own field and thus
submerges, in a sort of hypnotic continuum in which all possibility
of discourse is abolished, the relation of alternating eclipse which the
subject has to its own discourse; and this relation then demands to be
represented within the process of reading the film, which it duplicates"
(38). This is one of the most difficult passages in Oudart's "obtusely
written" essay (Fairfax 2020). I admit to being unsure in what sense
"all possibility of discourse is abolished," but the idea seems to be that
the process of abolishing the Absent One means that the spectator
in a sense repeatedly disappears as a subject. The second image in
a shot/reverse shot figure retrospectively indicates that the first shot
was, in a sense, somebody's view. It signifies the Absent One—who is
not the spectator (hence the spectator is displaced). But the reverse
shot, in abolishing the Absent One (by attaching the previous shot
to the gaze of a particular character), does not thereby reinscribe or
relocate the spectator. For a moment there seems to be no place for
the spectator; this, of course, is the aspect of suture that Dayan latched
on to. But for Oudart the process of reading the film as a series of
abolitions of the Absent One becomes a kind of "hypnotic continuum"
which the spectator cannot merely submit to, but which must also
itself be represented during "the process of reading the film." There
is a constant play between awareness and a lack of awareness at the
heart of suture, and the use of oblique angles (so that shot/reverse
shot figures relate to the gazes of the characters but do not duplicate
them) is essential to this process: "That the only possible position
for the camera should be that oblique angle, shows that the spectator
does not identify with any other character in the invisible field of the
film, but occupies a position out of alignment both with the character
and with the position of the Absent One which is only present in the
imaginary when the character, who takes its place, is not there itself"
(Oudart 1977, 45). In saying that Oudart's ideas of suture, by way of
Butte, are helpful with regard to *Alien* I do not by any means want to

argue that Scott's film aims consistently to reveal the "symbolic dimension" of its procedures of "representation," as Oudart claimed about Bresson. I do, however, want to argue that it does have something to do with this kind of process. *Alien* does not *simply* want to immerse the viewer in its narrative, in the goings-on of its "fictive subject[s] located in an illusory existential relationship with [their] surroundings," at the expense of all other operations. It also encourages an awareness of its procedures, one that becomes particularly rich with regard to something that its title leads us to expect to be central to the film: its exploration of alienness. The most interesting ways that it explores this idea, I want to claim, involve the intersubjective resources of the kinds of procedures that Oudart discusses under the rubric of suture.

Suture and Horror: Uncrossable Gaps

The central instance of intersubjectivity that I want to examine by means of the two scenes discussed earlier is that between Ash and the xenomorph. This certainly, I think, involves "strategies of . . . indirection," to use Butte's language (Butte 2017, 7). Ash, after all, never comes face to face with the mature alien. Their relationship is asymmetrical in that Ash is fascinated by the alien, whereas the xenomorph, as far as we know, never even becomes aware of Ash's existence. And yet there are connections between the two of them: neither of them is human, and both are made at least partly of silicon. Steven Mulhall notes that Ash's "body is composed of circuitry and silicon rather than flesh and blood" (Mulhall 2016, 17) and Ash observes at one point of the facehugger that it "has a funny habit of shedding his cells and replacing them with polarised silicon."

The editing pattern of the chestburster scene exploits a range of shot/reverse shot (or at least quasi-shot/reverse shot) relationships. To begin with, the scene is organized according to two shot/reverse shot exchanges operating roughly at right angles to one another: one between Ash and Kane, the other between Parker (Yaphet Kotto) and Lambert (Veronica Cartwright). When Kane becomes distressed and stands up the editing becomes more complex, but patterns of repetition and alternation between various camera setups consistently activate shot/reverse shot logics. Table 8.1 gives a full shot breakdown of the scene, indicating these patterns in detail.

Table 8.1. Chestburster scene shot breakdown (timings from Blu-ray edition of theatrical cut of Alien)

#	Timing	Shot type	Description
1	54'37"	Long shot	The entire crew eating their meal.
2	54'46"	Medium shot	Parker, Kane, and Dallas.
3	54'50"	Medium shot	Ash, in focus to the left, with Ripley out of focus to the right. Quasi-reverse shot of shot 2, albeit from a 90-degree angle to Ash's eyeline. Towards end of shot Ash looks intently towards Dallas with very slight camera movement in the direction of his attention.
4	54'56"	Medium shot	Same as shot 2, tracking in to frame Kane centrally.
5	55'07"	Medium shot	Lambert. Quasi-reverse shot of Parker's gaze, at a highly oblique angle (albeit less than the 90 degrees seen previously).
6	55'11"	Medium shot	Parker, Kane, and Dallas again (same as shots 2 and 4), serving as Parker's reverse shot to the previous shot of Lambert.
7	55'14"	Medium shot	Same as shot 5.
8	55'18"	Medium shot	Same as shots 2, 4, and 6. Towards end of shot, Kane begins to choke.
9	55'23"	Medium close-up	Ash framed frontally (hence a more conventional reverse shot of Kane's position). Jones the cat is visible, out of focus, to left of frame.
10	55'25"	Medium shot	Same as shots 2, 4, 6, and 8.
11	55'29"	Medium shot	Camera behind Kane's left shoulder, with Parker visible on right of frame. Not directly related to the point of view of any character.
12	55'33"	Medium close-up	Same as shot 9.

#	Timing	Shot type	Description
13	55'34"	Medium shot	Parker, Kane, and Dallas (with Brett just visible to the extreme left and Lambert to the extreme right); similar to the previous shots in this direction (2, 4, 6, 8) but with camera positioned higher, suggesting a standing rather than a sitting position, thus evoking the change in position of the crew (who are now all standing up in response to Kane's increasing distress).
14	55'37"	Medium close-up	Same as shots 9 and 12, but Ash now moves rapidly out of shot.
15	55'38"	Medium shot	Similar to shot 13 as Kane is laid on his back on the table. Camera moves to frame those helping Kane, rather than Kane himself.
16	55'48"	Medium close-up	Kane, stretched back on the table. Very similar to Dallas's point of view, though related to the point of view of all the characters helping to hold Kane down.
17	55'50"	Medium shot	Similar to shots 13 and 15, but now showing both Kane and Parker (who puts a spoon in Kane's mouth), with other characters also visible (Brett, Dallas, Ash's arm to right of the frame).
18	55'58"	Medium close-up	New position. Lambert rushing to assist. Related, albeit loosely, to the gaze of any number of the other characters.
19	56'00"	Medium shot	Similar to shots 13 and 15.
20	56'01"	Medium shot	Similar to shot 17.
21	56'03"	Medium shot	Back to shot 13/15/19 view of Kane.

continued on next page

Table 8.1. Continued.

#	Timing	Shot type	Description
22	56'04"	Medium shot	A new position, showing Parker's back to the left of frame and Ash to the right, helping to hold Kane down. Proximity to the characters and camera movement evoke sense of gaze of the various characters standing around the table, even if shot does not obviously relate directly to the gaze of any specific character.
23	56'06"	Medium shot	The shot 13/15/19/21 view of Kane. The first spurt of blood from Kane's chest.
24	56'07"	Medium shot	Similar to shot 22 with Lambert now visible centrally in the frame, recoiling from the blood.
25	58'08"	Medium shot	Similar to shots 17 and 20. Parker and Dallas are stunned.
26	56'14"	Medium shot	The shot 13/15/19/21/23 view of Kane.
27	56'15"	Medium shot	Similar to shots 22 and 24.
28	56'16"	Medium shot	The shot 13/15/19/21/23/26 view of Kane.
29	56'18"	Medium shot	As shots 22, 24, and 27.
30	56'18"	Medium shot	The shot 13/15/19/21/23/26/28 view of Kane.
31	56'19"	Medium shot	As shots 22, 24, 27, and 29.
32	56'20"	Medium shot	Extremely brief shot of Kane with the xenomorph beginning to burst from his chest.
33	56'20"	Medium shot	New position, similar to shot 22/24/27/29/31. Parker, Ripley, Brett, and Dallas recoil.
34	56'21"	Medium shot	As shot 32; once again incredibly brief.
35	56'21"	Medium shot	As shot 33.
36	56'22"	Medium close-up	New position, to the right of the previous shot. Lambert, in medium close-up, is sprayed with blood.

#	Timing	Shot type	Description
37	56'23"	Medium shot	As shots 32 and 34 as the xenomorph emerges further; once again, incredibly brief.
38	56'23"	Medium shot	As shots 33 and 35, although slightly more widely framed.
39	56'25"	Close-up	The xenomorph slowly emerges from Kane's body, the camera moving to keep its head framed centrally. Reflects the visual attention of all characters save Kane.
40	56'34"	Medium shot	As shots 33, 35, and 38. Parker grabs a knife.
41	56'36"	Medium shot	New position, related to shot 36 but framed more tightly. Ash remonstrates with Parker, with Lambert out of focus in the background. Quasi-reverse shot to the previous shot (exchange between Parker and Ash).
42	56'38"	Close-up	As shot 39.
43	56'40"	Medium shot	As shot 41.
44	56'41"	Medium shot	As shots 33, 35, 38, and 40.
45	56'42"	Medium close-up	New view of the xenomorph howling, against an entirely out-of-focus background.
46	56'44"	Medium shot	New position. Wider shot, showing the table—with Lambert and Ash arranged roughly as in shot 41 in the background—as the xenomorph dashes away across the table.
47	56'44"	Close-up	New position. Ash looking at the retreating xenomorph in astonishment.
48	56'48"	Medium shot	New position, related to shots 33, 35, 38, and 40 but from a lower angle, looking up from the table. Related to the "point of view" of the dead Kane. Ripley, Brett, Parker, and Dallas huddle in astonishment, all looking in different directions.

continued on next page

Table 8.1. Continued.

#	Timing	Shot type	Description
49	56'52"	Close-up	As shot 47, but Ash now looks much more thoughtful and calculating (see fig. 8.3).
50	56'54"		End of scene.

At the beginning of the scene, then, what seems like a wide establishing shot of the crew sitting around their dinner table followed by closer shots showing various groupings is legible, with hindsight, as governed by a logic of shot/reverse shot between Ash and Kane (which is also briefly interrupted by a shot/reverse shot sequence between Parker and Lambert). The quasi-shot/reverse shot relationship here between Ash and Kane is indirect in more than one sense. It is at the limit of the camera's obliquity with regard to the gaze it is related to; as noted in table 8.1, the third shot of the sequence is at right angles to Ash's gaze, the exact midpoint between a frontal shot of Ash and his point of view. It is also asymmetrical in more ways than one. Ash is looking at Kane, while Kane pays no attention to Ash; but, also, Ash is not really attending to Kane at all—he is focused on what is inside Kane and what it will do next. David Thomson writes that the chestburster scene "ends on Ash's face, like a believer who has seen a saint, but who finds the image more beautiful and more terrifying than he ever fancied" (Thomson 2000, 49), but I do not find this description entirely convincing. The sequence actually ends with *two* shots of Ash, which are separated by a shot of the rest of the crew huddled together in bewilderment and horror. In the first of these shots Ash, like the crew, also exhibits bewilderment and horror—his emotional reaction seems to a large degree to "suture" him to the rest of the crew, to make him one of them (even if we can also, perhaps, see traces of the religious awe referred to by Thomson). But the second shot separates Ash from his fellow crew, his face expressing neither horror nor awe but instead a coolly calculating attitude, mulling over what he has just seen and pondering its possible implications; he is attempting correctly (by his lights, which of course we come to discover are very different from those of his fellow crewmembers) to interpret what has just happened (see fig. 8.3).

Figure 8.3. Our last view of Ash in the chestburster sequence. *Source: Alien* (1979).

The later sequence, once Ash's head has been plugged back in, takes the form of a straightforward shot/reverse shot sequence between Ash and Ripley (Sigourney Weaver), with Parker and Lambert also visible behind her. But the really important intersubjectivity at play here is presented only indirectly because it is, once again, that between Ash and the alien, as indicated by Ash's famous speech in response to Lambert's claim that he "admires" the xenomorph: "I admire its purity. A survivor, unclouded by conscience, remorse, or delusions of morality." Robert M. Mentyka takes this rather at face value, commenting that thanks to this speech of Ash's, "we learn a lot about the creature that has been stalking the crew of the *Nostromo*" (Mentyka 2017, 189). What we learn, apparently, is that "[t]he nature of the Xenomorph illustrates some of the core principles of Nietzschean philosophy" (190). But to say so is to take "Nietzschean philosophy" as something much stabler and simpler than it is, and to neglect—unfortunately, given the absolute centrality of the notion of interpretation to Nietzsche's thought—that what "we learn" from Ash is *Ash's* interpretation of the xenomorph. Despite the fact that Ash never meets the alien, my claim is that the issues of intersubjectivity that are highlighted in Oudart's discussion of suture (and in Butte's discussion of Oudart) help us see how this relationship (which is not really a "relationship" at all, as we shall see in a moment) is part of the film's broader economy of operations of rupture and suture.

For Thomson, it is when Ash expresses his admiration for the xenomorph "that we detect the possible soul in the machine, the desire for the new level of life to be recognised, or appreciated. Ash is alien too, but oddly touching" (Thomson 2000, 57). Or we might put it another way and say that the film indicates that "nonhuman" is not synonymous with "alien." The cat Jones is also nonhuman, but not alien. Jones is simply an animal, whereas the xenomorph—despite the fact that it has a human father (and/or mother, in a sense)—is genuinely alien. (How might we possibly come to know whether or not this particular alien is "more human" than "normal"?) And what about Ash? He is not human, but he was built by humans. He thus behaves like a human, but as it were "from the outside in," rather than "from the inside out"—because he was built to *behave* like a human, rather than because he *is* a human. The very fact that Ash can admire anything at all comes, presumably, from the fact that he was built that way. I want to suggest that Ash admires the alien precisely because it is what he could never be, and *knows* he could never be. Ash does not have the kind of connection between conscience and consciousness that is characteristically human. And yet, if he can feel admiration, and also contempt—see his final sarcastic remark to Ripley, Lambert, and Parker that "you have my sympathies"—then he is more human than he would like; he can recognize the difference but can do nothing about it. Though he masks it with sarcasm, he is not so very different from the sickly figure described by Nietzsche who gives a "surreptitious glance imparting a deep sadness . . . that glance which is a sigh. 'If only I were some other person!' is what this glance sighs: 'but there's no hope of that. I am who I am: how could I get away from myself? And oh—*I'm fed up with myself!*' " (Nietzsche [1887] 2007, 89–90 [*On the Genealogy of Morality*, third essay, §14]; emphasis in original). Ash, presumably, thinks that his lack of compassion makes him superior to his crewmates—more similar to the xenomorph—but in so doing he neglects Nietzsche's insistence that if "great *compassion* for man" is a "calamity," then "great *nausea* at man" is equally so (89; emphases in original).

The very presence of emotion in Ash (whatever form it takes), then, both distinguishes him from the alien, and generates his admiration: he can sense both his distance from and closeness to humanity and obviously would like to be able to amplify the distance, to generate a real rupture between himself and humanity, tearing apart the last few stitches. But this is impossible because he is the creation of humanity: that he is aware of wanting this indicates the very impossibility of achieving his desire. (*Alien: Resurrection* [1997] raises the question of what happens when androids are built by other androids, though it does not pursue it very far.) Whereas, even though the alien is (as Ash calls it) "Kane's son," there is for it no question of a rupture with humanity because it has nothing to do with "humanity"; it simply used a human body in which to incubate. Materially, the alien has had more to do with human beings than Ash has, and yet it is devoid of humanity (it is, as Nietzsche would have put it, beyond good and evil) in a way Ash could never be. Not all gaps, then, are ruptures; Ash *admires* the alien (rather than, say, merely being *interested* in it) precisely because, despite the silicon they have in common, the gap between them is uncrossable. The relationship between them can be neither ruptured nor sutured because it can never truly be a relationship. (In claiming that Bresson neglects suture in *Au hasard, Balthazar*, to the film's detriment, it is rather curious that Oudart does not mention the scene at the circus containing Balthasar's exchanges of gaze with the other animals. What kind of suture is possible in *this* nonhuman situation?) Elsewhere, Nietzsche writes:

> For we could think, feel, will, remember, and also "act" in every sense of the term, and yet none of all this would have to "enter our consciousness" (as we say figuratively). All of life would be possible without, as it were, seeing ourselves in the mirror; and still today, the predominant part of our lives actually unfolds without this mirroring. . . . Consciousness is really just a net connecting one person with another—only in this capacity did it have to develop; the solitary and predatory person would not have needed it. (Nietzsche [1887] 2001, 212 [*The Gay Science*, §354])

Neither, of course, does the xenomorph! Unlike the xenomorph, then, Ash both *has* consciousness and is aware that he doesn't *need* it. Though we can never know for sure, there is no reason to think that the xenomorph possesses consciousness in anything like our sense; to echo Butte's language from earlier (Butte 2017, 7), perhaps it cannot "misread" because it never "read[s]" in the first place. It has no need for consciousness because it has no society to suture. It may well want us—it reaches out for Dallas (Tom Skerritt)—but not in a way that we could ever really understand.

It is, then, clear that despite having a violent rupture at its heart, *Alien* puts cinematic suture to extensive use. If we understand suture along the lines of Dayan's account—in which the procedures of suture trap (or even trick) viewers into participating in certain ideological operations—we could say that *Alien* uses suture mainly (and of course, for a great many viewers, hugely successfully) in order to engross, to thrill and to horrify its audience; the editing of the chestburster scene is an exemplary instance of this (see table 8.1 once more). But if we see suture more along the lines suggested by Oudart and Butte, in which it involves continual movement between unselfconscious and self-conscious awareness, then we can say that *Alien* finds in suture, as both rhetorical figure and thematic device, a remarkably rich resource for the exploration and dramatization of situations in which rupture may be impossible because suture is *also* impossible. As I noted earlier, not all gaps are ruptures. The film gestures towards the notion of an uncrossable gap very early on with a kind of fake suture; we are presented with a sequence of shot/reverse shot figures involving only computer screens and empty helmets, the reflections on the visors parodying the notion that we have ideas "in our heads" (fig. 8.4). Via the shot/reverse shot editing, we are presented with the conventional form of cinematic intersubjectivity in the absence of any real subjects. But what is a "real" subject anyway?

Figure 8.4. Intersubjectivity without subjects. *Source: Alien* (1979).

Alien, as I have been reading it in the light of Oudart's understanding of suture, relates in intriguing ways to what (as we saw in chapter 5) Cavell calls active and passive skepticism about other minds—the twin anxieties that we may never be able to *know* another, or to *be known by* another. Cavell explores these issues most extensively in *The Claim of Reason*, a book in which Nietzsche makes regular appearances, and which also suggests the usefulness for the understanding of the history of skepticism of "tales of the fantastic and of horror" (Cavell 1979b, 476). It would take at least another chapter properly to unpack this line of thought, but here is a paragraph that—despite its density and enigmatic qualities—I hope at least hints at the connections I see between Cavell's work and this chapter's subject:

> Is the cover of skepticism—the conversion of metaphysical finitude into intellectual lack—a denial of the human or an expression of it? For of course there are those for whom the denial of the human *is* the human. . . . Call this the Christian view. It would be why Nietzsche undertook to identify the task of overcoming the human with the task of overcoming the denial of the human; which implies overcoming the human not through mortification but through joy, say ecstasy. If the former can be thought of as the denial of the body then the latter may be thought of as the affirmation of the body. . . . [S]uppose my identity with my body is something that exists only in my affirmation of my body. . . . Then the question is: What would the body *become* under affirmation? What would become of *me*? Perhaps I would know myself as, take myself for, a kind of machine; perhaps as a universe. (492–93; emphases in original)

The claim that "the denial of the human *is* the human" is more or less what I have claimed about Ash and what I think we could call the "fantasy of the vanishing of the human" (468) that the xenomorph prompts in him. If my suggestion that we consider the xenomorph as a demonstration of what it might look like to live a life "without, as it were, seeing ourselves in the mirror," as Nietzsche puts it (Nietzsche [1887] 2001, 212), is at all plausible, I want to make the further suggestion that this means that it might be productive to explore whether the xenomorph can be thought of as an instance of what we might, following Cavell, call an affirmed body—a body that has overcome the human by overcoming (or discarding) the denial of the human. Does the xenomorph provide at least some hint as to what it might look like for someone to know themselves as "a kind of machine; perhaps as a universe"? Despite (or, rather, because of) the difficulty in knowing what this could possibly mean, I think it is as clear in Cavell as it is in *Alien* that this is a terrifying prospect.[4]

In closing, I want to propose that, odd as it may sound, we might say that the most disturbing instance of shot/reverse shot in *Alien* occurs when Jones the cat watches the xenomorph kill Brett (Harry Dean Stanton), something which is later briefly collapsed into a single shot of xenomorph and cat looking at each other (see fig. 8.5). The cinematic figuration here is straightforward. But what kind of suture could possibly be going on between these two nonhuman beings, despite their evident similarities (both of them are clearly, to reuse Nietzsche's words, "solitary and predatory" [Nietzsche [1887] 2001, 212])? What place is there here for our own subjectivity as viewers? Is this a vision of Cavellian skepticism confirmed? It surely leaves no room for any form of what Cavell would call acknowledgment, and yet the encounter points towards something like it in the way it suggests similarities between such vastly divergent creatures. The wary stillness on the cat's face, in the first encounter, and the way the xenomorph's movements suggest curiosity, in the second,

Figure 8.5. Impossible suture? *Source: Alien* (1979).

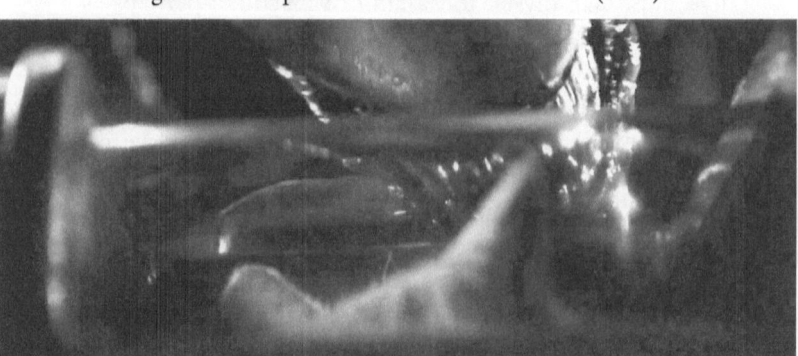

generate—through our awareness that these descriptions can only be anthropomorphic projections—a kind of pun on the possibility that xenomorph and cat *might* somehow acknowledge one another as fellow predators. *Alien* doesn't propose answers to the questions raised earlier in this paragraph, but even to raise them is a disorientating and bewildering achievement, something that would be impossible were we to understand the film's operations of suture wholly in Dayan's terms, rather than in Oudart's. The truly alien horror of the encounters between feline and xenomorph, emblematic of that which permeates the whole film, lies not in any violent rupture (say, that of Brett's body), but instead in the fact that no rupture is possible between that which can never even be sutured.

9

Hypnosis-Images

Indiscernibility and Hypnotic Agency in Gilles Deleuze's *Heart of Glass*

Werner Herzog's 1976 film *Heart of Glass* (*Herz aus Glas*) is set in eighteenth-century Bavaria.[1] Clearly indicating its aesthetic debt to the paintings of Caspar David Friedrich, the film begins by showing its protagonist sitting on a rock, enveloped in mist, apparently looking towards a herd of cows and some bare, somewhat stunted trees (see fig. 9.1). The conjunction of a human figure seen from behind, mist, and leafless trees with the more mundane image of a herd of cows suggests a combination of Friedrich's famously sublime paintings—such as "Wanderer above the Sea of Fog" or "The Abbey in the Oakwood"—and his somewhat more pastoral side, as is visible in the cows in "Landscape with Mountain Lake, Morning." Does the herd of cows in Herzog's film undermine the image's sublimity, juxtaposing the sublimely ineffable with the ridiculously familiar? Or might it be better described as complicating it, raising the question of why we might assume that a cow must be bathetic? After all, the fog and the stately, curiously suspended mood defamiliarize the cows' pastoral associations, as does the soundtrack's combination of vocal music based on yodeling with shimmering metallic percussion that abstractly evokes the sound of cowbells. The medium close-up of a group of cows that is the film's second shot shows them from side-on, almost as abstract silhouettes; and yet one of them periodically turns its head to look directly at the camera. These are familiarly ordinary cows, but the film also presents them as powerful and even mysterious creatures. As will become clear in what follows, it is highly appropriate that the register of the film's very first images is ambivalent.

The film also subtly sets up one of its central concerns in its opening sequence's ambiguities of vision. The man sitting on the rock is a seer or prophet named Hias (Josef Bierbichler), based on a legendary figure from Bavarian history.[2] The sequence involves a sly variation on shot/reverse shot conventions. Rather than showing us the face of a character, and then what they are looking at (or even showing us a scene and then revealing that a character is looking at it) we are simultaneously shown the character *and* what we presume they are looking at and yet, when—after a medium close-up of the cows—we eventually see Hias's face, it is disconcertingly blank. Admittedly, a herd of cows might not be expected to provoke a strong reaction, but it is far from clear that Hias even *is* seeing what we surely presume him to be seeing. Is he, instead, glumly lost in his own thoughts, staring blankly at nothing in particular as if in a trance? Or perhaps—as we may later come to suspect—he is having some kind of prophetic vision or hallucination. Hias visits a small town whose glass factory once produced a famous ruby glass, the secret of whose manufacture has been lost upon the death of Mühlbeck, the master glass blower. The factory's owner (Stefan Güttler) is obsessed with the secret of the glass and descends into madness, eventually murdering

Figure 9.1. *Heart of Glass*'s opening figure of vision . . . Source: *Heart of Glass* (1976).

his maid Ludmilla (Sonja Skiba) to find out if her blood can produce the red glass before burning his factory down, an event which Hias had foretold. Hias and the factory owner are both imprisoned, only for us to see Hias within a snowy forest battling an invisible (or imaginary) bear, after which he sits at a campfire and relates a vision concerning a group of men rowing out, surely to certain death, in search of the edge of the world. The film ends by showing us this vision (see fig. 9.2).

The Place of *Heart of Glass* in *Cinema 1* and *Cinema 2*

Heart of Glass is referred to in each of Gilles Deleuze's two enormously influential books on cinema. In the second half of this chapter, I will look in some detail at the film in relation to Deleuze's accounts of it, particularly in terms of the distinction he makes between the hallucinatory and the hypnotic, as well as his claims about its so-called crystal-images. (These are aspects of the film's figuration, as I have been using that term.) I will argue that these different aspects of Deleuze's thought come together in the aspects of "indiscernibility" and "reversibility" that he finds so powerful in *Heart of Glass*. Before this, to set up the stakes and terms of my reading of the film, I want to situate Deleuze's remarks about *Heart of Glass* in relation to their situation within his wider claims about cinema, motivating and elucidating these claims (so far as I am able), as well as noting some tensions between the accounts we are offered in *Cinema 1* and *Cinema 2*.

Figure 9.2. . . . and its final prophetic vision. *Source: Heart of Glass* (1976).

When we first encounter the film in *Cinema 1*, Deleuze declares that Herzog's is an "action cinema," and that it is "an extreme case" of the way that the "Ideas" of "the Small and the Large," although "distinct," are "capable of passing into one another" (Deleuze [1983] 1986, 188). This claim needs to be understood in the context of the proposition (which we find in chapters 9 and 10 of *Cinema 1*) that what Deleuze calls the action-image takes two main forms. In the work of certain directors—Victor Sjöström, King Vidor, Howard Hawks (some of the time), Elia Kazan—we see a preference for representing a movement "from the situation to the transformed situation via the intermediary of the action," a process which he notates as SAS' and calls "the large form" (146). Other directors, however—Charlie Chaplin (particularly in his silent films), Ernst Lubitsch, Howard Hawks (at other times), Anthony Mann—prefer to move "from the action to the situation, towards a new action," which Deleuze calls "the small form" and designates ASA' (164).

In the simplest terms, what these two forms serve to designate is that in the large form action is situated within a "determinate, geographical, historical and social" situation; eventually, by the end of the film, the situation is somehow transformed—or not, if the variant form SAS is employed, such as Deleuze finds in *Nanook of the North*, in which "the grandeur of Nanook's actions lies less in modifying the situation than in surviving in an impervious milieu" (148). In the small form, on the other hand, we begin with an action from which we infer or deduce its surrounding situation.[3] Punning on the French word "ellipse," which can mean either ellipsis (that is, gap or omission) or ellipse (the geometrical figure), Deleuze emphasizes both the more economically sketched narratives of "small form" films compared with those that partake of the large form (though both forms are equally realistic; see 145) and—more importantly, it seems to me—the notion that "a very slight difference in the action, or between two actions, leads to a very great distance between two situations" (166). Thus, at the heart of the small form is a sense of incongruity or disproportion, a kind of irony that becomes apparent in the perception of quite how similar two actions can *seem* to be, only for their noncoincidence to give rise to very large differences indeed.[4] As the case of Hawks demonstrates, a director can operate according to either strategy in a given film. In Herzog's work, however, Deleuze discovers the possibility of moving between the two forms, or of exacerbating them such that the distinction between them ceases to be as clear as Deleuze thinks it otherwise is (see 167). This productive confusion takes two forms in Herzog, involving either a discovery of the small within the large or vice versa; only the former is our concern here, because it is this that is exemplified by *Heart of Glass*.

Despite the evident complexities of Deleuze's ideas, it is worth noting that his point here is, in the first instance, a simple one, namely, that in these films the action "is not required by the situation" but is "a crazy enterprise, born in the head of a visionary" (188). In films such as *Heart of Glass*, as well as *Aguirre, Wrath of God* (1972) and *Fitzcarraldo* (1982) "a man who is larger than life frequents a milieu which is itself larger than life, and dreams up [*conçoit*] an action as great as the milieu. It is an SAS' form, but a very special one: the action, in effect, is not required by the situation, it is a crazy enterprise, born in the head of a visionary, which seems to be the only one capable of rivalling the milieu in its entirety" (188). The actions we are dealing with are not straightforward realities but are projects initiated by men verging on (or often, in fact, fully tipped over into) megalomania; these actions are therefore in a sense both actual and virtual, and this not only in some rarefied philosophical sense, but also in terms of the films' narratives.[5] We are, that is, not simply shown "external" reality in these films; instead Herzog presents us with "Visions which deserve even more to be called Ideas" (188). These films' protagonists want to rival the immensity of their environment—hence their "largeness"—and yet this desire in a sense shrinks everything down to the contents of one man's head, and thus we are also dealing with "smallness." There is a kind of blurring or indiscernibility between the apparent grandeur of the goings-on in these films and their purely egotistical origins.[6]

Deleuze distinguishes two main aspects of these crazy schemes: there is both "a *hallucinatory* dimension, where the acting spirit raises itself to boundlessness in nature and a *hypnotic* dimension where the spirit runs up against [*affronte*] the limits which Nature opposes to it" (188; my emphases). Deleuze claims that the action in these films "divides in two"; the first, hallucinatory, dimension corresponds to "the sublime action, always beyond," while the second, hypnotic, dimension corresponds to "a heroic action which confronts the milieu on its own account, penetrating the impenetrable, breaching the unbreachable [*franchissant l'infranchissable*]" (188). In *Heart of Glass* specifically, these dimensions are distinguished according to the types of landscape which the film shows us: "[T]he Bavarian landscape harbours [*abrite*] the hypnotic creation of the glass ruby, but goes still further beyond itself in the hallucinatory landscapes which prompt the search for the great abyss of the Universe" (188, 189; translation modified). The distinction between hallucinatory and hypnotic images, it seems, has to do with human action in relation to nature and whether nature and action both appear unbounded (the hallucinatory) or whether action is constrained by the limits that nature imposes (the hypnotic). Once again there is something simple lying behind at least part of this account, namely, the notorious fact that during the filming of *Heart of Glass* most of the cast were indeed hypnotized (see Herzog 2014, 132–39).

The way that this distinction manifests in the film is complicated. For example, despite the ambiguities of their presentation, it is clear enough that the images of clouds and waterfalls that we see after our first encounter with Hias and the cows somehow represent his visions or hallucinations, and yet, as Herzog himself points out, the waterfall images in particular have a hypnotic quality: "The opening images of the waterfall are there almost to put audiences into a trance. Staring directly into the moving water and listening intently to the suggestions of the voice in German—reading the English subtitles doesn't really do the job—makes you feel as if the waterfall is standing still and it's you who are floating upwards" (Herzog 2014, 138).[7] Rather than undermining Deleuze's distinction between the film's hallucinatory and hypnotic dimensions, this reveals a crucial ambiguity or reversibility at play within the distinction. This is not so much an instance of the passage between altered images that we explored with the help of Nicole Brenez in chapter 7 as it is a matter of images that are already multiple, that contain alteration within them. (This is relevant to the discussion of crystal-images to follow later in this chapter.) One could say that it is a question of internal or external views. Are we dealing with an image that is hallucinatory—or that might hypnotize us—or with an image of somebody having a hallucination, or who is in a hypnotic state? The film often shows us actors who are, quite literally, hypnotized, while its imagery is frequently hallucinatory. We might say that for much of the film's duration we see hallucination "from the inside" and hypnosis "from the outside." Towards the end of the film, however, when Hias fights an imaginary bear, we are finally given an external view of hallucination, an image—simultaneously bathetic and strangely dignified—of what it looks like when someone is hallucinating. While there is undoubtedly something ridiculous about this sequence, the camera's framing and Bierbichler's committed performance make it, at one and the same time, curiously powerful. It might even prompt us to wonder how sure we are that we are dealing with an imaginary bear rather than a bear that is invisible (at least to us). How could we distinguish a diegetically hallucinated bear from, say, the film's adoption of a strategy—as might be very effective in the theater—in which we are simply to take it from the actor's performance that there *is* a diegetic bear present? (After all, the use of hypnosis has by now entirely accustomed us to the film's willingness to adopt extremes of stylization.) The indiscernibility that is central to Deleuze's account of the "small form" of the action image, a species of movement-image in which (as is certainly the case in this scene) we deduce the situation from the action, and wherein "a very slight difference in the action . . . leads to a very great distance between two situations" (Deleuze [1983] 1986, 166), is folded into the complications about the relationship between actual and virtual that are so important to the time-image.

The question of the relationship between will and action is at the heart of the interest of hypnosis. Herzog has (for example, in the discussion with Norman Hill that is available as a commentary track on the DVD and Blu-ray releases of *Heart of Glass*) disputed the idea that his interest in it was a reflection of his own directorial megalomania, insisting that hypnotized actors are much more difficult to control than unhypnotized actors.[8] He also makes the familiar point that somebody under hypnosis will not do something that is fundamentally contrary to their character, claiming that "if I ask a hypnotised person to take a knife and kill his mother, he would refuse" (Herzog 2014, 138). In his early work *Time and Free Will*—before he developed the ontological account of memory that is so central to Deleuze's work on cinema—Henri Bergson drew from this same point a conclusion that Todd Cronan calls "astonishingly counterintuitive"; namely, that because nothing done under hypnosis can conflict with who one most fundamentally is, "[e]very suggestion that worked or took hold of the subject was simply eliciting something already at work deep within that individual," and thus an act done under hypnotic suggestion was a perfect example of a "free act" (Cronan 2013, 80). Bergson also drew a parallel between the experience of art and the experience of hypnosis: "In the processes of art we shall find, in a weakened form, a refined and in some measure spiritualized version of the processes commonly used to induce the state of hypnosis" (Bergson [1913] 2001, 14). It is not clear to me to what extent Deleuze might have been directly influenced by these ideas in his references to hypnosis but, questionable as they are, their paradoxical account of agency resonates with Deleuze's treatment of questions of activity and passivity, or actuality and virtuality, and the reversibility between them that Deleuze sees as characteristic of the time-image. But I am getting ahead of myself; I shall return to these ideas at the conclusion of this chapter.

Heart of Glass reappears in *Cinema 2* in the chapter on the crystal-image. The latter is Deleuze's term of art for a cinematic image that is disconnected from chains of action—of cause and effect—that operates by means of a relation to what he calls its own virtual image. We are told that an "opsign"—which is "an image which breaks the sensory-motor schema, and where the seen is no longer extended into action" (Deleuze [1985] 1989, 325), and of which the most straightforward instances appear to be memories or dreams (67)—"finds its true genetic element when the actual optical image crystallizes with *its own* virtual image"; when this happens, we have "a crystal-image" (67; emphasis in original). Deleuze insists that he's not simply talking about a kind of muddle: "[T]he confusion of the real and the imaginary is a simple error of fact, and does not affect their discernibility: the confusion is produced solely 'in someone's head.' But indiscernibility constitutes an objective illusion; it does not suppress the distinction between the two sides, but makes it unattributable, each side taking the other's role in a relation which we must describe as reciprocal presupposition, or reversibility" (67). Deleuze gives a clear example of what he's talking about by using the example of mirror images in films: "[T]he mirror-image is virtual in relation to the actual character that the mirror catches, but is actual in the mirror which now leaves the character with only a virtuality and pushes him offscreen" (68; translation modified). From one point of view, the character is real and their mirror image is virtual (is only an image). But, of course, film is made of images, so if we see a character's reflection while the actor "themselves" remains offscreen, it makes sense to say that in this case the mirror image is actual (is an actual onscreen image), while the character becomes in a sense virtual—we infer their presence and location solely from their image in the mirror.

A comparable kind of reversibility is important for Deleuze's account of *Heart of Glass*: he claims that the actual can, from certain points of view, become virtual, and vice versa. To complicate matters, however, Deleuze declares that two other figures are also important to the crystal-image: as well as the actual and the virtual, there is "the limpid and the opaque" and "the seed and the environment" (72). Deleuze introduces *Heart of Glass* in *Cinema 2* directly after a discussion of Orson Welles: "In a famous sequence in *Citizen Kane*, the little glass ball breaks apart when it falls from the hands of the dying man, but the snow that it contained seems to come towards us in gusts to impregnate the milieux that we will discover. We do not know in advance if the virtual seed ('Rosebud') will be actualized, because we do not know in advance if the actual environment enjoys the corresponding virtuality" (72; translation modified). (In fact, when the glass ball breaks, liquid splashes towards the camera; Deleuze is, I suspect, thinking of the images of snow that are superimposed over the globe *before* it breaks, as well as over the image of Kane's lips pronouncing "Rosebud.") Deleuze then suggests that "[p]erhaps this is how we should understand the splendour of the images in Herzog's *Heart of Glass*, and the film's double aspect" (72; translation modified), which leads to the longest passage on the film in either of the two books:

> The search for the alchemical heart and secret, for the red crystal, is inseparable from the search for cosmic limits, as the highest tension of the mind and deepest level of reality. But the crystal's fire will have to transmit itself to the whole factory in order for the world, for its part, to stop being an amorphous, flattened environment which stops at the edge of an abyss, and for it to reveal infinite crystalline possibilities in itself ("the earth rises up from the waters, I see a new earth . . ."). (72–73; translation modified)[9]

It is, to say the least, not entirely clear how this passage relates to the preceding discussion of *Citizen Kane*. In what sense do Deleuze's remarks about the snow globe suggest how we should understand *Heart of Glass*? Since he says that the snow seems to "impregnate [we might also say 'sow'] the environment ['ensemencer les milieux']," the idea seems to be that the snowflakes are like a collection of little seeds or sperm which, in a visual metaphor, spread the seed of "Rosebud" throughout *Citizen Kane*. Deleuze reads the spreading of the snow as a dissemination of the secret. (Note the etymology both of "ensemencer" and "disseminate.") Perhaps, therefore, the connection with *Heart of Glass* has to do chiefly with the *spreading*, with the affinities between the "sowing" of the bits of fake snow and the way the fire spreads to the whole factory. Also clearly important, however, is the idea of *not knowing*. Deleuze says that we don't know in advance whether, in *Citizen Kane*, the seed will become actual, and then remarks in the very next sentence that "perhaps this is how to understand *Heart of Glass*" (72). The claim must also, it seems, be about an absence of guarantees, but the sequences of events in Herzog's film and in Welles's are *so* different that the parallel is quite hard to make out. One possible interpretation would be that the search for the secret of the glass is like the search for the secret of Rosebud: it is a search for the wrong thing, or, more accurately perhaps, is based on a mistaken expectation of what discovering the secret would achieve (see fig. 9.3).

Immediately after the long passage about *Heart of Glass* quoted above, Deleuze makes an extraordinary evaluative claim: "In this film Herzog has set out the greatest crystal-images in the history of cinema" (73).[10] Crystal-images are, of course, crucial to Deleuze's claims about the post–World War II innovations of the time-image and the ways in which it breaks with the assumptions and procedures

Figure 9.3. Spreading snow in *Citizen Kane* and spreading fire in *Heart of Glass*. Source: *Citizen Kane* (1941) and *Heart of Glass* (1976).

of the movement-image; crystal-images reveal "a direct time-image, and no longer an indirect image of time deriving from movement" (95). To claim that *Heart of Glass* contains the "greatest" examples of crystal-images "in the history of cinema" implies that *Heart of Glass* is in some sense a privileged text in Deleuze's most well-known and influential contribution to the study of film, namely, his account of the distinction between movement-image and time-image. We might therefore expect that he would see the film as wholly distinct from the cinema of the movement-image, and yet, as we saw above, he also sees the film as a very interesting instance of what he calls the action-image.[11] Indeed, even in his remarks in *Cinema 2*, Deleuze still speaks in terms of cause and effect; as we have seen, in his account, the burning down of the glass factory around which the narrative revolves is necessary for the world to reveal its "infinite crystalline possibilities" and to stop being "a flat amorphous environment which ends at the edge of a gulf" (73; translation modified). And yet this latter remark is a reference to the parable of four men who row out to see whether the world is flat or not which occurs at the end of the film, *after* we have seen the factory burn down. For Deleuze, it seems, a cinematic sequence can be said somehow to *prevent* that which, in literal terms, follows it in the film.

A Partial Account of *Heart of Glass*, Guided by Deleuze

After the film's opening image of Hias among the mist and the cows we see time-lapse photography of clouds moving above forested Bavarian hills, culminating in a remarkable image in which the clouds passing through a valley take on the form of a river.[12] A peculiarly lurching transition—a dissolve appears to begin, only to be followed by a hard cut—takes us to an image of Hias, once again seen from behind, slightly silhouetted in the sunshine as he lies on his back on a hillside overlooking a valley, extending his right hand as if in blessing and proclaiming an apocalyptic vision: "I look into the distance, to the end of the world."

We continue to hear Hias's prophecy as Bavarian landscape is replaced by images of boiling mud and of waterfalls that share a bluish tint and a curious texture, almost as if they were photographed through a piece of fabric (see fig. 9.4). The images clearly represent

Figure 9.4. Hypnotic visions at the beginning of *Heart of Glass*. Source: *Heart of Glass* (1976).

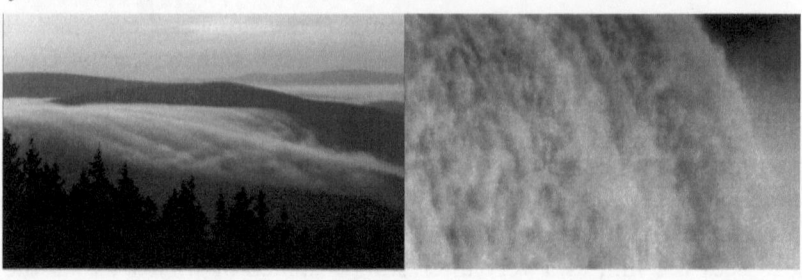

Hias's vision, and yet there is already ambiguity at work. Do the images show us what Hias is "literally" seeing (in his prophetic trance), or are they instead a kind of visual analogue, evoking in images that which the words also evoke? Another ambiguity involves the status of these images in relation to the earlier time-lapse clouds. Even if we decide that the blue-tinted images *do* represent what Hias is seeing, what about the clouds we saw previously? After all, Hias goes on to say that "the clouds will begin to race." This suggests, I think, one reason why Richard Roud is mistaken in his claim that the landscapes in *Heart of Glass* supplant the humans who are the film's "ostensible subject" (Roud 1980, 487), which is that the film continually prompts us to think about the relationship between the landscapes and the human subject, to keep asking *whose* view of the landscape—and what kind of view—we are being given. (We saw at the start of the chapter that this is true from the very beginning of the film—the opening three shots suggest that our view aligns with that of the character we initially see from behind, only to challenge that suggestion.) We are barely five minutes into the film and distinctions (such as that between a "real" image and a vision or hallucination) have been put into play while simultaneously having the boundaries between them blurred or rendered ambiguous, recalling Deleuze's notion of forms and conceptions that are "distinct, but capable of passing into one another" (Deleuze [1983] 1986, 188).

Eventually the rock music by the band Popul Vuh that has accompanied Hias's vision rises euphorically, and then fades to silence. We are then presented with a clear image of rocks in bright sunshine at the foot of a kind of ravine, surrounded by deep darkness. The camera pans up the ravine, revealing two bridges crossing its summit. Hias encounters four villagers (the first hypnotized actors we have seen), who are terrified by a giant they think one of their fellow villagers has seen. Hias tells them that it is all a matter of perspective (another instance of indiscernibility, or reversibility), and that the giant "was just the shadow of a dwarf." Hias then tells them, a little obliquely, about his vision of the burning factory: "I see a fire. And I see the glass factory." The next scene gives us the first instance of a visual mode that runs through much of the rest of the film, in which an interior is lit in dramatic chiaroscuro, showing characters and candles in a warm orange light surrounded by expanses that are often quite startlingly black, once again evoking eighteenth-century painting,[13] as well as demonstrating the virtuosity of the cinematographer Jörg Schmidt-Reitwein. The sense of heightened concentration on a limited number of objects which this visual presentation encourages is perhaps intended to evoke the experience of hypnosis. The glacial development of a bar fight between two hypnotized actors, which is the first thing we see filmed in this mode, and to which we return periodically over the next few minutes of the film, is both darkly comic and unsettling in its genuine oddness.

The film now begins to be organized according to a kind of parallel editing. Various narrative threads are interwoven, developing gradually. (These include the story of Wudy and Ascherl and their fight; the factory owner's increasingly mad search for the secret of the glass; what happens to Mühlbeck's wife; and Hias's wanderings in the woods.) We see Hias in the woods talking about the town's growing madness, which is followed by another lyrical sequence showing unpeopled landscapes (including images of Yellowstone National Park). The factory owner orders that Hias be sent for; thus, when he eventually arrives there is a sense of convergence, of the coming together of narrative threads according to what Deleuze would call a sensorimotor schema. (Hias is sent for; Hias arrives.) And yet the first thing Hias tells the factory owner is that he needs a hunter to kill a bear that is threatening the local bulls. It turns out that the impression of a causal link was just that—an impression generated by a fallacious *post hoc ergo propter hoc* inference. Hias visits the factory owner for his own reasons, and it just happens that he had also been sent for. (We are given no indication that he ever received the summons.) But despite this use of narrative misdirection—making coincidence look like causality—the film is much less narratively fragmentary and freewheeling than it first appears. Instead, we might say that it is low in redundancy; crucial pieces of narrative information are mentioned only sparingly, contributing to an atmosphere in which rationality seems alternately just within, or just out of, reach. We are likely to wonder what lies behind this strange, unexpected mention of a bear. Perhaps it has a symbolic or prophetic meaning? Our unpreparedness for this narrative detail allows the film to hide in plain sight its most straightforward interpretation—that Hias really believes that the village is threatened by a bear. The status of what we are seeing and hearing is, yet again, hard to make out; the clues that would clarify the status of the various possible interpretations approach indiscernibility, at least on one's first viewings of the film.

Although Deleuze does not explicitly acknowledge this, *Heart of Glass* differs from his accounts of *Aguirre* and *Fitzcarraldo* in that there is not a single hero who engages in an activity that is both heroic and sublime, depending on one's perspective. Instead, both the factory owner and Hias are engaged in quests of their own. Deleuze does not make explicit which actions in *Heart of Glass* are sublime and which heroic, as he does in his remarks about *Aguirre* and *Fitzcarraldo*. However, given that he refers to "the hypnotic creation of the glass ruby" and "the hallucinatory landscapes which prompt the search for the great abyss of the Universe" (Deleuze [1983] 1986, 189)—and recalling that the hypnotic dimension corresponds to "a heroic action which confronts the milieu on its own account," whereas the hallucinatory is connected to "the sublime action, always beyond" (188)—the implication is surely that the search for the secret of the ruby glass is heroic, while the quest for the edge of the world is sublime. *Heart of Glass*, however, does not present us with the same kind of megalomaniacal protagonist as do *Aguirre* and *Fitzcarraldo*, which of course take their names from these very protagonists. This dissimilarity between *Heart of Glass* and the other two films might also account for the oddity that, despite the apparent equation between the hypnotic dimension and the heroic action, Deleuze's example of the way in which "[t]he visionary's sublime plan failed in the large form" is that "the fire at the glass-works had no conclusion other than workmen picking up the pieces" (Deleuze [1983] 1986, 190), suggesting that the search for the ruby glass is instead the film's sublime aspect.

Deleuze describes the factory owner as "the visionary," but given that such a description applies much more readily to Hias, it seems more plausible to suggest that in this film the figure of the visionary is split in two. The details of the film's construction that we have been examining encourage us in the first instance to think that the madness lies wholly on the factory owner's side, so that Hias's "search for the great abyss of the Universe" (Deleuze [1983] 1986, 189) is uncontaminated by it. And yet we eventually come to realize that Hias has been motivated by a quest to destroy a nonexistent bear, an undertaking that seems just as mad as the factory owner's search for the secret of the glass. (It is important that the search for "the great abyss" is, of course, *not* Hias's search, but that of the men in the vision of his which ends the film.) The search for the secret of the glass and the search for the edge of the world are equally fruitless, but for different reasons. The secret of the glass has simply been lost, whereas a sphere has no edge. Though his means become increasingly insane, the factory owner's quest is the more rational of the two. The most charitable interpretation here seems to be that the confusion between the nature and status of the film's various quests is not an indication of the limitations or artificiality of Deleuze's categories so much as a further development of the film's exploration of indiscernible or reversible distinctions. (One might even speculate that the division of the "visionary" in two has a parallel in the connection, mentioned above, that Deleuze sees between *Heart of Glass* and *Citizen Kane.* Do the various quests in Herzog's film refract different aspects of the quest for Rosebud?)

As I mentioned at the start of this chapter, *Heart of Glass* ends with another of Hias's visions. Unlike the film's opening visions, the status of this one might initially appear relatively unambiguous. Having "killed" the "bear," Hias sits staring into a campfire, and begins relating his visions once again. There is an edit after he says "I see it quite clearly," showing us just what he has been describing. (He tells us, for example, "I see a man at the top of the cliffs," which is precisely what the film shows us.) But, as we have noted, Deleuze's interpretation is temporally rather peculiar, amounting—in another sense of "reversibility"—almost to running the film backwards. He tells us that for the world to stop being "an amorphous, flattened environment" (Deleuze [1985] 1989, 73; translation modified) such as we see at the end of the film (the lonely boat in the middle of a featureless sea, beneath a sky containing nothing but birds and a few unemphatic clouds) it needs to pass through the fire at the factory which we saw earlier, in order "to reveal infinite crystalline possibilities in itself" (73). The words Deleuze quotes to illustrate this revelation of possibilities ("the earth rises up from the waters, I see a new earth") come from Hias's opening prophecy, right at the beginning of the film. This temporal strangeness, or confusion about the relationship between sequentiality and causality, is not merely imposed by Deleuze onto the film. Hias himself renders the temporal status of his final vision problematic by announcing that he is seeing it "again," and the very reason that Hias is thrown into prison by the villagers after the fire is that they cannot distinguish between an event that precedes and an event that causes—committing their own *post hoc* fallacy, they reason that because he told them about the fire before it happened he must have been in some way responsible for it.

With regard to Deleuze's system, it would seem that the crucial question to ask about the film's concluding images is whether they are movement-images or time-images; and yet we have seen that the film as a whole partakes of both categories. Jacques Rancière has famously pointed out that "[t]he very same examples . . . can be used to illustrate the constitution of the any-space-whatevers of the affection-image and the constitution of the pure optical and sound situations of the time-image" (Rancière 2016, 112). Noting that Robert Bresson is another director whose work is discussed in both of the *Cinema* books, Rancière observes that "[i]t seems impossible . . . to isolate in the model filmmaker of the 'time-image' *any* 'time-images,' any images endowed with properties that would distinguish them from the 'movement-image'" (112; emphasis in original). The philosopher Anton Ford, however, notes that not all forms of generality operate according to the possibility (or the lack thereof) of pointing out the presence or absence of distinguishing features. Ford calls this kind of generality "accidental generality," distinguishing it from two other forms, one of which he calls "categorical generality." One cannot show what makes a horse an animal by subtracting everything that makes it a horse and seeing what is left over; there will be nothing remaining. Nor, Ford argues, can one define a horse by a list of "distinctive qualities," because "these qualities will be such as to logically depend on the species, in which case they cannot contribute to a non-circular account of it" (Ford 2011, 89). One might, for example, say that horses have four feet—but clams and mosquitos also have feet, and thus one will either underdetermine the characteristics of a horse's foot, or one will have to appeal to the concept "horse" in defining a horse's foot.[14] Ford's points apply to the ways we distinguish genus from species, not to how we distinguish different species within a genus. We can, of course, distinguish horses from clams and mosquitos, hence for Ford's argument to be relevant the time-image would have to be a species of the genus *movement-image*, or vice versa. Rancière's claim that the lack of distinguishing features means "that movement-image and time-image are by no means two types of images ranged in opposition, but two different points of view on the image" (Rancière 2016, 112–13) is, therefore, not conclusive. If we can think of one type of image as a species within the genus of the other type, then there could be no distinguishing features to point to in the first place.

Deleuze would presumably have rejected this account, given his insistence on the absolute distinction between the two types of images. But it seems to me that we might productively combine this idea with the *indiscernibility* which is at the heart of the account Deleuze offers of the "small form" of the action-image as well as the *reversibility* that is characteristic of the time-image.[15] Could it be that the "greatest crystal-images in the history of cinema" (Deleuze [1985] 1989, 73) come about because of the indiscernibility, or reversibility, of genus and species between movement-image and time-image? Is it plausible that what Deleuze finds so powerful about *Heart of Glass* is precisely the difficulty of deciding whether the final images of the boat sailing towards the horizon and the certain death of its occupants are *either* (1) a movement-image (the physical activity of rowing, the boat's progress)[16] as a species of time-image (the undecidable temporality of Hias's vision) *or* (2) a time-image (an archetypal representation of fruitless striving) as a species of movement-image (the aftermath of Hias's failure to effect any change within the village, epitomized by his failure to save the life of Ludmilla)?

These ambiguities relate directly to the film's ambiguities of agency and its investigations both of hypnotic imagery and hypnotized action. Just as the status of the images is so often reversible (movement-image versus time-image; actual image versus virtual image; hallucination versus hypnotic suggestion), we continually encounter actions with an apparently undecidable status. (The purest example of this is the question of whether Hias is fighting an imaginary bear or imagining that he is fighting a bear.) Bergson's early ideas about hypnosis, to which I referred earlier—according to which a hypnotized action is the purest possible example of a free action—might help us understand a remark which Raymond Bellour calls "mysterious and extreme" (Bellour 2014, 21); in the context of his discussion of Alain Resnais, Deleuze declares: "It is hypnosis which reveals thought to itself" (Deleuze [1985] 1989, 120). This suggests, it seems to me, a Cartesianism that both philosophers perpetuate despite themselves, according to which the self—our thinking—must be something fundamentally other than our bodily action in the world.[17] The logic of the early Bergson's ideas about hypnosis is that, were one never to be hypnotized, one might never express one's true self; note the absolute incompatibility between such a view and the formula that Elizabeth Anscombe offers in her remarkable analysis of intention: "I *do* what *happens*" (Anscombe [1957] 2000, 52 [§29]; emphases in original).[18] Contrast, also, Anscombe's account with Deleuze's claim that subjectivity "appears as soon as there is a gap between a received and an executed movement, an action and a reaction, a stimulation and a response" (Deleuze [1985] 1989, 45). Such an account appears to preclude the notion that subjectivity might appear precisely *in* "an executed movement." (See the introduction for more discussion relevant to this point.) Hypnosis "reveals thought to itself" because, for Deleuze, it is only by suppressing the normal situation—in which action (so it appears) expresses thought—that we can access pure thought, thought in itself; that thinking can truly come face to face with thinking.[19]

A skeptic might retort that *Heart of Glass* demonstrates exactly what the world would look like if Bergson and Deleuze were right about this. The film's disturbingly ambivalent sense of agency reveals how human action would appear if subjectivity were separable from it, if we were unable to be confident that we see people in what they do.[20] The hypnosis we see so often in, for example, Weimar films such as *The Cabinet of Dr. Caligari* (Robert Weine, 1920) and *Dr. Mabuse, the Gambler* (Fritz Lang, 1922) might disturb our confidence regarding free will, but it does not attack the idea of agency in itself; what appears to be the agency of one character turns out ultimately to have been the agency of another, namely, the scientist-hypnotist (Caligari or Mabuse). But, although the startling counterintuitiveness of Bergson's account of hypnosis certainly has its appeal, experiencing *Heart of Glass* and its world of hypnosis *sans* hypnotist (there is no hypnotist within the diegesis) ultimately reaffirms the commonsense notion that a hypnotized world would not be a world of pure free action but a world without agency.[21] The ambiguities of movement-image versus time-image that Deleuze discovers in *Heart of Glass* leave indeterminate in what sense anything can truly be said to *happen* in the film at all; these ambiguities highlight crucial aspects of the figuration at work in the film, but its sheer strangeness is better elucidated by Anscombe's account of agency than by that which Deleuze finds in it. Herzog's movie is thus both a beautiful instantiation of some of Deleuze's most important ideas about film and a profound challenge to their implications for our understanding of human activity.

Part Four

Tarkovsky and Reichardt

10

"You Can't Imagine How Terrible It Is to Make the Wrong Choice"

Faith, Agency, and Self-pity in Andrei Tarkovsky's *Stalker*

IN ANDREI TARKOVSKY's *Stalker* (1979), the eponymous protagonist leads two other men into and out of a mysterious Zone containing an equally mysterious Room at its heart.[1] The question of how best to understand both *Stalker* and the Stalker is a matter of continuing critical debate. As a contribution to this debate, this chapter fundamentally disagrees with Mark Le Fanu's claim that "if one regards the supernatural a jot less sympathetically than Tarkovsky and his protagonists do . . . the whole of his drama, and with it a great part of his claims as a film-maker, dissolves into a bundle of gestures" (Le Fanu 1987, 95–96). My approach has resonances, instead, with that of Michael J. Griffin and Dara Waldron, who respond to Fredric Jameson's famous accusation that *Stalker* is a "lugubrious religious fable" (Jameson 1992, 92) with the proposition "that what might be perceived as the lugubriousness of Tarkovsky's adaptation is part of its poetic point" (Griffin and Waldron 2007, 257). My aim is to show that one can regard certain aspects of *Stalker*—in particular the character of the Stalker himself, played by Alexander Kaidanovsky—with a great deal less than full sympathy, and nonetheless be left with a powerful and coherent film. We might usefully view it as *about* faith rather than as *requiring* faith in order to be appreciated.[2]

This chapter takes certain puzzling and unattractive features of *Stalker*'s protagonist—centrally, his self-pity—and traces what happens if we think them through to their conclusions, rather than either ignoring them, explaining them away, or dismissing them as a failing. Critics, whether sympathetic to the film or not, have for the most part taken it as largely symbolic, or at any rate as not legible in terms of subtleties of motivation. They have thereby tended to take the Stalker at what is supposed to be "face value," encouraged by some of the director's comments about the film. This chapter argues that to do so is in fact to accept what certain characters in the film—notably his wife—believe about him as well as, crucially, what he believes about himself. But if we can open up a distance between film and character then rejecting these accounts in no way entails rejecting the film as a whole. It will, however, entail an attention to the ironies and ambiguities that the Stalker's self-pity creates, and to the fresh perspective it affords on the film's other ironies and ambiguities.

Self-pity is not a subject that has received a great deal of attention in film, even though, as Glenn W. Most puts it, "there seem in general to be few passions which in our daily lives we have such ample opportunity to observe expressed so richly, so deeply, so sincerely, both around us, and within us, as self-pity" (Most 2003, 58). I hope to show some ways in which it is a rich subject for inquiry, particularly because it reflects on our understanding of agency, and on an agent's relation to their own agency. This chapter follows Robert Pippin (not to mention G. W. F. Hegel and G. E. M. Anscombe) in assuming that

> the meaning of agency ... is not properly understood as a timeless metaphysical issue, that the line between agents and impaired agents and nonagents is one that communities draw in all sorts of different ways over various periods. ... [A]gency is something like one of those "thick" concepts [his other examples are loyalty, moralism, self-righteousness, freedom, self-deceit, honor, justice, betrayal, selfishness; I propose to add self-pity], a norm of sorts, the conceptual content of which we can only understand in its variegated and complex uses for a community at a time. (Pippin 2012, 24–25)

The question of what we might learn about conceptions of agency and self-pity as they were specifically understood in Soviet society towards the end of the 1970s is beyond both the scope of this chapter and my own competence, but it is a question that would be well worth exploring, and one for which the study of films would be valuable. (One plausible suggestion is that the fact that *Stalker* "explores themes of disaffection, alienation, and demoralisation, which make action less and less possible" has its roots in "the collective loss of belief in historical agency driven by . . . above all, the Thaw—and a related scepticism towards the overarching cultural-political ideology of Socialist Realism" [Powell-Jones 2015, 77].) But while I will not attempt such wider contextual research here, I can and will attempt to clarify the notions of agency and self-pity such as they appear in this particular film. My itinerary is as follows: I shall first discuss the Stalker's self-pity, and explore some of its interpretative and methodological consequences, before expanding the focus to include the Stalker's companions. I then explore aspects of the film's reflexivity, showing how to do so is not to depart from the kind of naive reading defended in this book's introduction, before concluding the discussion by reflecting on its implications for our understanding of agency.

Fool, Pseudo-fool, or Dangerously Deluded?

A number of critics have seen self-pity in the Stalker. Le Fanu observes that "[t]ime and again Kaidanovsky's features, the whole posture of his body, seem to be wracked by perplexity: more than this, by self-pity" (Le Fanu 1987, 98). Vida T. Johnson and Graham Petrie see this as a kind of mistake on Tarkovsky's part that somewhat undermines what they take to be his intentions for the film:

> Though this "breaking" [of the "intellectual and spiritual hardness" of Writer and Professor] does seem to happen, at least to some extent, by the end of their journey, he [Stalker] appears—surprisingly—not to accept or recognize this. His expressions of despair to his wife on his return home, and his sense of failure as he condemns his companions for their lack of belief and their materialism and complains that no one needs him or the Room, have

the effect of undercutting this sense of possible change for the viewer and help to give the film a bleaker and more despairing tone than Tarkovsky seems to have intended. (Johnson and Petrie 1994, 149)

In keeping with the approach taken elsewhere in this book, however, I suggest that we will do better to discover Tarkovsky's intentions *in what is accomplished in the film*.

It has often been noted that the Stalker has affinities with that peculiarly Russian figure, one which continually appears in Tarkovsky's cinema, namely, the *iurodivyi* or holy fool. Indeed, he is explicitly referred to as such by Writer (Anatoly Solonitsyn), and, as Robert Efird explains, in her monologue towards the end of the film the Stalker's wife (Alisa Freindlikh) "describes her husband as *blazhennyi*, or blessed, a rather explicit reference to the most famous of all Russian holy fools, Vasilii Blazhennyi, and a term widely used interchangeably with *iurodivyi*" (Efird 2014, 4). With no further context than cinema and literature—thinking of other holy fools in Tarkovsky's cinema, such as Durochka (Irma Raush) in *Andrei Rublev*, or of figures that draw on the idea in Russian literature, such as, most famously, Prince Myshkin in Dostoyevsky's *The Idiot*—one might assume the Holy Fool to be simply a kind of saintly innocent. In fact, however, the notion is more complex and involves a fundamental paradox, as Sergey A. Ivanov explains: "The Orthodox Church holds that the holy fool voluntarily takes upon himself the mask of insanity in order that he may thereby conceal his own perfection from the world and thereby avoid the vanity of worldly praise" (Ivanov 2006, 1–2). Stalker's abject behavior and acceptance of Writer's description of him as a "louse" might indeed be an attempt to "avoid the vanity of worldly praise." His profession (or vocation) of Stalker draws him to company, albeit limited company: those people he leads through the Zone to the Room. Tarkovsky's own defense of the Stalker is based on his idiocy, on the notion that his faith is an "unconscious force," one "that leads him away from being common, that renders him ridiculous, idiotic, but that reveals to him his own singularity, his spirituality" (Gianvito 2006, 168). But the notion "that the holy fool voluntarily takes upon himself the mask of insanity" substantially complicates this idea.

How calculated, then, is then Stalker's behavior? Why, for example, does he force his companions to go before him? In the screenplay, Stalker suggests a fairly plausible practical reason: "If anything happens to me, you'll never get out of here" (Tarkovsky 1999, 403). Surely, though, sending them first renders them more vulnerable to the Zone's dangers; does he, instead, want to test their faith? There would be no test of faith if Writer and Professor (Nikolai Grinko) were already confident of their safety, having seen Stalker pass safely in front of them. The existence of border guards indicates clearly enough that some kind of Zone really exists, even if it tells us nothing of exactly what it is or why it is fenced off and defended, but we have only Stalker's word for the specific dangers to be faced in the Zone. Writer says in his long monologue in the Dune Room that "all this is someone's idiotic invention."[3] Stalker confirms this, in a way, when he informs his companions that "at each moment, it's as if we construct it according to our state of mind." Outside the Room, Writer asks Professor: "Who told you about the Zone, about Porcupine, about this Room?" and gets the answer, "he did," meaning Stalker. The question comes after Writer elucidates the reason that Porcupine, Stalker's former teacher, killed himself: he visited the Room which supposedly grants one's deepest wish in the wake of his brother's death, but instead of his brother coming back to life Porcupine found himself becoming immensely rich. The story of Porcupine could conceivably be an invention of Stalker's, which he hopes that his companions will decipher. This raises the question of whether Writer, at this point, understands something that Stalker hadn't seen, or succeeds in a hermeneutic task set for him by Stalker. If the answer is the former, then Stalker comes to seem rather dim; we might ask ourselves whether Stalker as we see him appears to have the imagination to have made up the story himself, although we should also remember the abundance of books that the Stalker's house contains which, Alina Birzache argues, show that "this broken man . . . is actually a well-read intellectual" (Birzache 2016, 89). But if the answer is the latter, why is Stalker so disappointed by what must surely be the understandable decision of Writer and Professor not to enter the Room? Why does he not consider the possibility that their decision shows humility rather than a lack of faith? We shall return to this question.

Robert Bird articulates a very likely response to the Stalker's possible manipulations when he discusses the "loop" via which Stalker and Writer find their way back to Professor: "[I]t is difficult to rid oneself of the suspicion that he was actually leading the Writer, so to speak, up the garden path. The Stalker's strictures are improvised, not to protect his visitors from unknown dangers, but solely to stamp his authority on their quest" (Bird 2008, 163). There is also the business with the matches, when Stalker suggests they draw lots to see who will go first through the tunnel called the Meat Grinder. Stalker simply ignores Writer's suggestion that a volunteer would be preferable, and the way that he throws away the second match out of sight of his companions means we are likely to conclude that Writer's later accusation has some merit: "Do you think I didn't see you offer me two long matches?" The evidence on this point is equivocal. We do in fact see Stalker break the matches (he faces us, shielding the matches from the others with his body), but it is unclear (at least to me) whether he breaks them both to the same length or breaks only one. The shooting script, adapted by Arkady and Boris Strugatsky from their 1972 novel *Roadside Picnic* with Tarkovsky's uncredited input, is more explicit about the fact that Stalker *does* cheat with the matches, but it also more clearly relates his reasons to his faith. In that script, the sequence that in the film takes place in the Dune Room happens before the Meat Grinder, and thus Stalker is impressed by the fact that the Zone lets Writer through: "The matches—that was nonsense. Back there, in the hall, the Zone took pity on you. It became obvious that if anyone were fated to pass through the mincer, that person was you. Only you!" (Tarkovsky 1999, 408). But in the finished film the Dune Room, where Writer is "let off," is where the characters arrive *after* going through the Meat Grinder, thus making Stalker's manipulation, if that is what it is, harder to understand.

Stalker's petulance and self-pity come through most strongly towards the end of *Stalker*, but in so doing they are the culmination of an emotional trajectory that runs across the entire film. At the beginning, Stalker ignores his wife's pleas that he stay behind with a calm determination. At one point he looks at her with what appears to be genuine sympathy, then pulls away firmly but not violently. He does not appear irritated; rather, her words can simply have no effect on his resolution to visit the Zone once again. When she tells him that he'll end up in prison again, his reply, "I'm imprisoned everywhere" is delivered with a small quaver in his voice that could represent a self-pitying fatalism, but his back is to the camera, underplaying this emotional dimension. In the bar and during the dangerous journey to the outskirts of the Zone in the jeep, Stalker appears both nervous and determined. When they do arrive in the Zone, he exhibits pure, peaceful joy as he lies in the grass, his eyes closed, gently exhaling his tension. When he returns to his companions he is, for almost the only time in the film, calm, cool and collected. Subsequently, however, his wretchedness increases with the emotional intensity. The first real sign of petulance is, perhaps, when he screams at the other two: "I demand discipline!" Later, when he stands up after being thrown down by Writer, he snivels and wipes his nose, his face covered in water, tears, and blood, his eyes looking bleakly offscreen. His voice becomes more and more wracked by sobs, angrier but also higher in pitch and more imploring. After being again thrown to the ground and berated by Writer we see Stalker from a higher angle, looking up pathetically at his companions, eyes red with tears, his speech tumbling out like a child attempting to justify itself.

These less attractive aspects of his character reach their greatest intensity in his final scene, as he lies in bed, tended to by his wife. Covered in sweat, eyes painfully screwed up, he berates his companions.

Figure 10.1. Petulance. *Source: Stalker* (1979).

If there have, earlier, been certain indications of a parallel between Christ and Stalker—most prominently in Stalker's recitation of the story of the road to Emmaus (to be discussed below), and Writer's presumably parodic fashioning of a crown of thorns—then Stalker's last appearance almost seems like a parody of Jesus's agony in the garden of Gethsemane. He doesn't ask for the cup to be taken away from him, while agreeing to accept it if it is truly his lot. Rather, he whines that nobody seems to want a messiah any more: "Nobody believes. Not only those two. Nobody." (Though there is certainly something unattractive in the Stalker's wife's vision of married life as involving unconditional devotion to her husband, in her final monologue she avoids self-pity more successfully than he does, instead expressing the beauty of joy that is surrounded by sorrow. She gradually masters her tears, her voice strengthens, and it seems like conviction rather than special pleading when she declares that "if there were no sorrow in our lives, it wouldn't be better. It would be worse. Because then there would be no happiness either.")

Figure 10.2. Self-pity. *Source: Stalker* (1979).

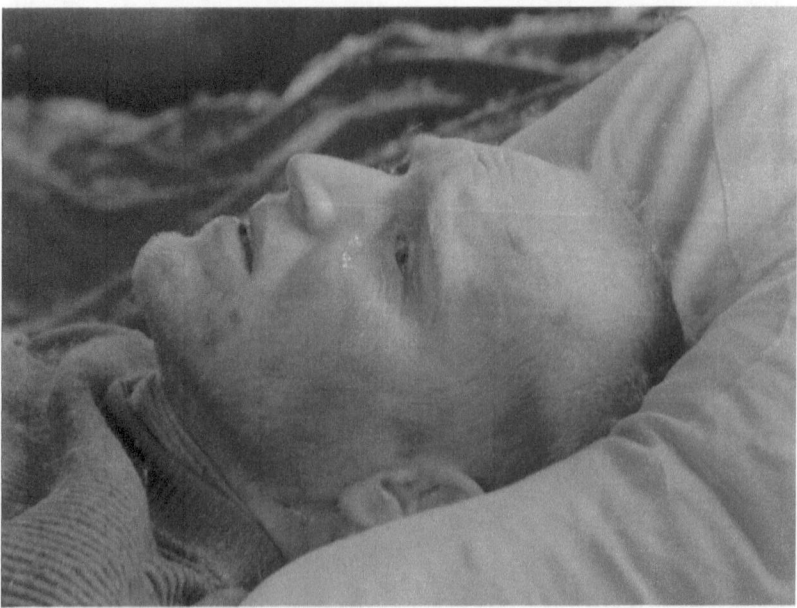

We might ask whether or not self-pity is compatible with the essential humility that so many have seen in the Stalker. At one point he extols softness (the same Russian word is also translated as weakness) as a virtue, associating it, in his prayer for his companions, with youth and flexibility: "May they laugh at their own passions. . . . But above all, may they believe in themselves and become as helpless as children. For softness is great and strength is worthless. When a man is born, he is soft and pliable. When he dies, he is strong and hard. . . . That which has become hard will not triumph." The elements of this prayer concerning softness and hardness derive from the ancient Chinese philosopher Laozi (Tarkovsky 1994, 147). But Stalker's petulance might be seen less as the expression of a childlike innocence than of a much more culpable childishness. Why does Stalker not recognize in himself the very same failing he berates his companions for? He certainly never seems even close to "laugh[ing] at [his] own passions," as he prays that his companions may do; his own devotion to the Zone seems to have become extremely "hard," hence his final despair. Given the film's explicit references to Christianity we should remember that despair is a sin; for Catholics it is a mortal sin. Although Orthodox Christianity does not have quite the same notion, despair is a very serious sin in eastern forms of Christianity as well.

So, too, is idolatry. (See chapter 6 for more on the subject.) What happens to the aforementioned parallels that the film draws between Stalker and Christ when we pay heed to the fact that Christianity clearly exists in the film's world, as indicated by the citations from scripture? What should a faithful Christian's attitude to the Zone be? In a Christian allegory such as C. S. Lewis's *Chronicles of Narnia* this particular problem never arises because Jesus does not exist as such in Narnia; to worship Aslan *is* to worship Jesus. But here the question is more delicate and generates another paradox or, at least, an ambiguity. If there were no Christian material in the film, the allegory could be straightforward, but since there is, the question is raised as to whether Stalker's faith is idolatrous. Is his final despair related to his inability to recognize that his faith has been misdirected? This notion does in fact have some support from the director. His diary entry for August 26, 1977, as translated by Kitty Hunter-Blair, refers to the character of the Stalker, rethought from the version that appears in the source novel, as needing to be "a slave, a believer, a pagan of the Zone"

(Tarkovsky 1994, 147). Johnson and Petrie claim that this "makes little sense," and offer instead "a believing slave and apostle of the Zone" (Johnson and Petrie 1994, 304n2, 138). But a middle ground is offered by Muireann Maguire's translation of Evgeny Tsymbal's account of the film's preproduction, where the passage appears as "the Zone's slave, disciple, pagan" (Tsymbal 2015, 276).

At the close of the extraordinary dream sequence in the center of the film, Stalker mutters the story of the road to Emmaus from the Gospel of Luke (Luke 24:13–18), in which Jesus appears after his resurrection to two disciples, who initially do not recognize him. Johnson and Petrie analyze this sequence as follows:

> As he speaks there is a cut to Professor lying down, with his eyes closed, and the camera then tracks slowly along his body to show Writer resting his head against Professor, also with his eyes closed. The camera stops on Writer's face with the words "But their eyes were holden that they should not know him"—at which point Writer opens his eyes. The camera then tracks back to Professor's face and stops there on the words of Cleopas, as he speaks to, but does not recognise, Jesus. Although Professor's eyes are now open, the very specific matching of camera movement and words here clearly suggests that Writer has the capacity for redemption (opening his eyes) while the more pragmatic Professor has the capacity to see but does not yet use it. (Johnson and Petrie 1994, 146)

This analysis seems to me a little far-fetched, and to underplay the ambiguity of the scene. On what basis does the fact of Writer opening his eyes override the text ("their eyes were holden") whereas in the case of Professor the text takes precedence over the fact that his eyes are open (he has, after all, opened them since we last saw him, earlier in the very same shot)? The sequence begins with Stalker waking up, opening his eyes (looking directly into the camera), sitting up and glancing across at his sleeping companions (checking that they are still asleep?) before beginning his recitation from Luke. The subsequent gazes of both men are directly at the camera, and thus directly at Stalker, and both are quietly penetrating (not quite accusatory but certainly with a note of gentle skepticism) despite the fact that the two men have just woken up (see fig. 10.3). The shot that pans over the men as they wake up is an echo of the film's very first horizontal dolly from above, which moves from a bedside table, over Stalker's wife, his daughter, and Stalker himself in bed, and back again. When we first pass over the wife, her eyes are already open, but only just, such that one could mistake them for being closed (we see only her right profile). When the camera passes back over her, she has not changed the position of her body but her eyes are now wide open.

There is, then, an ambiguity as to whether the gazes of Writer and Professor indicate that they recognize Stalker's resemblance to Christ or catch him out thinking that he resembles Him. After both men look at Stalker we cut to the same view of the back of his head we saw before when he began his recitation. He turns round and asks, "You awake?" Did he interrupt his quotation of Luke *because* they woke up? I find here—mostly from the quality of the gazes of Writer and Professor, but also from the way that Stalker's question might express uncertainty over whether or not he has been overheard—a hint that Stalker has been caught out by the other two, suggesting that he may have delusions of grandeur. Geoff Dyer describes the situation well, in his deliberately facetious style: "They really are sitting there listening, both thinking the same thing: Has this Stalker of theirs got a Messiah complex?" (Dyer 2012, 135). The wife's monologue at the end of the film renders almost explicit the parallels between Christ and Stalker ("when he came up to me and said 'Come with me,' I went"; compare, for example, Matthew 4:19–20). But we would do well to consider how disconcerting the fact that he tells the Emmaus story *himself* might be for that interpretation. The Stalker seems to

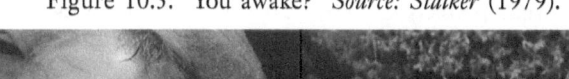

Figure 10.3. "You awake?" *Source: Stalker* (1979).

exhibit signs not only of sinful despair and idolatrous devotion (to the Zone) but also a possibly blasphemous hubris.

Before leaving this subject, we should not forget the diary entry Tarkovsky wrote on January 28, 1979, when the film was very nearly completed, concerning his idea of making another version of the film with the same actors in which "Stalker starts forcibly to drag people to the Room and turns into a 'votary' a 'fascist.' 'Bullying them into happiness'" (Tarkovsky 1994, 169). This might seem like a project for a kind of reversal or inversion of the film, but I hope to have shown why it could also be considered less as a negative image of *Stalker* than as a way of strengthening threads that are, in the film as we have it, present but understated.

Inner and Outer Realities

Efird is correct that "there are indications that the room itself may be solely the invention of the Stalker as a means for testing the faith of his companions—though the film, much like the character, is perhaps deliberately murky in this area" (Efird 2014, 5). In saying this one has the director's imprimatur: Tarkovsky told Aldo Tassone that "in the Strugatsky story, the desires were truly fulfilled, whereas in the script this remains a mystery. You don't know whether this is true or whether it's the Stalker's fantasy" (Gianvito 2006, 55). Not only were the fantastic science fiction elements of the original narrative pared away, but so was any confirmation of the existence of the miraculous, with just two possible exceptions: the mysterious voice that calls Writer back and the telekinetic powers of Stalker's daughter Monkey (Natasha Abramova) in the final scene. This puts the emphasis on faith itself; if the Room were proved to be efficacious, not to believe in it would be irrational, rather than a sign of lack of faith.[4]

In questioning the precise status of the Zone and the Room we are dealing with a question both of diegesis—because the question is active for the characters in the fictional world—and of narration in the broadest sense, which is to say a question concerning the film's narrative mode: realist, fantastic, allegorical, and so forth. The Zone, and the Room, can be interpreted as reflecting the Stalker's consciousness both diegetically, in terms of the plot (are they his inventions?), and formally, as a kind of pathetic fallacy (does the way the film represent them give us access to the way Stalker sees them?). Self-pity provides a way of articulating these two aspects. In a 1965 article on self-pity, the psychiatrist Eugen Kahn writes that "[t]he oversensitive person"—a type to which the Stalker could very reasonably be said to belong—"feels himself, as it were, constantly threatened by the malice of the environment" (Kahn 1965, 447). Self-pity serves, in *Stalker*, both as a means for creating particular kinds of narrative ambiguity (is the Zone dangerous or is the Stalker so self-pitying that he sees danger everywhere?) and as an object that these same ambiguities can be used to explore (what kinds of self-pity are displayed in the film?).

It is, then, possible to interpret *Stalker* not merely in affective or allegorical terms, but by taking account of a *character's* outlook, their own acts of (conscious or unconscious) narrativizing. This involves a complex series both of blurrings and of separations; it requires us to interpret the film's action as taking place in some kind of world, about which we can make judgments concerning truth and falsity, honesty and hypocrisy, self-knowledge and the lack thereof—judgments which would be either impossible or inappropriate with respect to a purely affective or allegorical reading. To perceive a character's narrativizing as such, we need a distance between the character and "the film" that a strictly allegorical reading will find hard to maintain. This is a point of contact between *Stalker* and some of the aspects of film noir that Pippin addresses. Pippin defends the ending of Orson Welles's *The Lady from Shanghai* (1947)—in which Michael O'Hara (Welles) departs the funhouse leaving behind a dying Elsa (Rita Hayworth)—against Andrew Britton's claim that it is "indisputably, one of the cinema's most disgraceful endings" (Britton 1992, 219). Pippin insists that "we are given several indications throughout . . . that we are, in effect, *in Michael's novel* and that one of the purposes of that novel seems to be to allow him to put this sort of narrative together and try to make it credible, above all to himself" (Pippin 2012, 72; emphasis in original). Even though he may be an intellectual, the Stalker is certainly not a novelist; but *Stalker*, too, gives us access to the way that its protagonist constructs his world. For Michael that process is largely retrospective, whereas the Stalker actually tries to bring people with him *into* his own world ("Here we are, home at last," are his first words upon entering the Zone). A major contrast between Michael and the Stalker is that Michael keeps telling himself that he is a fool (or a "boob"), that he was deceived (including by himself), which the Stalker never does. But Pippin's argument is that Michael thereby avoids recognizing other crucial ways in which he was self-deceived, specifically concerning his own capacity for agency: he blames his foolishness rather than his failure to act differently. My claim is that the Stalker's self-pity is similarly exculpatory, and enables him, too, to avoid any really honest assessment of his own actions.

The very way the film represents the entry into the Zone can even be read as a dramatization of what we might call the passage into pathetic fallacy, a process both gradual and sudden. During the long sequence on the trolley car, close-ups on the faces of the three protagonists emphasize their psychology but leave inaccessible exactly what they are thinking about. The sound is very gradually transformed electronically, introducing reverberations that generate an altered sense of space but are also clearly artificial; we are entering "another" kind of space. Suddenly the image changes, the exact moment unpredictable no matter how many times one has seen the film, and we pass from sepia into color, into a world of green that is somehow both faded and ordinary *and* wholly extraordinary. After an initial, unpeopled, point-of-view shot that dollies left to represent the moving trolley, pauses, and then pans right to represent the gaze of the protagonists (ending up by emphasizing a partly collapsed electricity pylon that looks distinctly like a crucifix), the film's second color shot is in mid-long shot, placing the three protagonists in the landscape, yet not expansively so. There is a prominent foreground, littered with debris; we cannot clearly see the vista that the characters, placed at the top of a ridge, would be able to see. The result is an unstable balance between figure and environment, between seeing a character in a situation and seeing how the character sees their situation. This kind of blurring of inside and outside, which the film exploits increasingly from now on, is supremely suited both to allegorical and psychological ends: the outside either *signifies* the meaning inside (allegory) or it *expresses* it (psychology). These two possibilities are not necessarily incompatible or mutually destructive. (Pippin makes some remarks to similar effect, commenting that the notion that "one has to choose between treating characters as persons *or* treating fictional entities as properties of or instantiations of structure, words, images, social or libidinal forces, and so forth" seems to him "a false duality" [Pippin

2012, 108; emphasis in original].) By emphasizing the possibility of other ways of reading *Stalker*, then, I certainly do not wish to deny its allegorical or symbolic dimensions.

Stalker and His Companions

It is a little strange how frequently one still encounters readings of the film that unquestioningly interpret the journey of Writer and Professor through the lens of the Stalker's own judgment. Efird, for example, observes that "though his two companions, known only as Writer and Professor, entrust their lives to this knowledge [that is, Stalker's knowledge of the Zone], they exhibit little faith in his competence and treat him derisively throughout" (Efird 2014, 4). In fact it is Writer who is derisive towards Stalker; Professor treats him with respect throughout. Even when disobeying the instruction not to return for his backpack, Professor—though clearly a little irritated at Stalker for not, he thinks, having made it clear enough that they were moving on—makes no aggressive or sarcastic remarks but simply slips away when the others are not watching. Comments such as Efird's are still encountered despite Johnson and Petrie's more accurate account, which is worthwhile quoting at length:

> Critics as varied as Maya Turovskaya, Peter Green, and Gilbert Adair all suggest that Writer and Professor learn little from their experience. . . . It does in fact seem to be the case that both Writer and Professor learn a good deal about themselves during their journey and that both change as a result. Professor listens to Stalker's pleas not to use his bomb and finally throws it away and, though Writer accuses him of being a time-serving careerist, Professor tells his boss on the phone that he is no longer afraid of him, and acts accordingly. . . . Writer's self-disgust is projected outward in his cynicism and sarcasm toward his companions, his readers, and the world in general (his caustic humor is inadequately rendered in the subtitles). . . . His theatrical bravado gives way to the simple gesture of putting his arm around Stalker—whom he had unmercifully ridiculed

and even beaten—while the thoughtful expression on his face on their return to the bar suggests that a genuine transformation has at least begun with him. (Johnson and Petrie 1994, 147–49)

The question for viewers of the film, then, is to what extent we feel, with Stalker, the other two's lack of faith, or whether—as I think is more plausible—we see Stalker as having, at least to some degree, convinced them with the example of his own faith. Returning to the issues addressed above, we might even consider that Stalker *himself* is shown as lacking faith, in the final analysis, precisely because he can't recognize this himself.

There are also more delicate paradoxes at work here. Johnson and Petrie note that Stalker successfully prevents Professor from destroying the Room. But would it be too convoluted to consider that Stalker's success in stopping Professor from detonating his bomb indicates Professor's *loss* of faith? It is Writer who paints him as an arch-rationalist ("miracles are outside your experience"), concerned only with soulless acts of measurement, but this expresses the Writer's conviction that scientific truth is mere tautology ("There's Triangle ABC, which equals Triangle A prime, B prime, C prime") more than anything about Professor himself. Professor identifies himself with science rather shruggingly: "I'd say I'm a physicist"; "in a sense, I'm a scientist." It is *Professor*, not Stalker, who first imposes the rule of not going back, when he prevents Writer from going back to get cigarettes in the bar. He might even appear a little credulous, passing on the story that Stalker's daughter has no legs when in fact she merely cannot walk. On a second or subsequent viewing, we should remember to read everything Professor says in terms of the dramatic irony that he is so convinced of the room's efficacy that he wants to destroy it. Writer also has a secret weapon with him, of course: we learn at the end of the Meat Grinder tunnel that he has been carrying a gun the whole time. But he relinquishes it without a struggle. (An aspect of the film that remains puzzling to me is Professor's attempt, at the end of part one, to get the others to leave him behind and go on to the Room alone. This must surely mean that he has decided not to go through with his plan to detonate his bomb. But why?)

Professor's initial faith is essentially political: he responds to Writer's paean to the selflessness of art by pointing out that people are still dying of hunger. But he is caught in the familiar paradox of wanting to be a dictator in order to rid the world of dictators. His response, before they even reach the Zone, to Writer's struggles with authentic self-knowledge—"I want world supremacy, at the very least"—is not, in truth, as sarcastic as he intends. When he eventually recognizes this he has in a sense lost the faith with which he entered the Zone, has become resigned to let things take their own course rather than to intervene in an attempt to make the world a better place.[5] Stalker's companions *are* changed, but he does not recognize it. He could be seen as a catalyst in a rather precise chemical sense: he changes the others without himself being changed.

The Reflexive Zone

We have, then, noted what seems to be a rather acute lack of self-awareness in the Stalker. We find rather more indications of self-awareness, not in Stalker, but in *Stalker*. Even though the wife's direct address to the audience was not the initial conception for the monologue, because "the scene was shot in the bar, with the speech clearly delivered to Writer and Professor, and was moved to its present position only during editing," the effect is not only striking but connected with other patterns in the film (Johnson and Petrie 1994, 283). To begin with, it is an echo of a less extensive direct address at the beginning of the film: Freindlich also looks directly into the camera just before the Stalker leaves, as the wife shouts after him, "Go, then! And may you rot there!" Another example comes during Stalker's monologue on the nature of the Zone at the end of part 1; when he repeats, "this is the Zone," he too looks directly at the camera.

Dyer notes the games played with montage and point of view soon after the entry into the Zone, giving the impression that we are sharing Professor's point of view, only for all three men to come into frame, thus creating "a disquieting sense of there being an extra pair of eyes . . . like an additional consciousness (that of the Zone itself?), alert and waiting" (Dyer 2012, 81). Another notable instance of this occurs during Writer's long monologue in the Dune Room, which is captured in a single long take. The camera slowly closes in on Writer as he sits on the edge of a large pipe, and then moves around him, consistently framing him from slightly above, which

Figure 10.4. "This is the Zone." *Source: Stalker* (1979).

combines with the way Solonitsyn regularly looks into the lens to give the impression that he is speaking to someone standing next to him. At the end of his speech, however, after a particularly sustained and intense look directly into the camera, Writer looks down and a cut shows Stalker and Professor in long shot, standing many yards away, still on the other side of the room, as they were when the monologue commenced. The film's tendency to blur the distinction between *what* a character sees and *how* they see is, in these instances, taken a stage further, in that they indicate somebody's seeing but not who that somebody might be. (Compare the discussion of suture in chapter 8.) Responding to these elements of the film, Bird remarks that the Zone "cannot simply be identified with the camera. The Zone is where one goes to see one's innermost desires. It is, in short, the cinema," while Dyer simply states that "[t]he Zone *is* film" (Bird 2008, 69; Dyer 2012, 81; emphasis in original). But, as Bird indeed warns, one should not be too simplistic regarding this kind of identification. The metaphor of the Zone allows these techniques to equivocate, or make some kind of equivalence, between designating these uncanny unlocalized gazes as representations of the Zone (a fantastic yet diegetic explanation), as an engagement with the audience (direct address), or as an acknowledgment by the film of itself (reflexivity).

The notion that connects *Stalker*'s reflexivity with its theme of faith—that connects the Zone as cinema with the Zone as the Stalker's pathetic fallacy—could, more neutrally, be called belief. (Self-pity, as I have already suggested and will say more about later, is shown by the film to be a means of avoiding confrontation with a lack of self-belief.) I disagree with David Foster's characterization of "*Stalker*'s foregrounding of reflexivity, at the expense of maintaining a coherent narrative and narrative space," because the film's reflexivity is profoundly connected with the way that it generates its narrative space (Foster 2000, 315). Our sense of the Zone—which is not *only* a narrative issue, but is nonetheless central to the narrative—comes about, in part, precisely *through* reflexive techniques. Dyer links Stalker's insistence on belief to our belief, as viewers, in the final scene of Monkey's telekinesis. We can't see how it's done no matter how closely we look, he claims, and "that's the wonder of cinema."[6] In fact it *is* at times possible to just about see the wire that pulls the jar and glasses. We are helped in this by the presence of the white fluffy seeds that drift through the air in this scene (as they also did in the previous scene of Stalker in bed). The mechanics of the scene could, had Tarkovsky wished, have been made harder to perceive (if the fluff had been left out). The poem by Fyodor Tyuchev that Monkey reads is all about the gaze (even though it claims that there's "greater charm" in "lowered" eyes), and so is the scene. Monkey's gaze makes the glasses move and, perhaps, makes the dog be quiet. Through our gaze as viewers we interpret the scene, and wonder how it is done; what Bird calls "the crossing of gazes" is crucial (Bird 2008, 223). I do not think it would be going too far to compare the final sequence with the Club Silencio sequence in David Lynch's *Mulholland Dr.* (2001), where it is demonstrated how willing we are to believe in cinematic illusion no matter how many times it is pointed out as such. We believe, despite knowing perfectly well that it is an illusion. But rather than believing *despite* this knowledge, we can also believe *because* of it. The fact that cinema can be so powerful when its artifice is perceptible is more remarkable than if its power was predicated solely on the successful concealment of artifice. *Stalker*'s reflexivities can be seen as acknowledgments of this fact; the film demonstrates, contrary to what the Stalker himself believes, that unquestioning devotion is not the most effective basis for belief.[7]

Agency and Self-pity

I have tried, above, to trace a process in which we move from wondering if the Stalker is manipulative or hypocritical (either inventing dangers or manipulating situations in which there are dangers), to the question of his self-delusion (his messiah complex) and how this contrasts with the film's own self-knowledge. All these threads culminate, emotionally and structurally, in the final sequences of self-pity which indicate the Stalker's fundamental lack of awareness, both of self and of others. Throughout this chapter I have been asking to what extent we might say that Stalker is deceitful, hypocritical, or self-deceived. It is possible that he is none of these, any one or two of them, or all three. The evidence is strong that he is deceitful to some degree, though ambiguity about the exact degree is central to the film's texture. As to the other two characteristics, I think the most plausible and interesting possibility is that he is essentially self-deceived without being hypocritical, despite Writer's accusation that he is a "hypocritical louse." (We might note that Stalker accepts the designation of "louse" but denies hypocrisy.) Bird rightly remarks that it is "unlikely that the Stalker's entire quest is intended to be seen as a mere sham" (Bird 2008, 168). A lack of hypocrisy also goes some way to explaining the continuities between Stalker's behavior when he is with his companions, and when they are sleeping or absent, as in his final scene.

The combination of self-deception with an essential lack of hypocrisy brings us again to the kinds of questions Pippin finds so well addressed in film noir. Even though at the end of the film the Stalker look back on his activity, the narration of Tarkovsky's film doesn't have the kind of retrospective temporality by means of which the archetypal noir protagonist attempts to represent events as fated, in order to diminish their own agency. But the prominence of self-pity in the Stalker does, nevertheless, use the resources of filmic narration and characterization to address agency and self-knowledge in ways that have more parallels with certain film noirs than one might have expected; compare the Stalker's statement that "I never choose. You can't imagine how terrible it is to make the wrong choice," with Michael O'Hara's claim that "I never make up my mind about anything at all until it's all over and done with." Pippin writes with reference to Robert Mitchum's character Jeff Bailey in Jacques Tourneur's *Out of the Past* (1947) that "Jeff and other noir heroes and antiheroes must sort out for themselves when exculpatory appeals like 'I couldn't help myself,' 'I had no choice,' 'I didn't intend to' *are* in fact reasonable excuses and when they are self-deceptions, evasions, or self-serving lies" (Pippin 2012, 49; emphasis in original). Writer raises this same kind of question when he admits that his earlier claim about wanting to visit the Zone for inspiration was false: "But how can I put a name to what it is that I want? How am I to know I don't want what I want or that I really don't want what I don't want?" He wonders how it is that we can say whether our actions are or are not willed if we don't have access to what it is that we desire or intend—if, that is, we have no way of discovering whether our sense of our own motivation is accurate or not. The fact that these lines are also self-indulgent drunken ramblings does not reduce their pertinence. For one thing, they help indicate why seeing agency *in* what people do, as discussed towards the end of chapter 9, should not result in behaviorism: to say that our intentions do not lie *only* in our heads does not entail that what we think about what we do is irrelevant. This can often be clarified, ironically enough, by examining situations in which an agent's sense of their agency is blocked or occluded; this is to draw the opposite conclusion to that which, as we also saw in chapter 9, Deleuze draws from Herzog's *Heart of Glass*. Films, as well as literature, offer abundant examples of such situations. The distinction that Pippin makes between hypocrisy and self-deception is helpful in understanding the character of the Stalker. Of Michael in *The Lady from Shanghai*, Pippin writes: "He reveals that he is simply incapable of registering and acknowledging his own culpability. . . . His viewing himself as such a diminished agent . . . constitutes him as one . . . and so his own relation to his deeds becomes for him constituted by such a self-image. . . . Michael is self-deceived, not hypocritical, and he is self-deceived because of what he is, and he is what he is because of what he can and cannot admit about himself" (Pippin 2012, 73). It is the Stalker's obsessive faith, rather than (as is usually the case in noir) an encounter with a *femme fatale*, that has generated a "power that robs a man of his free will, or initiates an *amour fou*, an obsessional, irrational, all-powerful desire" (50). This power renders Stalker incapable of registering, not perhaps his culpability per se, but rather the very possibility that his own failings might enter into the equation. Is *that* the real reason he does not even begin to question himself as he lies in spiritual agony at the end of the film? There is a dialectic of selflessness and selfishness here: that Stalker does not even consider himself and his own actions at the end of the film is a selflessness so extreme that it becomes a form of selfishness bordering on solipsism. (His language also at times indicates a more straightforward selfishness: "Don't deprive me of what's mine!" he implores outside the Room, and he tells his wife at the end that "the most terrible thing is that . . . all my efforts are in vain.") The fact that Stalker manipulates his companions in order to test their faith does not mean that he is a hypocrite if he is so simultaneously self-absorbed and lacking in self-understanding that he does not even consider the role that his own agency plays; he sees himself as haunting the world. Stalker views himself as such a "diminished agent," so enamored is he of his holy passivity in the face of the ineffable activity of the Zone, that he thinks he has no need to make any decisions at all. Bird makes some observations that are relevant here: "It is doubtful whether any of Tarkovsky's characters are shown in their authentic 'being.' . . . Only *Solaris* asks directly: who is this person with whom I share space?" (Bird 2008, 116). My central claim could be expressed in the form of the proposition that *Stalker* can be read in terms of the *failure* of the protagonist to ask this very question. (In the terms of chapter 2, this is a failure of redescription.)

To conclude, I want to ask whether we learn anything about self-pity from *Stalker*. The crux comes at the end of the film. The wife says that Writer and Professor "should be pitied, not abused." The film explicitly raises the idea that Stalker's pity, like his faith, is misdirected. This makes the Stalker both harder to like *and* harder to condemn; we know we are all subject to self-pity. But *Stalker* shows that self-pity is not merely a bad habit that some of us indulge more than others. The film demonstrates the connection between self-pity and the questions of what it is that we can want, and what can we know about what we want. This is what really binds *Stalker* to the questions of agency that preoccupy Pippin. Outside the Zone, Writer—recalling his earlier remarks about knowing whether we really want what we think we want—says that we can't really *want* things like world peace, but can only recommend them, abstractly: "These aren't desires but an ideology, actions, concepts." Writer has become cynical again after his own apogee of self-pity in the Dune Room, but that doesn't mean he's wrong; nor need it demean or diminish ideology, actions, or concepts to point out that they are not the same as desires. For an action to be an action it has to be able conceivably to result in the outcome towards which it is directed: "Someone who believes that by dressing beautifully every day, he is promoting justice in the world is doing something, but he is not doing *that*" (Pippin 2012, 21; emphasis in original). A name for dealing with this truth—the truth that if we want to work towards, say, peace, we cannot do so simply on the basis of our inner desires—might be "politics." If so, in that self-pity can help one to avoid examining the relation of one's desires to one's actions, to one's thoughts, and to the actions of others, it might all too easily result in an evasion of politics (in the broadest sense).

If this is at all plausible, then despite the hope that may be represented by Monkey's wondrous powers (the film's final ambiguity concerns whether or not Stalker will recognize these powers and, if he does, whether he will see them as a reward for his faith or as still further evidence of the world's slide into godlessness), despite a wife's powerful love for her husband, and even despite the lessons that Writer and Professor have at least begun to learn, *Stalker* might represent, for Stalker himself, something close to tragedy. But how close exactly? Stalker refuses to consider that he could have acted otherwise, whereas the tragic figure wishes that he had. The ironic complication here is that the Stalker's fatal flaw, what Aristotle calls *hamartia*—although this translation of the Greek term has been strongly challenged, it has also been argued that "the word has a range of applications, from 'ignorance' at one end to 'moral defect,' 'moral error,' at the other" (Stinton 1975, 221)—is, precisely, his inability to conceive of altering (or of having altered) his own behavior. In another irony, for Aristotle the hero's *hamartia* leads to a growing intensity of pity and fear in the audience, but here the flaw leads primarily to *its own increase* in the character (see Russell and Winterbottom 1989, 222–23, 226–27). Stalker is prone to self-pity, which events serve only to intensify to the point of paralysis. In an interesting philological twist, *hamartia* also has a theological meaning, which in its simplest form just means sinful acts, as in the Epistle to the Romans 5:12, "all have sinned."

Stalker could therefore be read as a kind of cautionary Christian tragedy: we all commit sin (*hamartia* in Saint Paul's sense), and self-pity (Stalker's particular *hamartia* in Aristotle's sense) is one of the sins we all commit—if not to such an extreme degree.

We need not be Christians ourselves, however, to see in *Stalker* a compelling portrait of a developing moral and psychological paralysis, rather than an accidentally bleak portrayal of a saintly figure. When he correctly deciphers the story of Porcupine, Writer declares: "Conscience, spiritual torment—this is just an intellectual invention. He understood that, and hanged himself."[8] That agonies of conscience are not in themselves virtuous might be the true lesson of the Zone, and both Writer and Professor are able both to learn this and to embrace the flexibility, the "softness," needed in order *not* to kill themselves in response. But Stalker can see no link between their reasons for not entering the Room and the reason why he doesn't want his wife to go there: "What if you fail, too?" In a final ironic twist, he wants to prevent her from trying, in order to sustain his faith, but illogically understands the fact that Writer and Professor made the very same decision as evidence of their *lack* of faith. William Empson writes in *Seven Types of Ambiguity* that "people, often, cannot have done both of two things, but they must have been in some way prepared to have done either; whichever they did, they will still have lingering in their minds the way they would have preserved their self-respect if they had acted differently" (Empson 1972, 66). Stalker uses his self-pity to neutralize this "lingering" sense, indulging in the consolatory effects of the emotion and blocking any consideration of the possibility of acting differently. The "hardness" of his devotion means that he cannot understand what, according to the logic of his own position, the Zone has to teach, and therefore avoids even *raising* the question of what the appropriate response might be. He comforts himself with self-pity, with the result that his self-pity becomes his only remaining companion.

11

Kelly and Andrei in the Zone

Two men on the verge of middle age are taking a road trip to visit some hot springs in the middle of a wood. One of them has been singing the praises of the springs (referring, for example, to their "otherworldly peacefulness") and has persuaded the other to come along for the ride, leaving his pregnant wife behind. The relationship between the men is not quite what it was. They've drifted apart—made different life choices—and things are just a little awkward between them. Finding the legendary springs proves harder than expected and they get decidedly lost. Having left the city a long way behind them, surrounded by a panoply of different kinds of green (leaves, pine needles, grasses, mosses), they are repeatedly forced to turn their car about. At one point, upon discovering that a road sign is "literally blank," one of the men announces, in playful tones of mock awe, "We've entered a whole other zone!"

At this point during my first viewing of Kelly Reichardt's 2006 film *Old Joy*, of which the preceding passage is a description, I immediately thought of another film involving a group of middle-aged men, one of whom has also left his wife behind, whose relationships are strained and fractious, and who end up going round in circles during a kind of "road trip" from the city into a green world in search of a legendary location. The world that these men enter is explicitly named "the Zone" and the film, of course, is Tarkovsky's *Stalker*. Both films also feature very significant canine performances, alongside some rather slimier creatures. (I've circled the snail in the second image from *Stalker* in figure 11.1 as it's otherwise hard to make out.)

Figures 11.1a, 11.1b, 11.1c, and 11.1d. Creatures of the watery Zone. *Source:* For 11.1a, *Old Joy* (2006); for 11.1b, *Stalker* (1979); for 11.1c, *Old Joy* (2006); for 11.1d, *Stalker* (1979).

Having associated these two films, though, what are we to make of the connection? Does it offer anything more than a piece of cinephile cleverness? I certainly have no "smoking gun" to prove that either Reichardt or Jonathan Raymond, who wrote the screenplay to *Old Joy* based on his own short story (in which the term "zone" does not, I think, appear), intended any reference or homage to Tarkovsky. Still, there are some obvious connections to be drawn between the work of these two directors from such different times and places. There are affinities in the way they use color, for example, in that both of them have the ability to wring a great deal of intensity and subtlety from palettes that, compared tone-for-tone with those of other filmmakers, might seem subdued. (The effect of the shift to color in *Stalker*, breathtaking no matter how many times one has seen the film, is a perfect case in point.) Both of them also tend to operate at a slower pace than mainstream cinema has accustomed us to, so much so that they are frequently spoken of as exemplifying a form of art cinema known, precisely, as "slow cinema."

Slow cinema, it is often assumed, operates by taking the emphasis away from classical priorities such as character and narrative. It puts much more weight on sheer perceptual experience, so that the viewer is not encouraged to concentrate on, say, motivation but, rather, to focus on what it feels like to submit to the colors and rhythms of these films over long—very long—stretches of time. There are two broad modes that such films are held to operate in. Tarkovsky represents one of them, which we might call the "mystical" mode, in which the boredom that our action-hungry selves feel on initially encountering films that operate so differently gives way—for those who are prepared to go with it—to an almost-transcendent sense of aesthetic unity, even bliss ("otherworldly peacefulness," perhaps). The other mode, with which Reichardt is often associated, might be called the "political" mode. Here boredom is intended to be functional, to make us think, ultimately, about power and agency in late capitalist America. For Elena Gorfinkel, for example, Reichardt's films involve "dedramatised scenarios in which incident replaces event, and sheer profilmic happening challenges structures of legible or discrete causality," all with a view to revealing "the linkage of quotidian activity and forms of arduous, painful labour with temporalities of exhaustion and dispossession for subjects on the margins of American life" (Gorfinkel 2016, 124–25).

As plausible as it can sometimes be to see Tarkovsky and Reichardt as exemplifying these two very different ways of resisting the logic and pacing of mainstream—"classical"—cinema, automatic assumptions about "slow cinema" and what it entails can also obscure as much as they reveal. Jonathan Rosenbaum thinks that the association of Reichardt's films with slow cinema has—together with seeing her work through the lens of "neorealism" and a tendency to confuse "the personal with the autobiographical"—led to some "unfortunate viewing habits" (Rosenbaum 2022). One of the things, I want to claim, that thinking about *Old Joy* and *Stalker* together might help clarify is how important character, in a traditional sense, is to both Tarkovsky and Reichardt.

Consider how elusive (how hard to pin down with language), and yet how wonderfully precise, is the emotional texture of the sequence in *Old Joy* in which Kurt (Will Oldham) and Mark (Daniel London), the two protagonists, return to their car after finally locating, and bathing in, the hot springs. They walk along the path through the trees in silence, side by side, their hands hanging loosely. We get a sense that they are comfortable with one another, and yet somehow not truly relaxed; note the way that Kurt drops his rucksack on the ground while waiting for Mark to open the car door, the irritability that their silence hints at, and the loneliness evoked by the way the film holds the image of trees and road, after the Volvo has driven off, for just a fraction of a second longer that one expects. Some kind of renewed connection has surely been established between the two men (whether or not there was any kind of literally sexual encounter, Kurt's massaging of Mark is indubitably erotic), but the mood of the aftermath is rather bedraggled. Is this because of what happened (are they embarrassed?) or, instead, because it's over? Do the two men sense that, whatever happened, it was only—could only have been—momentary? That there is no way truly to recapture their "old joy"? The answers to these questions aren't clear, but what comes across beautifully is that it's not simply that the film doesn't know what they are—this has nothing to do with vagueness—but that Kurt and Mark don't know, either.

In the same piece I cited earlier, Jonathan Rosenbaum claims that "unfulfilled fantasies belonging to viewers and characters alike are present in all of Reichardt's features—namely, the failure of life and the world (nature, humans, society, even sometimes animals) to conform to the expectations molded by culture, genres, and many

Figure 11.2. *Old Joy*: aftermath. *Source: Old Joy* (2006).

other conditioned reflexes" (Rosenbaum 2022). *Old Joy* is very much about this, about the way that fantasy is not an alternative to reality, but rather part of reality; that what we hope for, or regret, or fear, cannot but affect how we experience the world and one another. (As Cavell puts it, fantasy "is precisely what reality can be confused with" [Cavell 1979a, 85].) The novelist M. John Harrison, best known for his work in science-fiction and fantasy, said of his supposedly nonfantastic novel about mountain climbing, 1989's *Climbers*, that his goal was "to show fantasy and reality as co-dependent" (Chouinard 2002). *Stalker* works in very similar territory. Even aside from its narrative of a Room that supposedly grants one's innermost wishes, many commentators on the film have explored the senses in which Tarkovsky's Zone seems to reflect the psyches of the characters exploring it, its dangers coming as much—if not more—from within as from without.

Here, however, we encounter another point of contact between Tarkovsky and Reichardt which has served as a stumbling block for some viewers, namely, the presence in their films of distinctly unlikable characters. Even as sophisticated a critic as Rosenbaum writes of the character Gina (Michelle Williams) in 2016's *Certain Women*, that "because we aren't privy to so many self-doubts" as we are in the short story by Maile Meloy on which it is based, in the film "her chiding of her husband and daughter seem more self-centered" (Rosenbaum 2022). (See chapter 12 for a detailed exploration of this character.) But what's wrong with characters that are a little self-centered? Aren't we all? Isn't that an important and also an interesting part of our lives?

The ending of 2013's *Night Moves* is a useful test case. For some viewers, the fact that Josh (Jesse Eisenberg) ends up trapped—his dreams of ecological heroism in ruins, guilty of a murder he committed simply not to be found out by the system, but now unable to get even the most menial of jobs precisely because he mustn't be found out by that very same system—will provoke a reaction of, "Who cares?" He's been selfish, thoughtless, and standoffish throughout the film, so why should we viewers care about him now? For me, however, the inexorability of his situation and the complete uselessness of his ever-deepening self-pity are both completely riveting and utterly terrifying, even if I certainly don't "like" the guy. Josh shares this self-pity with the eponymous protagonist of *Stalker*, something that critics have tended to see as a mistake, as detracting from the character's supposed purity, even saintliness. As I argued in chapter 10, Tarkovsky's film can be read precisely as a compelling exploration of self-pity.

There's some self-pity in *Old Joy* as well. Though it doesn't come through nearly as strongly as in *Night Moves* or *Stalker*, both Mark's fear of the impending demands of fatherhood and Kurt's admiration of Mark's more settled life ("So fuckin' brave man—I have never gotten myself into anything that I couldn't get myself out of") contain elements of self-pity. This might cue us towards a recognition that Reichardt's interest in friendship—one that runs through all of her films in one way or another—has more light-and-shade than is sometimes recognized. The double-edged quality of the epigraph to 2019's *First Cow* ("the bird a nest, the spider a web, man friendship") seems to me to have been rather underplayed. Yes, Blake's proverb indicates that friendship is in some sense our natural state, but what follows from this? The nest is where birds rear their young, but the web is where spiders ensnare their prey. (This is, after all, a Proverb of Hell.)

The trajectory of *Old Joy* takes us from one friend—Mark—alone in his garden, to the other friend—Kurt—alone in the city at night, some of the camera angles strangely canted. We are suddenly alone with Kurt for almost the first time in the film, just as the end of *Stalker* puts us alone in a room with the Stalker's daughter Monkey for the first time. Both films don't only tell the story of a journey to and from a special "zone" but also end with the discovery of new, hauntingly ambiguous zones. To decide whether either ending is or isn't a "happy" one would be as crude as it would be impossible. Just as Monkey's telekinesis could signal the arrival of a new form of humanity as easily as it could indicate the end of humanity as such, the end of *Old Joy*, in its quieter way, expresses loneliness (Kurt has nothing to do but wander among strangers) as much as it does human connection (he and the homeless man do speak to each other, however briefly).

Both *Old Joy* and *Stalker* emphasize the sheer range of human relationships. Loyalty and knowability (the doglike aspects of people, we could say) are as characteristically human as inscrutability and alienation (their slug- or snaillike aspects, perhaps, although that is not all that the invertebrates in these films signify). But to say that we can't decide whether the endings are "happy" or not isn't to say that happiness is irrelevant to these movies; quite the opposite. They are about human happiness, about the idea of happiness. That in *Old Joy* it can seem that we can only say "I was happy"—and in *Stalker* "I will be happy"—does not mean that happiness is merely an illusion. Both films suggest, instead, that happiness can only be an origin or a destination, not a permanent dwelling-place. We have to pass through the Zone, because we can't live there.

12

"A Fair Curve from a Noble Plan"

Kelly Reichardt's *Certain Women*

Shortly before the midpoint of Kelly Reichardt's 2016 film *Certain Women* there is an expression on an actor's face, an expression that is held—by actor and camera—for about two seconds; just long enough to be more than momentary (not all moments, I think, are simply momentary).¹ I am attracted and intrigued by this expression and by this moment. This is one frame from, or of, that moment (a moment excerpted from a moment):

Figure 12.1. A momentary expression. *Source: Certain Women* (2016).

I feel as if I know exactly what it feels like to give someone such a look, although I have no idea if I look like Michelle Williams in doing so. Presumably I do at least *a little bit*, or the expression wouldn't be legible, which is to say that we can understand facial expressions "from the outside" only because we can comprehend something of how they would feel "from the inside." (See chapter 4 for more discussion of this.) When watching this moment, as part of this sequence, I connect more closely to my feeling of "expressing such an expression" than to my memories of having had such glances shot my way (though these moments, too, must also play into my experience of the glance). This, perhaps, explains something of the pleasure that seeing this expression gives me; if I felt myself more clearly the object of the gaze then it would be a much more awkward and, perhaps, a less pleasurable experience. It might be possible to stop there: this moment is interesting and pleasurable because an actor skillfully evokes a familiar emotion (namely, irritation and anger at a loved one putting their foot in it). The pleasure comes from some combination of recognition and distance: the emotion is familiar (I have felt it), but I am not feeling it now (and thus in enjoying this expression I am able, to an extent, to laugh at myself).

What I have said so far has barely made reference to the narrative context in which this moment takes place, nor even to the character's name. For some scholars, this is to be expected, because—in reaction against more traditional aesthetic notions of the relationship between parts and wholes—it is characteristic of a distinctly cinephilic form of appreciation that the pleasure of a moment does *not* derive from its connection to the wider work. Rashna Wadia Richards, for example, suggests in her book *Cinematic Flashes* that there is something of a zero-sum game between investment in a film's narrative, or absorption in its diegesis, and the specific attractions of unusual moments. She writes that "cinephiliac moments may be regarded as moments of cinematic excess, insofar as they surpass their diegetic requirements," which is to say that such moments "offer tiny glimpses of points where the coherent system of representation breaks down" (Richards 2013, 24). Comparably, albeit in less forceful language, Tom Gunning argues that "if we dwell on the sense of *a moment* in its singularity, it seems less to evoke the momentum of a plot than something that falls outside the story and its pace" (Gunning 2010, 5; emphasis in original). I have no wish to deny the interest of such moments, or of thinking about moments in this way, and my intentions align in a way with Richards's in that I am not interested in "moments that are designed to be unforgettable" (Richards 2013, 24); the moment with which I began is, instead, something smaller and quieter that nonetheless has the potential of grabbing and arresting the attention. I do, however, wish to argue that such moments need not undermine "the coherent system of representation," or thrive in its gaps or fissures, but can instead derive strength and intensity from narrative and diegesis, as well as intensifying them (and our involvement in them) in return. In his book *Cinephilia and History, or The Wind in the Trees*, Christian Keathley makes the suggestion that "if the cinephiliac moment is among the most intense of cinematic experiences, it seems to draw its intensity partly from the fact that it cannot be reduced or tamed by interpretation" (Keathley 2006, 9). The thrust of this passage might seem to be similar to Richards's argument, and to be that the cinephiliac moment somehow escapes or eludes interpretation, that it represents an excess for which any system—or pattern—can only be inadequate. I want to suggest that we might also, however, read Keathley's remark not as implying that interpretation is hamstrung—or outrun—by such moments, but that they can serve as opportunities for demonstrating that "reduction" or "taming" need not (indeed *should* not) be the aim of interpretation.

My own aims are perhaps a little closer to those expressed by George Toles when he writes, in an article entitled "Rescuing Fragments: A New Task for Cinephilia," that he is "not suggesting that the stray luminous passages in otherwise disposable or broken narratives ought to be scavenged catch-as-catch-can with no regard for the film worlds which engendered them. . . . The fragments warrant being respectfully placed and considered within their narrative context; it is, after all, the *felt* combination of a given moment with its surrounding circumstances that allows it to 'lift off' emotionally" (Toles 2010, 161; emphasis in original). Rather than pursuing Toles's focus on the ways in which "the brief passages that rise above the rest are also, arguably, in communion with each other, sharing a higher pitch of awareness and a secret network of correspondences" (161), however, I am particularly interested in how moments such as this form part of a wider whole—in their relations to what surrounds them, rather than with other "special" moments—and specifically in how they contribute not only to our experience of the plans or schemes of the characters represented in them but also to what we might call the schemes of the films of which they are a part (which is to say the aesthetic, ethical, and other matters towards which they are directed). In talking about "the film's schemes" I mean something along the lines of Cavell's recommendation here: "Don't ask what the artist is thinking or intending, but ask why the work is as it is, why just this is here in just that way. . . . My formulation employing the work's thinking or intending or wanting something, is meant to emphasise the sense that the work wants something of us who behold or hear or read it" (Cavell 2005b, 186).[2] As I argue in this book's introduction, we need not think in terms of a zero-sum game between character and form, in which a film that focusses on character must do so at the expense of its formal structure, and vice versa; instead, moments such as Gina's glare might prompt us to consider the ways form can express character, or how character can shape form. Another way of putting this might be to say that form does not *contain* action so much as it *consists of* action.

This chapter is, then, concerned both with a critical discussion of certain aspects of *Certain Women*, focusing on and radiating out from a single moment, and with the place of this moment in relation to the expressive patterns that inform it and to which it contributes. What is the place of the moment in question? The segment of the film from which it is drawn is the second of the three lightly intersecting stories that make up *Certain Women*. Michelle Williams plays Gina, a businesswoman, wife, and mother, who plans to build a house in the Montana countryside for herself and her family, although, as she says, they "can't really move out here full time, at least not until our daughter gets through high school." She is sitting in the front room of a bungalow belonging to an elderly man named Albert (René Auberjonois) from whom, as part of her plan for the house, Gina wants to buy some "authentic" sandstone that he has in his front yard. The dirty look that she is shooting is directed at her husband, Ryan (James Le Gros). Although Albert has agreed to give the sandstone to them, Ryan has just told him that he doesn't have to sell the stone if he doesn't want to, thus threatening what had seemed to be the successful achievement of this part of Gina's plan.

Certain Women is based on some works of literature, specifically on three short stories by Maile Meloy, which Reichardt adapted herself. The corresponding moment in "Native Sandstone," the story on which this segment of *Certain Women* is based, both does and does not match its counterpart in the film. The dialogue preceding Gina's glance is almost identical, apart from changes to the characters' names: "'You

Figure 12.2. Gina, Ryan, and the sandstone. *Source: Certain Women* (2016).

don't have to sell it if you don't want to,' Clay said. 'Susan wants a house that's *authentic*'" (Meloy 2005, 36). In the film, Ryan says: "You don't have to sell it if you don't want to, it's just that Gina wants this new house to be *authentic*." The sentence in the short story that directly follows, and that corresponds to the moment under discussion, however, is "He grinned at her and she frowned." (36)

Ryan certainly does grin—and not just smile—at Gina:

Figure 12.3. "He grinned at her. . . ." *Source: Certain Women* (2016).

Ryan's raised eyebrows, furrowed forehead, widened eyes, and toothy grin all take his expression to the edge of the ridiculous, overstating his evident desire—and obvious invitation—for Gina to agree with him. I think we are to understand that by offering Albert the chance to back out, Ryan hopes in fact to convince him that he is not being railroaded into parting with the sandstone; the risk that Albert will indeed withdraw his offer is a calculated risk, on Ryan's part, intended to make this outcome *less* likely.[3] Gina, however, is furious at the prospect that what she thought to be in her grasp might now, owing to her husband's actions, slip through her fingers. We might also note that their differing strategies and reactions contribute to the sense that the stone means more to Gina than to Ryan. This fact is not simply something he accepts; he subtly deflects responsibility onto her: "*Gina* wants this new house to be authentic." It is also important to remember that the opening scene of the film shows us that Ryan is having an affair with Laura Dern's character, a lawyer also called Laura, and that he has, in a rather cowardly fashion, recently attempted to break off, or at least pause, their relationship. (Laura receives a phone call in which he says, evidently disappointed, that he was expecting her voicemail, and that, "well, it's just my situation being what it is, I just think, maybe . . .") So we might expect Ryan to go out of his way to help Gina achieve her goals, yet he cannot bring himself fully to acknowledge those goals as also his goals, perhaps because he is all too aware that for him they are merely instrumental, a means of rescuing his marriage. What exactly lies behind Gina's desire for the stone is, I think, rather more opaque, or at least difficult to pin down; later I will suggest that one reason for this is that her reasons are not entirely clear to herself.

It is, anyway, crucial to the effect of the film, and to what makes this moment memorable, that Gina does *not* frown, as Susan does in the story. Or that she somehow frowns without frowning, by freezing her face and intensifying her gaze—the muscles around her eyes and mouth tauten, without (unlike her husband) any furrowing of her brow. In contrast to his exaggerated expression, hers is on the edge of not being an expression at all; she is shooting him an unmistakably dirty look, and yet the differences between this look and a neutrally inexpressive glance are subtle. This contrast contributes both to the eloquence of the moment in expressing their relationship and to its comedy. A novel could of course explore such a pair of expressions, such a moment, in great detail and with great power, but to do so would require the reader to spend a period of time reading about the moment described that greatly exceeded the fictional duration of that moment itself. The sparseness of Meloy's prose has its own strengths, but our highly developed ability to interpret the facial expressions of other human beings means that only in the film can the moment in question be expressed with such nuance and detail, and yet still be represented *as a moment*. In his 1921 book *La poésie d'aujourd'hui, un nouvel état d'intelligence*, the twenty-three-year-old Jean Epstein compared film with modern literature, and claimed that although film was an "emerging, still-hesitant mode of expression," it "nonetheless stands as the most subtle one we have ever known, the most attuned to the moment" (Epstein 2012, 271). Film may have long since "emerged," but its attunement to the moment remains undiminished, as this particular moment helps to illustrate.

Critics routinely connect Reichardt's films to an aesthetic of the long take, and indeed she does make a powerful and distinctive use of long takes (perhaps most obviously in *Certain Women* during the scene in the film's third segment in which the rancher [Lily Gladstone] drives away from her final brave but disappointing and embarrassing encounter with Elizabeth [Kristen Stewart]). The sequence from which our moment comes involves three characters in a single room and could easily have been filmed in a single take. Instead, Reichardt—who edited *Certain Women* herself—uses different editing practices to move in and out of subtly different narrational modes (she once remarked that "the language of the film is outside the dialogue. It's where the cut is" [cited in Holmlund 2016, 265]). Close attention to the way that this sequence is edited will clarify our sense of the way that editing can serve both to isolate moments of a film, precisely *as* moments, and to connect them with, or embed them within, the wider film of which they are a part.

Visually, there are three distinct groupings of characters used in this scene. Sometimes we can see all three characters simultaneously; at other times we see Gina and Ryan together and Albert separately; and at still other times all three characters are seen separately. After Albert comes to the door and invites Gina and Ryan in, we see the three characters together in a single take; a mobile camera follows them as they cross the room to sit down. This take ends by framing Gina and Ryan together on a sofa, establishing them as a unit distinct from their host, Albert. There then follows a shot/reverse shot sequence between Albert (seen in one-shot) and the two-shot of the couple on the sofa. During the last two-shot in this sequence Albert stands up and moves into view. The camera moves so that we see the couple from behind the sofa; Gina's face is visible but we can only see the back of Ryan's head, as Gina stage-whispers to Ryan her response to Albert's story of having had a fall ("Poor Albert!"). Gina gets up to look out of the window, and we see her view, including her reflection in the window and some of the crucial sandstone. When Albert returns and sits down again, Gina asks about the stone for the first time, something we know her to feel to be an imposition, since she earlier asked Ryan to be the one to broach the subject; presumably he felt that this request was itself an imposition on him. Gina's request, which clumsily and transparently attempts to pretend that her aims align with Albert's ("Albert, so we were wondering about the sandstone in the front yard, and if you'd be willing to sell it to us. I mean, if you wanted to get rid of it we . . . we'd take it off your hands") is seen from the same behind-the-sofa setup as before, but when we cut to Albert listening to her, we enter an extended series of one-shots of each of the three characters, mostly filmed from fixed camera positions, that eventually ends with a return to the two-shot of the couple on the sofa, after Albert's question, "When do you need it?"

Figure 12.4. "When do you need it?" *Source: Certain Women* (2016).

The scene thus moves, gently and unobtrusively but rigorously, from visually representing all three characters as some kind of group, to setting the couple off against Albert, and finally to isolating them as three distinct individuals. We move, that is to say, from a "three," to a "two plus one," and eventually to "three ones." Then the pattern is reversed with a return to the two-shot of the couple and one-shot of Albert after which, as Gina and Ryan leave, we once more, albeit briefly, see all three characters together in a single frame. This editing strategy emphasizes the complexity of the three-way conversation that is going on here. Its symmetry also serves to increase the scene's intensity as it approaches its denouement, and then elegantly diffuse the tension as the scene draws to a close. As the scene progresses, the editing and framing gradually isolate the characters from one another, making us reconstruct their various relationships in our minds, as the film increasingly denies us the chance to see both action and reaction simultaneously (although at times we do hear one character and see another). The scene's range of intricately ironic patterns concerning what the characters (with varying degrees of self-awareness and self-consciousness) assume about each other, and assume that the other is assuming about them, is thereby emphasized. I have already discussed Gina and Ryan's different attitudes to the accomplishment of Gina's plan. Albert, for his part, gives something of a *performance* of a confused old man, responding with what might appear to be non sequiturs (about getting someone called Kyle to help build the house, for example); it later becomes clear that he was thinking hard about the sandstone all along. The differing priorities of the differing characters are often expressed in patterns of listening and not listening. For example, it is clear from the play of the muscles around her mouth that Gina's delight about Albert's acquiescence concerning the stone (a delight which she is attempting somewhat to repress, to avoid breaking into a grin) is distracting her from, even making her impatient with, Albert's story about the origin of the stone (it was formerly the old schoolhouse)—and this despite her professed interest in authenticity. Albert, for his part, has no interest in Gina's expressions of interest in authentic materials, and cuts right across her—"edits" her dialogue himself—to announce that the stone was already there when, in 1966, he and his now dead brother built the house in which he still lives, but which remains unfinished; it lacks a back porch, for example.

It is worth noting that Albert tends very much to direct his remarks and his questions towards Ryan, not Gina, thereby hinting at a generationally conditioned misogyny, or at least discomfort around women. Lucy Bolton's description of this moment is careful but, I think, incomplete: "Gina tries to be kind to Albert, asking if he needs anything, then she asks him if he wants to sell the sandstone in the garden and he ignores her completely. He will talk to Ryan, who says the same things to Albert that Gina says, and says he will give them the sandstone. Gina says she wants to pay him for it, but he just doesn't engage with her. Albert looks at Gina with suspicion and a lack of connection" (Bolton 2019, 180). One of the film's achievements in this scene is the delicacy and clarity with which it presents this misogyny without thereby upsetting the balance of the scene, in which it is Gina's ethical shortcomings with respect to Albert that are most at issue. The mere facts of Gina's confidence and assertiveness would, of course, be deemed threatening by some men. (Does Albert perhaps think Ryan is emasculated by working for his own wife?) *Certain Women* explores the relationship between the qualities of confidence and assertiveness, and aspects of their gendering, throughout. In the first segment Fuller's (Jared Harris) assertiveness masks his lack of confidence, exasperating Laura despite her sympathy for him. In the third segment the rancher's particular kind of confidence is expressed via an absence of assertiveness, which is set off against Elisabeth's (Kristen Stewart) different blend of these qualities; this relationship is also given other dimensions by the fact that in this case both parties are female, something that is Reichardt's own contribution (in Meloy's source story, the rancher is male).

Albert then states that since he is now seventy-six he is unlikely ever to finish the house. Giving up the stone, therefore, represents the evaporation of a scheme that Albert has had for half a century, the surrender of the unrealistic but comforting belief that it might one day still be enacted. (It is not clear that Albert actually intended to use the stone as part of his own house, but it still serves as a reminder of unfulfilled plans that are now, he admits to himself, unfulfillable.) It is in the context of all this that Gina's glare at Ryan takes place. The look is just starting to form on her face as we hear Ryan begin to say that Albert does not have to sell the stone; we then cut to Ryan, who—as we have already seen—grins ingratiatingly at Gina after making his remark. Reichardt then cuts back to Gina's dirty look, which barely changes across a two-second shot after which we cut to Albert, asking rather curtly, "When do you need it?" The editing thus isolates Gina's expression so as almost to epitomize it, and in so doing corroborates Jean Epstein's sense that "[o]n the screen, the essential quality of a gesture is that it does not come to an end" (Epstein 2012, 273). It is as if the editing separates the gesture so that we can imagine it lasting forever; we do not see it come into being or pass away, so that this one moment is crystallized in our memory. But this isolation does not *remove* it from its narrative context; on the contrary, it *intensifies* its relation to this context, enriches this moment and what it encapsulates about the relationships at play and their shifting dynamics.

One could, in fact, describe the editing (and generally the rhetoric) at this point in the film as broadly classical, in that their effects seem intended to be largely subliminal, or at the very least are not foregrounded; the editing does not call attention to itself in "modernist" fashion.[4] The narration is also classical in its concentration on plausibly real human beings, their interactions and motivations; there may be ellipses in the narrative, but these are all relatively easily filled, and do not generate the kind of aesthetic and epistemological dilemmas we find in the canonical examples of modernist cinema. But there is something of a puzzle in the critical reaction to Reichardt's work, in that this classicism is underplayed; the films tend instead to be received as instances of modern American realist art cinema, with the focus put on the relations—and tensions—between their realism and their status as high art. E. Dawn Hall, for example, states unambiguously that Reichardt "rejects mainstream form" (Hall 2018, 143). As we saw in the previous chapter, Elena Gorfinkel, for her part, argues that "Reichardt's autonomous creative practice and relatively low budgets have linked her style with international art cinema, both historical (neorealism) and contemporary (slow cinema)" and that she makes the kind of "slow films [that] evacuate eventfulness, in the pursuit of dedramatized scenarios in which incident replaces event, and sheer profilmic happening challenges structures of legible or discrete causality" (Gorfinkel 2016, 123–124). There is certainly an initial plausibility to this account in relation to much of Reichardt's work, and particularly as applied to the film Gorfinkel concentrates on, *Meek's Cutoff* (2010), her reading of which I find broadly persuasive. The danger, however, is that, precisely because *Certain Women* is unlikely to strike anyone familiar with Reichardt's films as a radical stylistic departure, one might—if one isn't careful—assume that such an interpretation of her aesthetics is equally applicable here.[5] But—to take one example—does the rancher's labor in *Certain Women* seem to relate to "the linkage of quotidian activity and forms of arduous, painful labour with temporalities of exhaustion and dispossession for subjects on the margins of American life" (Gorfinkel 2016, 124–25)? The answer can at most be a qualified "yes and no." The rancher is certainly, from any standard perspective, "on the margins of American life," but it is also made clear that she enjoys and, at least to a degree, fulfills herself in such labor; she has spent time with horses, for pleasure, since she was a girl. *Certain Women* often facilitates our understanding of character by means of, and in relation to, action in ways that indicate that Reichardt's style is more amenable to an at least relatively classical treatment of cinematic narration than accounts such as Hall's and Gorfinkel's might lead us to expect.

Figure 12.5. Working "on the margins of American life." *Source: Certain Women* (2016).

Certainly, motivation is unclear at various points in *Certain Women* (both to the audience and to the characters themselves), but this is not quite the same thing as a challenge to "structures of legible or discrete causality." When we first meet Gina she is on a run near to the site of the planned house in the country, but she is also smoking. The way that she buries her cigarette after finishing it and later sucks on a breath mint indicate that she is hiding her smoking from her family. It would be reasonable to assume that they know her once to have smoked, and so that what she is concealing is a failure to see a plan through, namely, to quit smoking and stay quit. After running through the lion's share of its three narratives one after another, *Certain Women* concludes by returning briefly to each narrative, in the same order as they first appeared. When we return to Gina and Ryan, they are having a lunch party with friends at the site of their projected new house. When we last see Gina, she is sitting with a glass of wine, smoking openly, after which the film leaves this narrative thread for the last time with a shot of the sandstone, now piled up near the site of the future house, at which Gina is gazing. It is unclear whether this is better read as an image of acceptance (Gina has come to terms with herself, and part of that self involves being a smoker) or resignation (she has simply given up trying to pretend that she is different from how she actually is).[6] Does the neat pile of sandstone—as opposed to the shapeless piles that lay outside Albert's house—represent the next stage on the way to the house, the midway point of a plan that is being fruitfully exercised, or will this pile still lie here decades from now, as Albert's did? All these possibilities are in play, but expressed in this way as mutually exclusive options they are too crude; the answer lies somewhere between them, or in their mutual plausibility.

We gain the most insight into Gina's character, I believe, if we see something like these possibilities as also available to her, as possibilities. She may not know quite why she is so determined to build the house, but the tautness, toughness, and defensiveness that characterizes her earlier in the film (see the way she tends to fold her arms across her chest) has somewhat diminished; it seems she has, at the very least, developed a flexibility that may help her to be more relaxed about not knowing, at every moment, exactly what she wants and how to get it. Just as was the case when we were first introduced to her, our last glimpse of Gina is accompanied by the sound of quail asking, as we have learned from Albert, "How are you?" The response—"I'm just fine"—is pointedly missing. The resonance of this is complicated, however, by the fact that we have seen that both Albert and Gina are familiar with this piece of folklore, and thus it forms the only real connection between the two of them; looking at the sandstone and listening to the quail Gina may well be thinking of Albert as much as of herself, and thus could be said—in a more straightforward reading of the character's "journey"—to have learned a lesson about selfishness and empathy (and their relation to self-acceptance) that she seemed, earlier, to be very much in need of.

Certain Women is (like all narrative films) a film about moments and their connections; the two main ways moments can be connected are as patterns or—if those patterns represent the way in which a goal may be achieved—as plans. A number of characters in the film have what we might call an impulse to a scheme, the feeling of having a plan, but not actually anything close to a fully worked-out plan. The two crucial instances of this bookend Gina's narrative; they are Fuller's hostage situation in the first segment and the rancher's trip to Livingston in the third. Both of these seem to me to be instances of activities directed towards goals (Fuller wants to get his insurance money; the rancher wants to see Elizabeth again; these desires are what motivate their actions) without quite being *plans*, because plans

Figure 12.6. Our last glimpse of Gina. *Source: Certain Women* (2016).

need to involve a sense of how exactly the actions will bring about the goal.[7] Both Fuller and the rancher, however, select actions where the need simply to take the next step precludes any genuine planning or reflecting. (The hostage situation descends into a ludicrous attempt to escape from the police, while the rancher's need simply to *find* Elizabeth allows her to avoid spending any time thinking about what exactly she will do when she does find her.) Gina's situation is a little different because it does involve making detailed plans for her house—but this in itself turns out to be something of an evasion, distracting her from, for example, really dealing with her relationships with her husband and daughter.

It may of course turn out that we are able to discover what our plans "really" are only by embarking on them, even if we are incapable of formulating them in a completely lucid fashion. Robert Pippin articulates this kind of possibility in explaining the sense of agency that he finds in Nietzsche (among other philosophers): "I may start out engaged in a project, understand my intention as X, and over time, come to understand that this first characterization was not really an accurate or a full description of what I intended; it must have been Y, or later perhaps Z. And there is no way to confirm the certainty of one's 'real' purpose except *in* the deed actually performed" (Pippin 2010, 78; emphasis in original). I think something like this is true of Fuller's intentions with regard to his hostage-taking, and what he comes to realize about them later in prison, though I do not have space to explore that aspect of the film here. One could also argue that *Certain Women* exhibits a rather Hegelian attitude to agency, along the lines described by Terry Pinkard, when he writes that "we *come to be* the kinds of agents we are; we *actualize* certain self-interpretations in the ways we carry them out in practice, and this 'negative' stance toward ourselves—of our never being just what we are, except insofar as we interpret ourselves as being that type of agent and sustain that type of interpretation—inflicts a kind of 'wound,' a *Zerissenheit*, a manner of being internally torn apart that demands healing" (Pinkard 2007, 5; emphases in original).

To be an agent both interpretation *and* action are crucial; it is not that we simply have to interpret correctly or can choose action *instead of* interpretation. Neither, of course, is it the case that we have some kind of abstract "true self" that we simply have to discover, but nor are we free to be whoever we want to be, because becoming "the kinds of agents we are" is a practical matter, and also involves who others take us to be. Pinkard goes on to argue that for Hegel "the status of 'being an agent' is not a metaphysical or empirical fact about us; it is a socially conferred, normative *status*, and becoming an agent is to be construed as an achievement, not as a metaphysical or empirical property we suddenly come to possess" (7; emphasis in original). According to this way of thinking, then, who we are involves at least three things—who we *think* we are, what we *do*, and who *others* think we are, and none of these three factors can be discarded or simply equated with who we "really" are. (It wouldn't make sense, for example, to say that who we are is only a matter of what we do, because we only do what we do because of who we think we are.) One key distinction concerns those situations in which acting is a way of *avoiding* confronting "what we are," and those in which it is a way of *accepting* or *becoming* who we are; the former just attempts to conceal or deny Hegel's "wound," while the latter attempts to come to terms with it, if not necessarily actually to heal it. The rancher's drive to Livingstone is intriguing because it seems at one and the same time to be both a means of avoidance (we might think of her purposeless wandering and looking in shop windows as a way of avoiding the difficult cognitive activity of self-interpretation) and of becoming (because it is a proactive attempt to achieve something, even if it deliberately does not ask how exactly it will achieve this).

I hope it is clear that my discussion above of the last glimpse that the film gives us of Gina could also be explored in these terms. Gina's scheme to get the stone represents, it seems, one of the most worked-out plans in the film. If so, the crucial thing is that Albert sees right through it. Gina's plan has been predicated on telling herself that she (and her plan) have his best interests at heart (what use could Albert possibly have for the stone?), all the time, of course, knowing at least at some level that this is not true. Her commitment to authenticity is not itself authentic, or at least not fully so. This may in fact be where some of the venom behind her dirty look comes from; it can be painful to be confronted with the gap between one's intentions and what one has been telling oneself about them. When she and Ryan take their leave, Gina says to Albert, "no more falling down," to which he replies, "I don't plan to." This is of course a joke, but how exactly does it work? It once again shows up Gina; her statement takes the form of a fairly familiar idiom in which a wish ("I hope you don't fall down") is expressed in the form of a mock-admonishment, as if Albert was responsible for falling over. It is perhaps a little cruel (or at least unsporting) of Albert not to play along with this idiom's game, but also entirely reasonable, because Gina is assuming an intimacy and a mutual understanding that is not merited; she is not, for example, actually promising to help, should he fall over again. Albert's statement is also, of course, literally true (he doesn't plan to fall over), which serves merely to underline that this makes no difference to the likelihood of it happening again; nobody's future can be entirely a matter of planning.

The relationship between agency and intersubjectivity in *Certain Women* is frequently expressed in terms of small promises that are broken.[8] Laura promises Fuller to tell the police he's got a gun so that he will have time to escape, but immediately tells them he is unarmed; we also learn later that she has promised to write to him in prison but has not done so. Gina and Ryan break their promise to their daughter to go home straightaway by visiting Albert to ask about the stone, and Elizabeth breaks some kind of implicit promise in not telling the rancher that she's given up teaching the night class. It turns out that, just as sometimes one simply finds oneself acting without a detailed plan, sometimes it is best if such promises are simply kept, without any complicated reasoning behind them; Fuller tells Laura that it doesn't matter if she has nothing to say, it's best just to write ("It doesn't have to be a tome").

Figure 12.7. "It doesn't have to be a tome." *Source: Certain Women* (2016).

Authenticity, then, doesn't seem to require elaborate planning. This is something that Gina might seem to come to understand, but to say that is not to say that she experiences any kind of dramatic moment of self-revelation; driving away from Albert's house, she still says to Ryan: "I thought he knew he wasn't gonna use it" (which is of course what she *wanted* to think). She doesn't want to give it back, though: "Someone else will just take it" (which still sounds like a self-justifying excuse). Thus: "We just have to think of something really good to do with it; then it won't feel so sad to take it." When they return to collect the stone, Gina waves at Albert and he—rather pointedly—does not wave back. It might, then, be possible to read Gina's final act of staring at the stone as her attempting to think of just such a thing ("something really good to do with it"), but the degree of relaxation that finally appears on her face at this point—the absence of either triumph or determination in her expression—seems to me to be a hint that something about Gina's attitudes *to* plans (which is to say something about the kind of agent she is), rather than just her plans themselves, has changed or is in the process of changing. Perhaps the real importance of the plan to build a house was simply to have a plan, to occupy, distract, and drive herself. That plan has not necessarily been abandoned but it is the prospect of the house itself, rather than the plan to build one, that is—just—beginning to come alive, and in the process Gina is becoming more authentically who she is.[9]

სა

Although I have argued that, in *Certain Women* at least, there is an under-recognized classicism in Reichardt's work, I have also been arguing that *Certain Women* might be said rather to undercut, or at the very least to complicate, the notions of the centrality to classical narration of goal-directed action most famously expressed by the likes of David Bordwell because, in Reichardt's film, desires and actions are not straightforwardly connected. Thus, the conclusion of Gina's narrative could be described as something of an "open" ending, but it does not seem to me primarily directed at, say, a demonstration of the artificiality of narrative closure, or even the need for every viewer to contribute their own interpretation of what is shown; its openness tells us something about its protagonist. Characters can, as I think is the case here, be clear *that* they want something, or want to do something, but not entirely clear *why*. (Drawing on Cavell's observation that "Hildy, in *His Girl Friday*, does not know why she has come back to see Walter" [Cavell 1981b, 163], Alex Clayton deftly teases out some of the crucial subtleties that can be obscured by thinking too rigidly in terms of characters' goals, even in the most classical of instances, in Clayton 2011 [32–37]; Robert Pippin has expertly explored related questions in another set of films that at least border on classical narration in Pippin 2012.) Beyond this, I want to claim that there is a certain kind of reflexivity in *Certain Women* between the schemes of the film's characters, and what I suggested at the beginning of this chapter that we might call the film's own schemes. But for all this, however, it is not a particularly—certainly not an aggressively—"modernist" reflexivity. (Compare the remarks in chapter 10 about *Stalker*'s reflexivity.)

We might find this reflexivity, in the first place, in the film's title (which comes from Reichardt, not Meloy). The film concerns "certain" women: not just any old women, not extraordinarily unusual women, just a *particular* choice of individual women. But the irony is that in many ways these women are not that "certain," in the sense of being clear and confident about themselves and their purposes. Or, rather, what certainty they have is—in each of the three narratives—challenged and complicated by the ensuing events. In order for us to understand this—in order for the characters' actions and decisions to be comprehensible and interpretable—the film requires a certain realism, or naturalism, or perhaps neorealism. For Katherine Fusco and Nicole Seymour, in their book-length study of Reichardt's films, "Reichardt updates neorealism with a relentless antisentimentality, retaining its 'revolutionary humanism'" (Bazin, 'Cinematic Realism,' 33) even as she alienates viewers from her characters through a focus on either unlikable or opaque protagonists. By making her characters less lovable than their neorealist predecessors, Reichardt draws attention to contemporary society's unwillingness to care for those with whom it may be difficult to identify" (Fusco and Seymour 2017, 23). *Certain Women* was only released as Fusco and Seymour were completing their manuscript, and thus does not receive extended discussion. But it is easy to see Gina as another example of a somewhat opaque and certainly potentially unlikeable protagonist. (Hall argues that this aspect of the character is intensified in the film, that she receives "a more sympathetic characterization in Meloy's story than Reichardt allows on screen" [Hall 2018, 137].)

The second sentence from Fusco and Seymour cited above seems to claim an allegorical purpose to Reichardt's films; the way the films challenge the viewer's ability to empathize with their protagonists allegorizes "contemporary society's unwillingness to care for those with whom it may be difficult to identify." As with Gorfinkel's claims about "sheer profilmic happening" I find such a reading potentially fruitful, but I would also argue that it would be unhelpful and distorting were it to be taken as recommending certain interpretational strategies to the exclusion of others. Thus, if we find it hard to identify or sympathize with certain characters in these films, that may well raise wider social questions about "care"; but we should by no means merely take it as given that these characters *are*, for all viewers, "either unlikable or opaque." Nor am I at all sure that *relentless* antisentimentality is the right description of Reichardt's work, and certainly not of *Certain Women* (see, for example, the character of Fuller, the clear injustice he has suffered and the way that his skill at carpentry is emphasized, or the way he extols the pleasures of getting a letter—any letter—while in prison). If one is open to them there are a rather large number of touching, bittersweet moments in the film. It is certainly true (some of the undergraduates to whom I have taught the film could serve as proof) that some viewers find the characters difficult to empathize and identify with, but it seems to me more that the film's challenge is for audiences to move beyond this and find things to like—even to love—in these characters, a challenge which certainly renders the film vulnerable should one *not* manage to do this.

As well as their "naturalism," however, Reichardt's films are also carefully, and highly, patterned; we have seen this in the rigor of the editing patterns during Gina and Ryan's visit to Albert. To give one more example: there is a motif that appears in both the first and third narrative segments in which an important character arrives in a car, seen out of focus in the background of an image with a shallow depth of field. We thus *feel* that someone is approaching before we really *notice* that it happens; our noticing thus somehow emerges gradually rather than abruptly intruding. And the simple fact of the pattern itself, of course, invites comparison between the two moments. Reichardt herself has observed that "I get lumped in with this 'neorealism' a lot, often with a lot of films that feel more 'flimsy' or experiential to me. I feel like my films are different, more structured. But it's all treated the same. And maybe it is! Maybe it's all realism. . . . I try not to follow the dialogue around and try to be as sparse as possible and rely on the filmmaking as much as possible" (Fusco and Seymour 2017, 114). So, as I suggested earlier, there seems a question as to whether or not "realism" is somehow in tension with a "more structured" form of filmmaking. In a straightforward sense, we could easily observe that realism (and particularly Reichardt's brand of it) is likely to seem less realistic if it is too obviously wrought, because such operations would be likely to be distracting. Hence, presumably, Reichardt's desire to "try to be as sparse as possible," to minimize distractions.

Beyond this, however, it might seem as though a certain kind, at least, of "realism" is fundamentally at odds with a certain mode of expressing meaning through formal patterning—the more pattern, the less realism, perhaps. I want to dispute any such claim. It is only by entering imaginatively "into" the film that we will fully be able to comprehend its "schemes"; we do not *first* understand its story and *then* appreciate how that story is "artistically" arranged. It certainly seems plausible to say that diegetic schemes (Gina's plan for her house) are connected, by a kind of reflexivity, with the broader aesthetic schemes of the film in which they are represented. This kind of relationship is also achieved with a degree of irony. When Fuller is weeping self-pityingly in Laura's car, we hear on her car radio the song "Boats to Build" (performed by Jimmy Buffett, written by Guy Clark and Verlon Thompson), which refers to achieving "a fair curve from a noble plan." Is the film's conclusion that we don't need "noble plans"? That "fair curves" and "nobility" are achievable by other means? Or perhaps that plans are not quite what we thought them to be, that there is not a zero-sum game between fully working out a plan in detail and acting without thinking? (This might be one reason why we can learn things, not only about our desires, but also about our plans, by acting "thoughtlessly.")

It is one of the many extremely impressive accomplishments of *Certain Women* that in it Reichardt achieves a harmony between form and content where the former does not exactly mimic the latter; nor

Figure 12.8. "Boats to build." *Source: Certain Women* (2016).

is the form always directly at the service of expressing the content. (For *Certain Women*'s form to have mimicked its content the film would probably have had to—like Fuller and the rancher—exhibit a gap between its goals and its plans for achieving them, but it is much too meticulously structured and delicately balanced for that kind of gambit.) But would it be quite right to claim, then, that the characters' schemes in *Certain Women* reflexively serve the film's artistic/narrative schemes? If anything, I suggest that it is the other way around. Reading films in the way I have attempted in this chapter and elsewhere in this book (particularly in chapters 4, 5, 8, and 10) can, for those films that respond to such a reading, be a way of maximizing interpretive richness, drawing on as much of our wider experience as is relevant and helpful while still remaining acutely sensitive to every aspect of a text, whether that be the rhythm of the editing or the emotional expression of a character; recall V. F. Perkins's remark, quoted in chapter 1, that "[i]t is not difficult to see the image on the screen simultaneously as a world and as a performance. We do it all the time" (Perkins 2020, 296). A focus on character, such as one finds in the naive reading I have been developing here (see the introduction) understands cinematic characters as human beings, but it does not involve confusing cinematic characters *for* real people. In *Certain Women*, the film's artistic "schemes" are directed at exploring the human schemes manifested in and by the characters in the film. These explorations of human scheming take a particularly vivid form at certain moments, a form whose sharpness is assisted, not hindered, by the wider aesthetic schemes to which these moments contribute. As viewers, we come to understand and engage with *Certain Women*'s exploration of human agency and subjectivity by tracing the "curves"—the form—of the film and the actions of its characters in relation to the "plans"—whether "noble" or otherwise—both of these characters and of the film as a whole.

An Afterword on Parts and Wholes

Especially given that "whole" is (or would otherwise have been) this chapter's final word, I want to offer a brief afterword to the chapter—and indeed to the book—about the conception of the relationships between parts and wholes in film that underlies it, addressing what Douglas Pye has called "the vexed question of 'wholeness'" (Pye 2023, 23). Doing so will bring us full circle to the remarks about coherence that are to be found in chapter 1. In a conference paper on *Certain Women* that engaged with the material of this chapter, Alex Clayton worried that my reference to "how moments such as [Gina's glare] form part of a wider whole" rendered "the identity of the 'whole' . . . far too notional" and also that "the very notion of wholeness seems to run counter to the film's ethos, which, I take it, is to accept non-fruition as a part of life" (Clayton 2022b). Clayton suggests that thinking in terms of, for example, "part and pattern" or "part and project" are likely to be more helpful than strategies insisting on "part and whole." The suggestion is excellent and suggests some refreshing critical avenues, but this, it seems to me, is because it highlights the fact that we often think about part/whole relations in limited ways rather than because there is something inherently problematic about the idea that a film—even a fragmentary, oblique, or lacunary one—comprises a whole.

Another way of heading off the kind of misunderstanding or misguided investigation that both Clayton and I are keen to avoid might be to speak about *aspects* of the whole, rather than parts. Certainly, it is rarely—if ever—helpful to think of the parts of a film as being parts in the sense that the pieces of a jigsaw puzzle are parts of the puzzle; this would suggest that the whole divides up in exactly one way, and one way only, and that each part has its definite place. The two issues Clayton points out are distinct; yes, *Certain Women* is fascinated by failure and incompletion, but this does not make the film fragmentary—its omissions are far too exquisitely crafted for that to be true. My references to the film's "whole" were intended along the lines that Robert Pippin sets out when he argues that some (certainly not all!) "movies embody some conception of themselves, a distinct form, such that the parts are parts of one organic, purposive whole. Just in the way that a bodily movement in space can count as an action only by virtue of the self-understanding embodied in and expressed in it, an artwork, including any ambitious movie, embodies a formal unity, a self-understanding that it is always working to realize" (Pippin 2020, 8). Clayton quotes a famous and wonderful passage from one of Henry James's notebooks about the end of *The Portrait of a Lady* in which James declares that "[t]he *whole* of anything is never told; you can only take what groups together. What I have done has that unity—it groups together. It is complete in itself" (James 1987, 15; emphasis in original). One of the distractions of the word "whole," in this context, is its connotation of comprehensiveness, of *including everything*. But this is not the kind of whole that is at issue—the point is precisely, as James puts it, that his novel "is complete in itself"; it is not a fragmentary novel just because it doesn't tell us everything. In just the same way, when Perkins writes that narrative films offer us "an assembly of bits and pieces from which to compose a world" (Perkins 2020, 282), this does not imply that films are incomplete!

Coming to terms with the whole that a successful film comprises—or to put it another way, with why it is *Certain Women* (for example) *is* complete—is a matter of critical achievement. The wholeness of a film cannot be divorced from an evaluation of it—not because a particular form of unity is to be preferred over other formal possibilities, but because it is in terms of the relations that the various parts of a film (or aspects, or whichever vocabulary one prefers) have to one another that the very identity of the film, as a film, stands or falls. Nor can the question of unity be simply abandoned. As I put it in chapter 1, there is a sense in which a successful film is *necessarily* coherent—meaning that its parts (or aspects, or dimensions . . .) are the parts, aspects, or dimensions *of a whole*. To repeat myself, this means that coherence (wholeness, unity, call it what you will) is a matter to be brought out at the conclusion of a critical investigation rather than a critical criterion in itself that provides any recipe for how it should be applied. The wholeness of a film is not an unhelpfully notional concept that we can do away with, but neither is it any kind of skeleton key to a film's meaning; it is both what we *investigate* and what we *discover* in a successful critical investigation. The work of the three critics—Perkins, Cavell, and Pippin—whose work underpins every chapter in this book (at times explicitly; always implicitly) offers abundant examples of such successful investigations. James Conant has singled out this very same group of critics as remarkable precisely because of their ability "to show how the whole of a movie is present in each of its parts and how seemingly negligible aspects of those parts are essential to the achievement of the whole" (Conant 2018, 292). I suspect, in fact, that—despite the continued trendiness of declarations to the effect that totality has been subverted, or revealed to be a sham—the most pertinent difficulties here have much less to do with the shortcomings of the concept "whole" than with the still-inadequate condition of our understanding of the enormously varied ways in which things can be part of other things.[10]

When I denied, at the beginning of this section, that there is anything inherently problematic about the idea that a film comprises a whole, I meant that it is perfectly meaningful to say that successful films comprise wholes, not that what we mean by saying so is entirely clear. The issues involved become enormously more complex and ramified—as well as fascinating—when we bring questions of wholeness in film together with the ways in which films, in being viewed, "compose a world" (Perkins 2020, 282), while simultaneously recognizing that films are part of the world, of *our* world. Bringing these questions together is what Stanley Cavell does in the paragraph that concluded the original edition of *The World Viewed* that occupied us for the entirety of chapter 3, when he proposes that "an importance of film—and a danger" is that we seem to see in films "[a] world complete without me which is present to me," which—because such a world is "the world of my immortality"—"takes my life as my haunting of the world" (Cavell 1979a, 160). Part of what makes narrative film such an important medium is that what Cavell describes here does not entail, as might appear at first glance to be the case, that taking films seriously can result only in sheer escapism. On the contrary, paying films the right kind of attention might help us understand important things about how and why we so often haunt the world.

Conant writes that "[a] well-made movie, perhaps more than any other art-form, activates our capacities for engaged reflection and intelligent response in ways in which the world itself does, by presenting us with and involving us in *its* world" (Conant 2023, 250; emphasis in original). I spoke in the introduction about naive film criticism. In contrast to the kind of sophisticated theorizing about film which sees its central task as disabusing film viewers of their naivety, this book has risked inviting the accusation of naivety (in, for example, the seriousness with which it takes the humanity and the intentions of characters in films such as *Certain Women*) precisely because it seems to me that the most damaging naivety—the greatest obstacle to an understanding of the operation and the importance of narrative film—is displayed not in the assertion that film "activates our capacities for engaged reflection and intelligent response in ways in which the world itself does," but instead in its denial.

Notes

Introduction

1. I, of course, claim no originality for this position; the spine of this book is the view that it is expressed with coherence and power in the work of V. F. Perkins and Stanley Cavell. Something similar has also been very cogently argued by Robert B. Pippin; see, for example, Pippin 2012 (1–4).

2. William Rothman makes the same point in deliberately Cavellian language when he writes that "without knowing—that is, acknowledging—our own experience of film, we cannot know the roles films play in our lives, we cannot know the reality of the world on film, we cannot know what films are" (Rothman 1997, xiv).

3. This point can be regarded not as something unusual, but merely as a clear example of the nature of the relationship between self-consciousness and objectivity in aesthetic experience. Some contemporary philosophers are currently attempting to demonstrate that self-consciousness and objectivity, in general, should not—indeed cannot—be understood as mutually exclusive, and thereby to demolish the idea that the more a judgment is self-conscious the less objective it must be. See Rödl 2018 for a particularly bold articulation of such an attempt.

4. I am very grateful to Rybin for his thoughtful engagement with my work. Just to make one correction to his article: the passage from William D. Routt quoted on pp. 4–5 of Rybin 2024 is not Routt's own view (a claim Rybin repeats on pp. 7 and 24) but, as I tried to make clear in my original chapter, his summary of what he and I would agree is a misguided way of approaching the subject; see Lash 2020 (94, 102).

5. The slightly congested potted definition of figuration that I propose in the book just mentioned is "signification that is significantly aligned with articulation" (Lash 2020, 95). As chapter 7 and various remarks dotted elsewhere in this book indicate, my thinking on these issues has been

markedly influenced by the work of Nicole Brenez, although I find her criticism as a whole somewhat less congenial than I once did.

6. Pippin is a third critic whose work is equally valuable in this regard, hence my reference to him in the previous paragraph. He makes relatively regular appearances here—and is particularly prominent in chapter 10—but I have concentrated on him less extensively because I have already written a book about him; see Lash 2022.

7. To repeat: there are of course many reasons to study films differently—as, for example, sociological data or historical evidence—but such approaches are not inherently superior in rigor or scholarly value, merely alternative. One might also add that without an understanding of the aesthetic appeal of cinema—which must be naive in the sense I have been using—it is difficult to discern the precise form of the value of movies for other investigations.

8. Perkins also notes his debts to the work of William Rothman and George M. Wilson.

9. That much contemporary film studies could only see a remark like this as an apologia for the retention of—or insistence upon—irrelevantly "subjective" responses indicates quite how far the field would have to go to absorb some of the central insights of Perkins and Cavell. Seeing the remark this way would imply an unconvincing alignment between the members of the pairs subjective/objective and irrational/rational. But the project of *Film as Film* is explicitly rational: Perkins is interested in claims that can be "rationally sustained" and declares that "a critical judgment is of value only when it can itself be criticized and tested against others' experience and perceptions" (Perkins 1972, 190).

10. Elsewhere in his work, Cavell's debt to Anscombe is often somewhat submerged, but can nevertheless be clearly detected. For example, although "On Brute Facts" is the only text by Anscombe cited in *The Claim of Reason*, the long paragraph on p. 324 echoes many of *Intention*'s most famous phrases. "What you are said to do can have the most various descriptions; under some you will know that you are doing it, under others not. . . . What we are responsible for doing, is, ineluctably, *what in fact happens*" (Cavell 1979b, 324; emphasis in original). Compare "a man may know that he is doing a thing under one description, and not under another" (Anscombe 2000, 11 [§6]) and "I *do* what *happens*" (52 [§29]; emphases in original).

11. It also makes less counterintuitive Perkins's remark that "[a]n authorship theory must find room for processes that may enable the director to take responsibility for discoveries, incorporating them into the film's intention" (Perkins 2020, 233). The phenomena listed by Perkins that I quote in this paragraph ("systems of rhetoric and viewpoint," etc.) exceed the intentions of any one individual, but they do not straightforwardly

overdetermine them; it is only because of the existence of descriptions of actions as intentional that they are intelligible. This point is related to the discussion of description in chapter 2.

12. Compare: "So intention is never a performance in the mind, though in some matters a performance in the mind which is seriously *meant* may make a difference to the correct account of the man's action. . . . But the matters in question are necessarily ones in which some outward acts are 'significant' in some way" (Anscombe 2000, 49 [§27]; emphasis in original).

13. Nick Zangwill, for one, has defended the claim that "moral philosophy can learn much from aesthetics" (Zangwill 2013, 198). He, however, sees aesthetic description as having lessons for philosophy description chiefly in its use of metaphor "to describe the indescribable" (202), whereas in my view what is central is not the presence of metaphor but the simple fact that for any situation there are always competing—or at least alternative—descriptions available, deciding on the pertinence of which requires interpretation. Philippa Foot is quite right to have said, as Zangwill reports, "that in many legal cases there is no room or need for endless redescription" (203), but the ways in which we decide that we can settle on a description have much in common whether the situation is primarily legal, ethical, or aesthetic. See chapter 2 for much more on redescription.

14. And in places they receive direct attention; chapter 5, for example, offers some clues as to what a more detailed account of criteria along the lines suggested above might look like.

Chapter One

1. Many thanks to Alex Clayton, Hoi Lun Law, Janet Lash, and Alastair Phillips for comments on earlier versions of this piece.

2. *Movie* originally ran intermittently until 2000. It was revived in 2010 under the auspices of the Universities of Warwick, Reading, and Oxford in an online format under the title *Movie: A Journal of Film Criticism* (https://warwick.ac.uk/fac/arts/film/movie).

3. Cavell writes that "whatever is meant by a medium's 'possibilities,' each is what it is only in view of the others" (Cavell 1979a, 73).

4. Wood was to change his mind about this; he came to see some instances of aesthetic incoherence in cinema as revelatory of contradictions that the film, to its credit, fails to paper over. See the chapter "The Incoherent Text: Narrative in the '70s" in Wood 2003. Perhaps the most sophisticated expressions of such an aesthetics can be found in the writings of Theodor W. Adorno, who wrote, apropos the music of Schoenberg, that "[i]mportant works of art are the ones that aim for an extreme; they are destroyed in

the process and their broken outlines survive as the ciphers of a supreme, unnameable truth" (Adorno [1963] 1998, 226). Such a position would have been alien to Perkins at any stage of his career.

5. See Lash 2020 (69–73) for a discussion of the differences between coherence, cohesion, and consistency in film.

6. See Virvidaki 2017 for an examination, explicitly informed by Perkins, into the ways in which "we can appreciate the achievement of coherence in narrative films characterised by strikingly baffling or opaque organisational principles" (203).

7. This account would have to be complicated by addressing the question of whether a film can be incoherent in some but not all of its aspects—coherent in diegesis but incoherent in ideology, for example—not to mention the matter of what kind of coherence we should expect to see *between* such aspects; see, again, Wood 2003. I will merely remark that giving rise to incompatible interpretations should not, in and of itself, be considered a mark of incoherence, lest coherence becomes a vanishingly (and unhelpfully) rare beast.

8. Perkins acknowledges that the first drafts of the book were at times excessively prescriptive: "To the extent that the published *Film as Film* retains any traces of the prescriptive formulations of my first drafts (minor but not blameless inflections of tone in discussing the details of some examples) those remnants are clearly inconsistent with the whole drive of the book's argument" (Perkins 1972, 147).

9. Noël Carroll has written, correctly, that "to find that a film is disunified in certain respects already requires the presumption that it is somehow unified in others" (Carroll 1998, 13).

10. A judgment I tend to agree with, though I would incline towards calling it "pedestrian" rather than "pretentious."

11. It is interesting to note that in *These Three* (1936), Wyler's earlier version of the same story, although the crucial revelation takes place not in the back of a car but in the grandmother's room, Mary still insists on whispering and therefore the audience is still prevented from hearing what she says. But the fact that no physical screen separates us from Mary and her grandmother at this moment means that there can be no plausible parallel device deployed later when the children are being removed from school; the later film is, in this specific instance at least, formally richer.

12. See James Conant's discussion of "patent" and "latent" virtuosity and intention in Hitchcock in Conant 2018.

13. I think Hoi Lun Law was almost certainly right when he suggested to me that Perkins would have been wary of the "interpretive anarchy" that devices like those used in *La notte* might, in his view, have tended to encourage.

14. Wood discusses the colour effects in these two films in terms of classical and Romantic traditions during his discussion of *Film as Film* in Wood 1976 (23–25).

15. I am here using *rhetoric* to refer to the way films are (unavoidably) *shaped*, and to the implications of such shaping, rather than specifically to instances where the film attempts to persuade. This is analogous to the way Paul de Man uses the word about poetry, referring to "the study of tropes and figures (which is how the term *rhetoric* is used here, and not in the derived sense of comment or of eloquence or persuasion)" (de Man 1979, 6; emphasis in original).

16. Robert Pippin has very interestingly repurposed Yacavone's distinction between the world-of and world-in a film in terms of the perspectives of a film's characters; see Pippin 2020 (8n6), and see Yacavone 2023 (143–44) for an appreciative response.

17. This possibility was surely the source of Pasolini's attraction to the concept of free indirect discourse.

18. A rather more circumspect comment on the issues addressed in the first sentence here can be found in Stanley Cavell's remark that "[o]n the stage, two trees may constitute a forest, and two brooms the two trees; for the screen, this would yield only two brooms" (Cavell 1979a, 199).

19. Perkins makes much of the consequences of a betrayal of logic. Certainly, in mathematics, an inconsistency in a proof (where both p and not-p turn out to be true) is calamitous, for it allows one to draw any conclusion one wants: precisely "anything can happen." But this is not the case in narrative cinema, where incompossible events *can* occur: consider *Last Year at Marienbad* (Alain Resnais, 1961) or *Tokyo senso sengo hiwa* (Nagasi Oshima, 1970).

20. Perkins's criticism of that which distracts is related to his stipulation that "no game worth watching changes its rules at the players' convenience" (123). Certainly there is a sense in which watching a film is *like* playing a game. But is it *actually* a game, either literally or perhaps in a sense closer to Wittgenstein's language games? I think Perkins relies too heavily on his metaphor here. The distinction that he wants to make a critical principle (that when the rules change we have a flawed film, because were this to happen in a game it would then cease to be a game in any proper sense) might even be what distinguishes fiction from games. What if it is part of a film's method to make us work to discover what the rules are? Is watching a film perhaps less like going to see a game with whose rules we are already familiar than it is like trying to work out the rules while (and by) watching? Soccer might be easier to come to grips with that way than cricket, but that does not mean that soccer is better than cricket.

Chapter Two

1. I am thinking of pieces including Clayton 2016 and Watter 2019. The first conference entirely devoted to Perkins's work, "*Film as Film* Today: On the Criticism and Theory of V. F. Perkins," held at the University of Warwick in September 2018, included a number of papers working along these lines. A very preliminary version of what has become this chapter was presented at that conference, and I am very grateful to all the organizers and to various of the delegates for their feedback. I would like to thank Hoi Lun Law and Adrian Martin in particular. I am also extremely grateful to two anonymous reviewers for the *New Review of Film and Television Studies* for their generous and constructive criticism.

2. In bringing together a number of different senses of description I am encouraged by the fact that Ludwig Wittgenstein argued that there is no such thing as description "in general" that we could use as a starting point. See Wittgenstein 2009 (15–16 [§24]): "Remember how many different kinds of thing are called 'description': description of a body's position by means of its co-ordinates, description of a facial expression, description of a sensation of touch, of a mood." One could describe my project in Wittgensteinian terms as an attempt to show that a small group of applications of the term "description" have family resemblances, rather than being simply equivocal. Wittgenstein's work was foundational for a number of the thinkers I will mention later (Elizabeth Anscombe and Cora Diamond in particular), and he had a profound interest in description. Delving into its details—including its connections to, but also profound differences from, Bertrand Russell's theory of descriptions—would, however, take me too far afield. Helpful discussion of the topic can be found in Gert 1997, including the claim, very suggestive for what I want to say about Perkins on description, that Wittgenstein's recommendation to philosophers was that they "should describe *descriptions*" (221; emphasis in original).

3. In the terms I use in this book (as outlined in the introduction), I would phrase this point by saying that describing emphasis involves—or, perhaps better, *is*—a form of judgment.

4. Although I do not have space to explore the issue here, the notion of redescription could also prove a fruitful avenue for approaching the still-controversial question of Perkins's classicism, the emphasis—particularly strong in *Film as Film*—on coherence and credibility, and their consequences for Perkins's accounts of modernist filmmaking. (These issues are addressed, to some extent, in the previous chapter.) We might see modernism as using formal devices precisely as explorations of the possibilities of redescription, and thereby challenge Perkins's reading of a film such as Godard's *Vivre sa vie* (1962) on his own terms, along the lines pursued by Klevan when he argues,

in response to Perkins's charge that Godard privileges his devices at the expense of their meaning, that the device "must attract attention because it is itself under scrutiny" (Klevan 2018, 216). For another critical but charitable reading of Perkins's position on these issues, see Smuts 2006.

5. A distinct strand within the so-called descriptive turn is related to the advocacy of "surface reading," as represented by the work of Stephen Best, Sharon Marcus, and others (see Best and Marcus 2009). I share Eugenie Brinkema's concern about this strand's "presumption that texts disclose themselves on and at the surface with a neutral good faith" (Brinkema 2022, 388). The account of description that this area of work proposes and advocates—described by Ellen Rooney as "reporting what the text says in its own words" (Rooney 2010, 115)—has little to do with the topic of this chapter.

6. There is, however, an interestingly expanding field of research concerned with audio description; see Matamala and Remael 2015 and Ramos 2015 for two examples.

7. I have been slightly devious in my quotation from Benson here. He actually writes "explain or critique," but I have deleted "explain" because Perkins's work is centrally concerned with aesthetic explanation, with *accounting for* the achievements of the films that most impress him. In contrast to much work within film studies, however, the kind of explanations that Perkins searches for are to be found within the films themselves, rather than in, say, archival documentation or historical contextualization.

8. Although, here as elsewhere, I think Perkins's writing does tend to bear out Benson's association of the descriptive mode with affirmation rather than critique, this is not definitional of the practice as I conceive it. Description can as easily be a form of critique as of praise; there are plenty of examples of this in *Film as Film* and elsewhere in Perkins's work (see Perkins 1993, 85, for a famous—and in fact, I think, rather dubious—example).

9. ". . . of those events" has been silently corrected to ". . . or those events," which is clearly what is meant.

10. D. P. Fowler has suggested that, if anything, it would be more accurate to put things the other way around: "There is an obvious sense in which description is more basic—one could theoretically imagine a narrative with only names in it, and no referring expressions, but it is practically impossible for any narrative of length not to contain description. In a deeper sense, however, as Genette noted in his article on the 'Boundaries of Narrative,' description in general is secondary, is *'ancilla narrationis*, the ever-necessary, ever-submissive, never-emancipated slave'" (Fowler 1991, 26).

11. Although understanding the ways that films achieve results analogous to what is accomplished in literature by narration and description is obviously both intriguing and important (see Rieser 2007 for another

example), drawing the distinction in the manner outlined in this paragraph has not always proved fruitful. Chatman's conclusion that films *cannot* describe (see Chatman 1980, 128) follows from his insistence that description pauses story-time; thus, if the story-time is not paused we must not be dealing with description: "For example, recall the scene in the middle of *Notorious* just at the moment when Cary Grant and Ingrid Bergman are flying into Rio de Janeiro. We see shots of the city from the air, typical street scenes, and so on. Yet our sense is not of a hiatus in the story-time but rather that Rio is down there waiting for Cary and Ingrid to arrive" (129–30). Were Chatman not so determined to insist that all description involves this kind of "hiatus" he might have been more prepared to explore the descriptive dimensions of this sequence.

12. Some relevant texts include Anscombe (1957) 2000, Hepburn and Murdoch 1956, Williams 1973, Diamond 1991, and Pippin 2008.

13. This insight has very wide-ranging consequences. Anscombe complains, for example, that Kant's "rule about universalizable maxims is useless without stipulations as to what shall count as a relevant description of an action with a view to constructing a maxim about it" (Anscombe 1981, 27).

14. That David Bordwell's book *Making Meaning* (Bordwell 1989) exhibits just such a view—to its detriment—is the substance of the charge made by Perkins in his 1990 article "Must We Say What They Mean?" (see Perkins 2020, 240–56).

15. Note how potentially filmic are the details that Diamond mentions in her discussion of Tolstoy: "The opening chapters of *Anna Karenina*—what do they give us so much as the texture of Stiva's being? His good-hearted, silly smile when he is caught at something shameful, his response to the memory of the stupid smile, the failure of his attempt to look pathetic and submissive when he goes back to Dolly—what he blushes at, what he laughs at, what he turns his eyes away from: this is Stiva" (Diamond 1991, 374). I will have much more to say about smiles later in this chapter.

16. I should acknowledge that I have not mentioned one of the most well-known philosophical endeavors that connects ethics with redescription, namely, the work of Richard Rorty. Rorty's notion of redescription is rather different from that which is my focus here, and exploring the relationship between Rortian redescription and the claims I want to make about Perkins's practice is beyond the scope of this chapter. Suffice it to say that nothing I say about Perkins is intended to imply any affinities with Rorty's understanding of the ethical role of redescription, according to which, as Brad Frazier puts it, "in the hands of an ironist, redescription is the engine of self-creation" (Frazier 2006, 462).

17. Such descriptive acts are, for Williams, a central hinge between the ordinary activity of being in the world, and the activity of the artist:

"This vital descriptive effort—which is not merely a subsequent effort to describe something known, but literally a way of seeing new things and new relationships—has often been observed, by artists, yet it is not the activity of artists alone" (Williams 1961, 40).

18. For an interesting recent discussion of Williams including material on his understanding of the relationship between text and performance in film, see Chandler 2020.

19. Earlier, Perkins writes that, in the score, "[q]ualities of movement are closely described and thus boldly displayed by an accompaniment that exerts itself to turn action into choreography" (Perkins 2020, 358).

20. For more on the notion of the "monstrator," see Gaudreault 2009. Talking about what "the film does" has recently been described as not strictly accurate (Stevens 2022, 4) and even as "nonsensical" (Barrowman 2023). On the contrary; as long as we are clear what we are claiming, such language is not only acceptable, it is often the *most* appropriate way of talking. For a concise take on the theory of such issues, see Pippin 2013.

21. I should note that in saying this I do not intend thereby to take up a position on how best to understand the relationship between film narration and the notion of the narrator. George M. Wilson has thought deeply, but not in my view unproblematically, about this issue; see Wilson 1986 and 2011, Pippin's reworking of Wilson's ideas in Pippin 2013, and also the related discussion of self-conscious seeing in Lash 2022 (41–49).

22. Another interesting use of the word "gloss" can be found in Perkins's book on Renoir's *La règle du jeu*; he writes of the general's "appraisal of the marquis' behaviour under the most testing circumstances, when Robert has succeeded in putting an acceptable gloss on the slaughter of Jurieu" (Perkins 2012, 36). It would take at least another chapter fully to trace the functions of description and redescription in Perkins's account of Renoir's film; for a sketch of what this would have to involve, see Lash 2021b. I will content myself here with pointing out that, for Perkins, the film *begins* with a failure of redescription—"André seems to have turned back the clock on aviation to convert his solo flight into a knightly quest, performed to show him worthy of a lady's favour" (Perkins 2012, 28), something which is undermined by Christine's failure to meet him upon his return—and that description seems to get harder and harder as the film progresses: "Renoir arranges the drama so as to avoid narrowing the terms of our understanding. The surprises that he springs do not simply exchange one set of assumptions for another. Rather they produce a less and less easily defined complex of fact and possibility" (65).

23. Even if this account is convincing, it needs to be complicated by the recognition that the film is also the story of Kazan's own family, and so part of the story of how it was that Kazan came to be in a position to be able to make the very film that ends with this ambiguous smile. Various

interpretations are possible, but the ironies of the film are clearly complex enough that an unequivocal proclamation as to whether Stavros's final situation is, in the final analysis, "good" or "bad"—of whether or not the trip was "worth it"—would miss the point.

24. See Ford 2017 on the philosophical implications of the ambiguous genitive in "representation of action."

Chapter Three

1. The 1979 edition of *The World Viewed* consists of the unaltered text of the 1971 edition with a new afterword, "More of *The World Viewed*." Many thanks to Alex Clayton, Michelle Devereaux, Catherine Wheatley, and an anonymous reviewer for their comments and encouragement regarding previous drafts of this chapter.

2. For an exception to this tendency, see Robert Mankin's claim that "[t]here can be no better introduction to the method of Stanley Cavell and to *The Claim of Reason* than the sentence with which it closes" (Mankin 1985, 66).

3. He does, admittedly, refer in a late piece to the "defenses against comprehensibility" that he finds in Walter Benjamin, Emerson, and Thoreau, but in arguing that these should not be "underestimated" the implication is clearly that a clarity achieved too cheaply is no clarity at all (Cavell 2005c, 86).

4. *The World Viewed* is much concerned with skepticism in its broadest sense; this is precisely the import of passages such as the following: "Our condition has become one in which our natural mode of perception is to view, feeling unseen. We do not so much look at the world as look *out at* it, from behind the self" (Cavell 1979a, 102; emphasis in original). The term itself is, however, scarcely to be found in the original edition; the much-quoted slogan that "[f]ilm is a moving image of skepticism" first appears in the later "More of *The World Viewed*" (188).

5. There are fascinating and complex philosophical issues at play which I cannot explore in any detail here. As a placeholder for future investigations, I will simply note that Gareth Evans's article "Things without the Mind" (influenced by P. F. Strawson, and subsequently influential upon John McDowell) explores in detail the notion that the very idea of an objective world requires a subject that is *within* that world; see Evans 1985 (249–90). One reason, then, that film can be seen as "a moving image of skepticism" (Cavell 1979a, 188) might be that film gives us an image of objectivity according to which it could only truly be achieved by a subject that is not part of the world viewed. Such views are very widespread; Evans's

work helps show why they must be skeptical. A consequence of thinking along these lines is that the just-cited reading of Cavell that Pippin offers can be seen inadvertently—and contrary to Cavell's intentions—to confirm the skeptical perspective according to which participation in the world and objectivity are mutually exclusive.

6. Solipsism is never mentioned in *The World Viewed*, nor in "More of *The World Viewed*." It is true that in the latter text Cavell remarks about some other sentences towards the end of his book that in writing them he "was counting on having earned the right to expect my reader to take these expressions symbolically" (Cavell 1979a, 211). But taking Cavell's words symbolically is not equivalent to reading him as making the claim that a certain experience—that of watching movies—is itself symbolic.

7. *Haunting the World* ends with a few thoughts about this question.

8. There are also obvious connections between watching films and another philosophical fantasy that crops up a few times in *The Claim of Reason*, that of the "experience I have called 'seeing ourselves as outside the world as a whole,' looking in at it, as we now look at some objects from a position among others" (Cavell 1979b, 236).

9. Neither Annette Kuhn and Guy Westwell's entry on psychoanalytic film theory in their *Dictionary of Film Studies* nor Todd McGowan's extensive bibliography for *Oxford Bibliographies* contain any reference to Cavell. Joseph Smith and William Kerrigan's *Images in Our Souls: Cavell, Psychoanalysis, and Cinema* (1987), the collection in which "Psychoanalysis and Cinema" originally appeared, has had little impact within film studies.

10. It is also, in a different way, central to Hegel's thought. Hegel is an important, if often rather submerged, influence on Cavell; his affinities with Hegel are emphasized in Pippin 2019.

11. Cf. Timothy Gould's pregnant, if rather compressed, remark: "As the presences of film tend to conceal the absences they refer to, so the immediacy of the responses that film elicits tends to conceal (and of course might still reveal) the depth of our craving for those vivid absences and for the anxious privacies they conceal" (Gould 1998, 134).

12. Elsewhere, Cavell entertains the thought that criticism itself is a kind of afterlife. He raises the question of the relation between some critical remarks he offers about the music of Mahler and "what we have experienced of this music," suggesting that we might "say they are the afterlife of such a work," which then leads him to ask: "And what if this is the only afterlife we are given to know?" (Cavell 2022, 286)

13. As Marian Keane and William Rothman rightly point out: "The danger in his taking the world on film to be the world of his immortality, Cavell's words literally say, is that it takes his own life to be a haunting of the world" (Keane and Rothman 2000, 254).

14. Recall Cavell's suggestion that a "fantasy of necessary inexpressiveness" might compensate for a fear that "if I were expressive that would mean continuously betraying my experiences" (Cavell 1979b, 351). And compare: "Whatever in me I have to conceal I may betray exactly by the way in which I conceal it" (459). Note also that in *Contesting Tears* Cavell brings together remarks by Wittgenstein, Hegel, and Emerson concerning "the sense that the human body is expressive of mind" with the claim that "Freud's twist on the philosophers here is registered in his idea of our expressions as betraying ourselves" (Cavell 1996, 104–5).

15. It is, of course, true that the second paragraph of the book's preface suggests that one of its author's "motive[s] for writing it" was to pursue the question "What broke my natural relation to movies?" which might seem to imply that modernism is an interference with, rather than a basis of, Cavell's thinking about film (Cavell 1979a, xix). However, my interpretation of the book's concluding paragraph diverges from that of even such informed and insightful commentators as Keane and Rothman, who paraphrase our paragraph's remarks about denying the coherence of the world as indicating that Cavell "has reason to want nature to turn away from film, for film to turn away from its own nature, for his 'natural relation' to movies to end" (Keane and Rothman 2000, 255). This does not resemble what I find in this paragraph. Saying that the claim that "there is reason for me to want the camera to deny the coherence of the world" expresses a desire for "film to turn away from its own nature" skips too many steps, not least of which is the way such an argument surreptitiously moves from the idea that one might have a "natural relation to movies" to the question of "film['s] . . . own nature." I think Morgan's emphasis on modernism gets us closer to the right track.

16. Cf. also Cavell's reference to Freud's "Analysis Terminable and Interminable" in Cavell 1996 (111–13).

17. It is also un-Hegelian. Thinking of ontology this way, as is extremely common, might be an expression of what Cavell calls "our unappeasable discomfort (Hegel, I believe, calls this restlessness) with finitude" (Cavell 2022, 96). Earlier in this chapter we have already seen Cavell discover the theme of restlessness in the work of both Kant and Wittgenstein. See also the discussion in "Performative and Passionate Utterance" of the relationship between "human conventions" and "whatever there is, human or otherwise" (Cavell 2005c, 159).

18. Compare the passage in "Music Discomposed" in which Cavell notes that "the succession of art styles is *irreversible*, which may be as important a component of the concept of progress as the component of superiority" (Cavell [1969] 2015, 170; emphasis in original).

19. Compare the remarks in *The World Viewed* about "the myth of youth itself, that life has not yet begun irretrievably" (Cavell 1979a, 68).

Chapter Four

1. Many thanks to Alex Clayton for extremely helpful comments on an earlier version of this chapter, as well as to those people who offered feedback after I delivered a version of it at the 2023 BAFTSS conference at the University of Lincoln. I believe the preposition "on" in the English title doesn't have an equivalent in the Hungarian. *Body and Soul* might have been a punchier choice of translation; perhaps the aim was to downplay any associations with Johnny Green's jazz standard.

2. The quotation from Enyedi derives from press kit materials that are no longer available at the URL supplied in Walton 2020.

3. Enyedi has expressed her interest in Jungian ideas in relation to this film (see, for example, Leonard 2020, 160), and yet what is interesting about the dreams in *On Body and Soul* is precisely that they are neither exactly "collective" nor "unconscious"! The dreams are shared by precisely *two* people, both of whom retain full awareness of their dreams while they are happening and can remember them in detail when awake.

4. See also this remark in *The Claim of Reason*: "Being human is aspiring to being human. Since it is not aspiring to being the only human, it is an aspiration on behalf of others as well. Then we might say that being human is aspiring to being seen as human" (Cavell 1979b, 399).

5. This is not to say that we literally see what they see; Alex Clayton has pointed out to me that the perspective of the dreams remains in the third person, and that there are things we learn about the dreams from the film's dialogue which we are not shown directly. But I would still maintain that we are shown what they dream, and in such a way as to, if not undermine, then at least render questionable, the notion that the content of a dream must in some essential or fundamental way always remain incommunicable.

6. Gábor Gergely has pointed out to me that I may be reaching in my reading of the mash, because the sorrel dish that Endre eats at the beginning of the film has very different associations, to a Hungarian, from the mashed potato into which Mária puts her hand.

7. Further discomfort is provoked by inclusion of one scene between Endre and his daughter, which makes it evident that not only is he old enough to be Mária's father, she is in fact even younger than his daughter.

8. The philosopher Gareth Evans helpfully counters the possible view that inference might, instead, get into the picture at an earlier stage. As opposed to the kind of "information-acquiring transaction" in which "the subject would have been regarded as receiving data, intrinsically without objective content, into which he was supposed to read the appropriate objective significance by means of an (extremely shaky) inference," Evans declares that "[t]he only events that can conceivably be regarded as data for a conscious, reasoning subject are

seemings—events, that is, already imbued with (apparent) objective significance, and with a necessary, though resistible, propensity to influence our actions" (Evans 1982, 122–23; emphasis in original). Evans's account leaves open the possibility of the kind of inference that Wittgenstein and Merleau-Ponty deny, but importantly combats the idea that our engagement with the world rests on some kind of fundamental ground-level inference.

9. This paragraph should not be taken to imply that the two philosophers' positions are identical, at least when it comes to film. In "The Film and the New Psychology," Merleau-Ponty writes that "the movies can be so gripping in their presentation of man" because "they do not give us his *thoughts*, as novels have done for so long, but his conduct or behavior" (Merleau-Ponty 1964, 58; emphasis in original). One certainly understands the distinction—and the subsequent claim that "[f]or the movies . . . dizziness, pleasure, grief, love, and hate are ways of behaving" is not, of course, by any means to be understood as reductive behaviorism—but I think, nevertheless, that neither Wittgenstein nor Cavell would have wanted to express things thus, by denying that films present us with thoughts.

10. See the last part of chapter 2 for a discussion of smiles in Elia Kazan's *America, America* (1963).

11. This is sometimes expressed as a difficulty with inference. For example, Catherine S. Ames and Christopher Jarrold write that "if a child with autism finds it difficult to focus their attention and to learn which cues are most reliable in predicting a particular outcome, then the ability to use cues to infer meaning will be difficult to acquire" (Ames and Jarrold 2007, 1774). I would prefer to put the matter by saying that the difficulty stems from the autistic child's need to infer in the first place, because of the difficulty they experience in seeing expressions *as* meaningful.

12. Importantly, however, this moment contrasts with the way the female deer appears in the dream sequences, in which it is not at all clear that either of the animals is any less resourceful or more helpless than the other. Thanks to Alex Clayton for emphasizing this point.

13. Her description is also not entirely convincing: Mária at no point "stare[s] unabashedly at the camera."

14. I do not intend this description to prejudge whether a cow's eyes might or might not be able to express all these things, only that we cannot see them in its gaze with such clarity and immediacy.

15. The moment when she leaps out of the bath has something distinctly comic about it, which is a brave decision to take when the film seems to be preparing us for a tragic ending. That it seems to me to come off is an indication of the complexity of the film's tonal achievement. (It is helped by our having already heard the affecting Laura Marling song "What He Wrote" that Mária listens to in the bath, so that its initial emotional

impact has somewhat subsided when we hear it again. It is also prepared for by the slightly bathetic moment when the CD sticks and stops playing, leaving Mária in the bath in silence—her perfectly choreographed suicide has already begun to unravel.)

16. Another productive line of thought concerning the function in the film of the graphic scenes in the abattoir might be to explore the resonances between the consent that human beings can give one another and the consent that animals cannot give—to be slaughtered, for example—as well as the consent that we must give (if we eat meat) to the perpetuation of situations in which consent cannot be given. Cavell writes that "[t]he public circumstances in which I live, in which I participate, and from which I profit, are ones I consent to" (Cavell 1990, 108). Thanks are again due to Alex Clayton for some thoughts along these lines, as well as for offering the observation about the editing which I placed at the end of the previous paragraph.

17. Still later, Cavell explores the possibility that "he rips open my shirt and snaps off my chest to reveal (I glance down) some elegant clockwork" (Cavell 1979b, 408).

18. Compare Cavell's discussion of what would happen if "after a thousand instances of receiving me to tea" you "next time lay out the toy tea set that belongs to your child's doll, and proceed to pour" (Cavell 2005c, 136). Mária and Endre do not experience any crises in their relationship, in their mutual (mis)understanding, as severe as this would be.

19. To the idea that "'If the human body is a machine then a machine has sentience' is no better an inference than 'If the human body is a machine then the body does not have sentience,'" Cavell's response is that this "is not an inference at all. It is the result of absent logic" (Cavell 1979b, 414).

Chapter Five

1. Many thanks to Dan Flory, George Toles, and two anonymous reviewers for their comments and encouragement concerning earlier versions of this chapter.

2. The idea of "production for use" is, of course, made much of in one of the definitive remarriage comedies, *His Girl Friday* (Howard Hawks, 1940); see Cavell 1981b (174).

3. In spite of Cavell's reservations about "features," the list of "defining characteristics" that Wheatley provides is very helpful (Wheatley 2019, 108). We might note in particular that in *Phantom Thread* too the plot "gets resolved in a move to a world of nature"—Woodcock's country house—and that the film most certainly ends by "stressing remarriage as repetition," something I will return to at the end of this chapter (108).

4. I concentrate here on the relationship between Reynolds and Alma but a full treatment of the film's relation to the remarriage comedy would have to explore the relationship between Reynolds and Cyril, not to mention between the two women.

5. And yet it would not have taken much to turn the film into a variation on unknown woman melodrama instead; think of what happens to Alma's predecessor, Johanna (Camilla Rutherford).

6. Much is made of Reynolds's taste and its supposed inflexibility, but it is also hinted that this is to an extent a convenient device for retaining control. At the breakfast in which Alma irritates him by scraping her butter knife too loudly he is eating one of the pastries that he told his previous girlfriend, Johanna, were too "stodgy" for him.

7. To expand briefly on the point made above: although any careful reading of Cavell should make it clear that he does not intend "the truth of skepticism" to mean that skepticism is true, too many commentators still make this assumption. The phrase means something much closer to "what it is that skepticism gets right"—chiefly, that the existence of other people is not a matter of knowledge. Similarly, the final phrase quoted above means precisely what it says—not that skepticism cannot be combatted, but that combatting it cannot be a matter of refutation. For Cavell it is, instead, a matter of acknowledgment. For a sophisticated version of this kind of misreading, see Marie McGinn's chapter "The Everyday Alternative to Scepticism" (McManus 2004, 240–59), and Cavell's comments in rejoinder (278–91, and especially 282–87), where he is explicit that by "the truth of skepticism" he does *not* mean "that I think skepticism is more or less true" (287).

8. Note, for example, that Cavell's reading of *It Happened One Night* explicitly connects the way that the film's "Wall of Jericho" reflexively evokes the cinema screen to the issues of other minds and acknowledgement; see Cavell 1981b (109). We might further note that Macarthur does not accurately represent the difference between theater and cinema in these respects. To say that "unlike the theater, screen actors are not right there in front of us such that we could, if we wished to break with artistic convention, confront them" (Macarthur 2016, 125) is to ignore Cavell's warning against "imagin[ing] that you could enter the actors' space in a theater by crossing the footlights. But of course all you would accomplish would be to stop the performance" (Cavell 1979a, 155).

9. I will relegate a further disagreement with Macarthur to an endnote, because it is not essential for the thrust of my argument. In keeping with many references by a range of critics to Cavell as an heir to (an often-misinterpreted) Bazin, Macarthur I think over- (or mis-) emphasizes the role and importance to Cavell of the mechanical automaticity of film. He

writes: "In the second use, 'automatism' stands for 'what gives significance to this physical basis . . . artistic discoveries of form and genre and type and technique' ([*The World Viewed*] 105). I shall leave this secondary sense of the term aside" (Macarthur 2016, 125). But I think one could make a good case that this sense of automatism is better thought of as Cavell's *primary* sense. Martin Shuster rightly argues that when Cavell writes that "[t]he depth of the automatism of photography is to be read not alone in its mechanical reproduction of an image of reality, but in its mechanical defeat of our presence to that reality" (Cavell 1979a, 25), "[i]t is this [second] point, and not the point about the automatic nature of the camera, that is central" (Shuster 2015, 1076). Immediately after the passage Macarthur cites, Cavell writes: "It may seem perverse of me . . . to use the concept of automatism—anyway, the term automatic—also in the description of film's physical basis. . . . In part it has to do with the identity of film itself—the fact that the medium just does have this manufacturing medium at its basis. In part it has to do with the fate of modernist art generally. . . . This is also why, *although I am trying to free the idea of a medium from its confinement in referring to the physical bases of various arts*, I go on using the same word to name those bases as well as to characterize modes of achievement in the arts" (Cavell 1979a, 105; my emphasis). The passage I have emphasized should give us pause when we read Macarthur saying that "[f]or the purposes of this paper, I will not challenge Cavell's contention 'that the basis of the medium of movies is photographic' ([*The World Viewed*] 16)" (Macarthur 2016, 133n10). In the passage cited Cavell is in fact characterizing the thought of Panofsky and Bazin, and in "More of *The World Viewed*" he refers to "my discomforts with [Panofsky's and Bazin's] unabashed appeals to nature and to reality" (Cavell 1979a, 166). As I have already argued in the introduction and in chapter 3, Cavell clearly does not believe that one can say *anything* substantial about the ontology of film, in his sense, without watching a great many films and staying as close to, as faithful to, the experience of so doing as possible; many of his critics seem to think otherwise, believing that one can explore the ontology of film simply by reflecting on the cinematic apparatus and its implications. (There is further discussion of Cavell's understanding of cinema's ontology and its automatisms in chapter 6.) See Shuster 2015 (1087), and note also Cavell's ironic remark that "to trace the intellectual history of philosophy's concentration on the meaning of particular words and sentences, in isolation from a systematic attention to their concrete uses would be a worthwhile undertaking. . . . A fitting title for this history would be: Philosophy and the Rejection of the Human" (Cavell 1979b, 206–7).

10. Although Macarthur here uses criteria and standards interchangeably, Cavell—and, he argues, Wittgenstein—see a crucial distinction between them. See the introduction for more on this.

11. See the discussion of Anscombe and friendship (in contrast to, for example, revenge) in the introduction.

12. Usefully comparable lists produced by Cavell himself can be found in Cavell 1979b (209) and Cavell (1969) 2015 (48).

13. In the screenplay, Reynolds asks Alma, "What will you be when you finally grow up?" to which she replies, "I want to be a Mother and I want to be a Wife" (*Phantom Thread* screenplay, p. 12). The film is the richer for not being so explicit about her plans and her own sense of them.

14. See the discussion of the end of Hitchcock's *Rear Window* in Lash 2020 (25–26).

15. Note that for some reason simply leaving is not an option for Alma—she must either wait for Reynolds to expel her or find another solution: "What I am doing here? I'm standing around like an idiot . . . waiting for you to get rid of me, to tell me to leave. So tell me, so I don't stand around like a fucking fool." I am reminded of Cavell's discussion of houses "which are unleavable and hence unlivable" in Poe and Hawthorne; see Cavell 1986 (113).

16. A glance through viewer reviews on IMDB will readily provide examples of all three readings.

17. The answer, of course, is that the remarriage can only be achieved through *conversation*, as Cavell continually insists in *Pursuits of Happiness*; here, that means making the poisoning and its rationale explicit. Apropos of apparent formlessness in Anderson's work, George Toles has written that "stability or coming to rest, 'the momentary stay against confusion' that is form's animating desire, must not be worn too cheaply. Art can turn counterfeit, negligible, or vaporous if form closes the dialogue with formlessness prematurely, or if it too readily accepts those elements that the artist has previously 'used up' because they are manageable and familiar" (Toles 2016, 122). He argues that "[w]hat we cumulatively behold [in *The Master* (Paul Thomas Anderson, 2012)] is a defeat of form's concerted long-term effort to control, or at least find an enduring shape for, the dragon of chaos" (Toles 2016, 123). *Phantom Thread*, it seems to me, tells the other side of this story, a victory for form, but a victory wherein form's fragility and provisionality are clearly marked.

18. We see a building from the outside in the Alps, but we never see inside it; we do see both the outside and the inside of the Victoria Hotel, but that is where Reynolds meets Alma and the transformation is set in motion.

19. Note that Cavell links ideas of "satisfaction" and "oscillation" with philosophy and its sense of the strangeness, the uncanniness, of the everyday in Cavell 1986 (101–2).

20. Whereas Meyer focusses on happy endings that are anxious in the sense that it is not clear "that all problems have been or can be solved"

(Meyer 2008, 85), the disorientation and anxiety that linger at the end of *Phantom Thread* center around whether what we witness should even *count* as a happy ending.

21. I am reminded here of a remark of Cavell's in which he declares that he sees "Wittgenstein's construction and destruction of the possibility of a private language as revealing the barrier to narcissism, facing us with that reciprocity and exchange apart from which separate human beings cannot acquire the force so much as to name themselves, to create the realm of the private" (Cavell 1981b, 74).

22. There is something of the Addams Family in the way this aspect of the film's humor works.

Chapter Six

1. Kubrick's unmade film about the Holocaust, *Aryan Papers*, might perhaps have combined all these dimensions. Many thanks are due to Hoi Lun Law for his very insightful comments on an earlier draft of this chapter.

2. Lest the repetition of surnames prove distracting, I should say that there is indeed a relation, and that Nicholas Lash was my father. He died in 2020 so I had no opportunity to discuss this chapter with him; I can't say that I recall him ever expressing an opinion about Kubrick's work. But it has been a great pleasure engaging academically with his work, something I have not previously had the opportunity to do.

3. Note that this does not entail any kind of behaviorism, despite the persistence of such charges against Wittgenstein; neither Anscombe nor Lash—nor, indeed, Wittgenstein—deny the existence of "mental goings-on."

4. It is interesting to consider this point in relation to the German distinction between "Erfahrung" and the more private and immediate "Erlebnis" which was so important to the work of the Frankfurt school (of whom more shortly), but Lash's critique cannot be responded to simply by replacing the latter with the former. See the discussion in Hansen 2012 (xiv).

5. Andrea Kern has claimed that the notion that there is such a thing as raw sensory experience must have skeptical consequences, arguing that "one cannot account for the objectivity of our knowledge of the world by claiming that it is logically possible for us to enjoy the very same sensory experiences we do, yet without enjoying knowledge through them" (Kern 2017, 269).

6. Vincent Descombes, drawing on both Wittgenstein and Anscombe, describes this bewitchment very well when he writes that "[a] correct expression of the intentionality of our acts, therefore, should not be ontological but grammatical: their common factor is to be signified by

verbs, all of which require a direct object" (Descombe 1986, 127). We are bewitched if we unknowingly take this grammatical requirement to signal something ontological.

7. See the related claim that "it is arguable that the only instruments that could provide data for a theory of film are the procedures of criticism" (Cavell 1979a, 12).

8. An understanding of his films' relationship to genre is clearly key to a full appreciation of Kubrick's cinema, though I will not focus on the issue here.

9. Mast lays precisely this charge at the door of Kracauer, Cavell, and others in the first chapter of Mast (1977) 1983.

10. And *not*, as is commonly assumed, in his emphasis on reality and the automatic functioning of the filmic apparatus. As we have already seen earlier in this book, in "More of *The World Viewed*," Cavell explicitly declares his "discomforts" with the "unabashed appeals to nature and to reality" that he finds in Erwin Panofsky and in Bazin (Cavell 1979a, 166).

11. The idea of "a film's idea of itself" is what Robert Pippin calls its reflective form; see Pippin 2020.

12. This is not to deny that such procedures may go awry; for example, by descending into special pleading. But that this may happen does not—in and of itself—impugn the methodology.

13. This would be true even of an entity of "pure energy and intelligence with no shape or form," as Kubrick put it; energy is materially real, and a disembodied "intelligence with no shape or form" would not be divine but fantastical (Kubrick 1980).

14. The ordinary, we should note, is also a crucial term in Cavell's philosophy. Lash's *Easter in Ordinary* was published the same year as Cavell's *In Quest of the Ordinary* (see Cavell 1988).

15. Although I would dispute a number of its specific claims, Taylor's analysis is detailed and intriguing. Unfortunately, the article's philosophical underpinnings are hamstrung by completely neglecting Cavell's account of skepticism, as well as the Wittgensteinian insights that lie behind so much of it. (For example, Taylor appears completely to miss the attack on the idea of the soul as something lurking inside human bodies which underlies the famous claim that the human body is the best picture of the human soul; see Taylor 2016, 6.)

16. Calling the films' rhetoric "weak" is, of course, not a pejorative claim, any more than it was when Deleuze and Guattari called Kafka's work "minor." Compare also Cavell's important dispute with Saul Kripke about the interpretation of Wittgenstein's famous remark about his spade being turned (*Philosophical Investigations* §217; Cavell 1990, 64–100). In Cavell's view Wittgenstein's gesture should be seen as "acknowledging a necessary

weakness," in contrast to Kripke's perception of "a show of power" (Cavell 2005c, 113).

17. The remark in question forms the conclusion to *On the Genealogy of Morality*, namely that "man still prefers to *will nothingness*, than *not* will" (Nietzsche [1887] 2007, 120 [third essay, §28]; emphases in original).

Chapter Seven

1. Many thanks to Alex Clayton, Andrew Klevan, Hoi Lun Law, Douglas Pye, and an anonymous reviewer for the substantial improvements to this chapter brought about by their comments and suggestions. Any obscurities or examples of wonky thinking that remain are all my own work.

2. The definition states that figuration is the "symbolic game or process aiming to establish a fixed, evolving or unstable correlation between the plastic, aural and narrative parameters able to elicit fundamental categories of representation (such as the visible and invisible, mimesis, reflection, appearance and disappearance, image and origin, the integral and the discontinuous, form, the intelligible, the part and the whole . . .) and other parameters—which may be the same parameters, depending on the particular type of determination effected—relating to fundamental categories of ontology (such as being and appearance, essence and apparition, being and nothingness, same and other, the immediate, the reflective, inner and outer, . . .)" (translated by Adrian Martin and cited in Martin 2012, 8).

3. I shall concentrate in this chapter on the notion of *figuration*, rather than attempting to define what a *figure* might be. This is because, as I attempt to make clear in the course of the chapter, figuration is, for Brenez, so fundamentally processual that defining the noun associated with, or resulting from, such processes would involve us in complexities that are not to the point here.

4. Thanks to Alex Clayton for prompting me to think harder about this resonance between Perkins and Brenez and suggesting these examples.

5. This phrase should not be seen as implying than Perkins was any kind of naive realist; it indicates, instead, his resistance (at the time he wrote *Film as Film*) to certain aspects of modernism. This resistance finds expression in the stipulation—which this phrase reflects—that once the rules of the film world are set up, whatever they may be, then it is important for the film to abide by them, lest the viewer's experience be unhelpfully disrupted. Chapter 1 discusses these issues in much more detail.

6. The film draws connections between the acts of painting and (murdering by) drilling, and both activities reach a culmination in the final monochrome, which is both a "painterly" image and a metonym for

blood—once again the two senses of figuration (plastic and rhetorical) are entwined.

7. Smuts's last line is quite accurate, but only in a certain sense. The filmmaker must "remain out of mind," for Perkins, in that the film must not direct attention away from itself towards its creator, but the film is also the test of the filmmaker precisely because a successful film is an intentional achievement, and must be understood as such; see the introduction for more on Perkins and intention.

8. This habit of writing without always clearly indicating the boundary between specific and general claims derives largely, I suspect, from the work Gilles Deleuze, and in particular from his book on Francis Bacon, wherein we can find many sentences that are comprehensible as detailed analyses of Bacon's paintings but are written in such a way that they could easily be mistaken for strange and arbitrary general claims: "From the start, the Figure has been a body, and the body has a place within the enclosure of the round area" (Deleuze [1981] 2003, 11).

9. In a later piece Brenez maps these oppositions onto the distinctions between literal and figurative and between realistic and exaggerated: "Laurie is a believable working girl. . . . Laurie is the referent, the literal version of Thana, the concrete expression of daily resistance and oppression; while Thana is the compensatory figure whose exacerbation manifests itself in direct proportion to Laurie's suffering" (Brenez 2012, 132). The claim about Laurie as a "compensatory figure" is interesting, but by treating "believable" as essentially equivalent to "literal" Brenez merely confuses matters.

Chapter Eight

1. Many thanks to Hoi Lun Law and to two anonymous reviewers for their generous and valuable comments on earlier versions of this chapter.

2. In referring to "layers of experience," Butte's account here is, I think, compatible with the understanding of film experience that is in operation in chapter 6. Oudart is discussing something the experience of which must be individual but is not private; it is an experience *of the film* in question.

3. Butte interestingly explores the "homology . . . between film's oblique angle in shot/reverse shot continuity editing and print fiction's free indirect discourse" (Butte 2017, 100) in some film adaptations of Henry James; see Butte 2017, 73–119.

4. This curious phrase of Cavell's might provide a hint as to why Ash's admiration seems at times to border on a kind of worship (Thomson is, I think, onto something with the remark quoted earlier about "a believer who has seen a saint" [Thomson 2000, 49] even if I find he somewhat misdescribes the specific moment he is referring to). Ash does not emphasize

the xenomorph's machinic qualities—he is, after all, a machine himself—but rather its *inhuman* qualities. To worship a machine sounds rather like madness, whereas worship might be precisely the appropriate relationship to have towards a universe, insofar as a universe is the kind of thing one can have a "relationship" with at all. Compare the discussion of idolatry in chapter 6.

Chapter Nine

1. Thanks to Laurence Kent, Hoi Lun Law, and Dan Morgan for their invaluable input on earlier versions of this chapter.
2. The film is also derived from part of a 1975 novel by Herbert Achtenbusch called *Die Stunde des Todes* (The Hour of Death).
3. At one point, Deleuze admits that the name small form "is not entirely helpful" and that he employs it "merely to contrast the two forms of the action image" (Deleuze [1983] 1986, 167). Perplexingly, however, a mere fifteen pages later we find Deleuze insisting that "one should bear in mind that Small and Large are used in Plato's sense" (182). Equally puzzling is the claim that the small, "in Plato, is no less Idea than is the Large" (190). This is particularly curious given the late Plato's use of largeness and smallness to demonstrate some of the paradoxes to which the theory of forms gives rise; Parmenides gets Aristoteles to agree that "smallness will never be in anything which is . . . nor will anything be small except smallness itself" (Plato 1997, 39); see Plato's *Parmenides*, 149d–151e.
4. The reason Deleuze feels he can link this to the ellipse is that, geometrically speaking, an ellipse can be formed by taking two fixed points, choosing a value, and then marking all the points the sum of whose distance from the two fixed points equals that value. A simple example of what Deleuze is talking about here can be found in the scene in Chaplin's *The Idle Class* in which Chaplin, "deserted by his wife, seems to be shaking with sobs, but as soon as he turns round we see that he is in fact shaking himself a cocktail" (Deleuze [1983] 1986, 173).
5. The virtual is a crucial concept for Deleuze; see Ansell-Pearson 2005 for an account of how Deleuze's understanding of it builds on his readings of Bergson, both in the *Cinema* books and elsewhere.
6. Compare the remarks by Cavell about knowing oneself "perhaps as a universe" (Cavell 1979b, 493) that were discussed at the end of the previous chapter.
7. Herzog has also suggested that the film shows what it might look like for a *landscape* to be hypnotized, claiming that "the trance was not within the actors alone; the film is permeated by image (and music) of a Land in Trance" (Greenberg 2012, 200).

8. One might, of course, see this as special pleading. For the prosecution's case, see the article by Eric Rentschler in Corrigan 2014; the piece by Alan Singer that immediately follows it presents the case for the defense. I note only that the film's extreme stylization renders highly improbable Rentschler's claim that Herzog "espouses a cinema" that prompts the viewer to, as Christian Metz puts it, "perceive as real the represented" and "to pass over [the representation] without seeing it for what it is" (Rentschler in Corrigan 2014, 164; the Metz passage is quoted from *The Imaginary Signifier*). To be fair to Rentschler, though, he goes on to point out, quite rightly, that *Heart of Glass* "is not as narratively random or structurally chaotic as previous critics have claimed" (164).

9. The English translation is particularly unfortunate here, rendering Deleuze's reference to the glass factory burning down as the barely coherent "the crystal's fire will have to connect with the whole range of manufacturing" (Deleuze [1985] 1989, 73).

10. We might also note that in *Cinema 1* Deleuze claims that Herzog is "the most metaphysical of cinema directors" (Deleuze [1983] 1986, 189), which again is high praise indeed coming from a philosopher who told Arnaud Villani that he felt himself to be a "pure metaphysician" (Villani 1999, 130).

11. David Deamer calls the two types of images "two polarities," seeing the movement-image as "a tendency of the cinema to describe ways in which the world and its bodies capture up, organise, and structure pure memory and spontaneous thought through the sensory-motor system," whereas the time-image represents "a tendency of the cinema to discover means to escape, unground, disrupt and disturb the sensory-motor system through pure memory and spontaneous thought" (Deamer 2016, 5). We will return at the end of this chapter to the question of the relationship between the two categories of image.

12. Herzog describes the production of these images in Herzog 2014 (139).

13. Heringman 2012 interestingly compares the film to the work of Joseph Wright of Derby.

14. Ford makes an exemplary—failed—attempt to define a horse's foot without reference to the concept "horse"; see Ford 2011 (90).

15. One objection to this account might be that it renders impossible Deleuze's claim that the advent of the time-image represents a rupture in the history of cinema. Setting aside from the question of whether this claim can be substantiated, I do not think that the objection stands. It might even make things more plausible: the time-image represents a novel species within the genus *movement-image*, whose advent leads to the question of whether the whole structure of cinematic images has not been reorientated, so that it then becomes equally plausible to see the time-image as the genus. This

would be to say that new discoveries in cinema can reorientate the whole history of the artform, which is surely plausible; any claim for the existence of an aesthetic revolution proposes something similar.

16. Perhaps a perception-image: "a set of elements which act on a centre, and which vary in relation to it" (Deleuze [1983] 1986, 221).

17. It is a mark of the grip of such a picture that denying it so readily attracts the charge of behaviorism, such as in the case of Wittgenstein.

18. Our deep resistance to this way of thinking is indicated by Anscombe's remark that "everyone who heard this formula found it extremely paradoxical and obscure" (Anscombe [1957] 2000, 53 [§29]). Compare this from Hegel's *Phenomenology of Spirit*: "Whatever the individual does and whatever happens to him, it is he who has done it, and it is himself" (Hegel 2018, 232 [§403]).

19. These are of course extremely complicated matters of which I can touch on here only in an extremely compressed form. For a contemporary version of the kind of account that Deleuze's approach seems to preclude, see this claim by Sebastian Rödl: "An action expresses a thought about what to do, not in the sense of being its effect, but in the sense of being this thought. Actions do not point to a state of mind as to their cause. Acting intentionally *is* being of a certain mind" (Rödl 2007, 49; emphasis in original). For another, see Charles Taylor's remark that in the case of what he calls "happy action," such an "action doesn't just enable us to see the desire; it *is* the desire, embodied in public space" (Taylor 1979, 87; emphasis in original). If, as I believe, such accounts of agency and mindedness are more compelling than Deleuze's, Jennifer Fay suggests a challenging further thought: "Cinema has taught us to see signs of the mind principally through the previously imperceptible or simply silly, embarrassed movements of the body. It is not thinking but thoughtlessness that eludes representation and belief. . . . What might the consequences be for this widespread 'thoughtfulness' thesis? How might we account for ordinary complicity and unradical acts of barbarism?" (Fay 2023, 250).

20. Anscombe's argument that "[w]e do not add anything attaching to the action at the time it is done by describing it as intentional" (Anscombe [1957] 2000, 28 [§19]) might help to show why subjectivity cannot be so separated. Rather than a way of getting to the truth of pure thought, Deleuze's claim that hypnosis "reveals thought to itself" seems closer to the defective situation Hegel describes in which "consciousness is . . . through its experience . . . become a riddle to itself," in part because such a consciousness thinks that "the consequences of its deeds are not its deeds themselves" (Hegel 2018, 212 [§365]).

21. One possible response to this which I do not have space to explore here is to see Deleuze's distinction between the movement-image and the time-image as responding to the sense that our world is *becoming* a world

without agency. As Robert Pippin puts it, the historical crisis to which the cinema responds "has especially to do with the trauma of the Second World War and a growing sense that our agential powers to transform the world in the service of some idea of the good, or even to control our own destinies, are far weaker than we would like to admit" (Pippin 2021, 139).

Chapter Ten

1. Thanks to Patrick Farmer, Miguel Gaggiotti, Hoi Lun Law, Adam O'Brien, and Ali Rasooli-Nejad for their comments on earlier versions of this chapter.

2. A comparable approach might be taken to other of Tarkovsky's films, concentrating on character psychology rather than attempting to reconstruct the director's own views. For example, in *The Sacrifice* (1986), rather than seeing incoherence in Alexander's doubled attempts to save his family (his prayer promising sacrifice, and his use of magic by sleeping with Maria who, according to Otto, is a witch), we might ask what it is about *Alexander* that leads him to believe that it was the prayer, rather than the magic, which did the trick.

3. Unless it is indicated otherwise, dialogue is quoted from the English subtitles to the 2017 Criterion Blu-ray edition of *Stalker* (Criterion Collection 888).

4. There are tensions between this account of faith and that which is in operation in chapter 6, but it is beyond the scope of this chapter to explore them.

5. Bird gives an alternative slant on this: "The Professor discards his device, not because he loses faith in the Zone, but because he comes to believe in it more than in his own judgement" (Bird 2008, 163).

6. Geoff Dyer, interview included on Criterion Blu-ray edition of *Stalker*.

7. At this point there start to be more affinities between my reading of *Stalker* and the discussion of faith and experience to be found in chapter 6.

8. I quote here from Tarkovsky 1999 (413); the version in the Criterion subtitles is this: "Conscience and soul-searching were all invented by the mind. When he realized all that, he hanged himself."

Chapter Twelve

1. Many thanks to Alex Clayton, Steven Roberts, and two anonymous reviewers for insightful comments on earlier drafts of this chapter.

2. Also relevant to my practice here is the discussion between Cavell and Andrew Klevan about criticism that begins from the critic's response to a specific moment (Cavell 2005b, 180–82).

3. Having said this, it is also certainly possible that at some level—probably related to the affair that he has been conducting, as I discuss below—Ryan would not be sorry to be free of the obligation to continue pursuing Gina's plans for the house. His remark to Albert, that is, might be an attempt to have it both ways.

4. In saying this I wish to claim that the editing is largely aimed at the *effects* at which classical editing aims, not that it uses a strictly classical style. Just as this scene avoids long takes, it also avoids using master shots and insert close-ups, which would have been a more classical way of proceeding. At points, too, the editing is very delicately balanced. After Gina first asks Albert about the sandstone, the film keeps his rather blank expression on screen for slightly longer than we might expect, after which it cuts back to Gina, who is still grinning; only then does her face begin to fall. It is not clear to me if this is best described as a "nonclassical" attempt slightly to stretch time (would a more classical editing style have cut back to Gina with her face already fallen?), or as a wholly "classical" method of representing quite how long Gina attempts to keep smiling, willing Albert to agree to her request. Thanks to Polly Rose for discussions on this point. See also the discussion in chapter 8 of suture and the question of medium awareness.

5. Though I will not pursue the argument here, I would suggest that if there is an anomaly to be found in Reichardt's oeuvre it is *Meek's Cutoff* rather than *Certain Women*.

6. I think Bolton underplays the complexity of Gina's final gaze, claiming that "[h]er demeanour is quietly excited as she confidently looks forward to the future" (Bolton 2019, 184). Hall also appears to have a more straightforward reading of this moment—"the sun is shining, the family is surrounded by friends and possibly family, and Gina seems to crack a genuine smile" (Hall 2018, 137)—but "seems" works against "genuine" to imply further complexity that needs accounting for.

7. See Anscombe's discussion of how, for example, neither "He killed my father, so I shall kill him" nor "I admire him so much, I shall sign the petition he is sponsoring" are "form[s] of reasoning," because "there is no calculation in these" (Anscombe 2000, 65 [§35]).

8. The film also gestures at a connection between promises among people and promise as what the future might offer (as that towards which plans are directed?). Before the rancher drives into town and first visits the night school, her television says: "It's a mysterious realm, full of danger and full of promise. A new frontier just waiting to be explored." Clayton 2022b

importantly connects this moment to others in the film that similarly present "an oblique connection to a forgotten history of colonial settlement."

9. The source text is itself rather ambiguous on this point. Although we are told that Susan "constructed the house . . . the stone turning corners and supporting ceilings in her mind," she does this only "[w]ith effort," after initially finding that "she couldn't picture the stone as part of a building, only as freestanding monuments on their undeveloped lot, upright versions of the ruin in Albert's yard" (Meloy 2005, 39). It is interesting that building a house—and doing so in the mind's eye—serves as a central example in Anscombe's exploration of practical knowledge (see, for example, Anscombe 2000, 82 [§45]).

10. A remark by the philosopher P. F. Strawson is suggestive in this regard: "It is helpful . . . to remember the startling ambiguity of the phrase, 'a body and its members'" (Strawson 1959, 115).

Works Cited

Adorno, Theodor W. (1963) 1998. *Quasi una fantasia: Essays on Modern Music.* Translated by Rodney Livingstone. Verso.
Affeldt, Steven G. 1998. "The Ground of Mutuality: Criteria, Judgment and Intelligibility in Stephen Mulhall and Stanley Cavell." *European Journal of Philosophy* 6 (1): 1–31.
Allen, Richard. 1995. *Projecting Illusion: Film Spectatorship and the Impression of Reality.* Cambridge University Press.
Alpers, Svetlana. 1983. *The Art of Describing: Dutch Art in the Seventeenth Century.* University of Chicago Press.
Ames, Catherine S., and Christopher Jarrold. 2007. "The Problem with Using Eye-Gaze to Infer Desire: A Deficit of Cue Inference in Children with Autism Spectrum Disorder?" *Journal of Autism and Developmental Disorders* 37:1761–75.
Anscombe, G. E. M. 1981. (1957) 2000. *Intention.* Harvard University Press.
———. *Ethics, Religion and Politics.* Collected Philosophical Papers, vol. 3. Blackwell.
Ansell-Pearson, Keith. 2005. "The Reality of the Virtual: Bergson and Deleuze." *MLN* 120 (5): 1112–27.
Austin, J. L. 1970. *Philosophical Papers.* 2nd ed. Oxford University Press.
———. 1975. *How to Do Things with Words.* 2nd ed. Oxford University Press.
Banerjee, Suparno. 2018. "*2001: A Space Odyssey*: A Transcendental Translocution." In *Understanding Kubrick's "2001: A Space Odyssey": Representation and Interpretation*, edited by James Fenwick. Intellect.
Barrowman, Kyle. 2023. "Alfred Hitchcock and the Moving Camera: Authorship, Style, and Declarative Aesthetics." *Offscreen* 27 (1–2). https://offscreen.com/view/alfred-hitchcock-and-the-moving-camera-authorship-style-and-declarative-aesthetics.
Barth, John. 1984. *The Friday Book.* Perigee.
Bellour, Raymond. (2009) 2014. "From Hypnosis to Animals." Translated and edited by Alistair Fox. *Cinema Journal* 53 (3): 8–24.

Benson, Stephen. 2018. "Description's Repertoire: The Journals of R. F. Langley." *English* 67 (256): 43–63.
Bergson, Henri. (1913) 2001. *Time and Free Will: An Essay on the Immediate Data of Consciousness*. Translated by F. L. Pogson. Dover.
Best, Stephen, and Sharon Marcus. 2009. "Surface Reading: An Introduction." *Representations* 108 (1): 1–21.
Bird, Robert. 2008. *Andrei Tarkovsky: Elements of Cinema*. Reaktion.
Birzache, Alina G. 2016. *The Holy Fool in European Cinema*. Routledge.
Bolton, Lucy. 2019. *Contemporary Cinema and the Philosophy of Iris Murdoch*. Edinburgh University Press.
Bordwell, David. 1985. *Narration in the Fiction Film*. University of Wisconsin Press.
———. 1989. *Making Meaning: Inference and Rhetoric in the Interpretation of Cinema*. Harvard University Press.
Brenez, Nicole. 1993. "The Ultimate Journey: Remarks on Contemporary Theory." *Screening the Past*. Accessed September 11, 2023. http://www.screeningthepast.com/2014/12/the-ultimate-journey-remarks-on-contemporary-theory/.
———. 1998. *De la figure en général et du corps en particulier: L'invention figurative au cinéma*. De Boeck & Larcier.
———. 2007. *Abel Ferrara*. Translated by Adrian Martin. University of Illinois Press.
———. 2011. "An Archaeology of the Figure and the Figural in Cinema after Kracauer." Lecture delivered at the Goethe-University, Frankfurt am Main, November 22. http://www.kracauer-lectures.de/en/winter-2011-2012/nicole-brenez/.
———. 2012. "A Critical Panoply: Abel Ferrara's Catholic Image Trilogy." In *Film Trilogies: New Critical Approaches*, edited by Claire Perkins and Constantine Verevis. Palgrave Macmillan.
———. 2023. *On the Figure in General and the Body in Particular: Figurative Invention in Cinema*. Translated by Ted Fendt. Anthem.
Brinkema, Eugenie. 2022. *Life-Destroying Diagrams*. Duke University Press.
Britton, Andrew. 1992. "Betrayed by Rita Hayworth: Misogyny in *The Lady from Shanghai*." In *The Movie Book of Film Noir*, edited by Ian Cameron. Studio Vista.
Butte, George. 2017. *Suture and Narrative: Deep Intersubjectivity in Fiction and Film*. Ohio State University Press.
Carroll, Noël. 1996. *Theorizing the Moving Image*. Cambridge University Press.
———. 1998. *Interpreting the Moving Image*. Cambridge University Press.
———. 2020. "Revisiting *The World Viewed*." In *The Thought of Stanley Cavell and Cinema: Turning Anew to the Ontology of Film a Half-Century after "The World Viewed,"* edited by David LaRocca. Bloomsbury.

Cavell, S. (1969) 2015. *Must We Mean What We Say: A Book of Essays*. Updated ed. Cambridge University Press.

———. 1979a. *The World Viewed: Reflections on the Ontology of Film*. Enlarged ed. Harvard University Press.

———. 1979b. *The Claim of Reason: Wittgenstein, Skepticism, Morality, and Tragedy*. Oxford University Press.

———. 1981a. *The Senses of Walden*. Exp. ed. University of Chicago Press.

———. 1981b. *Pursuits of Happiness: The Hollywood Comedy of Remarriage*. Harvard University Press.

———. 1986. "The Uncanniness of the Ordinary." Tanner Lectures on Human Values, delivered at Stanford University, April 3 and 8. https://tannerlectures.utah.edu/_documents/a-to-z/c/cavell88.pdf.

———. 1988. *In Quest of the Ordinary: Lines of Skepticism and Romanticism*. University of Chicago Press.

———. 1989. *This New Yet Unapproachable America: Lectures after Emerson after Wittgenstein*. Chicago University Press.

———. 1990. *Conditions Handsome and Unhandsome: The Constitution of Emersonian Perfectionism*. University of Chicago Press.

———. 1996. *Contesting Tears: The Hollywood Melodrama of the Unknown Woman*. University of Chicago Press.

———. 2003. *Disowning Knowledge in Seven Plays of Shakespeare*. Updated ed. Cambridge University Press.

———. 2004. *Cities of Words: Pedagogical Letters on a Register of the Moral Life*. Harvard University Press.

———. 2005a. *Cavell on Film*. Edited by William Rothman. State University of New York Press.

———. 2005b. "'What Becomes of Thinking on Film?' Stanley Cavell in Conversation with Andrew Klevan." In *Essays on Cinema after Wittgenstein and Cavell*, edited by Rupert Read and Jerry Goodenough. Palgrave Macmillan.

———. 2005c. *Philosophy the Day after Tomorrow*. Belknap Press of Harvard University Press.

———. 2006. "The Wittgensteinian Event." In *Reading Cavell*, edited by Alice Crary and Sanford Shieh. Routledge.

———. 2010. *Little Did I Know: Excerpts from Memory*. Stanford University Press.

———. 2011. "Responses." *Modern Theology* 27 (3): 517–25.

———. 2022. *Here and There: Sites of Philosophy*. Edited by Nancy Bauer, Alice Crary, and Sandra Laugier. Harvard University Press.

Chakravorty, Swagato. 2017. Review of *Film Worlds: A Philosophical Aesthetics of Cinema*, by Daniel Yacavone. *Film-Philosophy* 21 (1): 152–55.

Chandler, James. 2020. "I. A. Richards and Raymond Williams: Reading Poetry, Reading Society." *Critical Inquiry* 46 (2): 325–52.

Chatman, Seymour. 1980. "What Novels Can Do That Films Can't (and Vice Versa)." *Critical Inquiry* 7 (1): 121–40.

Chouinard, Gabriel. 2002. "A Conversation with M. John Harrison." *SF Site*, September. https://www.sfsite.com/12b/mjh142.htm.

Clayton, Alex. 2011. "Coming to Terms." In *The Language and Style of Film Criticism*, edited by Andrew Klevan and Alex Clayton. Routledge.

———. 2016. "V. F. Perkins: Aesthetic Suspense." In *Thinking in the Dark: Cinema, Theory, Practice*, edited by Murray Pomerance and R. Barton Palmer. Rutgers University Press.

———. 2022a. "Mind the Gap: Autistic Viewpoint in Film." In *On the Island: Autism in Film and Television*, edited by Murray Pomerance and R. Barton Palmer. University of Texas Press.

———. 2022b. "'What Groups Together': The Integrity of *Certain Women*." Unpublished paper delivered at the symposium *Philosophical Thinking and the Films of Kelly Reichardt*, Queen Mary University of London, November 5.

Conant, James. 2018. "Cinematic Genre and Viewer Engagement in Hitchcock's *Psycho*." *Yearbook of Comparative Literature* 64:228–322.

———. 2023. "Cinematic Invisibility: The Shower Scene in Hitchcock's *Psycho*." In *Philosophy of Film without Theory*, edited by Craig Fox and Britt Harrison. Palgrave Macmillan.

Corrigan, Timothy, ed. (1986) 2014. *The Films of Werner Herzog: Between Mirage and History*. Methuen.

Cronan, Todd. 2013. *Against Affective Formalism: Matisse, Bergson, Modernism*. University of Minnesota Press.

Dayan, Daniel. (1974) 1976. "The Tutor-Code of Classical Cinema." In *Movies and Methods*, edited by Bill Nichols. University of California Press.

Deamer, David. 2016. *Deleuze's "Cinema" Books: Three Introductions to the Taxonomy of Images*. Edinburgh University Press.

Deleuze, Gilles. (1981) 2003. *Francis Bacon: The Logic of Sensation*. Translated by Daniel W. Smith. Continuum.

———. (1983) 1986. *Cinéma 1: L'image-mouvement*. Éditions de Minuit. Translated by Hugh Tomlinson and Barbara Habberjam as *Cinema 1: The Movement-Image* (Continuum).

———. (1985) 1989. *Cinéma 2: L'image-temps*. Éditions de Minuit. Translated by Hugh Tomlinson and Barbara Habberjam as *Cinema 2: The Time-Image* (Continuum).

de Man, Paul. 1979. *Allegories of Reading*. Yale University Press.

Descombes, Vincent. 1986. *Objects of All Sorts: A Philosophical Grammar*. Translated by Lorna Scott-Fox and Jeremy Harding. Blackwell.

de Vries, Hent. 2011. "'A Greatest Miracle': Stanley Cavell, Moral Perfectionism, and the Ascent into the Ordinary." *Modern Theology* 27 (3): 462–77.

Diamond, Cora. 1991. *The Realistic Spirit*. MIT Press.
Dienstag, Joshua Foa, et al. 2016. *Cinema, Democracy and Perfectionism*. Manchester University Press.
Dumas, Louise. 2018. "*Phantom Thread*: Le coq de bois et les poupées de chiffon." *Positif*, no. 684, 7–8.
Durgnat, Raymond. 1982. "Film Theory: From Narrative to Description." *Quarterly Review of Film Studies* 7 (2): 109–29.
Dyer, Geoff. 2012. *Zona*. Canongate.
Eagleton, Terry. 1990. *The Ideology of the Aesthetic*. Blackwell.
Efird, Robert O. 2014. "The Holy Fool in Late Tarkovsky." *Journal of Religion and Film* 18, no. 1, article 45.
Eisenstein, Sergei. 1968. *Film Essays*. Edited by Jay Leyda. Denis Dobson.
Empson, William. 1972. *Seven Types of Ambiguity*. Penguin.
Epstein, Jean. 2012. *Critical Essays and New Translations*. Edited by Sarah Keller and Jason N. Paul. Amsterdam University Press.
Evans, Gareth. 1982. *The Varieties of Reference*. Oxford University Press.
———. 1985. *Collected Papers*. Clarendon Press.
Fairfax, Daniel. 2020. "A Stranger in the Hotel: Jean-Pierre Oudart and *The Shining*." *Senses of Cinema*, no. 95. https://www.sensesofcinema.com/2020/the-shining-at-40/a-stranger-in-the-hotel-jean-pierre-oudart-and-the-shining/#fnref-39606-5.
Fay, Jennifer. 2023. "Thinking on Film with Arendt and Cavell." *Critical Inquiry* 49 (2): 227–50.
Ford, Anton. 2011. "Action and Generality." In *Essays on Anscombe's "Intention,"* edited by Anton Ford, Jennifer Hornsby, and Frederick Stoutland. Harvard University Press.
———. 2017. "The Representation of Action." *Royal Institute of Philosophy Supplements* 80:217–33.
Foster, David. 2000. "Where Flowers Bloom but Have No Scent: The Cinematic Space of the Zone in Andrei Tarkovsky's *Stalker*." *Studies in Russian and Soviet Cinema* 4 (3): 307–20.
Fowler, D. P. 1991. "Narrate and Describe: The Problem of Ekphrasis." *Journal of Roman Studies* 81:25–35.
Frazier, Brad. 2006. "The Ethics of Rortian Redescription." *Philosophy and Social Criticism* 32 (4): 461–92.
Fusco, Katherine, and Nicole Seymour. 2017. *Kelly Reichardt*. University of Illinois Press.
Gaudreault, André. 2009. *From Plato to Lumière: Narration and Monstration in Literature and Cinema*. University of Toronto Press.
Gert, Heather J. 1997. "Wittgenstein on Description." *Philosophical Studies* 88 (3): 221–43.
Gianvito, John, ed. 2006. *Andrei Tarkovsky: Interviews*. University Press of Mississippi.

Gibbs, John. 2019. "Interview with V. F. Perkins, 22nd May 1997." *Movie: A Journal of Film Criticism*, no. 8, 45–52.

Gibbs, John, and Douglas Pye. 2005. Introduction to *Style and Meaning: Studies in the Detailed Analysis of Film*, edited by John Gibbs and Douglas Pye. Manchester University Press.

Gorfinkel, Elena. 2016. "Exhausted Drift: Austerity, Dispossession and the Politics of Slow in Kelly Reichardt's *Meek's Cutoff*." In *Slow Cinema*, edited by Tiago de Luca and Nuno Barradas Jorge. Edinburgh University Press.

Gould, Timothy. 1998. *Hearing Things: Voice and Method in the Writing of Stanley Cavell*. University of Chicago Press.

Greenberg, Alan. 2012. *Every Night the Trees Disappear: Werner Herzog and the Making of "Heart of Glass."* Chicago Review Press.

Greif, Mark. 2020. "Cavell as Educator." In *Inheriting Stanley Cavell: Memories, Dreams, Reflections*, edited by David LaRocca. Bloomsbury.

Griffin, Michael J., and Dara Waldron. 2007. "Across Time and Space: The Impulses of Andrei Tarkovsky's *Stalker*." In *Exploring the Utopian Impulse: Essays on Utopian Thought and Practice*, edited by Michael J. Griffin and Tom Moylan. Peter Lang.

Gunning, Tom. 2010. "Shadow Play and Dripping Teat: *The Night of the Hunter* (1955)." In *Film Moments: Criticism, History, Theory*, edited by Tom Brown and James Walters. Palgrave Macmillan.

Hall, E. Dawn. 2018. *ReFocus: The Films of Kelly Reichardt*. Edinburgh University Press.

Hansen, Miriam Bratu. 2012. *Cinema and Experience: Siegfried Kracauer, Walter Benjamin, and Theodor W. Adorno*. University of California Press.

Hegel, Georg Wilhelm Friedrich. 2018. *The Phenomenology of Spirit*. Translated by Terry Pinkard. Cambridge University Press.

Heller-Nicholas, Alexandra. 2017. *Ms. 45*. Wallflower.

Hemon, Aleksandar. 2018. "Why *Phantom Thread* Is Propaganda for Toxic Masculinity." *New Yorker*, April 8. https://www.newyorker.com/culture/culture-desk/why-phantom-thread-is-propaganda-for-toxic-masculinity.

Hepburn, R. W., and Iris Murdoch. 1956. "Symposium: Vision and Choice in Morality." *Proceedings of the Aristotelian Society, Supplementary Volumes* 30:14–58.

Heringman, Noah. 2012. "Herzog's *Heart of Glass* and the Sublime of Raw Materials." In *A Companion to Werner Herzog*, edited by Brad Prager. Wiley-Blackwell.

Herzog, Werner. 2014. *Werner Herzog: A Guide for the Perplexed, Conversations with Paul Cronin*. Faber and Faber.

Holmlund, Chris. 2016. "Mutual Muses in American Independent Film: Catherine Keener and Nicole Holofcener, Michelle Williams and Kelly

Reichardt." In *Indie Reframed: Women's Filmmaking and Contemporary American Independent Cinema*, edited by Linda Badley, Claire Perkins, and Michele Schreiber. Edinburgh University Press.
Hornsby, Jennifer. 1997. *Simple Mindedness: In Defense of Naive Naturalism in the Philosophy of Mind.* Harvard University Press.
Ivanov, Sergey A. 2006. *Holy Fools in Byzantium and Beyond.* Oxford University Press.
James, Henry. 1987. *The Complete Notebooks of Henry James.* Edited by Leon Edel and Lyall H. Powers. Oxford University Press.
James, William. (1909) 1977. *A Pluralistic Universe.* Harvard University Press.
Jameson, Frederic. 1992. *The Geopolitical Aesthetic: Cinema and Space in the World System.* Indiana University Press/BFI Publishing.
Johnson, Vida T., and Graham Petrie. 1994. *The Films of Andrei Tarkovsky: A Visual Fugue.* Indiana University Press.
Kahn, Eugen. 1965. "Self-pity." *American Journal of Psychiatry* 122 (4): 447–51.
Kant, Immanuel. 1998. *Critique of Pure Reason.* Translated and edited by Paul Guyer and Allen W. Wood. Cambridge University Press.
Keane, Marian, and William Rothman. 2000. *Reading Cavell's "The World Viewed": A Philosophical Perspective on Film.* Wayne State University Press.
Keathley, Christian. 2006. *Cinephilia and History, or The Wind in the Trees.* Indiana University Press.
Kern, Andrea. 2017. *Sources of Knowledge: On the Concept of a Rational Capacity for Knowledge.* Translated by Daniel Smyth. Harvard University Press.
Keuss, Jeffrey F. 2005. "Reading Stanley Kubrick: A Theological Odyssey." In *Cinéma Divinité: Religion, Theology, and the Bible in Film*, edited by Eric S. Christianson, Peter Francis, and William R. Telford. SCM Press.
Klevan, Andrew. 2011. "Description." In *The Language and Style of Film Criticism*, edited by Andrew Klevan and Alex Clayton. Routledge.
———. 2018. *Aesthetic Evaluation and Film.* Manchester University Press.
Kracauer, Siegfried. 1960. *Theory of Film: The Redemption of Physical Reality.* Oxford University Press.
Kubala, Robbie. 2018. "Grounding Aesthetic Obligations." *British Journal of Aesthetics* 58 (3): 271–85.
Kubrick, Stanley. 1968. Interview. *Playboy*, September.
———. 1980. Interview by Jun'ichi Yaoi. Eyes On Cinema @RealEOC presents: Eyes on UFOs, YouTube, posted June 19, 2018. https://www.youtube.com/watch?v=er_o82OMlNM.
Kügle, Markus. 2020. "50 Jahre *Suture*! Everything You Always Wanted to Know about the Beginning of Psychoanalytic Film Theory* (*but Were Afraid to Ask Oudart)." *ffk Journal*, no. 5, 206–22.
Langley, R. F. 2006. *Journals.* Shearsman.

Lash, Dominic. 2020. *The Cinema of Disorientation: Inviting Confusions*. Edinburgh University Press.

———. 2021a. "Kubrick, Optimism, and Pessimism." In *The Bloomsbury Companion to Stanley Kubrick*, edited by Nathan Abrams and I. Q. Hunter. Bloomsbury.

———. 2021b. "Failures of Redescription in *The Rules of the Game*." *New Review of Film and Television Studies* (blog), November 5. https://nrftsjournal.org/failures-of-redescription/.

———. 2022. *Robert Pippin and Film: Politics, Ethics, and Psychology after Modernism*. Bloomsbury Academic.

Lash, Nicholas. 1988. *Easter in Ordinary: Reflections on Human Experience and the Knowledge of God*. University Press of Virginia.

———. 1996. *The Beginning and the End of "Religion."* Cambridge University Press.

Law, Hoi Lun. 2021. *Ambiguity and Film Criticism: Reasonable Doubt*. Palgrave Macmillan.

Le Fanu, Mark. 1987. *The Cinema of Andrei Tarkovsky*. BFI.

Lennon, Kathleen. 2017. "Expression." In *Wittgenstein and Merleau-Ponty*, edited by Komarine Romdenh-Romluc. Routledge.

Leonard, Linda Schierse. 2020. Review of *On Body and Soul*, directed by Ildikó Enyedi. *Psychological Perspectives* 63 (1): 159–62.

Loughlin, Gerard. 2004. *Alien Sex: The Body and Desire in Cinema and Theology*. Blackwell.

Luckhurst, Roger. 2014. *Alien*. BFI Film Classics. Palgrave Macmillan.

Lukács, Georg. 1970. "Narrate or Describe." In *Writer and Critic and Other Essays*, edited and translated by Arthur Kahn. Merlin.

Macarthur, David. 2016. "Living Our Skepticism of Others through Film: Remarks in Light of Cavell." *SubStance* 45 (3 [issue 141]): 120–36.

Mankin, Robert. 1985. "An Introduction to *The Claim of Reason*." *Salmagundi*, no. 67, 66–89.

Martin, Adrian. 2012. *Last Day Every Day: Figural Thinking from Auerbach and Kracauer to Agamben and Brenez*. Punctum.

———. 2015. "The Havoc of Living Things." *The Third Rail*, no. 6. http://thirdrailquarterly.org/adrian-martin-the-havoc-of-living-things/.

Mast, Gerald. (1977) 1983. *Film/Cinema/Movie: A Theory of Experience*. University of Chicago Press.

Matamala, Anna, and Aline Remael. 2015. "Audio-Description Reloaded: An Analysis of Visual Scenes in *2012* and *Hero*." *Translation Studies* 8 (1): 63–81.

McGinn, Marie. 1997. *Routledge Philosophy Guidebook to Wittgenstein and the "Philosophical Investigations."* Routledge.

McManus, Denis., ed. 2004. *Wittgenstein and Scepticism*. Routledge.

Meloy, Maile. 2005. *Half in Love*. John Murray.
Mentyka, Robert M. 2017. "The Alien as Übermensch: Overcoming Morality in Order to Become the Perfect Killer." In *Alien and Philosophy: I Infest, Therefore I Am*, edited by Jeffrey Ewing and Kevin S. Decker. Wiley Blackwell.
Merleau-Ponty, Maurice. 1964. *Sense and Non-sense*. Translated by Hubert L. Dreyfus and Patricia Allen Dreyfus. Northwestern University Press.
Meyer, Michael J. 2008. "Reflections on Comic Reconciliations: Ethics, Memory, and Anxious Happy Endings." *Journal of Aesthetics and Art Criticism* 66 (1): 77–87.
Miller, D. A. 2016. *Hidden Hitchcock*. University of Chicago Press.
Miller, Jacques-Alain. (1966) 1977. "Suture (Elements of the Logic of the Signifier)." Translated by Jacqueline Rose. *Screen* 18 (4): 24–34.
Moran, Richard. 2017. *The Philosophical Imagination: Selected Essays*. Oxford University Press.
Morgan, Daniel. 2020. "Modernist Investigations: A Reading of *The World Viewed*." *Discourse* 42 (1–2): 209–40.
Most, Glenn W. 2003. "Anger and Pity in Homer's *Iliad*." In *Ancient Anger: Perspectives from Homer to Galen*, edited by Susanna Braund and Glenn W. Most. Cambridge University Press.
Mulhall, Stephen. 2005. "On Refusing to Begin." In *Contending with Stanley Cavell*, edited by Russell B. Goodman. Oxford University Press.
———. 2016. *On Film*. 3rd ed. Routledge.
Murray, Patrick, and Jeanne Schuler. 2007. "Rebel without a Cause: Stanley Kubrick and the Banality of the Good." In *The Philosophy of Stanley Kubrick*, edited by Jerold J. Abrams. University Press of Kentucky.
Murray, Paul D. 2007. "Theology 'under the Lash': Theology as Ideology Critique in the Work of Nicholas Lash." *New Blackfriars* 88 (1013): 4–24.
Naremore, James. 2007. *On Kubrick*. British Film Institute.
Nietzsche, Friedrich. (1887) 2001. *The Gay Science*. Translated by Josefine Nauckhoff. Cambridge University Press.
———. (1887) 2007. *On the Genealogy of Morality*. Translated by Carol Diethe. Cambridge University Press.
———. 2006. *Thus Spoke Zarathustra*. Edited by Adrian Del Caro and Robert B. Pippin; translated by Adrian Del Caro. Cambridge University Press.
O'Malley, Sheila. 2018. "Love, after a Fashion." *Film Comment* 54 (1): 24–29.
Oudart, Jean-Pierre. 1969a. "La suture." *Cahiers du cinema*, no. 211, 36–39.
———. 1969b. "La suture (deuxième partie)." *Cahiers du cinema*, no. 212, 50–55.
———. 1977. "Cinema and Suture." Translated by Kari Hanet. *Screen* 18 (4): 35–47.

———. 1978. "À propos d' 'Orange mécanique,' Kubrick, Kramer et quelques autres." *Cahiers du cinéma*, no. 293, 55–60.
Perkins, V. F. 1972. "A Reply to Sam Rohdie." *Screen* 13 (4): 146–51.
———. 1993. *Film as Film: Understanding and Judging Movies*. Da Capo.
———. 1999. *The Magnificent Ambersons*. Palgrave Macmillan.
———. 2012. *La règle du jeu*. Palgrave Macmillan.
———. 2020. *V. F. Perkins on Movies: Collected Shorter Criticism*. Wayne State University Press.
Perkins, V. F., Ian Cameron, Michael Walker, Jim Hillier, and Robin Wood. 1975. "The Return of Movie." *Movie*, no. 20, 1–26.
Pinkard, Terry. 2007. "Symbolic, Classical, and Romantic Art." In *Hegel and the Arts*, edited by Stephen Houlgate. Northwestern University Press.
Pippin, Robert B. 2000. *Henry James and Modern Moral Life*. Cambridge University Press.
———. 2008. *Hegel's Practical Philosophy: Rational Agency as Ethical Life*. Cambridge University Press.
———. 2010. *Nietzsche, Psychology, and First Philosophy*. University of Chicago Press.
———. 2012. *Fatalism in American Film Noir: Some Cinematic Philosophy*. University of Virginia Press.
———. 2013. "Le Grand Imagier of George Wilson." *European Journal of Philosophy* 21 (2): 334–41.
———. 2013. "The Idea That Films Could Have a Bearing on Philosophy." In *Inheriting Stanley Cavell: Memories, Dreams, Reflections*, edited by David LaRocca. Bloomsbury.
———. 2017. *The Philosophical Hitchcock: "Vertigo" and the Anxieties of Unknowingness*. University of Chicago Press.
———. 2019. "The Bearing of Film on Philosophy." In *Cambridge History of Philosophy, 1945–2015*, edited by Kelly Becker and Iain D. Thompson. Cambridge University Press.
———. 2020. *Filmed Thought: Cinema as Reflective Form*. University of Chicago Press.
———. 2021. *Douglas Sirk: Filmmaker and Philosopher*. Bloomsbury.
Plato. 1997. *Plato's "Parmenides."* Translated and edited by R. E. Allen. Yale University Press.
Porton, Richard. 2018. Review of *Phantom Thread*, directed by Paul Thomas Anderson. *Cineaste* 43 (3): 49–51.
Powell-Jones, Lindsay. 2015. *Deleuze and Tarkovsky: The Time-Image and Post-War Soviet Cinema History*. PhD dissertation, University of Cardiff.
Pratchett, Terry. (1986) 2012. *The Light Fantastic*. Corgi.
Pye, Douglas. 2023. "Perkins, Gombrich and Criteria." *Movie: A Journal of Film Criticism*, no. 11, 22–26.

Ramos, Marina. 2015. "The Emotional Experience of Films: Does Audio Description Make a Difference?" *Translator* 21 (1): 68–94.
Rancière, Jacques. (2001) 2016. *Film Fables*. Translated by Emiliano Battista. Bloomsbury.
Richards, Rashna Wadia. 2013. *Cinematic Flashes: Cinephilia and Classical Hollywood*. Indiana University Press.
Rieser, Klaus. 2007. "For Your Eyes Only: Some Thoughts on the Descriptive in Film." In *Description in Literature and Other Media*, edited by Werner Wolf and Walter Bernhart. Rodopi.
Rödl, Sebastian. 2007. *Self-Consciousness*. Harvard University Press.
———. 2018. *Self-consciousness and Objectivity: An Introduction to Absolute Idealism*. Harvard University Press.
Rohdie, Sam. 1972. "Review: *Movie Reader, Film as Film*." *Screen* 13 (4): 135–45.
———. 2006. *Montage*. Manchester University Press.
Rollet, Sylvie. 2007. "Imaginary Lands and Figures of Exile in Elia Kazan's *America, America*." In *Diaspora and Memory: Figures of Displacement in Contemporary Literature, Arts and Politics*, edited by Marie-Aude Baronian, Stephan Besser, and Yolande Jansen. Rodopi.
Rooney, Ellen. 2010. "Live Free or Describe: The Reading Effect and the Persistence of Form." *Differences* 21 (3): 112–39.
Rosenbaum, Jonathan. 2022. "Crossing Kelly Reichardt's Wilderness." December 14. https://jonathanrosenbaum.net/2022/12/crossing-kelly-reichardts-wilderness/.
Rothman, William. 1976. "Against 'The System of the Suture.'" In *Movies and Methods*, edited by Bill Nichols. University of California Press.
———. 1997. *Documentary Film Classics*. Cambridge University Press.
———. 2021. *The Holiday in His Eye: Stanley Cavell's Vision of Film and Philosophy*. State University of New York Press.
Roud, Richard. 1980. *Cinema: A Critical Dictionary*. Vol. 1, *Aldrich to King*. Secker and Warburg.
Rudrum, David. 2013. *Stanley Cavell and the Claim of Literature*. Johns Hopkins University Press.
Russell, D. A., and Michael Winterbottom. 1989. *Classical Literary Criticism*. Oxford University Press.
Russell, Francey. 2018. "I Want to Know More About You: On Knowing and Acknowledging in *Chinatown*." In *Stanley Cavell on Aesthetic Understanding*, edited by Garry L. Hagburg. Palgrave Macmillan.
Rybin, Steven. 2024. "Blake Edwards, François Truffaut, and Figuration: Two Versions of *The Man Who Loved Women*." *Quarterly Review of Film and Video* 41 (2): 260–84.
Seaton, Lola. 2023. "That Which Haunts." *Sidecar*, October 26. https://newleftreview.org/sidecar/posts/that-which-haunts.

Shatz, David. 2021. "Science, Theology, and the Purpose of Creation." *Tradition* 53 (3): 250–59.
Shaw, Daniel. 2017. "Stanley Cavell on the Magic of the Movies." *Film-Philosophy* 21 (1): 114–32.
Shuster, Martin. 2015. "The Ordinariness and Absence of the World: Cavell's Ontology of the Screen—Reading *The World Viewed*." *MLN* 130 (5): 1067–99.
Siemienowicz, Rochelle. (2018) "A Guide to the Worst Takes on *Phantom Thread*." SBS, February 22. https://www.sbs.com.au/movies/article/2018/02/22/guide-worst-takes-phantom-thread.
Sinnerbrink, Robert. 2020. "Between Skepticism and Moral Perfectionism: On Cavell's Melodrama of the Unknown Woman." In *The Thought of Stanley Cavell and Cinema: Turning Anew to the Ontology of Film a Half-Century after "The World Viewed,"* David LaRocca. Bloomsbury Academic.
Smith, Joseph, and William Kerrigan, eds. 1987. *Images in Our Souls: Cavell, Psychoanalysis, and Cinema*. Johns Hopkins University Press.
Smuts, Aaron. 2006. "V. F. Perkins' Functional Credibility and the Problem of Imaginative Resistance." *Film and Philosophy* 10:85–98.
Sontag, Susan. 1977. *On Photography*. St. Martin's.
Spice, Nicholas. 2020. "Diary." *London Review of Books* 42 (11): 36–37.
Stevens, Brad. 2004. *Abel Ferrara: The Moral Vision*. FAB Press.
Stevens, Kyle. 2022. "Introduction: The Very Thought of Theory." In *The Oxford Handbook of Film Theory*. Oxford University Press.
Stinton, T. C. W. 1975. "*Hamartia* in Aristotle and Greek Tragedy." *Classical Quarterly* 25 (2): 221–54.
Stockhausen, Karlheinz. 1989. *Stockhausen on Music*. Marion Boyars.
Strawson, P. F. 1959. *Individuals: An Essay in Descriptive Metaphysics*. Methuen.
Tarkovsky, Andrei. 1994. *Time within Time: The Diaries, 1970–1986*. Faber and Faber.
———. 1999. *Collected Screenplays*. Faber and Faber.
Taylor, Aaron. 2016. "Blind Spots and Mind Games: Performance, Motivation, and Emotion in the Films of Stanley Kubrick." *Velvet Light Trap*, no. 77, 5–27.
Taylor, Charles. 1979. "Action as Expression." In *Intention and Intentionality: Essays in Honour of G.E.M. Anscombe*, edited by Cora Diamond and Jenny Teichman. Harvester.
Thompson, Michael. 2008. *Life and Action: Elementary Structures of Practice and Practical Thought*. Harvard University Press.
———. 2022. "Forms of Nature: 'First,' 'Second,' 'Living,' 'Rational,' and 'Phronetic.'" In *Reason in Nature: New Essays on Themes from John*

McDowell, edited by Matthew Boyle and Evgenia Mylonaki. Harvard University Press.
Thomson, David. 2000. *The Alien Quartet*. Bloomsbury.
Tokarczuk, Olga. 2017. *Flights*. Translated by Jennifer Croft. Fitzcarraldo.
Tőke, Lilla. 2024. "A Certain Kind of Happiness: Women and Disability in Recent Hungarian Cinema." *Studies in Eastern European Cinema* 15 (1): 37–52.
Toles, George. 2010. "Rescuing Fragments: A New Task for Cinephilia." *Cinema Journal* 49 (2): 159–66.
———. 2016. *Paul Thomas Anderson*. University of Chicago Press.
Tomasulo, Frank P. 1996. "Narrate and Describe? Point of View and Narrative Voice in Citizen Kane's Thatcher Sequence." In *Perspectives on Citizen Kane*, edited by Ronald Gottesman. G. K. Hall.
Tsymbal, Evgeny. 2015. "Tarkovsky and the Strugatskii Brothers: The Prehistory of *Stalker*." *Science Fiction Film and Television* 8 (2): 255–77.
Turvey, Malcolm. 2022. "The Medium Matters! In Defense of Medium-Specificity in Classical Film Theory." In *The Oxford Handbook of Film Theory*, edited by Kyle Stevens. Oxford University Press.
Villani, Arnaud. 1999. *La guêpe et l'orchidée: Essai sur Gilles Deleuze*. Éditions Belin.
Virvidaki, Katerina. 2017. *Testing Coherence in Narrative Film*. Palgrave Macmillan.
Wallace, Lee. 2020. *Reattachment Theory: Queer Cinema of Remarriage*. Duke University Press.
Walton, Saige. (2020) "Sleeping away the Factory, Healing with Time: Gaston Bachelard, the Poetic Imagination and *Testről és lélekről/On Body and Soul* (2017)." *Paragraph* 43 (3): 348–63.
Watter, Seth. 2019. "On the Conception of Setting: A Study of V. F. Perkins." *Journal of Cinema and Media Studies* 58 (3): 72–92.
Wheatley, Catherine. 2019. *Stanley Cavell and Film: Scepticism and Self-Reliance at the Cinema*. Bloomsbury.
Williams, Bernard. 1973. *Problems of the Self: Philosophical Papers 1956–1972*. Cambridge University Press.
Williams, Raymond. 1961. *The Long Revolution*. Pelican.
———. 1968. *Drama in Performance*. New ed. C. A. Watts.
Wilson, George M. 1974. Review of *The World Viewed*, by Stanley Cavell. *Philosophical Review* 83 (2): 240–44.
———. 1986. *Narration in Light: Studies in Cinematic Point of View*. Johns Hopkins University Press.
———. 2011. *Seeing Fictions in Films: The Epistemology of Movies*. Oxford University Press.

Wiseman, Rachael. 2016. *Routledge Philosophy Guidebook to Anscombe's "Intention."* Routledge.
Wittgenstein, Ludwig. 2009. *Philosophical Investigations*. Rev. 4th ed. Translated by G. E. M. Anscombe and edited by P. M. S. Hacker and Joachim Schulte. Wiley-Blackwell.
Wood, Robin. 1976. *Personal Views: Explorations in Film*. Giles Fraser.
———. 2003. *Hollywood from Vietnam to Reagan . . . and Beyond*. Exp. and rev. ed. Columbia University Press.
Yacavone, Daniel. 2015. *Film Worlds: A Philosophical Aesthetics of Cinema*. Columbia University Press.
———. 2023. ". . . Heterocosmic Connections: On the Many Worlds and World Values of Cinema." In *What Film Is Good For: On the Values of Spectatorship*, edited by Julian Hanich and Martin P. Rossouw. University of California Press.
Zangwill, Nick. 2013. "Moral Metaphor and Thick Concepts: What Moral Philosophy Can Learn from Aesthetics." In *Thick Concepts*, edited by Simon Kirchin. Oxford University Press.
Zehle, Soenke. 2011. Video interview with V. F. Perkins. Accessed March 28, 2017. https://vimeo.com/28979836.

Filmography

2001: A Space Odyssey (Stanley Kubrick, 1968)
Aguirre, Wrath of God (Werner Herzog, 1972)
Alien (Ridley Scott, 1979)
Alien³ (David Fincher, 1992)
Alien: Resurrection (Jean-Pierre Jeunet, 1997)
America, America (Elia Kazan, 1963)
Anatomy of a Murder (Otto Preminger, 1959)
Andrei Rublev (Andrei Tarkovsky, 1966)
Au hasard, Balthazar (Robert Bresson, 1966)
Barry Lyndon (Stanley Kubrick, 1975)
Battleship Potemkin (Sergei Eisenstein, 1925)
The Blackout (Abel Ferrara, 1997)
Body Snatchers (Abel Ferrara, 1993)
Bringing Up Baby (Howard Hawks, 1938)
Caught (Max Ophüls, 1949)
Certain Women (Kelly Reichardt, 2016)
The Children's Hour (William Wyler, 1961)
Citizen Kane (Orson Welles, 1941)
A Clockwork Orange (Stanley Kubrick, 1971)
The Criminal (Joseph Losey, 1960)
Dangerous Game (Abel Ferrara, 1993)
Dr. Strangelove or: How I Learned to Stop Worrying and Love the Bomb (Stanley Kubrick 1964)
The Driller Killer (Abel Ferrara, 1979)
Eyes Wide Shut (Stanley Kubrick, 1999)
First Cow (Kelly Reichardt, 2019)
Fitzcarraldo (Werner Herzog, 1982)
The Funeral (Abel Ferrara, 1996)
The General (Buster Keaton, 1926)
Heart of Glass (Werner Herzog, 1976)

Hiroshima mon amour (Alain Resnais, 1959)
His Girl Friday (Howard Hawks, 1940)
Holy Motors (Leos Carax, 2012)
The Idle Class (Charlie Chaplin, 1921)
In a Lonely Place (Nicholas Ray, 1950)
Invasion of the Body Snatchers (Don Siegel, 1956)
Invasion of the Body Snatchers (Philip Kaufman, 1978)
It Happened One Night (Frank Capra, 1934)
Johnny Guitar (Nicholas Ray, 1954)
King of Kings (Nicholas Ray, 1961)
King of New York (Abel Ferrara, 1990)
La notte (Michelangelo Antonioni, 1961)
The Lady from Shanghai (Orson Welles, 1947)
Last Year at Marienbad (Alain Resnais, 1961)
Les carabiniers (Jean-Luc Godard, 1963)
Letter from an Unknown Woman (Max Ophüls, 1948)
The Magnificent Ambersons (Orson Welles, 1942)
Marnie (Alfred Hitchcock, 1964)
The Master (Paul Thomas Anderson, 2012)
Meek's Cutoff (Kelly Reichardt, 2010)
Ms .45 (Abel Ferrara, 1981)
Mulholland Dr. (David Lynch, 2001)
My Darling Clementine (John Ford, 1946)
Nanook of the North (Robert J. Flaherty, 1922)
New Rose Hotel (Abel Ferrara, 1998)
Night Moves (Kelly Reichardt, 2013)
Old Joy (Kelly Reichardt, 2006)
On Body and Soul (Ildikó Enyedi, 2017)
Out of the Past (Jacques Tourneur, 1947)
The Passion of Joan of Arc (Carl Theodor Dreyer, 1928)
Phantom Thread (Paul Thomas Anderson, 2017)
Pickpocket (Robert Bresson, 1959)
Pierrot le Fou (Jean-Luc Godard, 1965)
Play (Dusan Vukotic, 1962)
Rebel Without a Cause (Nicholas Ray, 1956)
The Reckless Moment (Max Ophüls, 1949)
Red Desert (Michelangelo Antonioni, 1964)
The Rules of the Game (Jean Renoir, 1939)
The Sacrifice (Andrei Tarkovsky, 1986)
Sergeant Rutledge (John Ford, 1960)
The Shining (Stanley Kubrick, 1980)
Solaris (Andrei Tarkovsky, 1972)

The Son (Jean-Pierre and Luc Dardenne, 2002)
Stalker (Andrei Tarkovsky, 1979)
A Star Is Born (George Cukor, 1954)
Strike (Sergei Eisenstein, 1925)
Sunrise (F.W. Murnau, 1927)
These Three (William Wyler, 1936)
Tokyo senso sengo hiwa (Nagasi Oshima, 1970)
The Trial of Joan of Arc (Robert Bresson, 1962)
Vivre sa vie (Jean-Luc Godard, 1962)
Wild Strawberries (Ingmar Bergman, 1957)
The Wizard of Oz (Victor Fleming, 1939)
Woman of the Year (George Stevens, 1942)

Index

2001: A Space Odyssey (Kubrick), 129–30, 136–38, 145–47
Adorno, Theodor W., 39, 277n4
Affeldt, Steven G., 107–8, 117–18
agency, 42, 48–50, 201–202, 211–13, 218–19, 230, 236–40, 243, 263–66, 271, 299n19, 299n21
Aguirre, Wrath of God (Herzog), 199, 208
Alien (Scott), 172–75, 180–93
Alien³ (Fincher), 174
Alien: Resurrection (Jeunet), 189
Allen, Richard, 177
Alpers, Svetlana, 47
Althusser, Louis, 41, 172, 177–79
America, America (Kazan), 56–61
Anna Karenina (Tolstoy), 282n15
Anscombe, G. E. M., 7–8, 11, 48–49, 68, 132, 136, 212, 213, 218, 276n10, 277n12, 280n2, 282n12, 282n13, 293n3, 293n6, 299n18, 299n20, 301n7, 302n9. See also intention
Antonioni, Michelangelo, 29–30
Aristotle, 239–40
Arnheim, Rudolph, 21, 22
Austin, J. L., 44, 74, 139

Banerjee, Suparno, 129

Barry Lyndon (Kubrick), 129, 133
Barth, John, 25
Bazin, André, 68, 73, 134, 267, 290n9, 294n10
Beckett, Samuel, 33, 86, 130
Bellour, Raymond, 212
Benjamin, Walter, 135, 284n3
Benson, Stephen, 44–46, 281n7, 281n8
Bergson, Henri, 201–202, 212–13, 297n5
Bird, Robert, 221–22, 234–36, 238, 300n5
Birzache, Aline, 221
Body Snatchers (Ferrara), 158–61, 163–66
Bolton, Lucy, 258, 301n6
Bordwell, David, 20, 41, 96, 177, 178, 266, 282n14
Brenez, Nicole, 20, 44, 48, 57, 151–170, 200, 276n5, 295n3, 296n9
Bresson, Robert, 176–77, 181, 189, 210
Brinkema, Eugenie, 281n5
Britton, Andrew, 229
Butte, George, 173, 178–81, 187, 189–90, 296n2, 296n3

Capra, Frank, 75, 94
Carroll, Noël, 41, 68–69, 70, 72, 74, 79, 81, 177, 178, 278n9
Caught (Ophüls), 96, 157
Cavell, Stanley, 3, 65–147 passim, 173, 252; *The Claim of Reason*, 9, 10, 66, 71–72, 75–76, 93, 97, 101, 104, 108, 114–115, 118, 120–21, 127, 139, 191–92, 276n10, 284n2, 285n8, 286n14, 287n4; 289n17, 289n19, 290n9, 292n12, 297n6; *Contesting Tears*, 5, 13, 73, 92–93, 112–13, 125, 286n14, 286n16; *In Quest of the Ordinary*, 77–78, 114, 294n14; *Must We Mean What We Say?*, 5, 7, 8, 76, 86, 130, 142, 147, 286n18, 292n12; *Pursuits of Happiness*, 13, 92, 93–94, 110, 113, 120, 267, 289n2, 290n8, 292n17, 293n21; *The World Viewed*, 5, 15, 65–87, 115, 124, 133, 134, 173, 245, 273, 277n3, 279n18, 284n1, 284n4, 284n5, 285n6, 286n15, 286n19, 290n8, 290n9, 294n7, 294n10
Certain Women (Reichardt), 245, 247–271
Chakravorty, Swagato, 20
Chaplin, Charlie, 198, 297n4
Chatman, Seymour, 47, 281n11
Children's Hour, The (Wyler), 26–29
Citizen Kane (Welles), 46, 203–4, 209
Clayton, Alex, 12, 51, 96, 267, 271–72, 280n1, 287n5, 288n12, 289n16, 295n4, 301n8
Clockwork Orange, A (Kubrick), 129–30, 142–46
coherence, 23–24, 25, 31, 33, 65, 70–71, 72, 74, 116, 156, 161–64, 172, 271–73, 277n4, 278n5, 278n6, 278n7, 280n4, 286n15

Conant, James, 97, 273–74, 278n12
Criminal, The (Losey), 30–31, 162
criteria, 6–11, 99; Cavell on, 107–127; and coherence, 24, 273; Perkins on, 22–23, 35–36, 54
Cronan, Todd, 201

Dangerous Game (Ferrara), 166
Dayan, Daniel, 171–78, 180, 190, 193
de Man, Paul, 279n15
de Vries, Hent, 139–40, 144
Deamer, David, 298n11
Deleuze, Gilles, 157, 195–213, 237, 294n16, 296n8, 297n5, 298n15, 299n19, 299n20, 299n21; *Cinema 1*, 198, 201, 206, 208–209, 297n3, 297n4, 298n10, 299n16; *Cinema 2*, 202–203, 205, 209, 211–12, 298n9
Derrida, Jacques, 82
Descartes, René, 7, 77, 139, 212
Descombes, Vincent, 293n6
description, 8, 23, 41–61, 117–18, 166–67, 170, 238, 263, 276n10, 276n11, 277n12, 277n13, 280n2, 280n3, 280n4, 281n5, 281n6, 281n8, 281n10, 281n11, 282n13, 282n16, 282n17, 283n22
Diamond, Cora, 48–49, 282n15
Dienstag, Joshua Foa, 124
Dr. Strangelove (Kubrick), 129–30, 142
Dumas, Louise, 114
Durgnat, Raymond, 46–47
Dyer, Geoff, 227, 233–35

Eagleton, Terry, 35
Efird, Robert, 220, 228, 231
Eisenstein, Sergei, 33–35
Emerson, Ralph Waldo, 77, 284n3, 286n14

Empson, William, 240
Endgame (Beckett), 86, 130
Epstein, Jean, 255, 259
Evans, Gareth, 284n5, 287n8
Eyes Wide Shut (Kubrick), 129

Fairfax, Daniel, 180
Fay, Jennifer, 299n19
figuration, 4, 151–70 passim, 172, 192, 197, 213, 295n2, 295n3, 295n6; defined, 275n5
First Cow (Reichardt), 246
Fitzcarraldo (Herzog), 199, 208
Foot, Philippa, 277n13
Ford, Anton, 210–11, 284n25, 298n14
Foster, David, 235
Fowler, D. P., 48, 52, 281n10
Frazier, Brad, 282n16
Friedrich, Caspar David, 195
Funeral, The (Ferrara), 166
Fusco, Katherine, and Nicole Seymour, 267–69

Gallagher, Tag, 152
Genette, Gérard, 281n10
Gergely, Gábor, 287n6
Gert, Heather J., 280n2
Gibbs, John, 23, 167
Glück, Louise, 14
Godard, Jean-Luc, 24, 37–38, 151, 280n4
Gorfinkel, Elena, 243, 259–60, 268
Gould, Timothy, 285n11
Gunning, Tom, 250

Hall, E. Dawn, 259–60, 268, 301n6
Hamlet, 15, 25, 65, 72, 79, 82, 116
Hansen, Miriam Bratu, 135–36, 293n4
Harrison, M. John, 245
Hawks, Howard, 109, 151, 198, 289n2

Heart of Glass (Herzog), 195–213, 237, 298n8
Hegel, G. W. F., 13, 48, 151, 218, 263–64, 285n10, 286n14, 286n17, 299n18, 299n20
Heidegger, Martin, 74, 78, 139
Heller-Nicholas, Alexandra, 168–69
Hepburn, Katharine, 113, 125
Herbert, George, 140
Hiroshima Mon Amour (Resnais), 78–79
His Girl Friday (Hawks), 267, 289n2
Hitchcock, Alfred, 3, 29, 31, 75, 151, 278n12, 292n14
Hopkins, Gerard Manley, 140
Hornsby, Jennifer, 1

immortality, 65–86, 116, 126, 273, 285n13. See also mortality
In a Lonely Place (Ray), 157
intention, 1, 7–8, 11, 48–49, 97, 132, 212, 219–20, 237, 263–65, 274, 276n10, 276n11, 277n12, 278n12, 296n7, 299n19, 299n20. See also Anscombe, G. E. M.
intersubjectivity, 177–81, 187, 190, 265
It Happened One Night (Capra), 94, 290n8
Ivanov, Sergey A., 220

James, Henry, 120, 272, 296n3
James, William, 131–32, 136
Jameson, Fredric, 217
Johnny Guitar (Ray), 34, 37, 51
Johnson, Vida T., and Graham Petrie, 219–20, 226, 231–33

Kahn, Eugen, 229
Kant, Immanuel, 68, 76–77, 139, 282n13, 286n17
Kazan, Elia, 56–61, 198, 283n23

Keane, Marion, 285n13, 286n15
Keathley, Christian, 251
Kern, Andrea, 293n5
Keuss, Jeffrey F., 137–38, 140
King of Kings (Ray), 20
King of New York (Ferrara), 167
Klevan, Andrew, 44, 52, 280n4, 301n2
Kracauer, Siegfried, 134–36, 294n9
Kripke, Saul, 141, 294n16
Kubala, Robbie, 43
Kubrick, Stanley, 129–31, 136–47, 293n1, 294n13
Kügle, Markus, 172, 176

Lacan, Jacques, 41, 171–72, 178–79
Lady from Shanghai, The (Welles), 229, 237
Lang, Fritz, 85, 212
Langley, R. F., 57
Lash, Dominic, 4, 36, 275n4, 275n5, 276n6, 278n5, 283n21, 283n22, 292n14
Lash, Nicholas, 129–147, 292n3, 292n4, 293n5, 294n14; *Easter in Ordinary*, 131–32, 136–38, 140, 294n14
Law, Hoi Lun, 142, 278n13
Le Fanu, Mark, 217, 219
Lennon, Kathleen, 95–97
Letter from an Unknown Woman (Ophüls), 5, 53–56, 73
Loughlin, Gerard, 147
Luckhurst, Roger, 173

Macarthur, David, 115–17, 290n8, 290n9, 291n10
Macbeth, 93
Magnificent Ambersons, The (Welles), 44, 45–46
Mankin, Robert, 284n2
Marnie (Hitchcock), 31, 34

Martin, Adrian, 152–53
Mast, Gerald, 133, 294n9
McGinn, Marie, 95–96, 290n7
Meek's Cutoff (Reichardt), 260, 301n5
Meloy, Maile, 245, 252–53, 255, 258, 267–68, 302n9
Mentyka, Robert M., 187
Merleau-Ponty, Maurice, 95–96, 178, 288n8, 289n9
Metz, Christian, 46, 298n8
Meyer, Michael J., 109, 292n20
Miller, D. A., 3
Miller, Jacques-Alain, 171
Moran, Richard, 108, 120
Morgan, Daniel, 79–80, 83–84, 286n15
mortality, 65–86, 116
Most, Glen W., 218
Movie (journal), 19, 24, 35, 51, 56, 152, 277n2
Ms. 45 (Ferrara), 167–70
Mulhall, Stephen, 66, 181
Mulholland Dr. (Lynch), 235
Murdoch, Iris, 48–50
Murray, Paul D., 145

Nanook of the North (Flaherty), 198
Naremore, James, 142
New Rose Hotel (Ferrara), 160–61
Nietzsche, Friedrich, 13, 23, 48, 125–26, 145, 187–193, 263, 295n17
Night Moves (Reichardt), 245–46
Notte, La (Antonioni), 29–30, 278n13

Old Joy (Reichardt), 241–47
O'Malley, Sheila, 109
Oudart, Jean-Pierre, 171, 172, 173, 175–81, 187, 189, 296n2
Out of the Past (Tourneur), 237

Panofsky, Erwin, 290n9, 294n10
Pasolini, Pier Paolo, 151, 279n17
Passion of Joan of Arc, The (Dreyer), 85–86, 176
Perkins, V. F., 3, 4–11, 19–61 passim, 96, 151, 157–58, 162–64, 169, 270, 272, 273, 275n1, 276n8, 276n9, 276n11, 278n4, 278n6, 278n8, 278n13, 279n19, 279n20, 280n4, 281n7, 281n8, 282n14, 282n16, 283n19, 283n22, 295n5, 296n7; *Film as Film*, 5, 6, 8–9, 19–39, 42–43, 161, 162, 164, 276n9, 278n8, 279n14, 280n4, 281n8, 295n5
Pinkard, Terry, 263–64
Pippin, Robert B., 3, 48, 49–50, 67–69, 72, 74, 99, 120, 126, 134, 218, 229–30, 236–39, 263, 267, 272, 273, 275n1, 276n6, 279n16, 282n12, 283n20, 283n21, 285n5, 285n10, 300n21; reflective form, 98, 177, 294n11
Plato, 297n3
Porton, Richard, 109, 122, 125
Powell-Jones, Lindsay, 219
Pratchett, Terry, 36
Pride and Prejudice (Austen), 179
Proust, Marcel, 43
Pye, Douglas, 6, 9, 19, 167, 271

Rancière, Jacques, 210–11
Ray, Nicholas, 20, 31, 34, 51, 157
Raymond, Jonathan, 242
Rebel Without a Cause (Ray), 31, 34
Reckless Moment, The (Ophüls), 157
Reichardt, Kelly, 241–271 passim
Renais, Alain, 38, 78, 212, 279n19
Rentschler, Eric, 298n8
Richards, Rashna Wadia, 250–51
Rödl, Sebastian, 275n3, 299n19
Rohdie, Sam, 33–35, 38

Rollet, Sylvie, 56–57
Rooney, Ellen, 281n5
Rope (Hitchcock), 29, 34, 37
Rorty, Richard, 282n16
Rose, Polly, 301n4
Rosenbaum, Jonathan, 243–45
Rothman, William, 5–6, 10, 177, 275n2, 276n8, 285n13, 286n15
Roud, Richard, 206
Routt, William D., 275n4
Rules of the Game, The (Renoir), 283n22
Russell, Betrand, 280n2
Rybin, Steven, 3–4, 275n4

Schoenberg, Arnold, 10, 277n4
Screen (journal), 41, 171
Seaton, Lola, 14–15
Shaw, Daniel, 107, 127
Shining, The (Kubrick), 129
Shuster, Martin, 290n9
Sinnerbrink, Robert, 134
skepticism, 67, 75–79, 101, 114–20, 126, 133, 137–41, 191–92, 284n4, 284n5, 290n7, 293n5, 294n15
Smuts, Aaron, 162, 281n4, 296n7
Solaris (Tarkovsky), 238
solipsism, 68, 72, 238, 285n6
Sontag, Susan, 38
Spice, Nicholas, 127
Stalker (Tarkovsky), 217–247 passim
Star is Born, A (Cukor), 154–55, 159
Stevens, Brad, 161, 163
Stevens, Kyle, 97, 283n20
Stinton, T. C. W., 239
Stockhausen, Karlheinz, 39
Strawson, P. F., 139, 284n5, 302n10

Tarkovsky, Andrei, 217–247 passim
Taylor, Aaron, 141, 147, 294n15
Taylor, Charles, 299n19

These Three (Wyler), 278n11
Thompson, Michael, 1
Thomson, David, 186, 188, 296n4
Tokarczuk, Olga, 43
Tőke, Lilla, 98–99
Toles, George, 251, 292n17
Tomasulo, Frank P., 46–47
Tracy, Spencer, 113, 125
Trial of Joan of Arc, The (Bresson), 176

Virvidaki, Katerina, 162, 278n6
Vivre sa vie (Godard), 280n4

Waiting for Godot (Beckett), 33, 36–37
Wallace, Lee, 61
Walton, Saige, 91, 99
Welles, Orson, 44–46, 203–204, 229
Wheatley, Catherine, 73, 109–10, 112, 114, 289n3
Williams, Bernard, 48

Williams, Raymond, 42, 50–52, 58, 282n17, 283n18
Wilson, George M., 66, 177, 276n8, 283n21
Winter's Tale, The, 114
Wiseman, Rachael, 7, 8, 48–49, 68, 71
Wittgenstein, Ludwig, 9–10, 48, 66, 71, 76–77, 82, 85, 92, 95–97, 105, 107, 114, 117–19, 132, 139, 141, 279n20, 280n2, 286n14, 286n17, 288n9, 293n21, 293n3, 293n6, 294n16, 299n17
Woman of the Year (Stevens), 113, 125
Wood, Robin, 19, 24, 277n4, 278n7, 279n14
Wyler, William, 26, 29, 31, 278n11

Yacavone, Daniel, 32, 279n16

Zangwill, Nick, 277n13

www.ingramcontent.com/pod-product-compliance
Lightning Source LLC
Chambersburg PA
CBHW020121240426
43673CB00038B/550